A FISCAL CLIFF

EDITED BY JOHN MERRIFIELD
AND BARRY POULSON

A FISCAL CLIFF

NEW PERSPECTIVES ON THE U.S. FEDERAL DEBT CRISIS

CATO INSTITUTE

Washington, DC

Print ISBN: 978-1-948647-87-8
eBook ISBN: 978-1-948647-89-2

Cover design: Jon Meyers

Library of Congress Cataloging-in-Publication Data

Merrifield, John, 1955– editor. | Poulson, Barry Warren, 1937- editor.
  A fiscal cliff : new perspectives on the U.S. Federal debt crisis /
John Merrifield and Barry Poulson, editors.
     pages   cm
  Washington : Cato Institute, 2020.
  Includes bibliographical references and index.
  ISBN 9781948647878 (Paperback) | ISBN 9781948647892 (eBook)
  1. Debts, Public--United States. 2. Public administration--United States.
  3. Fiscal policy--United States.
  HJ8101 .F47   2020
  336.3/40973--dc23   2020024862

Printed in the United States of America.

CATO INSTITUTE
1000 Massachusetts Avenue NW
Washington, DC 20001

www.cato.org

The book is dedicated to the memory of Milton Friedman, who laid the foundations for rules-based fiscal and monetary policies.

CONTENTS

FOREWORD

As the immediate former comptroller general of the United States and former head of the U.S. Government Accountability Office, I know a fair amount about the deteriorating financial condition of the U.S. government and its unsustainable fiscal outlook. I also have considerable experience in evaluating the financial condition and fiscal sustainability of various states and municipalities due to my experience as a managing director for PricewaterhouseCoopers's Public Sector. More important, as a father and grandfather, I have a deep personal concern about the future impact of today's irresponsible fiscal actions and inactions on our children, grandchildren, and future generations of Americans.

The federal government's financial condition and fiscal outlook have deteriorated significantly since the end of fiscal year 2000. During this period, debt subject to the debt ceiling limit rose from about $5.7 trillion, or about 57 percent of gross domestic product (GDP), to more than $22 trillion, or about 110 percent of GDP in 2019. In addition, annual federal deficits are approaching $1 trillion and rising. They are also projected to further increase the debt-to–GDP ratio in the future, absent significant spending and revenue reforms.

The truth is that federal policymakers have lost control of the budget. Today only about 30 percent of the federal budget is controlled by Congress (discretionary spending), down from 97 percent in 1913 when the income tax and the Federal Reserve were established. In addition, the percentage of discretionary spending is set to decrease further due to rising costs associated with Social Security, Medicare, Medicaid, and other mandatory spending programs, along with interest on the federal debt. Shockingly, discretionary spending includes all the items that are expressly enumerated as a role for the federal government in the U.S. Constitution, including national defense and homeland security. And the fastest-growing expense today is interest on the federal debt, for which we get nothing.

Both political parties are to blame for this mess. Too many Republicans focus on cutting taxes today in an attempt to stimulate the economy without understanding the longer-range fiscal implications. Unfortunately, not all tax cuts stimulate the economy, and very few tax cuts pay for themselves. Too many Democrats want to increase the size and role of the federal government without paying for new programs and without understanding the implications on incentives to work, to marry, and to follow the legal immigration process.

Many current and historical fiscal controls have proved to be short-sighted and ineffective. For example, the debt ceiling limit has been totally ineffective in constraining debt burdens. Past attempts to control spending have not withstood the test of time. More fundamentally, Congress regularly fails to pass timely budgets and appropriations bills, resulting in periodic government shutdowns. During these shutdowns, members of Congress continue to get paid, and those civil servants who do not work during a shutdown still get paid retroactively when the shutdown is over. In addition, the current unitary federal budget approach has served to discourage legitimate and much-needed infrastructure projects that can benefit several generations.

While the federal government has its own major financial and fiscal challenges, many states and localities do too. Surprisingly, while all states but one have a "balanced budget" requirement, a number of states and localities have negative net positions, and many face large and growing structural deficits in the future due primarily to huge unfunded pension and retiree health care obligations. Municipalities can file for bankruptcy to restructure their finances, but state and federal governments cannot do so. And while the federal government has been able to handle much larger debt burdens at relatively low interest rates in recent years, it would be imprudent to think it can to do so in the future without a day of reckoning at some point. Such a day of reckoning would likely come suddenly and with devastating consequences both in the United States and around the world.

This book includes a number of essays from a range of scholars who provide their personal views on the nature and scope of our fiscal challenges, lessons from others, and possible solutions. I hope this book will serve to stimulate some much needed and long overdue discussion regarding how best to put our nation's finances in order so that our future can be better than our past. In the final analysis, our executives must lead at all levels of government, and the applicable legislative bodies must act as well if we want to create a better future for all Americans. Doing nothing is not a viable option.

David Walker
U.S. Comptroller General, 1998–2008

PREFACE

In 2010, the Simpson-Bowles Commission issued a report with recommendations to address the nation's debt crisis. The bipartisan commission fell short of the supermajority vote required to submit its recommendations to Congress. Other commissions and think tanks continue to make recommendations, but we are no closer to a solution to the debt crisis than we were 10 years ago. In 2018, a congressional committee was appointed to recommend reforms in the budget process, but that committee could not agree on any recommendations to submit to Congress. Clearly new perspectives are needed if we are to solve the nation's debt crisis. The flaw in past recommendations was a focus on the outcomes of fiscal policy; a more fundamental question is whether the rules and institutions governing fiscal decisions are biased toward deficits and debt. The essays in this book approach this question from a public choice perspective. They suggest that unless we reform our fiscal rules and institutions, we are not likely to solve the debt crisis and restore sustainable fiscal policies.

Fortunately, there are precedents for the new fiscal and budget process rules necessary to reduce debt at both the national and the subnational level. But the United States is far behind the learning curve compared to other countries, such as Switzerland, that have successfully enacted these rules. The United States no longer has the fiscal space to respond to a major recession with expansionary fiscal policies as we did a decade ago. The fiscal rules now required to solve the debt crisis will require more stringent fiscal policies than those recommended by the Simpson-Bowles Commission.

Given the polarization and dysfunction in Congress, many question whether our elected officials are capable of enacting such fundamental fiscal reform. There is growing interest in allowing the states and citizens to propose amendments to the Constitution under Article V, such as a balanced budget amendment, to address the crisis. The essays in this book offer a menu of choices in designing new fiscal and budget process rules. They also explore the fiscal policies that would be required by the proposed rules.

The book is dedicated to Milton Friedman, who laid the foundations for rules-based fiscal and monetary policies. The ideas in this book are some of the better ideas lying around to solve the debt crisis, and hopefully elected officials, as well as citizens, will someday find them useful.

Barry Poulson

INTRODUCTION

The editors of this book organized a colloquium of scholars and policy-makers as part of the Friedman Project, an ambitious program to restore America's fiscal constitution. Some participants in the colloquium presented papers in sessions organized at the Western Economic Association and Southern Economic Association meetings in recent years. This book is a collection of papers written by these scholars, focusing on the U.S. debt crisis. The book is the first in a series of publications planned for the Friedman Project.

The United States has emerged as one of the most heavily indebted countries in the world, and it now faces fiscal constraints that it has never encountered in the past. Like other major debtor countries, the United States now has little fiscal space to pursue macroeconomic stabilization policies. If the United States responds to a recession with deficit spending, as it did in the 2008 financial crisis, interest rates will likely increase very sharply. Lack of confidence in the ability of the United States to meet these financial obligations risks default on the debt. The essays in this volume provide new insights into the origins of the U.S. debt crisis and a roadmap for addressing the crisis to restore America's fiscal constitution.

When we undertook this book project, federal debt was already at crisis levels; it was already a book whose time had come. Now, with the book nearing completion, we see that federal fiscal response to the COVID-19 pandemic will increase the already huge debt another 20 percent. Prior to that, we might have imagined that we could gradually achieve sustainability by "just" keeping spending growth below gross domestic product (GDP) growth. But debt fatigue is eliminating the fiscal space required to respond to these economic crises. The debt incurred in response to the pandemic increases the urgency for reform in our fiscal rules and fiscal policies. The essays in this book provide a road map for achieving a sustainable debt level and restoring fiscal responsibility.

Chapters 1 to 3 provide historical perspectives on the origins and pre-pandemic state of the crisis. Though huge, and growing rapidly (even more so via the pandemic response), the official debt vastly understates the difference between federal assets and total liabilities, even if the net cash value of federal mineral assets is included. National entitlement programs are all on paths to bankruptcy. Many states and cities face their own impending financial cliffs as years of overpromising wages and benefits to public workers and government programs collide with chronic underfunding of public pension funds and overtaxed citizens. The fiscal rules now in place at both the state and the federal levels have failed to constrain deficits and debt, resulting in unsustainable fiscal policies.[1]

The Congressional Budget Office's 2019 *Long-Term Budget Outlook* reveals that federal fiscal policies are not sustainable.[2] Debt held by the public is projected to increase to levels exceeding national income over the next decade, and to a level double national income over the next three decades. As debt rises to that level, the country will experience retardation and stagnation in economic growth and be exposed to financial crises and economic instability.

Closing the fiscal gap simply stabilizes the debt-to-GDP ratio at current levels; to achieve a sustainable fiscal policy requires more than this. If the United States is to avoid a financial crisis that would trigger instability in international financial markets, it must reduce the debt-to-GDP ratio to levels that existed prior to the recent financial crisis.

Chapters 4 to 6 analyze the U.S. debt crisis from an in-depth, international perspective. Other developed countries have enacted new fiscal rules to address their debt crisis. New fiscal rules were first enacted in

Switzerland and Sweden in response to deep recessions in the late 1980s and 1990s. The new fiscal rules were then enacted in other European countries and in the European Union. In many of these countries the new fiscal rules were ineffective, especially during the recent financial crisis. This led to a second generation of fiscal rules that has proved to be more effective in achieving a sustainable fiscal policy.

The second generation of fiscal rules limits discretionary fiscal policies, prohibiting governments from accumulating unsustainable levels of debt. In countries such as Switzerland, the new fiscal rules have enabled policymakers to significantly reduce their debt-to-GDP ratio. The rules have created the fiscal space to pursue a countercyclical fiscal policy without increasing the debt-to-GDP ratio, even during the recent financial crisis. Switzerland pursues a cyclically balanced budget, with deficits in periods of recession offset by surplus revenue in periods of economic expansion. However, the second generation of fiscal rules is now under attack, and the essays in this section explore the prospects for these rules. What is clear in the literature on fiscal rules is that one size does not fit all. A heavily indebted country, such as the United States, faces more constraints and has fewer options than a country with a low debt burden, such as Switzerland.

Chapters 7 to 9 explore the failure of current U.S. rules and propose new fiscal rules to address the U.S. debt crisis. Since the Gramm-Rudman-Hollings Act was passed in 1985, Congress has enacted statutory fiscal rules designed to limit deficits and balance the budget.[3] That act has been amended many times over the years. In some years these fiscal rules have been effective, and in the late 1990s the federal government eliminated deficits and balanced the budget. But since then the fiscal rules have failed to constrain deficits and debt. Each year the debt burden grows, and the challenge of stabilizing and reducing debt becomes more formidable. At this point the path to a sustainable fiscal policy is not clear.[4] New and innovative fiscal rules are proposed in this set of essays.

The proposed new fiscal rules would require fundamental reforms in fiscal policy. Chapters 10 to 13 propose fiscal policy reforms designed to significantly reduce deficits and debt. Chapter 10 explores the controversial issue of tax policy. The current debate focuses on the near-term impact of the tax cuts recently enacted by the Trump administration. This essay uses a dynamic simulation model to analyze the long-term impact of tax policies as part of the fiscal consolidation required to solve the debt crisis.

In addition to imposing stringent expenditures limits, the proposed fiscal rules would require reforms in fiscal policy generating additional savings each year. Chapter 11 explores the potential to raise significant revenues from the sale and leasing of federal mineral assets. To generate this savings would require fundamental reforms in mandatory spending programs, and most important, entitlement spending. Chapter 12 discusses potential reforms to reduce expenditures for Social Security and Medicare. One of the major flaws in current fiscal policy is the extent to which expenditures have been shifted off-budget. Chapter 13 proposes fiscal policies to curb rising disaster and emergency spending.

It is clear that the current budget process is broken, and Chapters 14 to 16 propose budget process reforms. The 1974 Congressional Budget Act requires Congress to agree on a budget resolution as the framework for tax and expenditure bills. As amended, the act requires Congress to set a revenue floor and an expenditure ceiling. The spending caps are enforced through sequestration. If Congress and the president can't agree on a budget consistent with these rules, sequestration requires across-the-board cuts in spending. The act also requires Congress to determine debt levels as part of the budget resolution, in conformity to debt limits.

For several years Congress failed to agree on a budget resolution and found many ways to circumvent the constraints imposed by budget process rules. Congress repeatedly suspended the spending caps and then set higher spending limits. Congress also routinely suspended the debt ceiling and raised the ceiling to allow more debt. Recent years have seen unconstrained spending growth and trillion-dollar deficits.

Chapter 14 proposes reforms to improve transparency and accountability in the budget process. Chapters 15 and 16 discuss the absence of a budget constraint and propose reforms designed to impose such a constraint.

Chapters 17 to 20 use public choice theory to examine the U.S. debt crisis. Experience with the second generation of fiscal rules has yielded many important insights, and a growing consensus among economists on many issues. Orthodox public finance theory cannot explain the debt crisis as an outcome of optimal fiscal policy pursuit.[5] Whatever the relevance of orthodox theories in explaining fiscal policy in the short run, they have little explanatory power in understanding the last half century of debt accumulation. Chapter 17, by Richard E. Wagner, questions whether rational budgeting is possible in a democratic society. He asserts that understanding the transactional nature of debt is the key to understanding the deficit bias of democratic societies.[6] Monopolistic elements of the polity may not have the same debt preferences as elected officials' constituents, and elected officials' pursuit of self-interest may cause them to advance the interests of the former at the expense of the latter.

Economists interested in the debt crisis have increasingly turned to political economy theories, and Chapter 18 discusses U.S. debt from this perspective. Political economy models are based on the shortsightedness effect on elected officials in the decision to issue debt. From this perspective the debt crisis is a public-sector failure, the failure to constrain fiscal policy in a democratic society.

The final chapters conclude that addressing the debt crisis may not be feasible without fundamental institutional change. Chapter 19 proposes restoration of the no-bailout principle to reduce moral hazard and create incentives for elected officials to enact effective fiscal rules and reverse the decline in dynamic credence capital. Chapter 20 argues that it will be difficult to reverse the federal fiscal trends generating higher debt levels, but it concludes with a note of cautious optimism that it is still possible for the United States to enact fiscal reforms and institutional changes required to avert a debt crisis.

CHAPTER ONE

THE FEDERAL FISCAL CRISIS: AN OVERVIEW

JOHN MERRIFIELD

Because its most noteworthy symptoms may arrive suddenly, the declared debt crisis—an outcome of policies widely described as "unsustainable"—has not gotten the attention a bona fide crisis deserves. Certainly, many publications have stated the growing scope of the debt problem, and some have proposed solutions, but the public, Congress, and President Trump are not paying much attention. Debt concerns were not a major issue in the 2016 campaign. President Trump did declare a crisis, and before that candidate Trump announced his support for federal mineral rights sales as part of the solution, but the follow-up has been nonexistent, or else a well-kept secret.

"Unsustainable" means that one or more of the following will eventually occur:

a. An actual default, meaning failure to make payments due (see Baker Spring's Chapter 9 in this volume) that will cause a huge financial crisis and hastily arranged spending cuts and tax hikes;

b. Printing money to avoid default, which may cause significant inflation;

c. Drastic spending cuts to avoid default;

d. Tax hikes to avoid default; or

e.   Some near-term combination of slower spending growth (perhaps rules-based), faster economic growth, and mineral asset sales.

In the abstract, most people favor the last option. But specifics, such as the challenges created by faster growth, managing rapidly increased access to mineral deposits, and naming the programs to be cut or grown more slowly, will increase the opposition. That may be enough to force one of the other options. This chapter will explore these options, and our dynamic simulation model will assess the scope of the challenge to avoid default, inflation, higher taxes, or huge, sudden spending cuts.[1]

Many people favor large spending cuts. They see a financial crisis as one of few feasible routes to the significantly smaller federal government they want. However, even drastic discretionary spending cuts will not be enough. As the next section shows, even total elimination of the cabinet departments created since World War II (except Health and Human Services) would not come close to eliminating the average Congressional Budget Office (CBO)–projected budget deficit.

The purpose of this chapter is to describe the pathways to a debt-to-gross domestic product (GDP) ratio of less than 60 percent by 2040 and some consequences of a failure to reach that ratio. To the extent there is a rough consensus on a sustainable level of debt for a developed country, a ratio of total debt to GDP of around 60 percent is it. Note that we don't accept the conventional wisdom that only the debt owed to the public matters; readers can learn more about this question in Chapter 15 by Marvin Phaup. The total U.S. debt-to-GDP ratio is already more than 100 percent, about 30 percentage points above debt-to-GDP counting only debt held by the public. Interest must be paid on 100 percent of the debt. That's a key reason why the debt problem is likely much more than a burden on future generations. Because rising debt together with higher interest rates can crowd out funding for government transfers and services or force accelerated debt growth, the options a to e named earlier will impact nearly everyone now alive.

In the next (second) section, we describe the mounting consequences of kicking the can down the road. We can do that without an inordinate use of space because we have published estimates for reaching total debt-to-GDP ratio of approximately 60 percent had we deployed the Merrifield-Poulson (MP) fiscal rule option with a 20-year time horizon starting in fiscal year (FY) 1994,[2] and another recent estimate for a 20-year time horizon, MP deployment in FY 18.[3] In the third section, we examine the prospects for, and alleged requirements of, significantly faster economic growth. The fourth section explores the 2040 results of reduced spending growth, whether total or just discretionary. The fifth section looks at the potential use of federal mineral rights sales—something candidate Donald Trump said was part of his deficit and debt reduction strategy—to impact the 2040 debt-to-GDP ratio.[4] Finally, prior to a summary and concluding remarks, the sixth section examines some consequences, good and bad, of imminent, or actual, default.

KICKING THE CAN DOWN THE ROAD

The planned FY 19 deficit[5] was nearly $1 trillion, which is about five times the combined budgets of five of the cabinet departments created after World War II: Education, Energy, Housing and Urban Development, Transportation, and Homeland Security. But the gross debt increased from 2018 to 2019 by $1.15 trillion. Typically, unplanned spending causes the national debt to grow by more than the planned deficit.

Had we adopted the MP fiscal rule in 1993, taking effect in 1994, the 2015 debt-to-GDP ratio would have been 54.5 percent; below the 60 percent level that is a rough consensus view of what is sustainable, especially when it is the total debt, not just the debt in the hands of the public. The MP rule is similar to the better-known Swiss debt brake.[6] The MP rule limits the rate of discretionary spending growth to a prescribed multiple of the population growth rate plus inflation, or less than that when total debt or debt growth is above prescribed tolerance levels. For example, suppose the debt-to-GDP tolerance level is 60 percent, and the actual debt to GDP of X percent is above 60 percent. $X - 60$ is part of the braking formula that determines how far below the prescribed multiple of population growth plus inflation the allowed spending growth rate is.

Keeping the debt–to–GDP ratio below the sustainable 60 percent level, compared to its actual 2015 value of nearly 100 percent, would have only required an approximate 2 percentage point cut in the growth rate of discretionary spending from its actual average value of more than 5 percent to 3.3 percent. Naturally, with our aging population, and the addition of the George W. Bush prescription drug entitlement, keeping the debt-to-GDP ratio below 60 percent going forward probably would have required a further cut in the rate of increase in discretionary spending. But having failed to seize that opportunity, the costs of attaining debt to GDP below 60 percent is now *much* higher.

With the CBO's *2017 Long-Term Budget Outlook* as the counterfactual,[7] it took an approximate discretionary spending freeze for 20 years just to keep the 2037 debt-to-GDP ratio where it is now, at about 100 percent. While that is far below the current-law CBO projection for 2037, 100 percent is still unsustainably huge. With the March 2017 outlook as the counterfactual, bending the CBO 2037 debt-to-GDP projection below 60 percent would require an approximate mix of discretionary spending growth limited to 1.35 percent per year, and $700 billion per year in combined asset sales and entitlement savings. The federal government's most valuable assets are mineral rights; it owns rights to more than $50 trillion in mineral assets by one current estimate.[8] Either (a) a discretionary spending growth rate of just 1.35 percent or (b) $700 billion per year in savings or extra revenues without higher tax rates would be a major achievement. Using the CBO's March 2017 projections, we need *both* to achieve a sustainable debt level by 2037. Even if we can defy the current conventional wisdom at the CBO and the estimates from Obama administration economists and regain the longtime norm of at least 3 percent GDP growth, it would still take holding discretionary spending growth to 1.2 percent per year and entitlement savings or asset sales of $300 billion per year to get the debt-to-GDP ratio below 60 percent by 2037. And that was before the deficit-increasing 2018[9] and 2019[10] "budget deals."

The CBO's *2018 Long-Term Budget Outlook* takes into account the 2017 tax cut, and the Trump administration–approved spending increases. With those policy changes and the passage of another two years, it takes an additional $100 billion per year ($800 billion vs. $700 billion) to reach debt-to-GDP ratio of 60 percent by 2037, or an additional two and a half years at $700 billion per year to get below the 60 percent threshold. That's alongside a 1.2 percent limit on the growth rate of discretionary spending. Kicking the can down the road has been very costly.

FASTER ECONOMIC GROWTH

Much faster economic growth is the only way to lower the debt-to-GDP ratio to a sustainable level without politically daunting, massive, savings-generating entitlement reform, or politically difficult, perhaps economically impossible levels of annual revenue from mineral asset sales. Despite recent quarterly growth at a 4.2 percent and a 3.5 percent annual rate, and 2.9 percent for all of 2018, the CBO has the annual growth rate quickly reverting to the 2 percent rate that many economists assert is the new normal. That school of thought says it would be very difficult to budge the fundamentals enough to even regain the longtime normal of just over 3 percent. And there is at least one analyst who believes that more than 3 percent is undesirable:

> President Trump promised to increase economic growth to 4 percent. That's faster than is healthy. Growth at that pace leads to an overconfident irrational exuberance. That creates a boom that leads to a damaging bust.[11]

We might need to risk that increased instability. Perhaps an overriding reality is that the debt crisis may force acceptance of many risks, or trade-offs, that might otherwise be unacceptable.

TAX RATE REDUCTION

Notable economists,[12] including longtime Fed chair Alan Greenspan,[13] argue that the 2017 tax cuts unleashed "animal spirits" that created sustainable momentum. Phil Gramm and Michael Solon make the same point.[14] The upshot of such effects is that tax cuts can be a key ingredient of a well-crafted economic policy reform that increases revenue more in the long run than it reduces revenue in the short run. Indeed, despite the 2017 tax rate cuts, FY 2018 revenue was still slightly higher than in 2017; though likely less in 2018 than without the rate cuts. Our analysis, via the calculator posted at www.objectivepolicyassessment.org /vetfiscalrules is that a tax cut of 1 percent of GDP, combined with fiscal restraint via the MP fiscal rule, yields much-accelerated economic growth; enough so that after five years, a tax rate cut yields more revenue than a tax rate increase of the same amount.

TRADE POLICY

President Trump appears to be attempting to be the first president to win a trade war. And it may not be just unrealistic with regard to hope triumphing over experience. If "victory" yields more than an elimination of the newly imposed trade barriers, economic growth and debt restraint will get a boost. Probably more important than the slight economic and fiscal boost emanating from freer trade is to avoid the consequences of the usual trade war stalemate where machismo and concentrated gains in import-competing industries prevent trade wars from terminating quickly or at all. Key historical examples include (a) how long it took to substantially erode the Smoot-Hawley tariffs that at least greatly deepened the Great Depression, or were a principal cause, and (b) the persistence of some trade barriers, such as the "Chicken Tax" that resulted from a trade dispute in 1964.[15] Because of French and German tariffs on U.S. chicken exports, President Lyndon Johnson imposed a 25 percent tariff on imported trucks that still exists, undiminished by successive General Agreement on Tariffs and Trade (GATT) and World Trade Organization (WTO) rounds of tariff reductions. Early signs point to noteworthy persistence of some of the recently imposed barriers, even if the Trump administration achieves its trade war objectives.[16] Higher costs to consumers and industries, alongside disruptions associated with industry adjustment to domestic sources of raw materials and intermediate goods, could induce a recession. Long-term malaise could result from not being competitive with countries that do not deny themselves access to the world's lowest prices. Since the CBO counterfactual that projects a 2040 debt-held-by-the-public to GDP of

124 percent—about 150 percent for total debt—does not include the effects of recessions, or greater malaise than already implied by the projected 2 percent growth rate, trade policies are among the most likely causes of fiscal and economic outcomes that are even worse than the terrible outcomes that the CBO projects without major policy change to induce fiscal restraint.[17]

IMMIGRATION POLICY REFORM

A wide-open immigration policy seems like a surefire strategy for large-scale debt reduction that many people favor, without its possible economic growth and fiscal benefits. Given Alex Nowrasteh's assertion that, "there is no strong fiscal case for or against sustained large-scale immigration,[18] it may take some wise targeting of immigration eligibility to significantly increase federal tax revenues more than outlays.

The most recent noteworthy attempt at immigration policy reform, 2013's S. 744, would have had many of the needed fiscal effects.[19] Still, even though S. 744's projected benefits were small in relation to the scale of the fiscal crisis, the projected fiscal benefits are worth examining. Two chapters in Benjamin Powell's *The Economics of Immigration* also asserted noteworthy effects that can be scaled up.[20] For example, Richard Vedder found higher rates of entrepreneurship in states with higher concentrations of legal immigrants. That replicated an earlier finding by Wadhwa and others that legal, skilled immigrants have started a disproportionate percentage of new engineering and technology companies.[21] Alex Nowrasteh noted that one CBO model determined that if S. 744 became law, it would lower the projected federal budget deficit by $875 billion over 20 years. A second, more dynamic, CBO model determined that if S. 744 became law, it would boost GDP by 5.1 to 5.7 percent over 20 years, and lower the projected federal budget deficit by $1.197 trillion over 20 years.[22]

The political factors underlying S. 744's cautious attempt to find a viable path to reform probably underlie William Galston's proposed path to faster growth—eligibility limited to the most productive—without stirring up too much controversy, that is, without increasing the aggregate level of immigration:

There is only one way to boost the growth rate of the workforce: expand dramatically the number of working-age immigrants admitted each year. If the U.S. prioritized working-age entrants the way most other advanced countries do, it would increase annual labor-force growth by up to 0.3 percent.[23]

The author of this introduction is a first-generation immigrant, but despite the fiscal benefits, he's conflicted about the mixed effects of large-scale proposals that would yield massive population growth. Obviously, his personal struggle with the pros and cons are but a microcosm of the reasons why immigration policy is extremely controversial. But uncontroversial is the fact that the deepening debt crisis significantly increases the importance of the effects of accelerated legal immigration. As we continue to see, the fiscal crisis may make otherwise unacceptable trade-offs more palatable or even necessary.

TAX BASE CHANGE

Given the difficulty of achieving accurate, uncontroversial dynamic scoring for every potential tax policy change, a useful part of a debt-reduction strategy would be to adopt likely growth-accelerating tax base shifts that are revenue neutral as judged by the static scoring required by law. The reasons we haven't already adopted such tax base shifts are being made less important by the debt crisis.

The two prominent candidates for tax base reform based on a likely debt reduction dividend are a carbon tax and a consumption tax. Set at levels that would offset foregone income tax revenue on a static scoring basis, both would likely more than offset loss of revenue from reduced taxation of business or individual income. Some people condition their support of a carbon tax on the total elimination of the income tax. They fear that, otherwise, income tax rates would gradually creep upward after the initial reductions. Indeed, even with total elimination of the income tax, upward creep in other taxes may become a matter of fiscal necessity—perhaps just to sustain existing spending levels, or to accelerate debt reduction. And it may be that a carbon tax large enough to offset all income tax revenue does not exist.[24] Or some increased revenue may have to offset shrinkage in the carbon use tax base, in part because of the tax, but also as technological improvements make renewable energy sources more competitive.

Consumption taxes are a less promising idea. A consumption tax large enough to offset enough income taxation (with static scoring) to yield economic growth benefits, or to eliminate income taxation entirely, might stir enough tax evasion and avoidance to prevent that potential from being realized.[25]

SLOWER SPENDING GROWTH

It's obvious that it is very politically costly to cut spending. Yet through well-crafted, enforceable fiscal rules, we can nonetheless create political cover for the spending cuts that must sometimes be made to facilitate increases in other categories of spending.[26] For example, a threat short of actual attacks that would yield emergency military spending might prompt faster defense spending growth than the average rate allowed by a fiscal rule. That could force some categories of nondefense spending to be cut; this would be a true cut, meaning fewer dollars in the next fiscal year. The fiscal rule forces the prioritization of competing uses of a fixed sum instead of the budget-busting practice of, in the face of disagreement, using debt to avoid difficult trade-offs.[27] Indeed, without the binding external constraint, the result is no longer a budget plan; it's just a spending plan. When years of failure to make tough choices precede the enactment of effective fiscal rules, it takes especially low rates of spending growth to restore fiscal sustainability.

Indeed, as was shown earlier, regaining sustainability in a 20-year timeline will require very low limits on discretionary spending growth, large savings through entitlement reform, and perhaps additional major policy changes, such as massive asset sales, to restore sustainability. Since we are still kicking the can down the road, a 20-year timeline means looking at the menu of possibilities to restore sustainability by 2040.

Some might argue that it is enough to just reverse course. Never mind specific goals such as a debt-to-GDP ratio less than 60 percent by 2040, just get the GDP growing faster than the debt. That may be all that we can achieve. Given the counterfactual of rapid increase in the ratio of debt to GDP, any reduction in debt to GDP will require significant fiscal restraint. Even with a return to the longtime normal of 3 percent annual real GDP growth, just a 1 percentage point per year drop in debt to GDP will require some combination of an annual cap on discretionary spending growth at 0.4 percent with no entitlement reform savings or asset sales, or discretionary spending at 2.4 percent per year with entitlement reform savings and asset sales yielding $500 billion per year. So, each $50 billion in entitlement savings or revenue from asset sales allows an additional 0.1 percent per year in discretionary spending growth. If the economic growth pessimists are correct, or the debt begins to slow economic growth, it will take more entitlement reform savings or asset sales.

But slow progress may not be an option. It may not be enough to prevent the drastic, sudden policy changes or financial crisis we hope to avoid. Or a strategy that seems capable of yielding some progress may disappoint. For example, without significant steps toward sustainability, higher interest rates might preclude the debt reduction that might otherwise result from small steps. The existing adverse U.S. fiscal circumstances[28] have already significantly raised the government's borrowing costs.[29] The United States pays 2.7 percentage points more than Germany pays to borrow money, a gap expected to rise above 3 percentage points in the near future. Three percent of approximately $22 trillion, and growing, is a lot of additional annual cost.

Only if the Trump administration manages to reach and sustain 4 percent real growth, double CBO's expected growth rate, can we, *relatively* painlessly, get the debt-to-GDP ratio to 60 percent by 2040. We would also double the size of the economy in 18 years, an unlikely achievement. With 4 percent growth, we can reach a debt-to-GDP ratio of about 60 percent in 20 years with a combination of $100 billion per year in asset sales and entitlement savings, while still increasing discretionary spending by 2 percent per year. It is important to note that in each of the scenarios described earlier, the MP fiscal rule sets aside funding sufficient to meet the emergency spending requirements of the last 24 years, a period that included the Great Recession, lesser recessions, and the off-budget spending that financed overseas military operations, especially the fighting in Iraq and Afghanistan.

With less optimistic economic growth scenarios, it will take much more entitlement reform or asset sales than described previously. With slightly improved, sustained economic growth—2.5 percent versus CBO's 2.0 percent projection—the MP fiscal rule will not yield debt-to-GDP of less than 60 percent in 2040 without $400 billion per year in entitlement reform savings (less spending by $400 billion per year than currently projected by CBO), alongside discretionary spending growth capped at 1 percent per year.

FEDERAL MINERAL RIGHTS SALES

The more conventional approach to generating money from federal assets is to sell land and buildings, and lease access to minerals. But the potential to generate significant sums lies in federal mineral rights sales. Even though candidate Trump expressed interest in mineral rights sales as part of a debt reduction strategy, and even though there is no other plausible alternative source of funds (likely not even higher income tax rates according to our dynamic simulation model), questions about the potential to convert mineral rights into significant cash mostly yield blank stares. If there are well-developed answers to that (Chapter 11 in this volume describes the challenges) or plans to pursue the policy changes that would be needed to realize that potential, they are a well-kept secret. We need to document the structural impediments to quickly selling or leasing federal mineral rights, and we must eliminate as many of those barriers as we can in a precrisis atmosphere.

We also have to recognize that even the best-case scenario for generating a significant cash flow from federal assets is no excuse for complacency. Having rights to more than $50 trillion[30] in oil, gas, and minerals does not make a $21 trillion, and rapidly growing, national debt acceptable. Those mineral rights may help us avoid a devastating financial crisis, but only as a partner to significant fiscal restraint, and only on a one-time basis. The mineral rights can be sold only once.

The property right to mine the assets is worth much less than the minerals themselves. The mining companies will pay a royalty only for access to the minerals; this will be a fraction of the difference between delivered market value and extraction cost. Much of the federally owned mineral wealth may not be profitably minable, and lower prices for some minerals will decrease the wealth in that category. That coal reserves are a large share of federal mineral wealth makes the assets' future value a major concern, which could grow in scope as climate change politics, actual policy changes such a carbon tax, and technology gains make renewable energy sources more competitive.[31] As noted by the *Wall Street Journal*'s Greg Ip, "Coal has become a sunset industry as cleaner energy sources rapidly get cheaper. In the U.S., coal is headed toward obsolescence."[32]

To a lesser extent, such issues impact the value of all of the federal government's fossil fuel reserves. The rate at which federal mineral rights are made available will also affect the total amount generated by those sales. Where the relevant industry associations are not already maintaining a current estimate of demand—properly seen as a function of all of its key determinants through a fully specified, multiple regression analysis—that work needs to be pursued so that we can determine the trade-off between the near-term annual rates at which mineral rights can generate revenue and the total amount generated from the salable assets.

IMMINENT OR ACTUAL DEFAULT

The leading edge of default is already visible. It can become a real default if the likely effects of the monetary expansion needed to meet payment deadlines are seen as unacceptable. Rising interest rates will be both a cause and an effect of increasingly unsustainable federal fiscal circumstances. Even without those ever-more-dire circumstances, the eventual gradual escape from the Great Recession–induced and pandemic-induced monetary expansions will raise the federal government's already huge borrowing tab. The dire circumstances have created a large and growing risk premium best seen in the soon-to-be more than 3 percentage point difference between the German government's and the U.S. government's borrowing costs—almost enough for the risk premium costs to possibly become solely responsible for U.S. debt growth.

Spiraling debt service costs can become the proximate cause of the drastic measures that will prevent the worst elements of a full-blown financial crisis. Or poorly conceived drastic measures can bring on the crisis and make it worse. Good decisionmaking, even in a crisis atmosphere, may be necessary before all the necessary reforms can become politically feasible. The same sort of good decisionmaking has been a central aim of the Friedman Project, whose goal has been to produce a thorough grasp of the U.S. federal government's dire fiscal circumstances and a fully vetted menu of fiscal rule options. The contents of this book address both those objectives.

Consider, for example, farm subsidies; these policies and expenditures are arguably unconstitutional and inarguably economically inefficient. Political inertia is the only argument for permanently retaining them. But in the midst or under threat of a financial crisis, can we go cold turkey on farm subsidies? Because the value of the subsidies is capitalized into land values, and because farmers borrow against the value of their land, yanking the subsidies could add widespread rural bank failures to an existing financial crisis. Beyond economic efficiency arguments and fiscal concerns, the sheer fact that farm subsidies may be dangerous to remove during a financial crisis should argue for a gradual end to farm subsidies, beginning immediately, but not for an abrupt end in a financial crisis.

Those are the kinds of issues we need to sort through in advance of a crisis atmosphere. Many spending cut recommendations have been derived from ideology, including concerns about the unconstitutionality of various programs. We need to reprocess the documented rationales for spending cuts into program rankings based on economic efficiency and short-term stability factors.[33] Rankings are complicated by scope considerations. For example, there are undoubtedly many programs that should be cut back but not eliminated.

After we learn what the Great Recession teaches about the new relationship possibilities for monetary expansion and inflation, we need to

examine the consequences of well-designed, damage-minimizing monetary expansion as part of a default-avoidance strategy. It may be a de
facto existing strategy that we need to improve as we seek to maintain
historic low interest rates in the face of still high levels of liquidity and
the crowding out effects of ongoing debt growth.

In the increasingly cited words of then–Obama administration
Chief of Staff Rahm Emanuel—"You never want a serious crisis to go
to waste. [. . .] It's an opportunity to do things you think you could not
do before"—we need to find some silver linings to the default cloud,
or near-default cloud.[34] In light of the typically immense difficulty of
cutting government programs, fear of default is a key opportunity to
seize no matter what someone's political preferences are. Even seekers of
significant government expansions, such as single payer health care, can
find programs worth cutting, if only to eliminate future competition
for the new government programs they want. Well-developed rationales
that will resonate in a crisis atmosphere need to be crafted well in advance of the frenzy. That comes back to the need to assess and rank programs in terms of core government functions such as defense and justice
and, secondarily, in terms of economic efficiency.

Pressure to raise taxes should be tempered by Hauser's law, which
basically says that it is very difficult for the federal government to collect
more than 20 percent of GDP.[35] I attribute Hauser's observation to our
de facto narrow federal income tax base. When marginal tax rates were
high enough to qualify as borderline confiscatory—until 1986—there
was a lot of tax avoidance, especially by the wealthy, and also maybe
more evasion than we believe. Then we enacted the 1980s tax reforms
that sharply lowered rates and took a lot of people off the tax rolls. We've
so narrowed the income tax base to the relatively wealthy that the nearly
half of total income earned by the bottom 80 percent of income earners
accounts for less than 15 percent of income tax revenue.[36] Approximately
87 percent of federal income tax revenue comes from the top 20 percent
of income earners. An actual or imminent debt-driven financial crisis
may create an opportunity to reduce or adjust the progressivity of a tax
structure that creates a seemingly dangerous political economic condition that may be a significant underlying cause of debt growth. There

is disagreement on the optimal degree of progressivity, but there can be no disagreement on the danger inherent in excusing a large share of the electorate from the fiscal costs of the increased government spending that they can vote for. As 2012 Republican presidential nominee Mitt Romney, now a U.S. senator, said, "everyone needs to pay something." And for efficiency, if not political expediency, everyone's tax payments should vary with the amount the government spends. Until the symptoms of the debt crisis are more widely seen, it will be politically difficult to increase the tax burden of the lowest income Americans so that everyone pays something. But likewise, it will be difficult to increase revenue just by increasing the rates applied to already heavily taxed higher-income taxpayers.

SUMMARY AND CONCLUDING REMARKS

Clearly, all possible avenues for avoiding or coping with a fiscal or financial crisis need to be fully explored for possible deployment on short notice. The real—as opposed to "just" political[37]—consequences of spending cuts need to be well-documented before we see strong pressure for huge cuts. Sadly, that pressure is not yet evident.

CHAPTER TWO

FEDERAL DEBT IN HISTORICAL PERSPECTIVE

CHRIS EDWARDS

The federal government will spend $4.6 trillion and raise $3.6 trillion in revenues in 2020. The resulting $1 trillion deficit will be financed by borrowing and add to accumulated federal debt of $17 trillion, which is more than $130,000 for every U.S. household.[1]

Federal debt has more than doubled over the past decade. When measured against the size of the economy, it is the highest in our nation's peacetime history. Rising debt will impose a huge burden on future taxpayers and could trigger a financial crisis that will further undermine our prosperity.

Historically, federal government debt spiked during wars but was always paid down when crises subsided. Today, lawmakers are running massive deficits even though the nation is not at war and is enjoying strong economic growth. Official projections show a nonstop gusher of red ink in coming years as federal entitlement programs balloon in cost.

This essay looks at the history of federal debt and describes five types of harm that it causes. It concludes that policymakers should cut spending to balance the budget and reduce debt. Spending cuts would spur growth by reducing the economic distortions caused by many programs. Cuts would also reduce the risk of a financial crisis and avert pressure to impose harmful tax increases down the road.

JEFFERSONIAN FISCAL PRUDENCE, 1790–1930

America was born with a hefty load of government debt, which had been issued to finance the Revolutionary War. Following Alexander Hamilton's plan, Congress transferred state government debts to the federal government in 1790, creating a total federal debt of $75 million. Hamilton and the Federalists were in no rush to pay off the debt, and by the end of John Adams's administration in 1800 debt had edged up to $83 million.

Thomas Jefferson assumed the presidency in 1801, promising to end internal taxes, restrain spending, and pay down the debt.[2] In a 1799 letter to Elbridge Gerry, Jefferson said, "I am for a government rigorously frugal & simple, applying all the possible savings of the public revenue to the discharge of the national debt."[3] Jefferson followed through on his promises with the help of his outstanding Secretary of the Treasury Albert Gallatin.[4] They kept total spending roughly flat over eight years and were able to pay down a substantial part of the federal debt, even with added borrowing to pay for the Louisiana Purchase.

Figure 2.1 shows federal debt as a percent of gross domestic product (GDP) back to 1790.[5] Debt fell from 30 percent of GDP in 1790 to 6 percent by 1811. But then the nation entered the War of 1812, and the government again began borrowing heavily. Debt increased to 10 percent of GDP by 1815.

After the war, policymakers were able to cut spending, and they began to focus on the goal of becoming "wholly free" of federal debt.[6] By the 1820s, policymakers were running surpluses in most years, and in his 1824 State of the Union message, President James Monroe said that federal debt could be fully paid off by 1835.

That prospect caught the imagination of many political leaders who believed in both the moral and the practical benefits of debt freedom. They associated government debt with corruption and the erosion of liberty. Debt freedom was also favored by the public, which strongly supported frugality in the federal government.[7]

With policymakers focused on debt elimination, numerous efforts to expand spending during the 1820s and 1830s were foiled. Some members of Congress—such as Henry Clay of Kentucky—wanted the government

FIGURE 2.1

Federal government debt held by the public, percentage of GDP

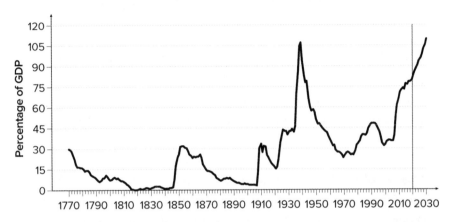

Sources: Congressional Budget Office (CBO), "Historical Data on Federal Debt Held by the Public," August 5, 2010; Amber Marcellino, "Updated Historical Budget Data Following BEA's Recent Update of the National Income and Product Accounts," CBO blog, August 12, 2013; CBO, "The 2013 Long-Term Budget Outlook," September 17, 2013.
Note: GDP = gross domestic product.

to fund "internal improvements." And President John Quincy Adams had grand plans to fund roads, canals, a national university, and many other items. However, such spending plans conflicted with the popular goal of debt freedom, and they were blocked in Congress. Opposition to spending came from members such as Martin Van Buren of New York and John Randolph of Virginia.

President Adams was replaced in 1829 by Andrew Jackson, who was a firm believer in debt freedom. In his first inaugural address, he promised "extinguishment of the national debt, the unnecessary duration of which is incompatible with real independence."[8] Jackson succeeded in his goal, making the period from 1835 to 1837 the only time in our history that the federal government has been debt-free.[9] Unfortunately, borrowing resumed when the economy plunged into recession after the Panic of 1837.

During the 1850s, the government ran surpluses nearly every year, and the federal debt plunged to just 1 percent of GDP. Massive spending during the Civil War caused debt to spike to 31 percent of GDP during the 1860s. But then the Jeffersonian tradition reasserted itself, and lawmakers reduced the debt in subsequent years to just 3 percent of GDP by the beginning of World War I. The government balanced its budget every single year from 1866 to 1893.

Debt peaked at 33 percent of GDP in 1919 as a result of the war, but it was then reduced under Presidents Warren Harding and Calvin Coolidge. The 1920s were the last hurrah for the Jeffersonian anti-debt tradition, which had been part of our unwritten "fiscal constitution," as numerous scholars have called it.[10]

KEYNESIAN PROFLIGACY, 1930–2020

In his 2014 book, *America's Fiscal Constitution*, Bill White argued that the anti-deficit stance of federal policymakers lasted from 1790 through Bill Clinton's presidency but then "collapsed" under President George W. Bush.[11] It is true that Bush presided over deficits and increased spending, but so have many presidents since Herbert Hoover. White's timing is off: the real dividing line in America's fiscal history was the 1930s.

Before the 1930s, policymakers kept federal spending very low. From 1790 to 1929, federal spending averaged just 2.7 percent of GDP, even including the war years during that period.[12] As late as the 1920s, spending was less than 4 percent of GDP. Yet starting in the 1930s, spending began a precipitous climb, reaching the current level of about 20 percent of GDP by the late 1970s.

Before the 1930s, policymakers not only kept spending in check, but also believed strongly that running deficits and racking up debt was immoral and bad for the economy. Those beliefs restrained the basic incentive politicians face to spend more on their constituents than the available tax revenue.

Two developments during the 1930s undermined the anti-debt ethos and shifted the federal government toward deficit spending. First, the creation of entitlement programs—such as Social Security—allowed for automatic annual spending increases without policymakers having to vote for them. Autopilot spending induces political irresponsibility.

Today, entitlement programs account for two-thirds of all noninterest federal spending.[13]

Second, the rise of Keynesianism beginning in the 1930s misinformed policymakers that deficit spending was good for the economy. Nobel Prize–winning economist James Buchanan points his finger at Keynesian economics for the decline in beneficial "Victorian fiscal morality," which had focused on balancing budgets and limiting debt.[14] With the rise in Keynesianism, the "modern era of profligacy" was born, Buchanan said.[15]

Figure 2.1 shows a sharp spike in federal debt in the 1930s and 1940s as a result of the Great Depression and World War II.[16] Federal debt peaked at 106 percent of GDP in 1946. But the importance of entitlements and Keynesianism grew over the decades, paving the way for almost continuous deficit spending since the 1970s.

In the figure, it appears that policymakers were fiscally prudent after World War II because the debt-to-GDP ratio falls rapidly. Actually, that fall was not due to policymaker frugality. Indeed, the government ran deficits in 7 out of 10 years in the 1950s.

Then what caused the fall in debt after the war? First, strong GDP growth helped produce a falling ratio of debt-to-GDP. Second, the debt was greatly reduced by inflation. Inflation reduces the real value of outstanding debt, and thus imposes losses on creditors. The ability to reduce the debt by inflation depends upon the debt's maturity and on whether creditors expect inflation. If the average maturity is long, the government can reduce the real debt load with an unexpected bout of inflation.

That is what happened following World War II. The federal debt-to-GDP ratio was cut almost in half between 1946 and 1955. Economists Joshua Aizenman and Nancy Marion found that nearly all of that drop was due to relatively high inflation during that period combined with a long average federal debt maturity of nine years.[17]

By the mid-1970s, the average maturity of federal debt had shrunk to just three years, so the high inflation in that decade resulted in little debt shrinkage.[18] The debt-to-GDP ratio started rising again in the

FIGURE 2.2

Percentage of years with balanced federal budget

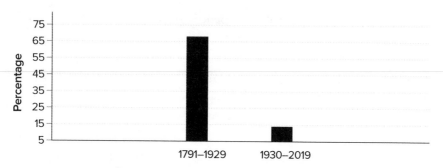

Source: Author's calculations.

1980s and peaked at 48 percent by the early 1990s. Debt fell during the late 1990s as a result of budget restraint and an economic boom.

In the new century, all fiscal restraint has been put aside, and debt soared to $17 trillion by 2019, or 78 percent of GDP.[19] This measure of debt is "debt held by the public," which captures the effect of federal borrowing on credit markets.

Today's federal debt ratio is easily the highest in America's peacetime history, and it will keep on growing unless Congress makes major budget reforms. Figure 2.1 shows that under the Congressional Budget Office (CBO)'s "alternative fiscal scenario" debt is expected to rise to 109 percent of GDP by 2030.[20] Thus, The United States could have World War II levels of debt just a decade from now, and even higher levels after that.

The bipartisan belief that balancing the budget is both prudent and morally proper largely disappeared after the 1930s. From 1791 to 1929, the government balanced its budget 68 percent of the years.[21] But from 1930 to 2019, the government balanced its budget just 14 percent of the years, as shown in Figure 2.2.

In his history of the Jackson-era effort to eliminate the federal debt, Carl Lane concludes, "Debt freedom, Americans in the Jacksonian era believed, would improve the material quality of life in the United States. It would reduce taxes, increase disposable income, reduce the privileges of the creditor class, and, in general, generate greater equality as well as liberty."[22] That is the type of sound fiscal thinking that we need to revive today.

THE PROBLEMS WITH GOVERNMENT DEBT

Over the years, numerous economists and pundits have argued that federal debt does not matter much because we "owe it to ourselves."[23] *New York Times* columnist Paul Krugman has disparaged analysts who express concern about deficits, and he has argued that high government debt is not at all like high family debt. He says that government debt does not hurt future generations because it is mainly "money we owe to ourselves."[24]

Krugman is wrong, and his view is a minority one among economists. The Congressional Research Service says that "the current consensus among economists is that the burden of the national debt is largely shifted forward to future generations."[25] Rising federal debt will impose real pain in the years ahead. Contrary to Krugman, the dangers of families and governments getting deep into debt are similar. Economist James Buchanan argued, "For citizens, the national debt is fully analogous to a private debt that has been incurred to finance a consumption spree in some past period."[26]

To understand the harm of debt, first consider the effects of government spending financed by taxes. Such spending may damage the economy in two ways:

1. *Spending distortions.* Most federal spending goes toward subsidy and benefit programs. Such spending distorts the economy, and thus reduces overall output and incomes.[27] For example, Social Security reduces private savings, welfare programs reduce work incentives, and farm subsidies induce overproduction. These distortions cause economic damage, which economists call "deadweight losses."

2. *Tax distortions.* The taxes to fund federal spending cause additional deadweight losses. That is because higher taxes induce

people to change their working, investing, and consumption activities, which misallocates resources. Economists estimate that the deadweight losses from each one dollar increase in federal income taxes is roughly 50 cents, including about 10 cents for the added compliance or paperwork costs.[28]

Suppose that the government spends $10 billion on a new subsidy program financed by income taxes. The program will cost the private economy about $15 billion when the deadweight losses of the higher taxes are included. If this new program creates distortions, or is poorly executed, it may produce benefits of perhaps just $5 billion. That would create an overall ratio of costs to benefits of three-to-one.

Economist Edgar Browning examined the effects of federal tax and spending programs in his book *Stealing from Each Other*. As a ballpark estimate for the overall federal government, he concluded that "it costs taxpayers $3 to provide a benefit worth $1 to recipients."[29]

Now consider the effects of federal spending financed by borrowing:

1. *More spending induced*. The deadweight losses caused by spending on subsidy and benefit programs are the same whether programs are financed by debt or current taxes. However, the availability of debt financing may induce policymakers to increase overall spending, particularly on low-value programs. Since borrowing makes programs appear to be "free" to citizens and policymakers, the government has less incentive to be frugal and prune low-value programs.[30]

2. *Tax damage moved to the future*. With borrowing, the deadweight losses from taxes are moved to the future when taxes are raised to pay the interest and principal on the debt. The damage from the funding of programs is imposed on people down the road because that is when the government will use coercion to extract the needed money from taxpayers.

3. *Reduction in investment*. Government borrowing may reduce national saving, and thus crowd out private investment, reduce the U.S. capital stock, and reduce future output and incomes.[31]

James Buchanan said, "By financing current public outlay by debt, we are, in effect, chopping up the apple trees for firewood, thereby reducing the yield of the orchard forever."[32] A decline in investment may be partly or fully averted if private saving rises to offset government deficits.[33] But the CBO concludes, "the rise in private saving is generally a good deal smaller than the increase in federal borrowing, so greater federal borrowing leads to less national saving."[34] Government debt may also deter investment as a result of business expectations. Businesses may be reluctant to make long-term investments if high and rising debt creates fears of tax increases down the road.

4. *Borrowing from abroad.* A decline in private investment as a result of government borrowing may be avoided by net inflows of capital from abroad. In recent years, huge federal borrowing has been facilitated by global capital markets. In 2018, 39 percent of federal debt was held by foreigners.[35] Borrowing from abroad may prevent a fall in domestic investment, but it does not prevent the shifting of costs to future generations. That is because some share of the future earnings of Americans will be taxed to pay the interest and principal on the debt held by foreign creditors. For this portion of federal debt, Americans certainly do not "owe it to themselves."

5. *Macroeconomic instability.* The CBO echoes many experts when it warns, "A large and continuously growing federal debt would . . . increase the likelihood of a fiscal crisis in the United States."[36] High levels of government debt tend to result in lower growth and increased financial fragility in nations and the global economy.[37] In their study of hundreds of financial crises in history, Harvard professors Carmen Reinhart and Ken Rogoff conclude, "again and again, countries, banks, individuals, and firms take on excessive debt in good times without enough awareness of the risks that will follow when the inevitable recession hits." Government debt, they find, "is certainly the most problematic, for it can accumulate massively and for long periods without being put in check by markets."[38]

James Buchanan uses a simple story to illustrate the error in the "we owe it to ourselves" claim.[39] Suppose a lender, L, lends $100 to a borrower, B, who spends it on consumption. L will have $100 less in cash but his "notes receivable" will go up $100. B has a liability of $100, but he has no asset because he spent the cash. Now let's say that L and B get married, and they combine their finances. B's liability and L's notes receivable cancel out. L and B "owed it to themselves" and the debt disappears.

However, the $100 that B spent initially is now gone. If that money had instead been put into a productive investment, the married couple would now be wealthier by $100 or more. Buchanan notes that incurring debt "to finance current consumption will permanently decrease the flow of potentially available income."[40]

It is true that the future net burden of federal debt would be reduced if government borrowing was used for high-value capital investments. But that is usually not the case: federal investments are often mismanaged and misallocated. Reporting on the government's $80 billion annual investment in information technology, the Government Accountability Office found that "investments frequently fail, incur cost overruns and schedule slippages, or contribute little to mission-related outcomes."[41] Other types of federal investment are similarly wasteful, such as capital spending by the Army Corps of Engineers and Federal Transit Administration.[42]

More importantly, only a tiny share of federal borrowing and spending is for capital investment purposes. Within the $4.6 trillion federal budget in 2020, just 3 percent will be spent on nondefense "major physical capital investments."[43] Thus, today's huge federal deficits are not being caused by investment spending but by consumption spending on benefit and subsidy programs.

CONCLUSIONS

Rising federal debt undermines economic growth and stability, and it imposes an unfair burden on taxpayers in the future. Policymakers used to understand the harms of debt better than they do today. Thomas Jefferson was right that "the multiplication of public offices, increase of expense beyond income, growth and entailment of a public debt, are indications soliciting the employment of the pruning-knife."[44]

Congress should take a pruning knife to the budget and identify programs in every department to terminate.[45] One factor that makes spending cuts a pressing issue is that even CBO's scary outlook of rising debt shown in Figure 2.1 may be optimistic. America may face unforeseen military challenges or endure another deep recession in coming years, which would make deficits worse than projected. Also, interest rates and other economic variables may not be as favorable as expected. The best way to prepare for the nation's uncertain future is to cut spending, end deficits, and begin paying down the debt before the next crisis hits.

To that end, we should consider structural changes to encourage policymakers to be more fiscally responsible. One option is adding a balanced budget amendment to the Constitution. In 1798 Thomas Jefferson wrote, "I wish it were possible to obtain a single amendment to our constitution . . . I mean an additional article taking from the federal government the power of borrowing."[46]

However, there may be better methods of restraining spending than a balanced budget amendment, as other essays in this book consider. One simple alternative would be to cap the annual percentage growth in total federal outlays.[47] Congress directly controls spending, not deficits, so spending is the best target for a budget limit. Perhaps a combination of structural reforms would be the best solution for the fiscal mess in Washington.

Channeling Thomas Jefferson, Franklin Roosevelt said in a 1932 radio address, "Let us have the courage to stop borrowing to meet continuing deficits. Stop the deficits. . . . Any government, like any family, can for a year spend a little more than it earns. But you and I know that a continuation of that habit means the poorhouse."[48] Unfortunately, when he was elected president later that year, Roosevelt put Jefferson aside, and imposed the pro-spending and high-debt policies of Alexander Hamilton, which still bedevil the American economy today.

CHAPTER THREE

THE DEBT CRISIS IN INTERNATIONAL PERSPECTIVE

BARRY POULSON

Over the past half century virtually every developed country has experienced a growth in debt in excess of its growth in income.[1] The upward trend in debt in the long term reflects a persistent bias toward deficit spending, with the growth in spending outpacing the growth in revenue. The fiscal rules and institutions, both formal and informal, which historically constrained debt, have proved to be ineffective in many countries.

What has emerged is a new era of fiscal rules.[2] The origin of these fiscal rules can be traced to sharp recessions experienced in Switzerland and Sweden in the late 1980s and early 1990s.[3] The fiscal stress experienced in these countries led them to begin experimenting with new fiscal rules, often referred to as debt brakes. in Switzerland, a debt brake was first enacted at the cantonal level and then at the federal level. By the early 2000s, the debt brakes enacted in Switzerland and Sweden were effectively constraining deficits and debt, and this led to the enactment of new fiscal rules at both the national and the supranational level in Europe.

The effectiveness of the new fiscal rules in constraining debt varied considerably, especially during the financial crisis that began in 2008.[4] These rules did not prevent heavily indebted countries, such as Italy, from continuing to pursue unsustainable fiscal policies. Critics questioned whether the new rules were a credible commitment to fiscal stabilization in Europe, and the default on debt, or threatened default, in several countries reinforced this view.

But the critics were too pessimistic regarding the effectiveness of the new fiscal rules in constraining debt. Some countries, such as Germany, modified their rules to make them more effective constraints on deficits and debt. Some countries, such as Sweden, introduced new fiscal institutions, such as fiscal responsibility councils, to provide more transparency and accountability in the budget process. What emerged was a second generation of fiscal rules that has proved to be more effective in addressing the debt crisis.[5]

Economists have learned a great deal from the experience with this second generation of fiscal rules, and at least on some issues, there is a growing consensus among economists. The debt crisis cannot be explained as the outcome of optimal fiscal policies in orthodox public finance theory.[6] In orthodox public finance, debt is incurred to stabilize spending over the business cycle, ensuring tax smoothing rather than the volatility in taxes that would be required if governments are not able to borrow. Whatever the relevance of orthodox theories in explaining fiscal policy in the short run, they have little explanatory power in understanding the last half century of debt accumulation. Eusepi and Wagner maintain that understanding the deficit bias in a democratic society requires piercing the veil of public debt in orthodox public finance theory, to reveal its transactional nature.[7] When monopolistic elements enter the polity, the preferences of elected officials in deciding to issue debt may differ from the preferences of their constituents. In a society characterized by political capitalism, economic and political elites may influence debt decisions to maximize their welfare at the expense of taxpayers.

Economists interested in the debt crisis have increasingly turned to political economy theories. Political economy models are based on the short-sightedness effect on elected officials in the decision to issue debt. From this perspective the debt crisis is a public-sector failure, the failure to constrain fiscal policy in democratic societies. These studies find evidence that a number of political variables contribute to the shortsightedness effect and deficit bias, including an aging population, political polarization, and electoral uncertainty.[8]

Political economy models are also used to explore the role of fiscal rules in democratic societies.[9] The leviathan model is based on time inconsistency in government preferences. It predicts that a current government wants to be fiscally irresponsible, but it wants future governments to be fiscally responsible. Current governments thus have an incentive to enact fiscal rules that are easily circumvented in the short run, but that are binding on future governments, restricting their ability to issue debt.

Other studies relax the assumptions of the leviathan model to explore the role of citizens in enacting fiscal rules to constrain fiscal policy. For example, the median voter model is used to capture the influence of citizens as well as elected officials and special interests in the design and enforcement of fiscal rules. The dynamics of this decision process are observed in the enactment of debt brakes in Europe. Debt brakes are an institutional innovation that can increase the ability of citizens to constrain the issuance of debt. But, in a monopolistic state, elected officials designing fiscal rules will be influenced by special interests as well as their own interests. Thus the effectiveness of debt brakes will depend upon these different transactions, which change dynamically over time.

The effectiveness of the second generation of fiscal rules differs considerably in different European countries.[10] There is a growing divergence between European countries that have successfully enacted debt brakes and highly indebted countries where debt brakes have had little impact in the long run. Highly indebted countries, such as Italy, continue to pursue unsustainable fiscal policies despite sanctions from the European Union for violating fiscal rules. Recent stress tests suggest that Italy has little if any fiscal room to respond to financial crises and other economic shocks.

Analysis of the success and failure of the second generation of fiscal rules has focused both on the design of the rules and on the political institutions within which the rules are enacted.[11] There is now a growing consensus regarding the design of effective fiscal rules. The second generation of fiscal rules is a hybrid, linking the instruments of fiscal policy to fiscal targets. For example, linking expenditure rules to debt targets is considered essential for fiscal sustainability in the long term. Tolerance levels are set for deficits and debt that can trigger more stringent spending constraints in the short term. The deficit and debt brakes provide guardrails to keep fiscal policy from going off track. This hybrid approach incorporates other fiscal rules that can resolve the trade-off between commitment and flexibility, rules such as emergency funds, escape clauses, and capital investment funds. With these fiscal rules in place, countries can not only achieve debt targets in the long run but also pursue fiscal stabilization policies in response to financial crises and other economic shocks in the near term.

Economists have turned to political economy models to explore the role of institutions in determining the effectiveness of fiscal rules.[12] There is less consensus on these issues, with some economists questioning whether the new rules are a credible commitment to fiscal sustainability. Critics point to the absence of supporting institutions, including a functioning capital market, a functioning interjurisdictional competition with tax and spending autonomy, and the absence of insolvency laws and no-bailout rules.

On the other hand, economists have identified some political institutions that can positively impact the effectiveness of fiscal rules. In Sweden, effective fiscal rules are implemented in a budget process providing transparency and accountability. New budget institutions, such as fiscal responsibility councils, have proved to be effective in providing both transparency and accountability in the budget process.

In Switzerland, strong institutions of federalism and direct democracy empower citizens at both the subnational and the national level. Swiss cantons have tax and spending autonomy and interjurisdictional competition. The initiative and referendum give Swiss citizens a voice in fiscal policy that is often missing in other countries that lack these institutions. Swiss economists maintain that the support for these rules within the polity has been decisive for the success of the debt brake. The Swiss debt brake was enacted through a referendum with an overwhelming majority vote. The Swiss debt brakes are also supported by other institutions, such as a strict no-bailout rule. Over time, the success of the Swiss debt brake has contributed to what the economist Charles Blankart refers to as "dynamically developing credence capital."[13]

Which brings us to the debt crisis in the United States. The United States has virtually abandoned fiscal stabilization and has emerged as one of the most heavily indebted nations in the world. Over the past half century, the federal government has continuously incurred deficits, accumulating a debt that now totals more than $21 trillion. Addressing this massive public-sector failure will require fundamental reform of our fiscal rules and policies. It will take decades for the federal government to balance the budget and restore a sustainable fiscal policy.[14]

Stress tests reveal that the greatest threat to fiscal and financial market stability is not weakness in the balance sheets of private financial institutions, but rather in the growing debt burden and balance sheet of the federal government.[15] Fiscal stress tests have been conducted by the Federal Reserve and by the International Monetary Fund (IMF). The Federal Reserve study, using simulation analysis of fiscal policy, reveals that in a major recession the federal government could experience even greater fiscal instability than it did during the recent financial crisis. The IMF study estimates that in a major recession the federal government's net asset position could deteriorate by 26 percent of gross domestic product.

In our research, John Merrifield and I simulate second-generation fiscal rules to estimate their potential impact on deficits and debt in the United States over the next two decades.[16] Our simulation analysis with these rules in place estimates the impact of a minor recession on revenue and spending. This stress test reveals that the United States has the space to pursue fiscal stabilization in response to a minor recession and still reduce debt to a sustainable level. However, this would require stringent spending constraints and significant savings earmarked for debt reduction. The United States now has little fiscal space to respond to a major recession.

Everyone agrees that the budget process in the United States is broken. The 1974 Congressional Budget Act requires Congress to agree on a budget resolution as the framework for tax and expenditure bills. As amended, the act requires Congress to set a revenue floor and an expenditure ceiling. The spending caps are enforced through sequestration. If Congress and the president can't agree on a budget consistent with these rules, sequestration requires across-the-board cuts in spending. The act also requires Congress to determine debt levels as part of the budget resolution, in conformity to debt limits.

For a number of years Congress has failed to agree on a budget resolution, and it has found many ways to circumvent the constraints imposed by these fiscal rules. Congress suspends the spending caps and then sets higher spending limits to sanction increased spending. Congress also routinely suspends the debt ceiling and increases the ceiling to sanction more debt. The outcome in recent years is unconstrained growth in spending accompanied by trillion-dollar deficits. Debt is projected to increase to unsustainable levels in coming decades.

In the 2019 session of Congress, elected officials congratulated themselves on restoring "regular order." All 12 appropriations bills advanced in both the House and the Senate, and most of the spending bills passed on the floor in each chamber. Congress avoided relying on a continuing resolution that allows them to postpone controversial spending decisions. When Congress relies on a continuing resolution, spending bills are often passed in an ad hoc manner; an omnibus spending bill is then passed late in the year without much input from Congress as a whole.

But Congress has passed these appropriations bills without agreeing on a budget resolution. Every appropriations bill calls for a significant increase in spending, and Congress continues to suspend the spending caps to allow increased spending. It is easy to reach bipartisan agreement on a budget when there is no budget constraint.

Elected officials know that the budget process is broken. In 2018 the House appointed a Joint Select Committee on Budget Process Reform. Yet that committee failed to agree on proposed budget process reforms and made no recommendations to Congress in its final report in November 2018.

Congress would do well to revisit the 2016 recommendations for budget process reform by the House Budget Committee, chaired by Republican Tom Price. The recommendations of the Price committee were very clearly focused on solving the debt crisis in the long run. In addition to strengthening existing fiscal rules, the committee recommended consideration of new fiscal rules that have proved to be successful in addressing the debt crisis at both the state and the national level. In particular, the committee noted the success of new fiscal rules adopted in the European Union. In those countries a debt target is set at a sustainable level. An expenditure limit is then imposed to achieve that debt target within a medium-term time frame. Annual budgets are adjusted according to the expenditures limit and the debt target. Guardrails are imposed in the form of deficit and debt brakes; when deficits or debt approach tolerance levels a more stringent spending limit is imposed.

The Price committee noted the success of European countries, such as Switzerland, that have imposed the new fiscal rules for several decades. These countries reduced debt levels significantly. This has given them more flexibility to pursue a discretionary fiscal policy in response to recessions and financial crises. The Swiss rules require a cyclically balanced budget with deficits in periods of recession offset by surplus revenue in periods of expansion. An emergency fund allows them to exceed the spending limit in response to unforeseen events. The committee noted that over this time period the United States has incurred higher levels of debt, which will make it more difficult to impose these fiscal rules. The committee concluded that failure to address the debt crisis with current fiscal rules underscores the need for the United States to consider new fiscal rules that have proved to be successful in other countries.

The United States is clearly behind the learning curve compared to other countries that have enacted the second generation of fiscal rules. Thus we are left with several unresolved questions, and the fiscal future of the United States is uncertain:

- Will the United States, like heavily indebted European countries, continue to pursue unsustainable fiscal policies alongside retardation and stagnation in economic growth?
- If the United States now has limited fiscal space to respond to economic shocks, will the next recession result in even greater economic instability than that during the recent financial crisis?

- If current fiscal rules have failed to curtail spending, what reforms and policies are required to solve the debt crisis?
- Should the United States enact its own debt brake to address the crisis?
- What reforms in financial markets are required to put effective fiscal rules in place?
- Do we need supporting institutions in the form of insolvency laws and no-bailout rules?
- Could budget process reforms provide better transparency and accountability in fiscal decisions?
- Should the United States introduce new budget institutions, such as a fiscal responsibility council?
- What political reforms are required for effective fiscal rules?
- Do we need stronger fiscal federalism with interjurisdictional competition and tax and spending autonomy?
- Do we need to strengthen institutions of direct democracy, relying more on initiatives and referendums in tax and spending decisions?
- If Congress fails to enact more effective fiscal rules, should citizens do so through an Article V constitutional convention?
- Would such a convention energize public support for effective fiscal rules in this country, as it did in Switzerland?

A colloquium of scholars provides new perspectives on the U.S. debt crisis in this volume. The chapters have a common theme: the failure of elected officials in Washington to address the debt crisis. The authors explore the questions I have raised, and while they may not have resolved these issues, their essays should stimulate a vigorous discussion and debate regarding the nation's debt crisis.

CHAPTER FOUR

INTERNATIONAL EXPERIENCE WITH FISCAL RULES

RYAN BOURNE

Preceding chapters explained the need for federal budget discipline, outlined how fiscal rules might help achieve it, and analyzed the political dynamics behind the dire federal debt outlook.

To recap, the federal budget deficit is projected to rise to above 5 percent of gross domestic product (GDP) by 2022, even with benign economic forecasts.[1] Federal debt held by the public is already at its highest level (at 78 percent of GDP) since just after World War II. Congressional Budget Office (CBO) projections show rapid federal debt increases as a share of GDP over the coming decades, primarily due to rising entitlement expenditure as the population ages.[2] Economists agree that fiscal consolidation—including reform of these programs or tax increases—will be necessary to stabilize or lower the debt-to-GDP ratio.[3]

Can we learn anything from other countries about how fiscal rules could help get the debt-to-GDP ratio back on a downward path?

Ninety-six countries have utilized fiscal rules, defined as "a long-lasting constraint on fiscal policy through numerical limits on budgetary aggregates" at some point in the past three decades.[4] Countries have experimented with spending, revenue, deficit, and debt targets and ceilings; with varying degrees of stringency; with different escape clauses; with rules applying to either budget plans or hard outcomes; and with exemptions for various types of spending and revenue. Reaching generalized conclusions about whether rules per se are effective, or which particular aspects of rules are successful, is therefore difficult.[5]

Individual country case studies are more instructive. This chapter therefore analyzes the experiences of Chile, Switzerland, the United Kingdom, and Sweden with formal fiscal rules. All have sought to lower debt-to-GDP levels or reduce budget deficits in the past two decades.

None experienced challenges completely analogous to the United States today. Switzerland implemented a constitutional debt brake after a period of rapidly increasing debt, but with accumulated debt levels much lower than the United States currently faces. The United Kingdom and Sweden adopted fiscal rules to reduce swollen budget deficits following banking crises that saw the need for significant near-term deficit reduction and a desire to then lock-in achievements from these efforts, whereas the United States is still running large structural deficits in benign conditions. More importantly, long-term imbalance in the United States is driven by spiraling costs of entitlement programs brought about by population aging. This unprecedented challenge is faced by most western economies and throws up different economic and political difficulties than reducing debt-to-GDP ratios in the aftermath of one-off crises.

Nevertheless, the experience of these countries can provide general lessons for effective fiscal rule design given the current U.S. debt outlook.

CHILE

Economists have written glowingly about Chile's fiscal rule, which appeared to reduce debt levels while allowing flexibility during downturns.[6]

In 2000, the Chilean government voluntarily adopted a structural balanced budget rule. This aimed to achieve a cyclically adjusted budget surplus of 1 percent of GDP each year. This target was lowered to 0.5 percent in 2007 and straight structural balance in 2009, after gross debt was virtually eliminated.[7]

In Chile, a committee of economic experts estimates potential GDP each year. A separate committee assesses copper prices relative to their trends, which strongly affect the public finances. These analyses are combined to estimate annual government revenues were the economy at full potential. This determines the maximum spending level allowed in budget plans for the year ahead. In other words, planned spending is capped at an estimate of cyclically adjusted tax revenues.

Unlike a strict balanced budget rule, the budget balance fluctuates over the economic cycle with revenues acting as an automatic stabilizer. Debt acts as a shock absorber to economic fluctuations. The government runs a deficit when revenues are below potential and a surplus if the economy is regarded as "overheating" with unsustainable growth. Provided economic potential is accurately estimated, this ensures the budget balances over the business cycle. Economic growth means the debt-to-GDP ratio gradually falls in the medium term.

Accurate estimates of the country's economic potential are crucial to the rule working. Chile's independent committees help mitigate against politicization and overoptimistic estimates of economic potential to justify higher spending. But the Chilean fiscal rule applies no sanctions or future adjustment to spending plans if within a year structural balance is breached.[8]

The Chilean fiscal rule was initially adopted voluntarily, before being formalized into law in 2006. How has it performed? Between 2000 and 2007, the International Monetary Fund (IMF) estimates Chile ran an average budget surplus of 2.8 percent of GDP, with an average structural balance of 0.6 percent of GDP.[9] General government gross debt fell from 13 percent of GDP in 2000 to 4 percent of GDP in 2007, and net debt swung from 3 percent to minus 13 percent of GDP. Chile's sovereign debt rating improved. Even the announcement of the rule in 2000 improved Chile's creditworthiness.[10] Importantly, public spending fluctuated much less than in previous decades, and GDP volatility declined substantially.[11]

The framework's virtues really became apparent before the financial crisis. Then-president Michelle Bachelet was under pressure to increase government spending given sustained strong GDP growth and a high

FIGURE 4.1

Chile general government fiscal balance

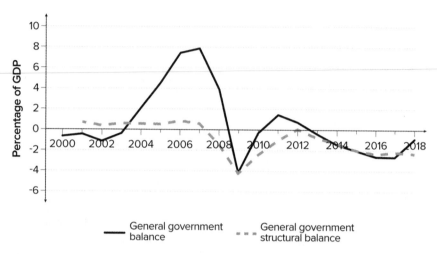

Source: International Monetary Fund, *World Economic Outlook*, April 2018.

world price of copper. Yet the government resisted, with the independent committees judging most of the strong budget performance as cyclical.[12] In 2007, Chile ran a budget surplus as large as 7.9 percent of GDP.

This conservatism proved prescient. By 2009 the budget had swung to a 4.2 percent deficit as the global recession hit. General government debt increased again, but Chile had been so prudent prior to the crash that even today gross and net government debt stand at 24 percent and 1 percent of GDP respectively.[13]

The limits of the framework have been exposed in the postcrisis period, however. From 2009 through 2011, the rule was temporarily abandoned, as the government cited extraordinary circumstances following the global recession.[14] No sanctions or commitments to a future tightening of policy were made, and the country ran structural deficits during this time, as shown in Figure 4.1.

Having returned to structural balance in 2012, the period since has seen sustained failure to meet the rule too, in part because "potential GDP" is difficult to calculate. Chile raised its corporate income tax rate from 17 to 20 percent under President Sebastián Piñera in 2011, and further to 27 percent under President Bachelet, with the intention of raising revenues for education and social spending.[15] But during this period of higher taxes and steep spending increases (overall spending has increased by 1.9 percentage points of GDP since 2011), annual real GDP growth underwhelmed expectations. Gross government debt therefore nearly doubled between 2013 and 2018, and net debt drifted back into positive territory, despite the pickup in the global economy.

Potential GDP is inherently difficult to assess, particularly when major supply-side policy change occurs. Calculating "potential revenues" requires accurate assessment of (a) the health of the economy in real time, (b) the "output gap"—that is, how far the economy is away from its potential, and (c) how moving to potential affects revenues. All are uncertain and difficult to calculate.

Faced with slower-than-expected growth, President Piñera downgraded the rule's stringency to a 1 percent of GDP structural deficit target by 2014. President Bachelet then diluted it further, targeting a structural deficit trajectory (aiming for it to fall by 0.25 percent of GDP per year). Despite a recent pickup in Chile's growth rate, which has reduced the overall deficit, the IMF believes the country will still run a structural deficit of 2.4 percent of GDP in 2018. Finally, in 2017, Standard & Poor's downgraded Chile's credit rating.[16]

The new government under President Sebastián Piñera has now pledged to return to structural balance over a six- to eight-year period.[17] But breaches and continual adjustments to the framework have undermined its credibility.[18] Chilean economic commentators and analysts have called for the Fiscal Council, which has overseen the independent committees since 2013, to be granted more binding powers.

Chile's experience thus highlights strengths and weaknesses of structural rules based upon potential tax revenues. When potential GDP is estimated accurately, a structural balance rule delivers countercyclical policy and a falling debt-to-GDP ratio. (The basic correlation between Chile's budget surplus and real GDP growth since 2000 is 0.67, see Figure 4.2.) But potential GDP is difficult to estimate. Overoptimism can

FIGURE 4.2

Chile's countercyclical fiscal policy

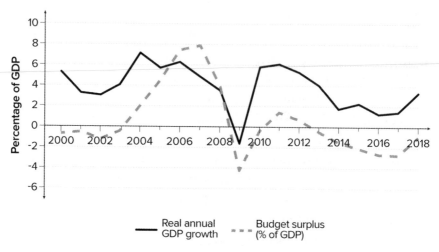

Source: International Monetary Fund, *World Economic Outlook*, April 2018.
Note: GDP = gross domestic product.

lead to unforeseen borrowing which, absent correction, raises debt-to-GDP levels.

Chile's rule proved effective in the build-up to the crisis. But it has proved less enduring since. Absent a constitutional underpinning, political will is required to ensure rules are not abandoned or diluted, and in the postcrisis period, Chile's framework has been relaxed. This may have been initially because the structural balance rule only allowed revenues, and not spending, to fluctuate with the business cycle. When crises hit, as after 2009, social protection spending tends to rise. But under Chile's rule other spending must be cut to allow for this. This absence of spending-side automatic stabilizers may have contributed to the political willingness to temporarily abandon the rule, ultimately undermining its credibility.

In Chile's case, with low debt levels, allowing bygones to be bygones and temporarily abandoning the rule might not have major consequences, but such mistakes could be problematic for a country such as the United States with already high levels of debt.

THE SWISS DEBT BRAKE

Proponents of fiscal rules often hold up Switzerland as an exemplar. Through the 1990s the Swiss national government ran sustained budget deficits, with gross government debt increasing from 34 percent of GDP in 1990 to 55 percent of GDP in 2000, and net debt rise from 13 percent of GDP to 34 percent.[19] Widespread concern saw the Swiss debt brake approved in a referendum by 85 percent of voters in 2001, applying in the country's constitution from 2003 onward.[20]

The debt brake requires structural balanced budgets annually. Annual federal spending is capped at an estimate of tax revenues multiplied by a business cycle adjustment factor (trend real GDP growth divided by expected GDP growth for the year).[21] This means spending levels stay relatively independent of the near-term state of the economy and are stabilized around a smoothed revenue trend.

This rule should be countercyclical by construction. When real GDP growth is expected to be below trend growth, the spending cap exceeds revenues. When real GDP growth for the year is expected to be above trend growth, the spending cap falls below revenues. Over the long run, the overall budget should balance, and hence the debt-to-GDP ratio should fall with economic growth. This sounds similar to the Chilean rule. But the Swiss fiscal framework differs in key respects.

First, the Swiss Federal Department of Finance uses backward-looking trends in real GDP growth in calculating planned spending caps. Spending caps are therefore much more formulaic and predicated on hard data and near-term forecasts, rather speculative estimates of economic potential. This eliminates ambiguity and potential sources of bias (though not entirely; the Swiss government admits there has been a bias error toward surpluses in application so far). By incorporating backward-looking data, the Swiss rule ensures balance is achieved in the long run, although it is possible the rule could result in near-term structural imbalance if the potential growth rate were to change from its historic trend.

Second, certain expenditures highly sensitive to the health of the economy, such as unemployment insurance, are excluded from the rule and spending cap altogether, as are social security expenditures (though the latter is bound by its own spending targets).[22] Automatic stabilizers therefore operate for both spending and revenue.

Third, the Swiss framework incorporates mechanisms to deal with outcomes differing from planned structural balance. Deviations in actual outcomes from plans are chalked up as debits or credits in a "compensating account," which must be adjusted for in future budgeting. Once debits exceed 6 percent of government spending, the excess must be eliminated in the next three budget cycles through cutting spending. Whereas in Chile there are no consequences for deviations from forecasts, in Switzerland deviations are factored into future policy to ensure the budget really does balance over time.

Finally, there is an escape clause for exceptional circumstances if a qualified majority in both houses of the Swiss parliament approves the exceptional spending. Yet even these emergency measures are "debited" to a special "amortization account" and must be compensated for within six years of the exceptional spending.

This rule practically guarantees a decline in the debt-to-GDP ratio over time, unless social security spending—which sits outside of it with its own rules—were to be increased significantly. In Switzerland's case, the rule also helps tame government size. Since some tax rates are constitutionally restricted, with change requiring approval of a majority of voters in a majority of cantons, structural balance is largely achieved through controlling expenditure.

How has the debt brake performed since 2003? Switzerland has run an average overall surplus of 0.2 percent per year since then. This is practically identical to the IMF's estimate of the average structural balance, showing that a balanced budget has broadly been achieved, with a slight surplus bias. As a result, after peaking in 2004, government net debt-to-GDP has more than halved (see Figure 4.3).[23] During this period, Swiss fiscal policy has been moderately countercyclical (with a correlation of 0.2).

The Swiss debt brake has largely worked as intended. Its constitutional backing, underpinned by the democratic mandate, gives the rule more authority and permanence than rules passed through ordinary legislation.

FIGURE 4.3

Switzerland government net debt: percentage of GDP

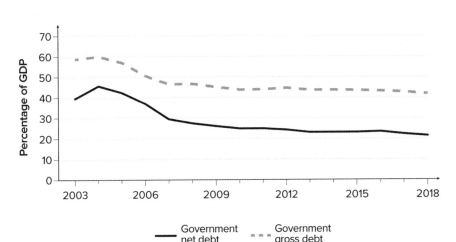

Source: International Monetary Fund, *World Economic Outlook*, April 2018.
Note: GDP = gross domestic product.

It is simple, transparent, and formulaic, adjusting over time to deviations from plans, making it robust to unforeseen events. It cannot be manipulated by continued overoptimistic assumptions about trend growth.

Yet as with all fiscal rules, it is difficult to answer whether it is the rule that is most important, or the supporting institutions and public support which generated it in the first place. Switzerland relies heavily on voter initiatives and referenda in fiscal decisions, has a strongly decentralized federalized system, and employs effective fiscal rules at the cantonal level. It is worth noting too that the country has a strong and open financial system, providing clear signals for when deficits and debt are not sustainable.

The rule may yet be tested if Switzerland experiences a major crisis. In the longer term, the exclusion of social security from the scope of the rules is likely to put upward pressure on government debt, as it would in most western countries facing aging populations, absent continuation of separate rules to rein in that spending growth, or constitutional changes to tax rate limits.

Critics regularly contend that the rule is too restrictive, not allowing enough countercyclical discretion to deal with crises and limiting the scope for productive public investment. But the example of the United Kingdom's experience with rules that exclude investment expenditure and the frequency of tinkering with fiscal rules in Chile, the United Kingdom, and Sweden, suggest that there might be some meaningful trade-off in sticking to transparent and simple frameworks at the expense of limiting flexibility.

THE UNITED KINGDOM'S EVER-CHANGING FISCAL RULES

The phrase "rules are made to be broken" could describe the UK's fiscal experience over the past two decades.

Between 1998 and 2007, the Labour government operated by a "golden rule" that only allowed borrowing for investment over the economic cycle. This was supplemented with a "sustainable investment rule" that said the net debt-to-GDP ratio should be kept below 40 percent.[24] By 2007 these rules had been completely discredited. The *Financial Times* wrote of its annual survey of economists: "Almost none use the chancellor's fiscal rules any more as an indication of the health of the public finances."[25]

The government used creative accounting to meet the golden rule. Consumption expenditure was redefined as investment spending. The government's growth forecasts, which underpinned the fiscal rules, proved continually overoptimistic about tax revenues. The methodology used to calculate cumulative budget surpluses for noninvestment spending was changed, and, according to the Institute for Fiscal Studies, "the estimated start date for the economic cycle was moved by two years at precisely the point at which, without this change, the government looked on course to break rather than meet the golden rule."[26]

The financial crisis led to a complete abandonment of this framework, as debt-to-GDP soared when the recession hit. Reassessments from the IMF found potential GDP had previously been grossly overestimated. The UK is now believed to have entered the crisis running a 5.2 percent of GDP structural deficit in 2007.[27] Adding to that a discretionary stimulus package caused the UK's structural deficit to soar to near 9 percent of GDP in 2009. Net debt rose from 37 to 68 percent of GDP between 2007 and 2010.

The incoming Conservative government recognized the unsustainability of this fiscal stance. It adopted two new rules in June 2010 as part of a fiscal mandate to reduce the deficit slowly over the five-year parliamentary term and to get the debt-to-GDP ratio back to falling by its end. These had no legal standing, but it was thought not meeting them would result in large political costs given the salience of the government finances in public debate.

The first rule said the government would eliminate the structural deficit, excluding investment spending, "within five years." The second, a firmer rule, pledged that the net debt-to-GDP ratio would be falling by 2015. The government planned a deficit reduction package of tax increases and spending restraint to hit these targets given growth and revenue forecasts. They created an independent Office for Budget Responsibility to oversee forecasting and assessments of compliance with the rules.[28]

These rules, ultimately, were abandoned. In 2011, the Office for Budget Responsibility revised down its estimate of the economy's potential capacity, revising up its estimate of the level of the structural deficit. The government did not adjust its tax or spending plans, pushing back the timeline for achieving structural balance. In the end, the structural deficit was only halved over the period it was supposed to be eliminated (see Figure 4.4).[29]

The net debt rule was also abandoned when it became clear it would bind. Though the net debt-to-GDP did begin falling from the end of the parliamentary term, the headline figure gave a false impression of long-term fiscal sustainability as the government improved the debt position through one-off asset sales.

Though the rules were abandoned, they were not completely useless. They kept focus on the need for deficit reduction. The primary reason for failure to meet targets was due to unexpectedly weak productivity growth and hence tax revenue shortfalls. This led borrowing to be significantly higher than planned. But despite huge political pressure

FIGURE 4.4

UK government debt-to-GDP levels

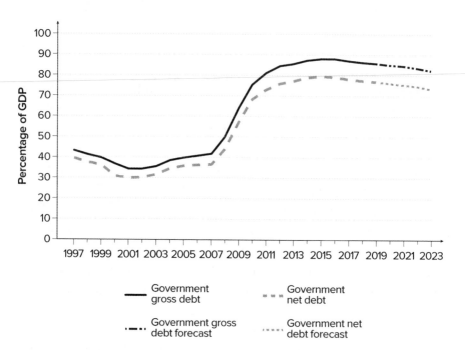

Source: International Monetary Fund, *World Economic Outlook*, April 2018.
Note: GDP = gross domestic product.

to jettison fiscal consolidation and spend more, the government actually delivered marginally lower nominal spending at the end of the Parliament than originally planned (£757.1 billion in 2014–2015, compared with plans for £757.5 billion).[30]

The main problem with the plan itself was a decision to ring-fence large areas from restraint, including health care and the state pension (where spending was increased).[31] This not only meant major cuts had to be made in unprotected departments, but some of the longer-term liabilities associated with an aging population were worsened.[32]

A new framework was adopted in 2015 to finish the job of near-term fiscal repair. The aim was to close the remainder of the budget deficit and deliver an overall surplus by 2020. From there, a legally binding surplus rule was planned, mandating an overall budget surplus every year, except when the economy encountered a negative shock (defined as when annual real GDP growth fell, or was forecast to fall, below 1 percent). The government argued that sustained overall surpluses were necessary to get the debt-to-GDP ratio down to historic levels over the long term, giving the headwinds of an aging population and likelihood of recessions.

This proposed rule was criticized by economists for being simultaneously both too stringent and too lenient. It could have resulted in large within-year spending cuts if growth forecasts proved overoptimistic, making it very procyclical at times, and it would have required targeting a large surplus to account for forecasting uncertainties. Yet when growth fell below the 1 percent threshold, the rule gave the government carte blanche to deviate from the target and decide when to return to it.

Again, this framework was abandoned before it ever bound. After the Brexit vote, the government pushed back the date for targeting a surplus, and it now promises one by the mid-2020s. The electorate appears fatigued by years of "deficit reduction," and demands for increased spending proliferate despite the tax burden rising to its highest level in 49 years.[33] The debt-to-GDP ratio is expected to fall only modestly over the coming half-decade (see Figure 4.4), assuming benign conditions. But with the headwinds of an aging population to come, British government debt levels are still highly elevated relative to historic norms and projected to rise substantially on unchanged policies in future.[34]

The UK's experience with fiscal rules is therefore an unhappy one. Absent constitutional constraints or independent assessment, politicians used creative accounting and overoptimistic forecasts to circumvent rules. Annual deficit targets proved difficult to plan for or hit given fluctuations of revenues, and structural consolidation plans were thrown off course by changing estimates of the productive potential of the economy. The UK government has continually promised future restraint through tough rules but then ignored failures to hit deadlines.

One political economy lesson appears to be that fiscal repair should be undertaken while there is political and electoral buy-in. Promises to be responsible sometime in the future are virtually certain to be abandoned as circumstances change and political will subsides. In the

UK, there were no consequences for failing to hit targets. This is in stark contrast to Switzerland where spending caps are largely based on past data or near-term forecasts, and where deviations from targets are worked into future budgets.

SWEDEN

Sweden reduced an extraordinarily high budget deficit in the 1990s and set a fiscal stance to ensure its debt-to-GDP ratio fell over the longer term, albeit from a lower debt-to-GDP level than faced by the United States today.

In the early 1990s, Sweden faced a severe banking crisis, which saw banks recapitalized, the unemployment rate increase from 2 to 11 percent, and three consecutive years of falling GDP.[35] The budget deficit soared, as Figure 4.5 shows, to just under 11 percent of GDP by 1993.[36]

A political consensus developed that the deficits were unsustainable, and substantial fiscal consolidation was required. Halting debt accumulation became a priority in 1993 for the Liberal-Conservative government and then the Social Democrats in 1994. Two deficit reduction attempts were made in 1992 and 1993, with more significant efforts delivered between 1995 and 1997. The aim of the 1995 program was to stabilize the debt-to-GDP ratio by 1996 and balance the overall budget two years later. Both were achieved, with a 0.8 percent of GDP surplus by 1998.[37]

It is beyond this chapter to detail the deficit reduction program. Economists have debated why the budget deficit fell so rapidly, with some crediting other factors, including an accommodative monetary policy stance, strong international economic growth, supply-side reforms of the tax system, competition policy, and public services reform.

But the crisis did create a climate conducive to developing a fiscal framework for Sweden's subsequent smooth downward path of debt as a proportion of GDP. This began with the National Medium-Term Budgetary Framework enacted in 1997–2000, and then formalized into fiscal rules.

Today, Sweden's fiscal framework is somewhat complex. But its outcomes stand out among advanced western economies. Between 1998 and 2018, Sweden averaged a general government surplus of 0.6 percent

FIGURE 4.5

Sweden budget balance, 1980–2023

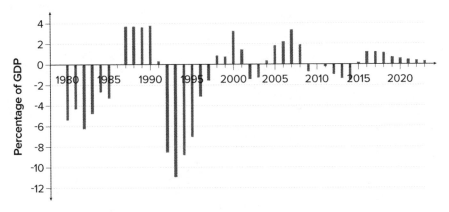

Source: International Monetary Fund, *World Economic Outlook*, April 2018.

of GDP per year. Gross debt has fallen from 66 percent to 38 percent of GDP, and net debt from 51 percent to just 7 percent (see Figure 4.6).[38] The country was running budget surpluses prior to the financial crisis, meaning that even the 2008 crash resulted in very modest deficits.

The current framework has built up in piecemeal fashion.[39] The main component is a "surplus target." Until recently, the central government was committed to running an average budget surplus of 1 percent of GDP across the economic cycle (since relaxed to 0.33 percent of GDP).[40] As the UK example showed, though, any rule that relies on estimates of the highly uncertain economic cycle is open to circumvention by politicians. The framework guards against this by using two indicators to assess whether the target is likely to be met.

First, each year a forecast of the structural budget balance is calculated and compared to the surplus target.[41] If the government believes it will not hit its structural surplus target annually, it must explain the deviation and outline how it intends to return to target, with plans incorporated into the next budget.[42] There are no sanctions or automatic adjustments if the target is forecast to be missed. In fact, in theory there is maximum flexibility for discretionary deviations in any year. The hope though is that clear and transparent analysis of the public finance

FIGURE 4.6

Swedish general government gross and net debt, 1993–2018
(outturns and projections)

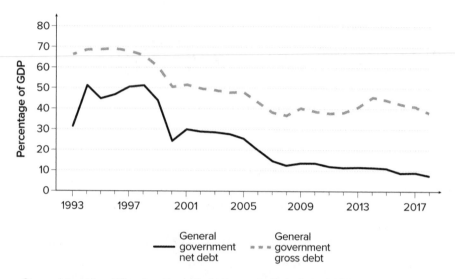

Source: International Monetary Fund, *World Economic Outlook,* April 2018.

position will cause politicians to pay a political cost for not being able to justify these deviations.

This evaluation is also supplemented with a backward-looking calculation of the budget balance across the previous eight years, used as a proxy for whether the rule is being delivered across the cycle. Again, any systematic deviations from the rule are highlighted, with suggestions for spending or tax decisions to adjust accordingly.

Absent systematic mistakes over assessments, this surplus rule ensures the debt-to-GDP ratio falls over time. The level of the surplus target is reviewed every eight years too, allowing governments to reassess what is needed to ensure sustainable debt-to-GDP ratios given changes to demographics and the outlook for the federal finances.

To hit this surplus target, Sweden operates a rolling "expenditure ceiling" covering all central government and old-age spending except for debt interest payments. This ceiling applies to spending in each of the next three years, protecting against governments permanently increasing spending after temporarily strong tax revenues. Flexibility for unforeseen events is granted through a "budget margin" of up to 3 percent of forecast spending for three years ahead.[43] But combined with the surplus target, the ceiling effectively caps total tax revenues and prevents situations where taxes must be increased to account for insufficient control of expenditure.

A Fiscal Policy Council staffed overwhelmingly by academic economists was created in 2007 to oversee and assess whether the surplus rule and expenditure ceiling are being met, to evaluate economic forecasts, to assess the justification for deviations from targets, and to set out what return to target is appropriate.

A "debt anchor" will be added in 2019, with a benchmark target for gross debt of 35 percent of GDP. If actual debt deviates more than 5 percentage points over this benchmark, the government must write to Parliament outlining how it will deal with it. If this is due to the surplus target not being hit, then the surplus target should be revised up in the next period.[44]

Overall, the framework appears to have been effective. Sweden has almost eradicated its net debt (Figure 4.6). It is in a strong fiscal position given future demographic challenges. The real question is whether these outcomes are due to rule design and implementation, or to the political consensus for fiscal conservatism born out of the 1990s crisis.

Some anecdotal evidence suggests the latter is important. In 2013 and 2014, opposition parties began undermining informal budgetary procedures. By 2015, the Social Democratic government was calling for a relaxation of the surplus target. Finance minister Magdalena Andersson explained that it "was never meant to last forever."[45] The surplus target was reduced to 0.33 percent of GDP, a reasonable move given low debt levels, but still showing the framework's malleability. Absent a constitutional underpinning, one could imagine future governments deciding to dilute the target further.

Sweden's overall target is more constrictive than the rules in Switzerland or Chile, but it allows far greater discretion and flexibility year-to-year in practice. This has advantages. It means, for example, that fiscal policy can be adjusted for unforeseen events. But it also makes a consensus behind meeting the rules incredibly important, and the recent changes suggests the rule is less secure than the one in Switzerland.

As the UK example shows, too, the technocratic Fiscal Policy Council is important to underpin the integrity of the framework, given the difficulty of estimating the business cycle and hence structural deficits. Sweden has appeared to be lucky so far in its outcomes, but the Chilean experience shows estimated structural balance is difficult to track accurately, making it hard to assess whether a surplus is consistent with the target within-year.

LESSONS FOR DEVISING A U.S. FISCAL RULE

The experiences of Chile, Sweden, Switzerland, and the UK provide some interesting lessons for fiscal rule design for the United States today.

1. Political will is needed to achieve fiscal discipline and sustain rules. The examples of Chile and the UK show that governments often abandon or circumvent rules when they bind, particularly absent constitutional underpinning. Well-designed rules, with public buy-in, can improve the functioning of a disciplined fiscal policy, providing cover for politicians to make tough budget decisions and resist pressure to increase spending substantially in cyclical upturns. But the desire for fiscal discipline is a prerequisite.

2. Rules must have provisions to deal with recessions or slower than expected growth. Inflexible rules, such as strict deficit targets or balanced budget rules, tend to be abandoned, revised, or suspended in difficult circumstances. If constraints are too tight, rules will not prove politically durable. What one needs is a rule by which the overall budget balance can fluctuate with the business cycle, but which balances budgets or runs surpluses over the long run and has pathways or institutions which help balance to return after temporary deviations from the rule.

3. The ultimate aim of a fiscal rule should be to keep the debt-to-GDP ratio at sustainable levels in the long term. Given that one

cannot directly target or control a debt-to-GDP level, intermediate targets and controls on spending, revenues, and ultimately budget balances are necessary over long periods to keep debt at sustainable levels.

4. A falling debt-to-GDP ratio is all but guaranteed by some form of structural balance rule. Provided that the nature of the business cycle is accurately estimated, structural balance can be achieved by capping annual spending either to a cyclically adjusted trend in revenues or to an estimate of revenues if the economy was operating at full potential, as in Switzerland and Chile respectively. The former ensures the effects of balanced budgets are delivered in the long term but may be less countercyclical in any given year, whereas the latter's effectiveness is determined by how accurate estimates of the productive potential of the economy are. To guard against overoptimistic prospects for the economy, the country can either set up fiscal councils or independent committees to undertake or evaluate forecasts and economic potential on behalf of the government or try to assess trend growth and revenues using historic data and shorter-term forecasts.

5. Fiscal rules should be neutral between revenues and spending and should work to affect the budget balance, not the size of government. Expenditure caps or ceilings, as seen in Switzerland and Sweden, have seemed most effective in delivering the structural balance that restrains the growth of debt. But that does not mean that governments should be restricted in what tax rates they can set over time by the fiscal rule itself. To command consensus, a fiscal rule must be neutral between tax revenues and spending. To prevent governments from running up irresponsible spending increases before demanding major tax hikes, the Chilean and Swiss fiscal rules in effect force the government to first raise structural tax revenues to facilitate higher expenditure ceilings.

6. A spending cap should be as broad as possible to minimize creative accounting and ensure debt sustainability. Rules that

exclude certain forms of expenditure, such as investment spending, have been prone to gaming by politicians. With the major driver of future imbalance being rising demands on entitlement spending, it makes sense to include old-age related expenditure within a rule, such that politicians are forced to consider reforms to these programs as their fiscal consequences begin to bite. The strongest argument for exclusion from spending caps are the cyclical components of social expenditure, which tend to rise during recessions. Absent flexibility with these, downturns force governments to cut noncyclical expenditure to cover this extra social expenditure. The Chilean example suggests that this rebalancing leads to political pressure to abandon the rule.

7. Any rule should not allow bygones to be bygones. Deviations in outcomes relative to the rule should not be ignored, but instead incorporated into future budgeting plans. The absence of consequences for missed targets creates an unhealthy political dynamic, incentivizing either continual overoptimism or leading to rules that fail to deliver fiscal sustainability. This is a particular concern for the U.S. federal government, where debt levels are already very high by historic standards.

8. Other restraints may be necessary to prevent current politicians worsening long-term budget outcomes. Structural balanced budget rules do not restrict politicians today from worsening the long-term fiscal imbalance by making entitlements more generous for future generations. This is a concern if the political consensus around fiscal discipline is expected to change. Therefore, restrictions that prevent new entitlement promises in future years would be beneficial. Some countries, such as Switzerland, exclude social security spending from their primary fiscal rule and subject it to its own rules. In the absence of this approach, rules could be designed requiring future entitlement promises to be worked into budget provisions today through compensating tax or spending adjustments.

9. There should be a clear but limited escape clause for genuine emergency situations. Otherwise there is a risk that the legislation

will be abandoned entirely when difficult circumstances arise. Some economists have proposed, for example, the relaxation of fiscal rules when the central bank's interest rate target hits the nominal bound of zero (when, they claim, the effectiveness of monetary policy is more questionable). But it is better that temporary suspensions require a high-threshold vote, and the framework should ensure a well-acknowledged pathway back to achieving structural balance.

10. The best way to obtain credibility for a fiscal rule is to get to the stage where it legally binds. As the UK example shows, preaching fiscal discipline like St. Augustine—"Lord give me fiscal discipline, but not yet!"—is not credible. Pushing further into the future the targets for achieving balance is especially dangerous given the risk of a changed political consensus and new economic downturns. In the United States, an initial discretionary program to reduce the structural deficit will be necessary before any structural balance can be delivered. The evidence from other countries suggests that this should be delivered relatively swiftly when the political will arises.

CHAPTER FIVE

THE UNITED STATES VS. SWITZERLAND AND SWEDEN: THREE APPROACHES TO FISCAL RESTRAINT

ROMINA BOCCIA

The United States is on a fiscal collision course. Projected spending, deficit, and debt levels are highly unsustainable and growing automatically due to statutory rules and structural demographic and programmatic factors. Absent presidential and congressional leadership through the regular budget process, fiscal restraints are necessary to invoke reforms to out-of-control federal spending and borrowing and avert a severe fiscal crisis in the United States. Existing U.S. institutions and budget procedures are inadequate for addressing current and future fiscal pressures. Switzerland and Sweden offer the United States valuable insights for what makes for a successful fiscal framework, including a stable political commitment to fiscal sustainability.

THE U.S. FISCAL OUTLOOK

The fiscal and economic projections by the Congressional Budget Office (CBO), published in its 2018 *Budget and Economic Outlook*, paint a clear picture.[1] Spending and debt are growing at an unsustainable pace, greatly increasing the risks of a sudden fiscal crisis during which investors could

FIGURE 5.1
U.S. public debt, 1900–2049

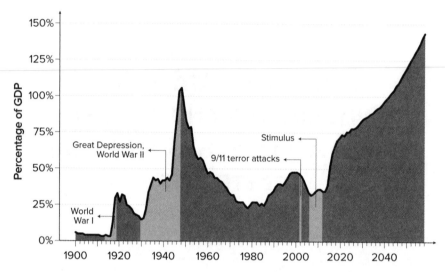

Source: Congressional Budget Office, "The 2019 Long-Term Budget Outlook," CBO Report, June 25, 2019, https://www.cbo.gov/publication/55331.
Note: GDP = gross domestic product.

demand much higher interest rates to continue lending to the U.S. government.

The CBO projects that outlays will grow in nominal dollar terms from $4.1 trillion in 2018 to more than $7 trillion in 2028. Moreover, spending growth is projected to outpace economic growth, as outlays are expected to grow by 3 percentage points from 20.6 percent of gross domestic product (GDP) in 2018 to 23.6 percent of GDP in 2028.

Meanwhile, tax revenues are projected to grow by approximately 2 percentage points, from 16.6 percent of GDP in 2018 to 18.5 percent of GDP in 2028. These projections assume that Congress will allow the 2018 tax cuts to expire on schedule. This is a highly unlikely proposition, as doing so would mean the imposition of significantly higher taxes on the middle class; a politically unpopular move regardless of which party has control of the government.

The outlook beyond 10 years is even more dismal (Figure 5.1) and demonstrates a highly unsustainable and worsening fiscal position for the United States over a 30-year horizon.[2] CBO projects that federal spending during the decade from 2029 to 2038 will be about 25 percent of GDP with federal revenues 6 percentage points below that level at about 19 percent.

By that time, publicly held debt borrowed in credit markets would far exceed the U.S. GDP, by more than triple the U.S. average historical level of debt over the past 50 years.

The primary drivers of growing spending as a share of GDP are well-known among those who study the U.S. federal budget. The aging of the U.S. population owing to rising life expectancies and the retirement of the baby boom generation is putting a growing strain on senior health care and retirement programs. Social Security and Medicare, as well as Medicaid spending on nursing care, are the key programmatic drivers of rising spending and debt.

In numbers, Medicare, Medicaid, health care subsidies, and Social Security make up more than half of the annual federal budget, and when combined with projected interest on the debt, they are responsible for 85 percent of the projected growth in spending over the next 10 years.[3] Given current projections, major entitlement programs—Medicare, Medicaid, health care subsidies, and Social Security, plus interest—will consume all projected tax revenues by 2041 (Figure 5.2).[4]

Rising interest rates and a larger overall debt accumulation will sharply increase the interest cost of the national debt.[5] Net interest is projected to more than double, growing by 2 percentage points of GDP, from 1.6 percent of GDP in 2018 to 3.6 percent in the decade from 2029 to 2038.[6]

In recent years, legislators have also taken actions that further weaken the U.S fiscal position by circumventing budget limits to appropriate additional funds to federal government agencies without making provisions for paying for the resulting increase in spending and by reducing tax revenues without corresponding spending reductions.

INSTITUTIONAL FAILURE

The Congressional Budget and Impoundment Control Act of 1974, also referred to as the Budget Act, governs the U.S. federal budget process.[7] The purpose of the budget process is to provide the framework for

FIGURE 5.2

Mandatory spending as a share of GDP and tax revenue

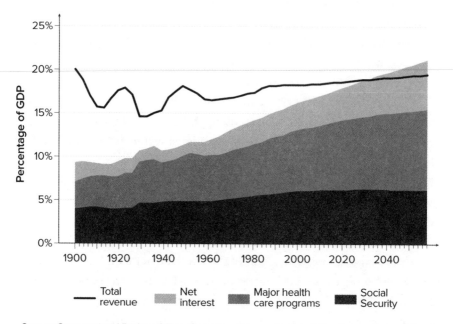

Source: Congressional Budget Office, Budget and Economic Data, https://www.cbo.gov/about
/products/budget-economic-data#1.
Note: GDP = gross domestic product.

the regular and orderly debate of fiscal issues to guide legislative action. A properly functioning budget process should encourage debate on
fiscal issues, set in motion negotiations over the trade-offs and considerations involved in congressional spending and taxing, and lead to
budgetary decisions.

The Budget Act lays out a clear timeline for this process: By the first
Monday in February of each year, the president is to submit a budget
to Congress. By February 15, the CBO issues its *Budget and Economic
Outlook* report for the upcoming decade. Congressional budget committees use the CBO report as a starting point for crafting the House
and Senate budget resolutions. The House and Senate debate these
resolutions until mid-April when Congress is to complete consideration
of the budget.

By law, the resulting concurrent budget resolution must pass both chambers of Congress before lawmakers may appropriate moneys for federal agencies, programs, and grants. The budget is important to this process because it sets the top-line spending figures for the upcoming fiscal year. Under regular order, the House is expected to have completed all floor action on appropriations bills by June 30. That leaves three months for the Senate to complete action and to reconcile the bills for the president to sign before the beginning of the fiscal year.

The budget resolution also triggers another critical budget tool: reconciliation.[8] The purpose of reconciliation is to expedite consideration of budget legislation that changes revenues or direct (mandatory) spending, such that those changes bring government finances in line with the levels prescribed in the congressional budget resolution. While reconciliation is typically seen as a deficit-reduction tool, especially at times of high and rising deficits, the process itself establishes no such requirement. Most often, reconciliation is not used as intended, but as a means for the majority party in control of both chambers of Congress to pursue partisan priorities. Examples include passage of the Affordable Care Act and the Tax Cuts and Jobs Act. Reconciliation also facilitates increases in the debt limit, including in the absence of deficit-reducing provisions.

To trigger reconciliation, Congress must include reconciliation instructions in the concurrent budget resolution and establish revenue and outlay baselines for a minimum of five years.

The reconciliation process enables Congress to fast-track mandatory spending and tax reform in the Senate, limiting debate and lowering the necessary vote threshold to a simple majority, instead of requiring 60 votes as is typical in the Senate to overcome a filibuster.[9]

Typically, the budget resolution covers a period of 10 years (11 including the current fiscal year). However, Congress is free to establish any budget window it chooses, as long as it covers at least five years.[10]

Legislators mostly followed the federal budget process for more than two decades, immediately following enactment of the Budget Act. For the most recent 21 fiscal years, from 1999 through 2019, however, the process has broken down as legislators have neglected to follow the process and compromise has become a seemingly lost art. Congress completed a budget resolution in only 10 years and pursued reconciliation instructions in only 8 years. Of these reconciliation bills, seven were enacted into law.[11]

While legislators are required to pass annual appropriations, the size and scope of the federal budget subject to such appropriations covers only about one-third of annual federal spending. Mandatory spending, or programs on "autopilot," make up more than two-thirds of annual federal spending, and they are the primary driver of growing deficits and debt. Budget reconciliation is one of the few effective legislative tools that allow for necessary spending adjustments in mandatory spending (though Social Security is exempt).

The reconciliation process requires active engagement by Congress. If Congress fails to make use of reconciliation, lawmakers face no immediate consequences as debt and spending continue spiraling out of control. The most recent instances of reconciliation used the process contrary to its intended goal of aligning current programs with the goals set out in the budget resolution. Instead, Democrats used the process in 2009 to pass the Affordable Care Act, adding a new entitlement to the already strained U.S. budget; and Republicans used it in 2017 to pass the Tax Cuts and Jobs Act, including a $1.5 trillion reduction in the revenue baseline.

At the same time that legislators have made less use of the congressional budget process, or used it primarily for pursuing narrow policy priorities, spending and debt have grown further out of control. This has led to various attempts at imposing fiscal restraints, including deficit targets and stopgaps to new spending.

INADEQUATE FISCAL RULES

As of 2019, three primary fiscal restraints governed the U.S. federal budget process. They are the Budget Control Act, pay-as-you-go rules, and the debt limit. Despite their promising names, they have largely proved inadequate.

THE BUDGET CONTROL ACT

The Budget Control Act (BCA) passed Congress in August 2011, after nearly eight months of negotiations with the Obama administration.

In January 2011, then–Treasury Secretary Timothy Geithner warned Congress that, sometime between late March and mid-May, the federal government would exceed its legal borrowing limit of $14.3 trillion.[12] Several months after the debt limit came into effect, an agreement was forged, and the BCA authorized a $2.1 trillion increase in the debt limit.

The BCA, in an effort to achieve enough savings to offset the $2.1 trillion increase in the debt limit, established discretionary spending limits for fiscal year 2012 through fiscal year 2021. The BCA further established defense and nondefense category caps within the overall funding levels. The BCA provided for the enforcement of these statutory caps by triggering an automatic sequester, with the sequestration of resources carried out by the Office of Management and Budget if Congress appropriated funds in excess of the caps.

However, the BCA spared some of the largest programs within the federal government's mandatory budget. The BCA specifically excluded Social Security, Medicaid, the Children's Health Insurance Program (CHIP), Temporary Assistance for Needy Families (TANF), and the Supplemental Nutrition Assistance Program (SNAP) from cuts. It also limits cuts to Medicare to 2 percent, in accordance with baseline projections, meaning after accounting for assumed spending growth in Medicare.[13]

While the caps limit overall discretionary funding, the BCA does allow for certain upward adjustments to be made for purposes such as Overseas Contingency Operations (OCO) funding, as well as disaster and emergency designated funding and program integrity initiatives.[14]

Congress has several times circumvented most of the components of fiscal restraint the BCA sought to impose (Figure 5.3). It decided that it was unable to adhere to the original restrictions on discretionary spending imposed by the BCA on defense spending without undermining U.S. military readiness. The resulting political dynamic gave big spenders leverage by holding adjustments to the defense caps hostage to funding increases for domestic spending. As a result, Congress delayed and partially canceled sequestration in 2013, and it revised the budget caps for each year afterward.[15]

FIGURE 5.3

Budget authority increases since 2014

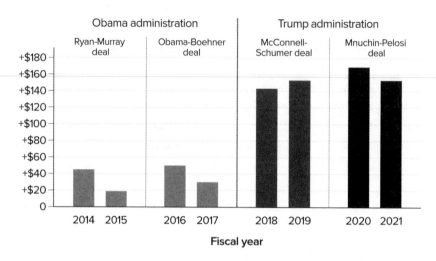

Source: Congressional Budget Office, "CBO Estimate for Senate Amendment 1930, the Bipartisan Budget Act of 2018," February 8, 2018, https://www.cbo.gov/publication/53556.

In addition to revising the spending caps themselves, Congress has also abused various emergency spending provisions by treating them as loopholes for other spending. Since the beginning of the 115th Congress, domestic spending classified as an emergency exploded from 5 percent of total domestic discretionary spending in 2016 to 22 percent in 2018.

Appropriations designated as an emergency by Congress are exempt both from the discretionary spending limits and from the pay-as-you-go law that requires all new mandatory spending to be offset by other mandatory spending cuts or revenue increases. Emergency spending is supposed to be reserved for spending on wars, disasters, and other events that are sudden, unexpected, urgent, and temporary. Congress regularly ignores these limitations, without facing any legal consequences.

Since 2013, Congress has authorized $255 billion in emergency spending on domestic programs including disaster relief, domestic spending for the Global War on Terror, and program integrity measures,

FIGURE 5.4
Uncontrolled spending surges

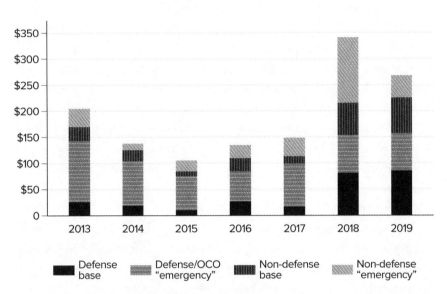

Source: Heritage Foundation calculations based on data from Office of Management and Budget.
Notes: OCO = Overseas Contingency Operations. Spending increases relative to original Budget Control Act levels, in billions.

along with $481 billion in emergency funding above the spending limits for national defense (see Figure 5.4).[16]

Spending limits are critical fiscal tools to encourage budgetary discipline. Spending limits can encourage Congress to prioritize among competing programs, facilitating greater transparency and encouraging legislators to more carefully examine and debate the trade-offs involved in federal spending decisions.

Yet statutory spending limits alone are not sufficient. Legislators must also have the will to abide by them, and constituents must hold them to their commitments.

PAY AS YOU GO (PAYGO)

While discretionary spending is controlled by the Budget Control Act of 2011 and the 302(a) allocations[17] (shares of authorized spending) provided in the congressional budget resolution, PAYGO controls changes in mandatory spending and revenues. Increases in discretionary spending are exempt from PAYGO.

The Statutory Pay-As-You-Go Act of 2010 requires that all legislation enacted during a session of Congress affecting mandatory spending or revenues must not increase the deficit over the 5- and 10-year budget window when considered cumulatively.[18] There is also a Senate PAYGO rule that prohibits the consideration of any direct (mandatory) spending and revenue legislation that would increase the deficit over a 10-year budget window.[19] Legislation that would increase direct spending or reduce revenues must also include equivalent amounts of direct spending cuts, revenue increases, or a combination of the two, to be considered deficit neutral.

The Senate Budget Committee can enforce the Senate PAYGO rule via a point of order. Any senator may raise the point of order to prevent the consideration of legislation that would increase deficits via changes to mandatory spending or revenues.

The statutory Pay-As-You-Go Act implements an automatic sequestration whenever Congress enacts legislation that increases the deficit via direct spending increases or revenue reductions, on net, during a session of Congress.

The Office of Management and Budget (OMB) keeps two cumulative scorecards, counting the cumulative budgetary effects of all PAYGO legislation, averaged over rolling 5-year and 10-year periods starting with the budget year. The OMB uses these scorecards to determine whether a sequestration is necessary. If Congress ends its session with a net PAYGO deficit on the 5-year or 10-year scorecard for that year, the statutory PAYGO Act requires the president to issue a sequestration order, meaning the cancellation of budgetary resources for certain non-exempt direct spending programs, as defined in law.

Similar to sequestration triggered by the BCA, a major shortcoming of the statutory PAYGO rule is that it applies sequestration to a very limited subset of mandatory spending programs. Many of the largest and fastest-growing programs are completely or partially exempt. Sections 255 and 256 of the Balanced Budget and Emergency Deficit

Control Act exempt Social Security, Medicaid, and food stamps (SNAP), among a host of other programs. Special rules apply to Medicare, limiting sequestration to no more than 4 percent of budgetary resources in any given year.[20]

As federal health care spending and Social Security are projected to drive more than half of the expected growth in spending over the next decade, current sequestration exemptions are woefully misguided. The threat of sequestration can spur debate over how to make deliberate reforms and cuts, to substitute for indiscriminate reductions ("sequestration") required by law. This allows Congress to replace arbitrary sequestration cuts with sensible, targeted reforms that secure benefits for vulnerable beneficiaries and reduce economic distortions driven by current program design. Without the threat of sequestration, the status quo favors inaction and automatic spending increases. Sequestration can turn that status quo upside down.

Another shortcoming is that the pay-as-you-go principle does not apply to mandatory spending increases or tax reductions that occur under current law. Increases in mandatory spending due to existing statutes and tax changes codified in law do not trigger PAYGO provisions and do not require offsets.

Last, Congress also routinely evades the existing pay-as-you-go requirements by including language in legislation excluding the costs from the PAYGO scorecard.[21] Statutory and rules-based fiscal restraints ultimately rely on political commitment to be effective.

THE DEBT LIMIT

The debt limit is a legislative fiscal restraint that imposes a limit on federal borrowing. It limits the amount of money or the dates during which the U.S. Treasury is authorized to borrow to finance federal deficit spending. At the debt limit, the Treasury could find itself unable to meet all federal payment obligations on time. Absent specific guidance by Congress, the Treasury Department and the president are confronted with a difficult decision: prioritize spending in accordance with the national interest (making judgments that will be closely scrutinized in courts and by the public) or delay payments across the board, paying bills in the order in which they come due when sufficient revenues are available, regardless of the nature of those bills. Current law does not dictate how the executive branch is to conduct its operations when confronted with a payment resource shortfall at the debt limit, when the issuance of Treasury securities financing deficit spending must cease. Alas such a situation has never occurred and is shrouded in uncertainty.

Several analysts and pundits argue that the debt limit is an archaic construct that serves no useful purpose.[22] They argue that because Congress authorizes all spending, it does not make sense to have a separate limit on borrowing that goes into effect after spending has already been obligated.

Ideally, congressional decisions to spend and borrow would align. However, there are at least three reasons why the debt limit serves a useful purpose: (a) the programs driving the majority of the growth in federal spending were authorized decades ago and are allowed to grow on autopilot with few congressional action-forcing deadlines to change those programs' trajectories; (b) the public does not understand that it is the most popular entitlement programs that are driving the growth in spending and the debt, and the debt limit debate can help elevate public understanding while at the same time providing political cover for lawmakers who seek to reduce spending on those programs; and (c) lawmakers control only some of the factors that drive the growth in the debt, and economic downturns or unanticipated increases in interest costs may mean that previously authorized spending should be reconsidered in light of factors outside Congress's control.

The debt limit provides an urgent and important deadline, enforced by possible painful fiscal measures, to motivate Congress to take action. At the same time, the debt limit provides the political cover necessary to make unpopular, but necessary, legislative decisions.

After all, it was a debt limit negotiation that motivated the Budget Control Act of 2011. Leveraging the debt limit to impose fiscal restraint requires a willingness by Congress to use this powerful tool.

Since passage of the BCA, Congress has failed to put a current-dollar limit on the debt, opting instead to repeatedly suspend the debt limit. A debt-limit suspension technically renders the debt-limit statute inoperative. It allows unlimited borrowing by the Treasury through a certain date.

Debt-limit suspensions are a convenient way for Congress to mask the consequences of its action. Taxpayers will not know until after the debt-limit suspension ends and Treasury has exhausted its extraordinary measures how much the debt increased as a result of Congress's earlier vote.

When the debt-limit suspension ends, the debt limit is automatically increased to reflect the amount of borrowing that occurred since the last debt limit came into effect. In many ways, a debt-limit suspension is like giving the Treasury a credit card with no limit, or a blank check to be cashed against younger and future generations, valid until a certain date.[23]

Lawmakers often argue that suspensions allow them to schedule a more opportune legislative moment at which to enact spending control. Recent history, though, shows that Congress does not, in fact, enact spending control following suspensions of the debt limit. Instead suspensions are politically easier to pass than debt limit increases and act similarly to a temporary debt limit repeal without incurring the corresponding political costs.

The debt limit itself is not sufficient to control the growth in the debt. Congress must act on its commitment to limit debt by controlling its key driver: out-of-control spending.

EFFECTIVE FISCAL RESTRAINTS: AN INTERNATIONAL PERSPECTIVE

Other countries face demographic and political challenges similar to the United States, and yet some of them have mustered a multiparty political commitment to fiscal sustainability and adopted better processes of addressing fiscal pressures than others. The United States can learn valuable lessons from considering two countries that have adopted successful fiscal restraints: Switzerland and Sweden.

SWITZERLAND

Following a large accumulation of deficits and debt in the 1990s, Switzerland adopted a constitutional balanced budget amendment based on a business cycle model in the early 2000s. This so-called Swiss debt brake was first applied to the Swiss budget in 2003.[24]

The debt brake enjoys overwhelming support among the Swiss population. The constitutional amendment was passed by popular referendum with 85 percent support. The Swiss public is broadly aware of and supportive of fiscal rules, a feature that rests in large part on the simplicity and transparency of the Swiss debt brake.

Each year, the Federal Finance Administration calculates a spending ceiling based on projected revenue and a GDP adjustment factor. Taxation is limited by the Swiss Constitution, and Swiss residents pay their taxes directly, rather than by automatic withholding, such that the Swiss are keenly aware of how much they are being taxed.

The GDP adjustment factor is based on the difference between real and potential GDP. Real GDP is an inflation-adjusted measure of the value of all goods and services produced by an economy in a year. Potential GDP is a theoretical construct that produces a projection of what real GPD would be if the economy was operating at full employment, usually defined as the lowest level of unemployment the economy can sustain without inflation accelerating.

The adjustment factor allows for spending to be higher than revenues during an economic downturn and reduces spending to below projected revenues during an economic boom. This allows the Swiss government flexibility to respond to macroeconomic shocks while building fiscal space during good times and maintaining overall budget balance.

The system uses a notional compensation account to track deficits. Net deficits accumulated over the course of a business cycle require a reduction in the spending cap during economic boom times to pay for previous borrowing.

If a surplus develops over a business cycle, this surplus will reduce the Swiss debt. As Switzerland has seen strong surpluses in recent years, the Swiss national debt has been reduced rapidly.

Swiss legislators also retain flexibility to allow for emergency spending above the spending ceiling, with the approval of an absolute majority in both chambers of the Swiss parliament. Emergency spending too is tracked in a notional amortization account. Similar to the compensation account, the Swiss debt brake imposes rules to ensure any emergency appropriations are paid back, rather than adding to the long-term debt.

Certain spending accounts with dedicated revenues (i.e., trust funds), such as unemployment insurance and social security, are exempt from the debt brake as spending on these programs is already limited by other means. Government health care spending is primarily provided for at the cantonal level with little expenditure by the Swiss central government.

According to interviews conducted by myself with representatives of the Swiss Federal Finance Administration in March of 2018, the debt brake is enforced by political consensus. More than a rule on paper, the debt brake codifies a popular, bipartisan commitment to fiscal prudence.[25] Swiss legislators abide by the fiscal rules in place, with support from the Swiss population who show a high level of support for the debt brake.

Larger-than-projected revenues in recent years have rapidly reduced the Swiss national debt, leading to the establishment of a review committee considering how to respond to the huge success in Swiss fiscal consolidation.[26] The group of experts recommended tax reductions, interpreting consistent budget surpluses as a sign that tax revenue is higher than necessary.

SWEDEN

Similar to Switzerland, Sweden imposed a new fiscal rules framework in the 1990s to address rising deficits and debt in central government finances. The Swedish fiscal framework consists of a surplus target, a spending limit, and a debt anchor.

The Swedish Parliament establishes its own surplus target, to be reviewed in every second electoral term. The Swedish Parliament also establishes a spending limit, for the following three years, intended to achieve the surplus target.

A debt anchor was introduced recently as a supplementary goal, without being an operational target. If the Swedish debt differs from the debt anchor by more or less than 5 percent of GDP, it triggers a reporting requirement.

Sweden also established a special Fiscal Policy Council, an outside body tasked with reporting on how well the Swedish government is complying with its fiscal rules.

According to interviews I conducted with representatives of the Swedish National Institute of Economic Research in April 2018, the Swedish fiscal framework is aided by less than full indexation of social benefit programs and notional accounts for the Swedish pension system with built-in triggers that reduce the generosity of pension indexation and rates of return to contributions to secure fiscal solvency. Sweden does not provide open-ended entitlement programs that grow automatically, regardless of available revenues.

The Swedish welfare state is structured to target those who require assistance while keeping disincentives to work at a minimum. Sweden has maintained a relatively constant ratio of social spending to GDP despite the country's more extensive commitment to governmental social welfare policy.[27]

Last, relatively high overall tax burdens have allowed Sweden to maintain fiscal balance despite large public spending commitments.

THE UNITED STATES LACKS A COMPREHENSIVE FISCAL FRAMEWORK

The U.S. fiscal framework suffers from several shortcomings compared to its Swiss and Swedish partners.

The United States has no constitutional amendment to guide legislative fiscal decisions. The Constitution puts Congress firmly at the center of spending, taxing, and borrowing decisions, but the founding document is silent concerning fiscal sustainability or budget balance.

There are no comprehensive fiscal targets to guide the U.S. budget process in statute. While the congressional budget process dictates that Congress is to set spending and revenue targets in the annual budget resolution, Congress rarely agrees on a budget resolution, and yet federal spending continues. Legislators may appropriate monies, and Treasury will pay out to cover entitlement program commitments, even in the absence of a budget resolution.

One primary cause for the institutional and procedural failure of the U.S. budget process to secure fiscal sustainability is the lack of a shared fiscal goal and the resulting absence of a corresponding political commitment. Other driving causes are deep political divides and a willingness by both parties to hijack the budget process to try to force their will. As government grows in size and scope, such divides grow deeper and become more prevalent.

Unlike Switzerland and Sweden, following the emergence of a significant fiscal gap in central government finances, there has been no serious attempt in the United States to adopt a comprehensive fiscal framework on the basis of targets enforced by spending limits, or to peg federal spending to some measure of GDP that corresponds with the economic cycle.

A few attempts have been made to implement a more comprehensive fiscal framework, though most of these were partisan plans with little support from legislators from either party, and none of them garnered sufficient support for passage.

THE PENNY PLAN

Rep. Mark Sanford (R-SC) and Sen. Mike Enzi (R-WY) introduced the Penny Plan, which would implement an aggregate spending cap and "cut a single penny from every dollar the federal government spends," in accordance with the plan's name.[28]

This plan would have imposed a spending cap or limit for total noninterest outlays minus 1 percent in year one. For each of the subsequent five years, outlays would be capped at the previous year's level (not including net interest payments) minus 1 percent. Beginning after five years and for all subsequent years, total spending would be capped at 18 percent of GDP, in line with the historical revenue average. Automatic spending cuts or sequestration would enforce the spending cap in the absence of more deliberate congressional reforms to achieve the spending target.

Unlike the current form of sequestration applied to the Budget Control Act spending caps, the Penny Plan would not exempt any of the programs listed under the Balanced Budget and Emergency Deficit Control Act of 1985, except payments for net interest. The Penny Plan was primarily successful as a political document with little legislative action toward its implementation.

THE MAXIMIZING AMERICA'S PROSPERITY ACT

The Maximizing America's Prosperity Act, introduced by Rep. Kevin Brady (R–TX) would cap federal noninterest spending as a percentage of full-employment GDP, or potential GDP, for cyclical adjustment. Lawmakers would be able to spend more during periods when the economy is weak, and deficits incurred to smooth out business cycles would need to be offset with surplus revenues when the economy is at full employment.[29]

Sequestration would be limited in size and scope, affecting only those programs not exempt from sequestration under the Balanced Budget and Emergency Deficit Control Act of 1985. One theory holds that, as discretionary programs financing domestic and defense priorities get squeezed, this will bring about the political consensus to address the key drivers of spending growth: health care and Social Security. The Maximizing America's Prosperity Act garnered little political support in Congress.

THE BUSINESS CYCLE BALANCED BUDGET AMENDMENT

This smart balanced budget amendment introduced by Rep. Justin Amash (R–MI) would cap federal noninterest spending at the average annual revenue collected over the three prior years, adjusted for inflation and population.[30] Congress would need to pass implementing legislation to carry out the necessary spending changes to achieve the savings determined by the outlay cap. The bill's authors would rely on public humiliation for breaching the caps to motivate spending reforms. This approach also garnered little support in Congress.

CUT, CAP, AND BALANCE

The Cut, Cap, and Balance Act would have placed statutory caps on federal spending and required the passage of a balanced budget amendment to the U.S. Constitution before increasing the nation's debt ceiling.[31]

The act would have imposed separate limits on discretionary spending and mandatory spending with exemptions for Social Security, Medicare, veterans programs, and interest spending. In each subsequent year, the act would have placed a spending ceiling on all noninterest outlays at a declining percentage of GDP until spending as a percentage of GDP was no higher than 19.9, over a period of 10 years. Automatic spending cuts or sequestration would have secured compliance with this spending cap, exempting payments for military personnel and health care, Medicare, military retirement, Social Security, veterans, and net interest. Cut, Cap, and Balance was part of the discussions during the 2011 debt limit impasse. President Barak Obama and then-Speaker of the House John Boehner ultimately settled on the Budget Control Act of 2011 instead.

To the extent that the United States has an effective budget process on paper, this process has been rarely if ever followed as intended over at least the past two decades. U.S. spending and borrowing operates largely on an ad-hoc basis.

Spending on social welfare and other mandatory programs is driven by programmatic criteria, irrespective of tax revenues, with irregular review by legislators. More than two-thirds of federal spending in the United States effectively operates on autopilot.

Discretionary spending requiring annual appropriations, meanwhile, has failed to abide by statutory fiscal commitments, most recently the Budget Control Act of 2011. In addition to political deals to revise previously established spending limits without adequate fiscal offsets, U.S. legislators have resorted to abusing budgetary exemptions intended for emergency needs to finance ongoing operations, in an attempt to further evade fiscal restraints.

Unlike in Switzerland, where emergency spending is tracked in a notional account and lawmakers are required to offset such spending in future years, emergency spending is exempt from fiscal rules in the United States with no provision to ensure future repayment.

The U.S. budget process is highly convoluted and complex. Federal legislative staff, and even legislators who are not in key positions on budget committees—as well as the public—lack a solid understanding of how the process works. A lack of transparency and simplicity facilitate an irresponsible spending process as constituents have difficulty assigning blame for fiscal failures and holding legislators accountable.

TOWARD EFFECTIVE FISCAL RESTRAINTS FOR THE UNITED STATES

The United States will soon reach a tipping point as unsustainable fiscal projections concerning deficits and debt could bring about a crisis. Now is the time for U.S. legislators to adopt a more sustainable fiscal framework to ensure a strong economy for the future. Such a framework, according to lessons from Switzerland and Sweden, should be structured so it would do the following:

- Rest on a popular base of support: Constituents are the ultimate arbiters of political success. In both Switzerland and Sweden, the population is highly aware and highly supportive of government policy to achieve overall budget balance. A lasting framework for fiscal sustainability will only work with popular awareness of the problem and support for restraining government budgets.

- Reflect a bipartisan political commitment: A lasting political commitment must reflect bipartisan recognition that fiscal sustainability is an important and timeless goal. Legislators of all parties must be committed to protecting younger and future generations from undue debt burdens.

- Be transparent: In order for legislators to follow the budget process and for constituents to be able to hold them accountable, a sustainable fiscal framework should be transparent. It should account for all spending and taxes, and the public should be able to access regular reports on the fiscal state of the nation. Moreover, a nonpartisan fiscal entity, such as the CBO, should provide regular, public updates on how well legislators are abiding by the fiscal framework.

- Establish and maintain fiscal targets: A sustainable fiscal framework should establish and maintain short-term, medium-term, and long-term fiscal targets. Targets for spending and revenues should drive a gradual decline from today's historically high levels of public debt to a level that reflects the U.S. historical debt burden and ensures a fiscally sustainable path. Lawmakers should regularly review fiscal targets and enforce them via budget process tools, including reconciliation and mandated savings.[32]

- Adjust with the business cycle: A sustainable fiscal framework should be responsive to economic fluctuations and resulting needs and pressures. During periods of economic weakness, a sustainable fiscal framework should allow for flexibility to respond to shocks with automatic stabilization policies. During periods of economic strength, the framework must exert sufficient discipline to allow the economy to flourish without excessive fiscal stimulus and to accumulate fiscal space for when economic crisis strikes next.

- Provide for emergencies: When natural disaster strikes or when a national security threat arises, legislators must be able to respond to unforeseen, sudden, and immediate needs. A sustainable fiscal framework should account for disaster assistance that is expected to occur on a regular basis in a designated disaster-related account, with specific guidance regarding the circumstances during which such funds become available. While hurricanes, floods, and wildfires are natural disasters, they occur with relatively predictable frequency in the United States and can thus be budgeted for. For large-scale, unforeseen disasters and threats, a sustainable fiscal framework should impose a sufficiently high voting threshold for emergency spending to require broad, bipartisan support and should account for such spending in a notional account that would be required to be made whole over a business cycle, to allow for the immediate expense without permanently burdening the fiscal account.

PROSPECTS FOR A SUSTAINABLE FISCAL FRAMEWORK
IN THE UNITED STATES

Recent actions by the U.S. Congress and the administration paint a grim picture for the prospects of a sustainable fiscal framework in the

United States. Political tensions are high, and legislators of both parties have resorted to making unfunded and unsustainable promises to their respective constituents concerning the preservation of current spending policies for popular entitlements, immediate tax relief, and the establishment of new entitlements such as paid family leave and Medicare for all.

As was the case in Switzerland and Sweden, prior to the adoption of their respective sustainable fiscal frameworks, it may take a crisis to awaken the U.S. constituency and their legislators to the highly unsustainable fiscal trajectory that characterizes current U.S. budget policy and to motivate necessary reforms. It remains to be seen whether the COVID-19 pandemic will elicit this response. The most recent fiscal restraint enacted by legislators in the United States came on the heels of the 2008 global financial crisis that led to a political movement in the United States, the Tea Party, which demanded better budget policy. The Budget Control Act of 2011 proved to be an inadequate fiscal framework for a more sustainable budget policy in the United States, and its success was short-lived and limited in scope. Legislators should learn valuable lessons from Switzerland and Sweden and adopt a sustainable fiscal framework that rests on popular support, reflects a bipartisan commitment, is transparent, is based on fiscal targets that adjust with the business cycle, and allows for a responsible emergency response.

CHAPTER SIX

UNDER THREAT: RULES-BASED FISCAL POLICY AND HOW TO PRESERVE IT

XAVIER DEBRUN AND LARS JONUNG

The demise of the Bretton Woods system[1] in 1973 inaugurated two decades of high inflation and rising public debts. As theory linked expansionary policy biases to policymakers' distorted incentives under discretion,[2] interest in rules-based policymaking grew. Even though theory framed the debate in terms of rules versus discretion, it was clear that in practice, a regime predicated on mechanical policy adjustments dictated by a rule would be as suboptimal as unconstrained discretion.[3] Thus, the concrete problem underlying the design of rules-based policy frameworks never was to find the optimal state-contingent rule, but to devise practical mechanisms containing the dark side of discretion—such as a neglect for long-term outcomes—while preserving the bright side of it—that is, the ability to quickly respond to unforeseen developments.

In the monetary realm, failures to stick to quantitative limits on the growth of monetary aggregates in the 1980s favored the spread of inflation targeting. Under inflation targeting, politically independent central banks are primarily mandated to achieve price stability expressed as a numerical goal for the rate of inflation. While policy instruments are not subject to any binding rule, the goal of achieving the inflation target over the medium term shapes current policy decisions. Since the early 1990s, successful inflation targeting regimes have proliferated, keeping inflation expectations anchored around the target and providing ample room for active stabilization policy in the short term.

Rules-based fiscal frameworks came later,[4] and often after the formal adoption of inflation targeting.[5] Historically confined to subnational governments,[6] fiscal rules only became the norm at the central level among the first group of European countries committed to adopt the euro in the 1990s. Beyond Western Europe, rules-based fiscal policy became increasingly popular after the beginning of the 21st century as more countries felt the need to reduce their public debt.[7]

In their most advanced form, fiscal frameworks combine numerical rules affecting key fiscal indictors with transparency requirements, strict budgetary procedures, and more recently, independent fiscal councils monitoring adherence to the numerical rules and assisting in their implementation. By setting quantitative limits on aggregate indicators such as government debt, the budget deficit, and public expenditure growth, fiscal rules aim to make deviations from these limits sufficiently costly to deter excesses. Costs include both formal sanctions and reputation losses associated with the breach of public commitments. Effective fiscal rules guide discretion in the short term and make future fiscal trajectories more predictable. Hence, successful fiscal rules create policy space in the short run because better anchored expectations reduce the risk of financial market stress whenever significant public-sector borrowing is required.

The potential role of independent fiscal councils to constrain fiscal discretion, often alongside fiscal rules, has been acknowledged more recently.[8] The appetite for such institutions quickly grew after the global financial crisis (GFC) of 2008–2009.[9] Whereas existing institutions operate primarily as watchdogs alerting stakeholders in the budget process, proposals to give them teeth have received new attention, notably in the form of a right to set binding deficit limits for the government[10] or to use specific fiscal levers to preserve public debt sustainability and promote fiscal stabilization.[11]

Our sense of the vast empirical literature on the determinants of monetary and fiscal policies is that explicit institutional constraints on discretion have on average contributed to improve policy outcomes. Central bank independence—and inflation targeting in particular—is widely credited for maintaining low and stable inflation in advanced as well as developing economies.[12] Although great caution remains in causally linking the adoption of fiscal rules to lower public deficits and less procyclical budgets,[13] the positive association between adequately constrained fiscal discretion and improved fiscal performance is strong.[14]

Despite this apparent success, rules-based fiscal policy has been harshly criticized to the point of facing an existential crisis. After the GFC, fiscal rules have been successively deemed too rigid to support the recovery and too lax to encourage the subsequent consolidation. More broadly, formal compliance with numerical limits has been consistently low, raising questions about the overall usefulness of rules-based frameworks.[15]

Although threats to rules-based fiscal policy can take various forms, they largely reflect the common presumption that fiscal rules, like traffic laws and speed limits, must be enforced. With enforceability seen as critical, efforts to make rules more flexible (i.e., contingent on a broader set of circumstances) result in more complex, less transparent setups. Escape clauses must be well defined; technical refinements must be codified in detail; and the related enforcement loopholes must be closed. Of the three basic properties of good fiscal rules—simplicity, flexibility, and enforceability—only two can be simultaneously achieved. In the end, complex and opaque rules stop being a reliable compass for policymakers, and the temptation to abandon them looms large.

As delegation of fiscal levers to independent institutions is likely to remain off the table in the foreseeable future, effectively constraining fiscal discretion requires more effective rules-based frameworks.[16] In a recent note, International Monetary Fund (IMF) staff see the scope for better combining simplicity, flexibility, and enforceability.[17] They suggest comprehensive reforms that (a) guarantee the internal consistency of fiscal frameworks, (b) exploit simpler ways to make rules more contingent (e.g., a greater reliance on medium-term expenditure ceilings), and (c) promote mechanisms raising the reputational costs of noncompliance. These proposals, however, amount to tweaking existing parameters, an exercise which, considering recent history, might fall short of mitigating the risk of a return to pure fiscal discretion.

Going beyond parametric adjustments, we propose a less constrained paradigm to guide the design and implementation of fiscal rules. Specifically, we argue that the enforceability of numerical limits should not be a binding constraint. This allows for rules that boil down to quantitative benchmarks whose impact on policy behavior rests solely on tangible reputational costs. In a sense, we suggest being open to so-called Taylor rules in the fiscal realm.[18] To enhance the reputational effects of such fiscal Taylor rules (FTR),[19] independent fiscal councils would have to be ruthless and vocal watchdogs debunking "fiscal alchemy," clearing the public debate of partisan smokescreens, and fostering popular support for sound fiscal policies.

It is worth clarifying two points upfront. First, the FTR idea is not new.[20] However, the originality of our proposal is to place the FTR at the center of a rules-based fiscal framework, without formal enforcement procedure (nor other traditional fiscal rules), and operating in symbiosis with independent fiscal institutions focused on amplifying the reputational effects of the rule. Second, our proposal is not premised on the claim that enforcement per se is useless and ought to be abandoned. Beyond the credibility of sanctions (or lack thereof), there is arguably a signal embedded in the activation of an enforcement procedure. A country willing to risk even elusive sanctions might reveal an intrinsically weaker commitment to fiscal soundness compared to a country unwilling to take such risk. If so, market participants would take note, and risk premiums would adjust accordingly. As such, enforcement procedures could promote market discipline even if actual sanctions are a low-probability event. That interpretation is consistent with the higher sovereign spreads resulting from entering the Excessive Deficit Procedure under the European Union (EU) Stability and Growth Pact.[21]

In the end, our qualm with the central role of enforcement in the current paradigm is that it can produce rules sufficiently opaque and intractable to threaten rules-based policy itself. Thus, the key differences between the current paradigm and our proposal consist in (a) breaking any mechanical link between the breach of a numerical limit and the threat of sanctions emanating from opaque procedures and arcane numerology and (b) actively amplifying reputational effects of rules through independent watchdogs. Our point is not that an FTR-based framework is always and everywhere preferable, but that it can offer a viable option for countries where the traditional speed-limit view of rules has failed or does not seem politically palatable. Our proposal and the underlying analysis are in the spirit of Bénassy-Quéré and others, who call for "a combination of streamlined rules, stronger institutions, and market-based incentives, with the aim of strengthening national responsibility."[22]

The rest of this chapter first elaborates on the trilemma that makes legally enforceable rules either too rigid or too complicated ("Designing Fiscal Rules: Mission Impossible?"). We then discuss the extent to which such a restricted paradigm can threaten rules-based fiscal policy itself ("Threats to Rules-Based Fiscal Policy"). Then, in the section "Rules-Based Fiscal Policy without Formal Enforcement," we illustrate the properties and potential benefits of simple fiscal Taylor rules.

DESIGNING FISCAL RULES: MISSION IMPOSSIBLE?

This section shows that the enforceability requirement at the core of the paradigm underlying the design of fiscal rules has made them ever more contingent (flexible) in the hope to improve formal compliance. The resulting loss of simplicity illustrates a trilemma between the three essential properties of good-practice fiscal rules: simplicity, flexibility, and enforceability.

ENFORCEMENT, COMPLIANCE, AND EFFECTIVENESS

Fiscal policy rules are generally nested in legal instruments, such as international treaties, constitutions, and fiscal responsibility laws. The dominant view is that the numerical constraints at the core of the rule should effectively bind.[23] This requires enforcement, that is, "the act of *compelling* observance of or *compliance* with a law, rule, or obligation."[24]

As illustrated in the appendix, the basic logic of the argument fits a bare-bones political-economy model of excessive deficits and fiscal rules.

In the classic Alesina and Tabellini two-period "partisan" model of optimal fiscal policy, a deficit bias emerges because citizens and politicians have different motivations.[25] Politicians care about reelection, which is intrinsically uncertain. Electoral uncertainty inflates the incumbent's discount rate (or makes him or her myopic), encouraging excessive expenditure compared to the case of certain reelection. As this extra spending is financed with new debt, it comes at the cost of lower future spending, which is socially undesirable.

Subjecting a myopic politician to a fiscal rule can then be socially beneficial. For instance, Beetsma and Debrun model the existence of a fiscal rule as a utility loss incurred when public debt d exceeds some socially optimal level $d^\star$ as follows $-\psi(d - d^\star)$. The total utility loss is proportional to the size of the fiscal excess and to a parameter ψ capturing the strength of the enforcement procedure (i.e., the marginal disutility of excessive public debt).[26] As formally illustrated in the appendix, there is an optimal value of ψ such that the elected politician will choose the socially optimal level of debt in period 1. Intuitively, the optimal enforcement parameter grows with politicians' incentives to accumulate excessive public debt, which depends on reelection prospects and on the (marginal) social value of future public spending.

However, this result is straightforward only because enforcement per se comes as a free lunch (i.e., it can deliver the first best policy by blindly cutting expenditure to address a debt bias). Experience points to a more realistic scenario where the rule is imperfect so that enforcing it fully would have negative side effects.[27] In this case, strictly sticking to the rule is costly, making it socially optimal to tolerate some deviation of d from $d^\star$. De facto, the desirable enforcement parameter ψ will be smaller than the $\psi^\star$ characterized under the assumption of no enforcement cost.

This simple example illustrates the difference between the *enforcement* of (and correspondingly, the formal *compliance* to) a fiscal rule and its *effectiveness* in fostering outcomes that dominate equilibrium policies under unconstrained discretion. It also suggests that a fiscal rule meant to be strictly enforced (or fully complied with) must not have any undesirable side effect. In practice, however, fiscal rules are neither fully state-contingent nor adjusted for possible collateral damage associated with forced policy change, and the economy is arguably better off with imperfect enforcement and compliance. By the same token, attempts to make the rule more contingent (i.e., less costly when enforced) would call for stricter enforcement. Beetsma and Debrun show this in a model where enforcement has adverse composition effects on public spending, and the same conclusion is implicit to Equation (6.A.8) in the appendix.[28]

The positive link between the flexibility of the rule (or its degree of contingency) and the desirable strictness of enforcement helps rationalize common arguments in existing analyses of fiscal rules. First, extreme enforcement options—such as the fines envisaged for EU member states in breach of the Stability and Growth Pact (SGP)—carry little credibility because they are suboptimal in most states of the world. Second, low levels of compliance with numerical rules[29] (see Figure 6.1) can be consistent with empirical evidence showing a broadly positive association between rules-based fiscal policy and fiscal performance.[30] Third, the flexibility-enforcement nexus echoes recent attempts in the EU to tighten the enforcement of rules loaded with a growing number of contingencies, augmenting the overall complexity of the fiscal framework. This suggests a trilemma that we now elaborate upon.

THE TRILEMMA AND AN EVOLUTIONARY TALE OF FISCAL RULES

Since the seminal insights of Kopits and Symansky, it is generally accepted that fiscal rules should ensure a credible commitment to the long-term sustainability of public finances without prejudice to other key policy objectives.[31] With this in mind, Kopits and Symansky argue that a good rule, on top of being discipline-inducing and *enforceable* as defined earlier, should be *flexible* (i.e., contingent enough not to conflict too often with other policy objectives) and *simple*. Simplicity is a key virtue because to foster policymakers' credibility, rules must shape expectations about future fiscal trends. As such, the rules should be clear to policymakers themselves and easy to communicate to markets and the public.

FIGURE 6.1

Compliance rates with fiscal rules by type and country group

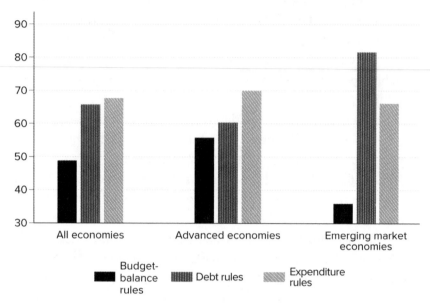

Source: International Monetary Fund (IMF) *Fiscal Monitor* (April 2014).
Note: Bars show the frequency of country-year characterized by compliance with fiscal rules in a panel of IMF member countries by type of fiscal rule.

However, of these three desirable properties, only two can be simultaneously fulfilled. Simple and enforceable rules (such as a constitutional balanced-budget requirement) are often bound to conflict with economic logic; hence they are inflexible. Simple and flexible rules cannot be subject to strict enforcement because, as discussed previously, flexibility itself can only stem from a tolerance for sensible (and potentially sizable) deviations from numerical limits. Finally, flexible and enforceable rules are complicated because many contingencies need to be spelled out, and the enforcement loopholes associated with exceptions, technical refinements, and escape clauses need to be closed. The resulting trilemma is described in Figure 6.2.

The trilemma suggests an evolutionary tale of fiscal rule design in history. *Enforceable* and *simple* rules have been common at the subnational level, where rules historically emerged. Classic examples are the

FIGURE 6.2

Designing fiscal rules (Stability and Growth Pact [SGP] 1.0): a trilemma

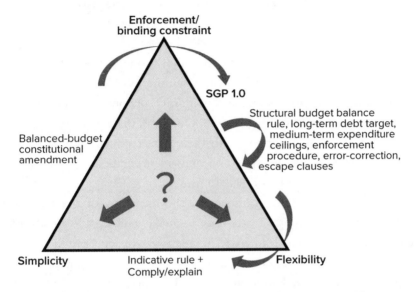

Source: Authors' application of trilemma (https://www.investopedia.com/terms/t/trilemma
.asp) to the Stability and Growth Pact (SGP).

constitutional amendments banning deficits in most U.S. states since the mid-19th century. Of course, while debt-fearing voters might consider such rules desirable, the lack of flexibility in the short term inevitably challenges strict enforcement. Tolerance for off-budget operations and allowing rules to bind only ex ante are just two common ways to allow for weaker enforcement while remaining formally compliant.

In the early 1990s, central governments started to show interest in rules-based fiscal policy, and greater complexity was allowed. Caps on public debts and deficits were combined with medium-term balanced budget requirements to leave room for short-term fiscal stabilization below the deficit ceiling. The original EU SGP adopted in Dublin in 1997 reflected these conscious efforts to enforce discipline without prejudice to using the budget as a macroeconomic shock absorber. However, by 2003, it had become clear that this arrangement had not been enforced as envisaged and was still perceived as inflexible.[32] This paved the way for the SGP relaxation in 2005.[33] The result was a more complex framework.

Today, the SGP, revamped once again in the aftermath of the GFC, features limits on the level and the first difference of practically every macro-relevant budget aggregate: debt, budget balance, structural balance, and expenditure growth.[34] Although formally strengthened, enforcement has remained challenging. Voluminous official documents are required to clarify how compliance with myriad potentially inconsistent caps and benchmarks can be assessed. On top of that, euro area member states must now be equipped with their own national fiscal rules that explicitly account for the cycle and must incorporate automatic adjustment mechanisms in case of deviations.

The journey of EU countries in the meanders of the trilemma shows how well-intended attempts to make enforceable fiscal rules more state-contingent lead to an increasingly opaque system as each wave of tensions in the system triggers amendments, refinements, exceptions, and codified interpretations. This process of sedimentation through partial reforms reflects the natural reluctance to overhaul a supposedly permanent system too often, the same dynamic that drives the ever-increasing complexity of tax codes. In fact, the fiscal alchemy famously decried by Leeper now appears to have metastasized from the exercise of discretion itself to the rules supposed to constrain it.[35] This is an impasse.

Interpreting history aside, the trilemma can also help us think about the future of rules-based fiscal policy. First, frustration about the inability to get the rules right and to enforce them motivates many specific arguments against rules-based fiscal policies. We discuss these threats in the next section. Second, accepting that only two of three desirable properties of a good fiscal rule can be simultaneously achieved should encourage us to explore the possibility of relaxing the enforceability constraint and to discuss the scope for simple and flexible fiscal rules. What would they look like and how could they shape the conduct of fiscal policy? The last section of this paper lifts the veil on what remains uncharted territory in the realm of fiscal rules.

THREATS TO RULES-BASED FISCAL POLICY

This section shows that the limitations associated with enforceability expose rules-based fiscal policy to a broad range of threats. First, attempts to get the rules "right" put a premium on finding the adequate calibration of the numerical constraints. After the GFC, uncertainty about the steady state of the economy (notably in terms of potential growth and natural interest rate) has made it potentially easy to build a plausible economic case against any given fiscal rule. Beyond technical issues, enforcement is ultimately about the possibility of forcibly constraining *elected* policymakers. This brings politics, public perceptions, and compatibility with the country's broader institutional setup into the picture. Such considerations can motivate arguments questioning the democratic legitimacy of rules-based fiscal policy.

GETTING THE RULE RIGHT

Because interest rates and nominal GDP growth are key drivers of public debt dynamics, uncertainty about their steady-state levels invites criticisms about the calibration of fiscal rules expected to deliver public debt sustainability.[36] The arguments mainly revolve around the persistently low borrowing costs experienced by many advanced economies post-GFC and the risks related to permanently lower nominal growth.

Lower borrowing costs. In many countries, unconventional monetary policies have been testing the lower bound of nominal interest rates. For governments still considered to be issuing safe securities, this means historically low borrowing costs and the possibility of keeping the dynamics of the public debt-to-GDP ratio under control without running significant primary surpluses, if at all. Expectations of persistently low interest rates could have lasting implications for the relevance of specific fiscal rules and for their resilience in the face of monetary policy normalization. In this context, recalling the basic drivers of debt dynamics is important.

In a deterministic setting, two basic relationships determine debt dynamics and the related assessments of debt sustainability (omitting time subscripts for convenience). The first is the period public–debt–accumulation equation:

$$\Delta d = \gamma d - p, \tag{6.1}$$

where Δ is the discrete first-time-difference operator, d is the debt-to-GDP ratio, p is the primary balance (also in percentage of GDP), and γ captures the growth-adjusted interest rate paid on public debt $\left(\gamma = \dfrac{r - \theta}{1 + \theta} \right)$, with r the (nominal or real) interest rate and θ the (nominal or real) GDP growth. The second key relationship describes the endogenous (sluggish) response of fiscal policy to public debt developments:

$$p = \lambda p_{-1} + \kappa + \rho d, \tag{6.2}$$

where λ captures the well-documented persistence in fiscal balances, κ is a constant, and ρ is the policy response (in terms of a change in the primary balance) to variations in the public debt. Two key indicators matter when assessing whether public debt is sustainable in the long term. The first is the requirement for stable debt dynamics:[37]

$$\rho > \gamma^{*}(1 - \lambda), \tag{6.3}$$

where a * superscript denotes steady-state values. Equation (6.3) states that public debt will revert to a finite steady-state level d^{*} if the strength of the primary balance's stabilizing response to variations in the debt ratio more than offsets the automatic debt buildup associated with interest payments. (Note that this is the relevant condition regardless of the sign of γ^{*}.) The second indicator is the steady state debt level implied by fiscal behavior as described in (6.2). It is given by:[38]

$$d^{*} = \frac{-\kappa}{\rho - \gamma^{*}(1 - \lambda)}. \tag{6.4}$$

A priori, the long-term debt level should not matter if it corresponds to a dynamically stable equilibrium—that is, if (6.3) is fulfilled. In practice, however, the level at which debt ultimately stabilizes matters if the primary balance is bounded upward. This assumption is at the core of the notion of "debt limit."

Ostry and others and Ghosh and others rationalize the existence of a primary balance upper bound by invoking "fiscal fatigue," that is, a limited ability to achieve and sustain high primary surpluses.[39] They provide empirical estimates of Equation (6.2), showing that the marginal response to debt is nonlinear and weakens as debt reaches very high levels—often well above 150 percent of GDP for advanced economies. Bi uses calibrated general equilibrium models to show that the combination of Laffer-curve effects on tax revenues and incompressible floors to public expenditures determines debt limits beyond which default is unavoidable.[40] Her simulations also point to high debt limits in advanced economies.

Formally, if Equation (6.2) is now written as $p = min(\lambda p_{-1} + \kappa + \rho d, \overline{p})$, there are *two* relevant long-term equilibria for the debt level: d^*, as described in (6.4), which prevails as long as the corresponding primary balance fulfills the condition $p^* \leq \overline{p}$, and a higher debt level $d^{**} = \dfrac{\overline{p}}{\gamma^*}$. Assuming dynamic efficiency in the long run ($\gamma^* > 0$), this is an unstable equilibrium (because $\rho = 0$). Hence d^{**} is literally the edge of a cliff beyond which the government loses control of debt dynamics.

We see two ways in which rules-based fiscal policy could be threatened by the current low–interest rate environment. The first is that low interest rates can undermine fiscal "prudence"—or encourage profligacy. Mauro and others propose measuring fiscal prudence by ρ, the endogenous response of fiscal policy to public debt.[41] The higher ρ, the more prudent the fiscal policy and vice versa. Using an estimated variant of (6.2), Debrun and Kinda find evidence that the budgetary "footprint" of public debt (i.e., the interest bill) matters for fiscal behavior.[42] Specifically, taking the public debt level and other standard determinants of the primary budget balance as given, the response to public debt is weaker when the interest rate is low than when it is high. If the low–interest rate environment is perceived as *temporary*, pressures to deviate from normal-time fiscal behavior would be short-lived, and they would not put into question the degree of fiscal prudence (and the corresponding long-term debt level) embedded in any given fiscal rule.

However, the damage to existing fiscal rules could be real if lower interest rates were a *permanent* development—that is, if $r^\star$ had fallen as well.[43] To see this, we can use the fiscal behavior specification estimated by Debrun and Kinda:[44]

$$p = \lambda p_{-1} + \kappa + \rho d + \chi rd, \qquad (6.5)$$

where rd is the interest bill and $\chi > 0$ (the sensitivity of fiscal policy to the latter), instead of (6.2). The corresponding long-term debt level is

$$d^\star = \frac{\kappa}{\gamma^\star(1-\lambda) - (\rho + \chi r^\star)}. \qquad (6.6)$$

Clearly, a change in the estimated $r^\star$ would affect the implicit public debt target $d^\star$, potentially conflicting with the debt norm prescribed by a fiscal rule. A priori, the marginal effect of a change in $r^\star$ on $d^\star$ is ambiguous:

$$\frac{\partial d^\star}{\partial r^\star} = \frac{-\kappa\left(\dfrac{1-\lambda}{1+g^\star} - \chi\right)}{\left(\gamma^\star(1-\lambda) - (\rho + \chi r^\star)\right)^2}. \qquad (6.7)$$

(recall that $\kappa < 0$ for $d^\star$ to be positive).

For lower interest rates to translate into a higher long-term debt level, the marginal impact of the interest burden on fiscal prudence should be large enough (χ high enough), fiscal policy should be sufficiently persistent (λ high enough) or the fall in $r^\star$ should mirror a decline in $\theta^\star$, leaving $\gamma^\star$ broadly unchanged.[45] Econometric estimates suggest that a rise in $r^\star$ would, *all else equal*, leave $d^\star$ unchanged.[46] That said, perceptions that permanently lower borrowing costs take place in the context of a secular-stagnation scenario—bringing a downward adjustment in $\theta^\star$ as well—would suffice to raise the long-run debt anchor implicit to fiscal policy behavior, potentially putting into question fixed prescriptions incorporated in rules.

A second channel through which low borrowing costs could test the resilience of fiscal rules pertains to the rules' basic design. In many cases, and certainly in all euro area countries, the emphasis on capping the overall budget deficit—cyclically adjusted or not—could create stress when interest rates normalize. A budget-balance rule (BBR) is a special case of (6.5) where $\lambda = 0$, $\kappa = -\overline{b}$, the overall *deficit* cap ($\overline{b} > 0$), $\rho = 0$, and $\chi = (1 + \theta^\star)^{-1}$. The corresponding long-term debt level is

$$d^\star_{BBR} = \frac{\overline{b}\left(1 + \theta^\star\right)}{\theta^\star} \, . \tag{6.8}$$

Under a BBR, savings on interest payments can be spent, whereas the costs of rising interest rates must be offset by tax increases or primary expenditure cuts. To the extent that (some of) the fiscal space created by a temporarily lower interest bill is used to finance structural increases in primary outlays, the fiscal rule is bound to come under pressure as soon as interest rate normalization occurs. The intensity of these pressures will depend on the actual maturity structure of existing obligations and on the speed at which the yield curve moves up.

Lower nominal growth. Intimately related to the threat described previously is the prospect of entering a period combining persistently low nominal growth and interest rates, or "secular stagnation."[47] The basic tenet of the secular stagnation story is that too much savings chases too little investment. With interest rates at their effective lower bound, the likely policy advice to exit this trap is for governments to use fiscal measures to invest in public infrastructures. If this strategy for escaping secular stagnation prevails, fiscal rules constraining public borrowing regardless of the quality of spending may quickly be seen as a counterproductive.[48]

Independent of the adequate policy response to an episode of protracted slow nominal growth, structural factors—including shrinking and aging populations—dampening potential growth can have a dramatic impact on the long-run properties of certain fiscal rules. For instance, Equation (6.8) shows that the Maastricht deficit ceiling of $\overline{b} = 0.03$ requires long-term nominal growth of 5 percent per annum ($\theta^\star = 0.05$) to be consistent with the convergence of public debt to a maximum of 60 percent of GDP ($d^\star_{BBR} = 0.6$). With real growth and inflation struggling to reach 2 percent in many advanced economies, the arithmetic is brutal: either the debt ceiling is too low, or the deficit cap is too lax. Either way, the two rules look increasingly inconsistent, weakening the foundation of rules-based fiscal frameworks.

Changing views about optimal fiscal policy. Aside from changes in the long-term technical properties of fiscal indicators under a given fiscal rule, the calibration and even the existence of a rule can be put into question if views about optimal fiscal policy change. As indicated earlier, the rise of rules-based fiscal policy in the 1990s reflected evidence that unconstrained discretion could lead to excessive deficits and ever-rising debts. Political-economy models of fiscal policy provided formal support to the idea that discretionary policies were plagued by a bias toward deficits because of short-sighted, opportunistic, and vote-maximizing politicians.

However, the first two threats discussed previously (i.e., lower borrowing costs and lower nominal growth)—that point to limited monetary policy space and expanded need for macroeconomic policy support—have started to push the pendulum back in favor of greater fiscal discretion.[49] The GFC and its aftermath have strengthened a preexisting tendency to view discretionary fiscal policy under a more positive light. The development of New Keynesian and dynamic stochastic general equilibrium models in the 1990s and 2000s brought back to the fore the stabilizing role that discretionary fiscal policy can play.[50] Beyond smoothing the business cycle, fiscal policy is now also seen as a tool to correct external imbalances, as countries with large current account surpluses are explicitly advised to pursue more expansionary policies.

It is hard to say how far the pendulum will swing back toward discretionary fiscal actions, but the raison d'être for rules-based fiscal policy could be under threat.[51] Indeed, as fiscal policy is expected, more than in the past, to achieve multiple objectives (internal and external balance on top of equity and efficiency), tensions between the prescription of fiscal rules and the perceived need for greater discretion are likely to increase. An expanded role for fiscal policy also complicates the formulation of sufficiently simple fiscal rules.

POLITICS, PERCEPTIONS, AND INSTITUTIONS

Adopting a rules-based fiscal framework and enforcing it in a consistent manner remain political decisions that depend on enabling factors being in place. Public support and an institutional ecosystem conducive to the enforcement of rules strike us as particularly important. Public support is likely to be high if the rationale for constraining elected policymakers' discretion is well understood and broadly shared. At the same time, and perhaps paradoxically, the public is more likely to back fiscal rules if there is a certain level of trust in governments' ability to define such rules appropriately and to ultimately stick to them.

Although these dimensions do not easily lend themselves to a rigorous analysis, we see risks that the publicly perceived rationale for fiscal rules may fade away. Also, we fear that laudable efforts, notably in the EU, to promote common standards for rules-based frameworks aligned on international good practice will meet the harsh reality of certain institutional environments not conducive to the enforcement of fiscal rules.

Perceived rationale for fiscal rules and public support. While shifts in the economic paradigm in favor of greater discretion might escape the public, broader perceptions that rules are introduced to perpetuate "austerity" can undermine the popular support required for their legitimacy and longevity. These perceptions reflect the fact that many fiscal rules and frameworks have been debated and introduced in response to debt overhang and fiscal stress—or at least the risk of it—and the corresponding need to credibly commit to lower debts and deficits. The risk that trust in government is low or falling when such reforms have to be made may further undermines support for rules-based fiscal policy.[52]

To gauge the relevance of the argument, we look at trust in government as measured by the Eurobarometer around 11 recent episodes of fiscal rule adoption at the national level in the EU between 1999 and 2017 (Figure 6.3). For each episode, the bars show the difference between the average level of trust measured during the three years before (gray) and the three years after (black) the adoption of the rule, and the level of trust measured the year of its introduction.

Rules were adopted under severe fiscal stress in only two cases: Greece (2010) and Spain (2011). In both countries, trust in government was falling rapidly during the entire seven-year period. In three other episodes, trust was relatively low at the time of adoption but rebounded thereafter. Finally, among the six episodes where trust at the time of

FIGURE 6.3

Trust in government before and after the adoption of national fiscal rules

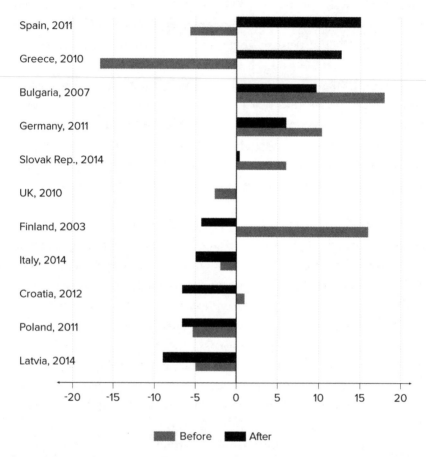

Sources: International Monetary Fund Fiscal Rules Dataset, Eurobarometer, and author's calculations.

Note: Trust is the percentage of positive answers to the question: "Do you tend to trust or not to trust the government?"

adoption was greater or equal to the average of the preceding three years, trust continued to grow in two cases (Finland, 2003, and Croatia, 2012, albeit marginally).

Overall, there is scant evidence that moving to rules-based fiscal policy was systematically done in a challenging context where low trust and an impending fiscal crisis would undermine broad-based popular

FIGURE 6.4

Trust in the national government across European Union member states
(2001–2017)

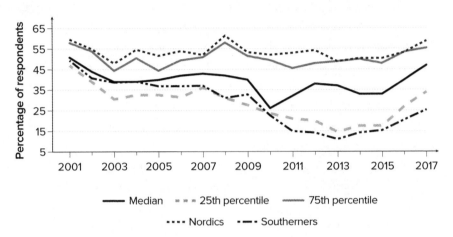

Source: Eurobarometer.

Notes: Trust is the percentage of positive answers to the question: "Do you tend to trust or
not to trust the government?" Countries included are Belgium, Denmark, Ireland, Greece,
Spain, France, Italy, Luxembourg, The Netherlands, Austria, Portugal, Findland, Sweden,
and the UK. Nordics = Denmark, Finland, and Sweden; Southerners = Greece, Italy, Portugal,
and Spain.

support from the start. That said, support for the many rules adopted
during or in the aftermath of the GFC remains vulnerable to the fading
memory of the fiscal stress of that time. Lessons learned under stress may
not always endure when normalcy returns,[53] so that even the proponents
of fiscal rules may eventually discount their long-run benefits and conclude that they are obsolete or irrelevant.[54]

Institutional ecosystem: Not always enforcement friendly. Beyond a strong
rationale for fiscal rules and some trust in a government's ability to design and operate them, some have argued that deeper country-specific
factors determine the extent to which a society values compliance with
rules—and correspondingly accepts enforcement as needed. These attitudes are partially reflected in the nature of government institutions
and the quality of governance, which should ultimately affect the level
of public trust in the governance system. Figure 6.4 offers another cut

at the Eurobarometer's measure of trust in national governments. Most striking is the cross-country difference in the overall level of trust between two groups of EU member states which we could a priori think of as having different attitudes with respect to rules-based fiscal policy, namely the Southern European members (Greece, Italy, Portugal, and Spain) and the Nordic members (Denmark, Finland, and Sweden).

While trust of government in the Nordic members has remained relatively high and quite stable since 2000, it collapsed among the Southern members, particularly after the GFC. Movements in unemployment and other crisis-related economic pain clearly explain time variations in this gap.[55] However, the possibility that certain cultural features translate into sound institutions and strong public trust is worth exploring. Trust in the democratic system, in the integrity and effectiveness of elected politicians and of civil servants, and in the rule of law arguably increase the chances of survival of an effective rules-based fiscal framework.

Purely for the sake of illustration, Figure 6.5 displays the unconditional correlation between a broad measure of fiscal performance—the average overall budget balance over 2000–2010—and a measurable cultural dimension that may shape attitudes vis-à-vis fiscal soundness as embedded in fiscal rules.[56] This dimension—which Hofstede, Hofstede, and Minkov label "masculinity"—assigns country scores reflecting the extent to which people value assertiveness and individual competition as opposed to cooperation and consensus building.[57] In the context of this paper, one interpretation is that a low masculinity score is likely to be associated with societies showing greater respect for institutions aimed at fostering cooperation and consensus around certain policy objectives. And this is exactly what a fiscal rule is supposed to achieve: coordinate people's expectations about future policy paths anchored in clear and broadly shared goals.

Looking at a broader sample of 25 advanced economies (among which 18 are EU members), we observe a clear negative correlation (−0.49) between the budget balance and the "masculinity" score. The slope of the simple bivariate regression line is significantly different from zero at the 1 percent level. What is also striking is that the two subgroups exhibiting contrasting levels of trust in their national governments in

FIGURE 6.5

Culture and fiscal behavior (in percentage of GDP, 2000–2010)

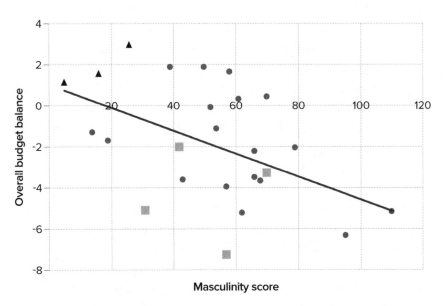

Masculinity score

Sources: Eurobarometer, https://www.eui.eu/Research/Library/ResearchGuides/Economics/Statistics/DataPortal/Eurobarometer; IMF *World Economic Outlook*; and authors' calculations. *Notes*: GDP=gross domestic product. Balance=−0.06 (***), Masc+1.05, R^2=0.24. Countries included are Belgium, Denmark, Ireland, Greece, Spain, France, Italy, Luxembourg, The Netherlands, Austria, Portugal, Findland, Sweden, and the UK. Nordics (▲)=Denmark, Finland, and Sweden; Southerners (■)=Greece, Italy, Portugal, and Spain.

Figure 6.4 (the Southerners and Nordics) have very different positions in the scatter plot. This is particularly evident in the case of the Nordics.[58] This line of reasoning suggests that a rules-based fiscal framework aimed to anchoring expectations of responsible fiscal policies may have a greater chance to emerge and survive in countries with public trust in governments and in rules.

WRAPPING UP: ENFORCEABILITY AND THREATS TO FISCAL RULES

Enforceable fiscal policy rules are vulnerable to a range of potentially existential threats. First, when their authors try to make them economically sensible, they will end up being to some degree more complex and opaque, obfuscating policy guidance and communication. Second, uncertainty around the steady state (and especially potential growth and the natural rate of interest) complicates the calibration of sensible binding rules, raising the risk of enforcing undesirable policy adjustments or being too lenient with policy mistakes. As such, they are exposed to widespread criticisms on technical as well as political grounds. Third, the possibility of forcing *elected* policymakers to take certain actions puts a premium on a strong and well-understood rationale for the rule as well as a broad public support for the framework (i.e., ownership).

If, for all these reasons, the voting public ultimately fails to fully grasp the benefits of fiscal rules, deviations from numerical caps will also carry little or no reputational or political costs for governments. Hence, when public support is low, simply abandoning the rule may not appear to be a costly proposition for a government unconcerned with macroeconomically sound policies.[59] As suggested previously, large and persistent cross-country divergences in average levels of trust in government institutions may suggest varying degrees of support for enforceable fiscal rules. Moreover, as fiscal rules tend to be adopted at or around times of fiscal duress, the return to normalcy might further erode the perceived rationale for keeping a rules-based fiscal framework.

To be fair, enforceability also comes with specific advantages to be weighed against the practical relevance of the previously discussed threats. In particular, the impact of an enforcement procedure exceeds the expected value of sanctions punishing violations of the rule. The mere activation of such a procedure could indeed trigger reputational effects. Even if sanctions lack credibility, the apparent readiness of a country to be caught reneging on its own public promises might signal an intrinsically weaker commitment to debt sustainability compared to a country actively avoiding being considered a violator. An enforcement procedure could thus be a useful device to coordinate market expectations, causing risk premiums to react accordingly. The higher sovereign spreads associated with the activation of Excessive Deficit Procedures under the EU Stability and Growth Pact are consistent with that role.[60]

In the end, it is only if attempts at enforcement carry sufficiently serious risks of abandoning rules-based fiscal policy (or if they severely undermine rule implementation) that consideration should be given to nonenforceable fiscal rules or benchmarks. In the monetary realm, a "rule" that is simultaneously simple, flexible, but not enforceable is a Taylor rule. The next section illustrates how a rules-based fiscal framework centered on a fiscal Taylor rule could work.

RULES-BASED FISCAL POLICY WITHOUT FORMAL ENFORCEMENT

This section expands the universe of possible rules-based fiscal frameworks to include those that do not rely on an enforceable numerical rule. We elaborate on the potential role for Taylor-type indicative rules to formally guide discretion in the short run and promote long-run debt sustainability. In a sense, we wonder whether a good compass might not be more useful than a heavy, unusable stick. After illustrating the basic features of such a rule, we discuss how an effective fiscal framework could leverage nonbinding benchmarks to improve the conduct of fiscal policy.

THE FISCAL TAYLOR RULE

The idea of using a simple formula to benchmark fiscal policy is not new. It directly emulates the use of Taylor rules in monetary policy discussions.[61] Taylor himself proposed such a fiscal rule for the United States based on a simple empirical model of the fiscal balance.[62] The rapidly growing use of dynamic stochastic general equilibrium models allowed characterizing similar policy rules with desirable welfare effects.[63] Other studies built on Taylor's original proposal to devise sensible benchmarks against which to assess the fiscal stance.[64] Here, we only illustrate how a simple formula with well-defined properties can indeed provide relevant benchmarks to assess fiscal policy; we do not look for a desirable—and even less an optimal—calibration.

Under the original fiscal Taylor rule, the nominal budget balance is such that a given structural surplus is maintained over the cycle, while the nominal balance benchmark fully accommodates the estimated effect of automatic stabilizers. In short, the rule makes the standard distinction between the cyclical and structural components of the budget deficit. That way, fiscal policy is anchored (public debt converges to some number deemed desirable), it provides support to aggregate demand when activity is below potential, and it cools down expenditure growth when the economy is above potential. Taylor's empirical estimates suggest that such a rule provides a good fit for the U.S. federal fiscal balance over the long term; his sample spans 1960–1999. He proposes a simple FTR that can be written as follows:

$$b_t = 0.5y_t, \tag{6.9}$$

where y_t symbolizes the output gap.

The normative value of (6.9) is even more controversial than its analogue in the monetary Taylor rule because the fiscal policy mandate extends well beyond macroeconomic stabilization under the constraint of debt sustainability.[65] Debt sustainability remains a constraint regardless of policymakers' goals, and short-term output stabilization is usually seen as desirable. And since the idea is to devise a sensible benchmark for good behavior, not a binding constraint subject to enforcement, one can be more relaxed about getting close to a characterization of the optimal fiscal stance.

For the sake of illustration, a more general FTR could be parametrized along the lines of (6.10), which we simulate for the United States and France:

$$b_t = \overline{b}_t + \beta y_t, \tag{6.10}$$

where β is the deficit allowance for cyclical stabilization and $\overline{b}_t = \dfrac{-\theta_t^\star}{1+\theta_t^\star} d_{FTR}^\star$ is a "long-term" objective defined as the nominal balance ensuring a convergence of the public debt-to-GDP ratio to a given number $d_{FTR}^\star$ if the output gap was always zero. Thus, $\overline{b}_t$ ensures that fiscal policy is *anchored* in the specific sense that public trajectories tend to converge to some desirable public debt level. For our illustrative simulations, we simply assume that $\theta_t^\star$ is the 10-year moving average of nominal GDP growth.

The FTR described in (6.9) is simulated in Figure 6.6 over the period 1990–2017, assuming a desired convergence to a public debt target of 60 percent of GDP ($\bar{b}_t = 0.6$) and two alternative responses to the output gap: $\beta = 0.5$ and $\beta = 1$. The reference value for the long-term public debt target is a rather common benchmark in assessments of long-term adjustment needs.[66] Lower numbers could be envisaged in accordance with precautionary motives, such as the need to create buffers to accommodate uninsurable fiscal risk.[67] For fiscal stabilization, $\beta = 0.5$ is a reasonable proxy for the effect of automatic stabilizers,[68] while $\beta = 1$ presupposes some systematically stabilizing response of discretionary fiscal policy.

Except for the two underlying objectives (debt and output stabilization), every dimension of this highly stylized calibration exercise is debatable. Using the output gap and potential growth, which are unobservable, makes the analysis vulnerable to possibly sizable revisions in potential output.[69] And little guidance exists on acceptable long-run public debt levels, or on the adequate degree of fiscal stabilization. Again, we do not try to define an optimal FTR, we illustrate how simple benchmarks explicitly incorporating desirable properties of fiscal policy suffice to support a meaningful narrative on the adequacy of the fiscal stance.

Several interesting lessons emerge from the simulations. First, while the U.S. budget balance oscillates around the benchmarks, France consistently underperforms, with deficits exceeding the benchmark every single year following the adoption of the Maastricht Treaty. Second, while France's performance initially remained close to the benchmark assuming a strongly stabilizing response, a performance gap opened abruptly after 1998, the year euro area candidates had to pass the Maastricht admission test to the currency union. That gap only started to close during the post-2009 adjustment. This suggests that when the Maastricht criteria were generally considered as binding, fiscal policy was broadly in line with the FTR benchmark, but that public finances never made up for the lack of improvement during 1999–2001. Third, in both countries, the FTR benchmarks fail to account for the exceptional fiscal stimulus and revenue losses associated with the Great Recession. Remarkably, however, there is a strong convergence toward the benchmarks after 2010 and in the medium-term forecast, suggesting that, as

FIGURE 6.6
France and the United States: actual fiscal balance versus FTR-based benchmark

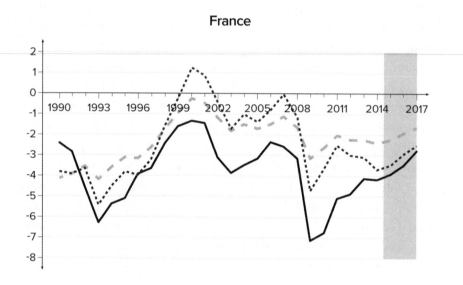

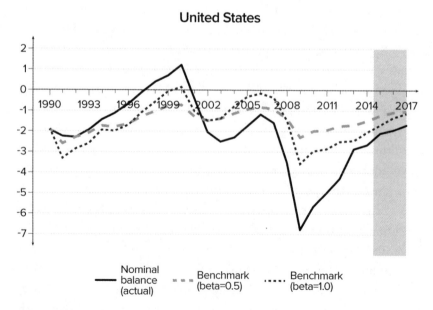

Source: Authors' calculations.
Note: FTR = fiscal Taylor rule.

FIGURE 6.7

France: FTR-based benchmarks against actual in "real time"

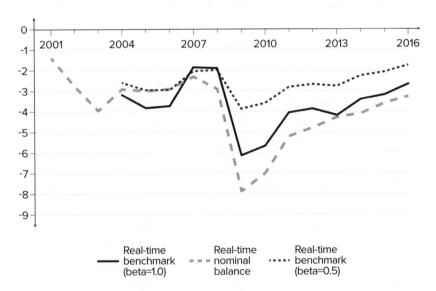

Real-time benchmark (beta=1.0) — Real-time nominal balance — Real-time benchmark (beta=0.5)

Sources: Author's calculations and Stability and Convergence Programs.
Note: FTR = fiscal Taylor rule.

output gaps close, deficits are moving back to levels consistent with the long-term debt objective.

As always, any formula–based benchmark is subject to limitations calling for judgment when interpreting deviations. For instance, assessments are sensitive to the data vintage. Figure 6.6 plots series reflecting the most recent data and, as such, they incorporate information on the output gap and the budget balance that was not available at the time policymakers planned and executed the budget or at the time fiscal performance against the rule could plausibly be assessed. To better gauge the relevance of the FTR benchmark, it is useful to look at how fiscal policy fared using the data that was available at the time an official assessment might have been carried out. In Figure 6.7, we use the data vintage of year $t+1$ (the earliest estimates possible during the year) to compare the benchmark to the actual balance estimated for t. As we use data from the Stability and Convergence Programs submitted to the European Commission, the results concern France only.[70]

Real-time benchmarks are generally closer to the estimated balance than when using the latest available data, particularly between 2004–2008. That period exhibits large differences between real-time output gaps—thought to be negative except in 2007–2008—and postcrisis estimates—which often exhibit positive numbers.[71] Symmetrically, real-time postcrisis estimated output gaps were much more negative than the most recent figures, resulting in larger and more protracted benchmark deficits.

Such differences illustrate the already difficult trade-off between maintaining sufficiently simple formulations of the FTR benchmark and the flexibility required in selecting the most relevant factors shaping sound fiscal policies. Still, the FTR could be a novel and constructive part of the communication strategy of a fiscal framework—an issue we turn to next.

FTR BENCHMARKS AND RULES-BASED FISCAL POLICY

The basic simulations discussed previously suggest that FTR benchmarks can identify episodes where fiscal policy is adequate and those where it is problematic. If defining simple and meaningful benchmarks is possible, the framework through which these could influence the conduct of fiscal policy is yet to be defined. In the absence of enforcement, there is no formal commitment device such as the threat of sanctions. Thus, the costs of deviating from an FTR are strictly reputational; any FTR-based framework should exhibit specific arrangements aimed at amplifying the reputational effects of the rule.

The recent emergence of independent fiscal councils (IFCs) suggests a promising avenue to ensure that significant reputational effects are associated with a nonenforceable rule. In most countries, and certainly in EU member states, IFCs are mandated (and in many cases well equipped) to make thorough economic assessments of fiscal policy.[72] By influencing the public debate and clarifying the meaning of traditional signals about fiscal policy—through official budget documents and statements, as well as parliamentary debates—IFCs inform all interested parties in the budget process, from parliaments to markets and the voting public. In doing so, IFCs can trigger meaningful discussions on the broad adequacy of the fiscal stance, and there is suggestive evidence that stronger fiscal performance has followed.[73]

Assessing fiscal policy informed by a simple and transparent FTR with well-defined properties would thus be a natural function of IFCs. A home-grown IFC mindful of the local political landscape should be able to raise alarm bells about unwarranted deviations from an FTR and usefully inform voters, market participants, and veto players in the budget process. Exposing unhealthy trends in public finances should trigger pressures—from members of parliament to civil society and sovereign markets—to correct them.

The approach is relevant in the European context. Heterogeneous political traditions and fiscal cultures are a clear threat to the Maastricht construct of supranational fiscal rules, making the enforcement of these rules complex and uneven across countries. Before some seize that opportunity to bury—de facto if not de jure—rules-based fiscal policy, the potential merits of an FTR-based framework are clear, and the idea has made its way in the debate on EU fiscal governance reforms. For instance, Carnot proposes an FTR-styled benchmark as a complement to existing rules at the EU level.[74] One might even argue that the Medium-Term Objectives embedded in the SGP are a form of FTR, although their role is currently blurred by enforcement-related complexities.[75] As greater reliance on national fiscal frameworks is a pillar of the last wave of fiscal governance reforms in the EU,[76] member states that find it in their best interest should be able to consider an FTR-based framework provided that it complies with the fundamental properties desired at the EU level (i.e., fiscal stabilization in line with automatic stabilizers and convergence of the debt-to-GDP ratio to 60 percent of GDP).

Who should define and periodically review the FTR? While the objectives of fiscal policy result from a political choice, the technical work of defining a benchmark consistent with these objectives belongs to an IFC. In the EU context, the European Fiscal Board—or a beefed-up variant of it—could be involved in the design of country-specific benchmarks consistent with the Maastricht prescriptions. Countries and their national IFCs should then be left with the task of operating national fiscal frameworks in line with the broad patterns of fiscal behavior embedded in the FTR. The specific procedures and means used by the IFC to adequately amplify the reputational effects of a well-defined FTR depend on the country's political environment. It seems clear, however, that such an IFC should be aligned with leading international practice.[77]

CONCLUDING REMARKS

Rules-based fiscal policy is facing existential threats. We connect these threats to the dominant view of fiscal rules as *enforceable* speed limits. We show that to be socially desirable, enforceability requires rather sophisticated rules that should ideally mimic optimal fiscal policy. Otherwise, weak enforcement (and correspondingly low formal compliance) is preferable, and at the limit simple rules should not be enforced at all. In practice, the focus on enforceable rules appears to have resulted in intractable complexity, to the point of putting rules-based fiscal policy at risk. The evolution of the EU fiscal framework illustrates this outcome and the related risk of de-anchoring fiscal expectations.

Acknowledging that strict enforcement is not a precondition for the effectiveness of a fiscal rule, we suggest that simple, flexible but nonenforceable rules could be potentially useful anchors for fiscal frameworks. Such numerical benchmarks à la Taylor (against which fiscal performance can easily be assessed) can only affect policymakers' incentives through reputational effects. Independent fiscal councils could play a key role in amplifying these effects. Specifically, unwarranted deviations from the benchmarks—if of course the latter are well-defined and receive broad popular support—should prompt the fiscal council to raise alarm, encouraging reactions from parliament, the voting public, and market participants that improve fiscal behavior.

Because enforcement procedures per se can also generate reputational effects, the adoption of a rules-based fiscal framework anchored in nonenforceable rules and benchmarks should result from a cost–benefit analysis. The perceived threats associated with enforcement (and the related risk of abandoning any constraint on discretion) must be weighed against the reputational effects achieved through the activation of enforcement procedures. Overall, a fiscal Taylor rule with strong independent oversight provides a potentially fruitful avenue to increase the set of effective rules-based frameworks.

APPENDIX: COSTLY ENFORCEMENT AND
COMPLIANCE—A SIMPLE ILLUSTRATION

To illustrate the basic logic of our argument in the main text, take the bare-bones two-period "partisan" model of optimal fiscal policy, indexed by Equations (6.A.1) and (6.A.2).[78] Citizens value the production of public goods as follows:

$$W = u(g_1) + u(g_2), \text{ with } u' > 0 \text{ and } u'' < 0, \tag{6.A.1}$$

whereas elected officials choose the path of public goods production to maximize their own utility, defined as:

$$U = u(g_1) + \pi u(g_2). \tag{6.A.2}$$

For simplicity, both the rate of interest and the subjective discount rate are equal to 0. The difference between citizens and elected officials is that the latter value their time in office and only extract utility from public goods when they are in charge. Equation (6.A.2) reflects the assumption that elections taking place at the end of period 1 have an uncertain outcome, with π capturing the incumbent's probability of reelection. The production of public goods is subject to obvious resource constraints and public debt (d) can only tilt the intertemporal profile of public consumption:

$$g_1 = \tau^o + d, \tag{6.A.3.a}$$

$$g_2 = \tau^o - d, \tag{6.A.3.b}$$

where τ^o is a given resource endowment of the government every period.

The social optimum (planner solution, denoted by a star superscript) and the political equilibrium (denoted by a two-star superscript) have the usual features:

$$g_1^\star = g_2^\star \text{ and } d^\star = 0; \tag{6.A.4.a}$$

$$g_1^{\star\star} > g_2^{\star\star} \text{ and } d^{\star\star} > 0. \tag{6.A.4.b}$$

In words, the risk of losing an election makes elected officials myopic, leading them to produce more public goods in period 1 than in period 2 and to accumulate public debt in the process.

Now assume a balanced-budget requirement framed in a credible legal instrument that triggers adequate costs for the elected official in case he or she borrows $d > d^*$. A policymaker subject to a fiscal rule defined in this way thus maximizes:

$$V = u(g_1) + \pi u(g_2) - \psi(d - d^*), \qquad (6.A.5)$$

where ψ symbolizes the marginal cost of an excessive deficit. That parameter encompasses the utility loss incurred when the rule is breached as well as the strength of the enforcement procedure. Assuming for the sake of the argument that the population—say through a referendum—can directly choose the (socially) optimal enforcement term, it will opt for the following:[79]

$$\psi^* = (1 - \pi)u'(g_2) > 0. \qquad (6.A.6)$$

Hence, the fiscal rule characterized by a debt ceiling d^* and an enforcement procedure delivering a marginal cost of deviation ψ^* can eliminate the debt bias because it encourages the provision of future public goods. Clearly, enforcement is instrumental for the effectiveness of the rule.

Now, if enforcing the rule is costly—for example, because spending cuts undermine the quality of fiscal policy—the period 1 resource constraint becomes as follows:[80]

$$g_1 = T(\tau^o, \psi) + d, \text{ with } T_\psi < 0; \ T_{\psi\psi} < 0, \text{ and } T(\tau^o, 0) = \tau^o. \qquad (6.A.7)$$

Enforcing the fiscal rule would now entail a negative "income effect" denting the gains from improved intertemporal substitution. Thus, citizens would find it optimal to trade off some suboptimal intertemporal substitution (i.e., a deficit) against lower enforcement costs, resulting in a weaker enforcement of the rule.

Formally, this means that the resource constraints now imply $\dfrac{\partial g_2}{\partial \psi} = T_\psi - \dfrac{\partial g_1}{\partial \psi}$. The first-order condition for optimal enforcement of the rule when enforcement is costly (denoted by **) then becomes

$$\frac{\partial W}{\partial \psi} = \left((\pi - 1)u'(g_2) + \psi^{**}\right)\frac{\partial g_1}{\partial \psi} + u'(g_2)T_\psi = 0. \qquad (6.A.8)$$

Since $u'(g_2)T_\psi < 0$ and $\dfrac{\partial g_1}{\partial \psi} < 0$, then the solution of (6.A.8) must satisfy $\psi^{**} < \psi^*$ by a sufficient margin. (Note that $\psi^{**} = \psi^*$ yields $(\pi - 1)u'(g_2) + \psi^{**} = 0$.) The result is an upward tilt in the time path of available resources for public good production. Weak enforcement results from the fact that pursuing a balanced budget as prescribed by the rule would not be socially optimal because the induced income loss of strict enforcement would more than offset the benefit from achieving an optimal intertemporal distribution of public consumption.

CHAPTER SEVEN

RULES FOR SUSTAINABLE FISCAL POLICY: THREE PERSPECTIVES

ED DOLAN

Everyone wants a fiscal policy that is sustainable, but just what does sustainability really mean? This chapter considers three different perspectives—sustainability as solvency, sustainability as constraints on the growth of liabilities, and functional sustainability. Each of these perspectives is useful in formulating rules for sustainable fiscal policy.

SUSTAINABILITY AS SOLVENCY

The first and simplest perspective makes sustainability a synonym for solvency—or strictly speaking, *equitable solvency,* which means the ability to meet financial obligations in full and on time. Individuals and private firms can easily become insolvent in this sense. If so, they may face legal sanctions or be forced into bankruptcy. Governments too can become insolvent if they fail to pursue responsible fiscal policy.

The adherents of modern monetary theory often emphasize the proposition that sovereign governments that follow certain rules are immune from equitable insolvency. As L. Randall Wray puts it, perpetual government sector deficits of any size are sustainable "in the sense that a sovereign government can continue to make all payments as they come due—including interest payments—no matter how big those payments become."[1]

To qualify, governments must adhere to what we might call the golden rule of solvency, namely, that all liabilities must be denominated in a currency that the government itself issues. If so, the government can meet any obligation, such as a maturing bond or an invoice for goods or services, by issuing monetary liabilities through the banking system or in the form of paper currency.

In contrast, countries that use a currency that they do not issue must have an external source for the currency that they will need to meet their obligations. Examples include members of the euro area and countries like Ecuador, which uses the U.S. dollar. Governments that issue their own currencies for domestic use but borrow in foreign currencies are a mixed case; they must have an external source to cover foreign-currency obligations, but they can meet their domestic obligations without limit. It is also important to note that the golden rule protects only a country's currency-issuing central government. It does not guarantee the solvency of local or regional units of government that issue liabilities denominated in the national currency.

Furthermore, the golden rule itself is subject to some important caveats. One is that even governments that issue their own currencies need to avoid self-imposed constraints on their solvency. For example, the U.S. government operates under a nominal debt ceiling. According to the U.S. Treasury, "Failing to increase the debt limit would have catastrophic economic consequences. It would cause the government to default on its legal obligations."[2] The debt ceiling is a "soft" constraint on solvency, since it can be, and regularly is, raised or suspended to ensure continuous service of the national debt. In the EU, not only euro area members but also countries like Sweden or Poland that have retained their own currencies are subject to similar soft debt ceilings.

Finally, although the golden rule protects a government against equitable insolvency, it does not protect it against other hazards of bad fiscal policy. Solvent governments can maintain an inappropriate degree of budgetary austerity, leading to inadequate aggregate demand, high unemployment, and slow growth. They can, instead, pursue inappropriately expansionary fiscal policy when their economies have reached the full-employment level of output, resulting in excessive inflation. They can pursue stop-go policies that alternate between these extremes, exacerbating rather than moderating the business cycle.

Finally, in extreme cases, sovereign governments that issue their own currency can fall victim to hyperinflation. Inflation, even hyperinflation, need not result in technical insolvency. It is always possible to honor all past nominal liabilities, no matter how large, by issuing currency or bank balances with a sufficiently large number of zeros. However, eventually people become unwilling to make new offers of goods or services in exchange for promises of any number of billions or octillions of nominal currency units. At that point, the game is over, and either the government falls or it relinquishes its unlimited power to issue currency in favor of some arrangement such as a dollarization or a currency board.

In short, maintaining equitable solvency is only the starting point for a discussion of fiscal sustainability, not the whole story.

SUSTAINABILITY AS CONSTRAINED GROWTH OF LIABILITIES

According to a second perspective, a fiscal policy is sustainable if it appropriately constrains the growth of government liabilities as a share of gross domestic product (GDP). Just what the appropriate constraint should be is open to debate. Those whose only concern is maintaining equitable solvency might set the ceiling for liabilities at a substantial multiple of GDP. Others would like to see a ceiling well below 100 percent of GDP, on the grounds that high liability ratios are associated with high interest rates, slow growth, or excessive inflation. The question of the optimal level of liabilities is beyond the scope of this chapter, which will focus on the more general question of the conditions under which the liability ratio will not increase without limit.

For purposes of this section, it is convenient to treat the entire central government of a country as a single unit. For the United States, that means consolidating the balance sheets of the Department of the Treasury and the Federal Reserve System (the Fed), along with other accounting entities such as government trust funds that hold government liabilities as assets. All liabilities of one government entity that are held as assets by another entity are netted out. What remains are government liabilities held by members of the public, that is, by households; financial and nonfinancial firms; and foreign, private, and government entities.

Liabilities of the consolidated government sector can be further divided into monetary and nonmonetary liabilities. In the United States, monetary liabilities include Federal Reserve notes, commercial bank reserve deposits at the Fed, and Treasury coin, which together are known as the *monetary base*. Nonmonetary liabilities include Treasury bills and notes, collectively known as government debt.

Over time, total liabilities outstanding change as a result of government expenditures and tax receipts. Expenditures, whether for purchasing goods and services, making interest payments, or making transfer payments, have the immediate impact of increasing monetary liabilities as payments by check or electronic transfer are cleared through the banking system. Tax payments by households and firms reduce outstanding monetary liabilities as they are deposited in the Treasury's account at the Fed.

Simultaneously with spending and taxation, or subsequently, the government may engage in further financial operations that affect the composition of its liabilities to public. For example, when the Treasury sells new securities at auction, the government's nonmonetary liabilities increase, and its monetary liabilities decrease by an equal amount. Similarly, nonmonetary liabilities increase and monetary liabilities decrease when the central bank sells securities from its own portfolio of previously issued Treasury securities (open market sales). Redemption of maturing securities by the Treasury and open market purchases by the Fed decrease the government's outstanding nonmonetary liabilities and increase monetary liabilities.

When the government uses taxation to offset the monetary impact of its expenditures, it is popularly said to be "financing its spending with taxes." When it sells securities for the same purpose, it is said to be "financing spending by borrowing." When it does neither, it is said to be "monetizing the deficit" or "financing spending by issuing money" or simply by "printing money."

Since our topic is the long-run sustainability of fiscal policy, this section will pay less attention to short-term changes in the values of the budget balance and government liabilities and more attention to their long-term relationships to GDP. Accordingly, we will focus on the "structural" or "cyclical adjusted" values of variables. Structural values are defined as those that would prevail when the economy is operating at "full employment," or more properly, at "potential GDP." During downturns, GDP falls below its potential level, unemployment rises, spending on unemployment insurance and poverty programs rises, tax revenues fall, and the deficit increases. In boom times, unemployment temporarily falls below the level consistent with potential GDP, outlays fall, revenue rises, and the budget balance moves toward surplus.

With these points of terminology out of the way, we are ready to explore the simple mathematics related to the ratio of liabilities to GDP. Over any period, the change in total liabilities is equal to the budget balance with the sign reversed—increasing when there is a deficit and decreasing when there is a surplus. For any given values of GDP growth and the initial level of liabilities, there is some "steady-state structural balance" that will hold the ratio of liabilities to GDP constant, on average, over the business cycle. The steady-state structural balance, stated as a percentage of GDP, is equal to the negative of the liability ratio times the rate of growth of GDP.

$$SBAL^* = -G(LBR), \tag{7.1}$$

where $SBAL^*$ is the equilibrium structural balance expressed as a percentage of potential GDP; LBR is the ratio of total government liabilities (monetary and nonmonetary) to potential GDP; and G is the rate of growth of potential GDP.

For example, suppose GDP is initially $10 trillion, the growth rate is 4 percent, and total liabilities are initially $5 trillion, or 50 percent of GDP. A $200 billion deficit, or 2 percent of GDP, would then be just enough to hold the liability ratio at 50 percent.

Instead, solving Equation (7.1) for the liability ratio, we can define a steady-state liability ratio, LBR^*, for any fixed values of the structural balance and the growth rate:

$$LBR^* = -SBAL/G. \tag{7.2}$$

Using the numbers from our previous example, the liability ratio remains constant at 50 percent of GDP when the growth rate is 4 percent and the structural balance is in deficit by 2 percent.

If there is a permanent change in the structural balance, the liability ratio will increase or decrease over time until it reaches its new equilibrium value. For example, beginning from our previous numbers, suppose that the structural deficit increases to 3 percent of GDP in 2010 and stays there. If the value of GDP at the beginning of 2010 is, say, $10 trillion, then over the course of the first year, it will increase to $10.4 trillion while liabilities increase by $300 billion to $5.3 trillion. That will raise the liability ratio to about 51 percent of GDP. The liability ratio will continue to increase each year after that, gradually approaching a new equilibrium level of 75 percent of GDP. In graphical form, the process would look like Figure 7.1.

The same math applies if the structural budget is permanently in surplus. For example, a change in the budget balance from a 2 percent deficit to a 2 percent surplus would gradually decrease the liability ratio over time. Following the practice of countries like Norway that have chronic budget surpluses, the annual surpluses would be invested in a sovereign wealth fund. By Equation (7.2), the steady-state value of the sovereign wealth fund would be 50 percent of GDP (LBR$\star$ = −50 percent).

These conclusions suggest two possible rules for fiscal sustainability: One would be to select a desired target value for the liability ratio and hold the structural budget balance equal to the corresponding steady-state budget balance as given by Equation (7.1). The alternative would be to select a desired value for the budget balance, allowing the liability ratio to rise or fall over time to its steady state value.

Mathematically speaking, any level for the structural deficit is sustainable so long as it is held constant as a share of GDP—even if growth is sluggish and the deficit is chronically large. For example, a deficit of 5 percent of GDP and nominal GDP growth of 2 percent would produce a steady-state liability ratio of 250 percent of GDP Those are roughly the numbers for Japan in recent years.

However, although mathematically valid, there is a major practical difficulty with a fiscal policy rule that tries to hold the overall budget

FIGURE 7.1

Evolution of liability ratio following a change in the structural balance

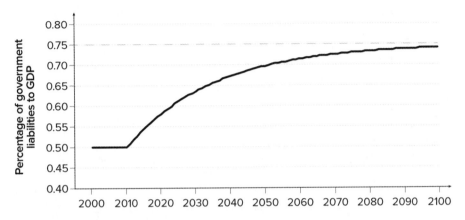

Source: Author's calculations.
Note: GDP = gross domestic product; LBR = steady-state liability ratio; SBAL = structural balance expressed as a percentage of potential GDP. Assumptions: G = 0. 5, Initial LBR = 0.5, Initial SBAL = −0.02, and SBAL after 2010 = −0.03.

balance constant. To understand why, we need to make a distinction between two types of government expenditures: *interest expenditures*, that is, the net interest paid or received by the consolidated government, and *program expenditures,* which includes all other outlays.

Program expenditures, whether for civilian or military purposes and whether for transfer payments or purchase of goods and services, are the part of the budget that produces the public benefits that motivate political decisionmakers. Interest expenditures produce no comparable political payoff.

With this distinction in mind, let's revisit the process of adjustment to a new equilibrium liability ratio following an increase in the deficit. As before, we assume GDP growth of 4 percent and an initial liability ratio of 50 percent. This time we will be more specific about the budget. We assume that tax revenue is 18 percent of GDP and total expenditures are initially 20 percent of GDP. We assume an interest rate of 4 percent, so that interest expense is initially 2 percent of GDP. Program expenditures are initially 18 percent of GDP. They increase to 19 percent in

FIGURE 7.2

Evolution of expenditures following permanent change in structural deficit from 2% to 3% of GDP

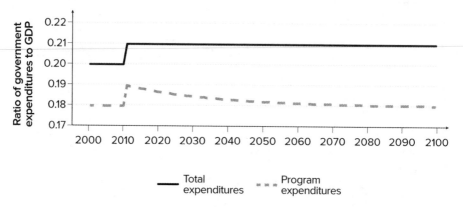

Source: Author's calculations.
Note: GDP = gross domestic product.

2010, bringing total expenditures to 21 percent of GDP. Under these assumptions, what will happen over time to expenditures and taxes if the deficit is held steady at its new level of 3 percent?

The answer is that something has to give. As soon as the deficit increases, total liabilities and interest expenses begin to rise. If taxes are held at 18 percent of GDP and the overall deficit is held at 3 percent, then program expenditures will be squeezed. As Figure 7.2 shows, by the time the liability ratio rises to its new equilibrium, program expenditures will be right back where they started.

Politically speaking, it would be much more desirable to be able to maintain both a constant level of program expenditures and a constant level of taxes. To do that, the fiscal policy rule would need to target not the overall structural balance, but the "primary structural balance," meaning taxes minus program expenditures, or equivalently, the overall structural balance minus interest expenditures. But such a rule raises a new question: Can we be sure that the liability ratio will have a finite steady-state value for any given primary structural balance, or is it possible that the liability ratio might increase (or decrease) without limit?

The answer, it turns out, depends on the relationship between the rate of growth of GDP and the interest rate. To see why, we can rewrite Equation (7.1), replacing the overall structural balance with the primary structural balance (PSB) minus interest expense, and writing interest expense as the interest rate R times the liability ratio LBR. That gives us

$$PSB - R(LBR) = -G(LBR). \tag{7.3}$$

Let PSB* be the steady-state value of the primary structural deficit, that is, the level of the primary structural deficit that will hold the liability ratio constant over time. For a given value of the liability ratio, the steady-state value can be written as

$$PSB^* = (R - G)LBR. \tag{7.4}$$

The interest rate and the growth rate can be expressed in either real or nominal terms, so long as both are done the same way. The examples that follow will use nominal values.

The first thing we see from Equation (7.4) is that when the interest rate is higher than the growth rate, PSB★ has a positive value, that is, a primary structural surplus is required to keep the liability ratio from increasing over time. In contrast, if the growth rate is greater than the interest rate, the liability ratio can be held constant even when there is a primary structural deficit.

A second important implication of Equation (7.4) is that an increase in the liability ratio raises the steady-state primary structural balance when the interest rate is greater than the growth rate, whereas an increase in the liability ratio lowers the steady-state primary balance when the growth rate is greater than the interest rate. That relationship has important implications for the stability of the liability ratio, as the following numerical examples make clear.

For example, suppose that the initial liability ratio is 0.5, the growth rate is 0.04, and the interest rate is 0.02. The steady-state primary structural balance will then be −0.01. Interest expenditures will also be 1 percent of GDP, so overall budget balance will be −0.02.

FIGURE 7.3

Evolution of liability ratio following a change in primary structural balance

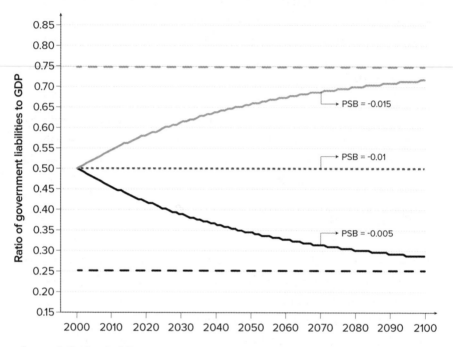

Source: Author's calculations.

Note: GDP = gross domestic product; PSB = primary structural balance; G = high growth; R = low interest rate; Assumptions: R = 0.02 and G = 0.04.

Suppose, now, that due to an increase in program spending, the primary balance falls a little farther into deficit, say, to −0.015. As a result, the liability ratio will begin to increase. In accordance with Equation (7.4), the greater liability ratio will begin to decrease the steady-state value of the primary deficit, PSB*. Eventually, when the PSB* reaches 0.015, the liability ratio will stabilize at a new equilibrium value of 0.75, as shown by the top curve in Figure 7.3.

If, instead, the primary structural balance moved toward surplus from its initial steady state value, say from −0.01 to −0.005, the liability ratio would begin to decrease. As it did so, PSB* would also increase until it reaches −0.005. At that point, the liability ratio reached a new equilibrium value of −0.25 (net assets), as shown by the lower curve in Figure 7.3.

To generalize, as long as the rate of growth of GDP is greater than the interest rate on government liabilities, the liability ratio will adjust to a new, finite equilibrium value following any change in taxes or program expenditures that increase or decrease the primary structural balance as long as the balance remains at its new value relative to GDP.

In contrast, if the interest rate is greater than the rate of growth, then a departure from the steady-state primary structural balance will have quite a different effect. To illustrate this possibility, suppose that the initial liability ratio is 0.5 as before, but the growth rate is 0.02, and the interest rate is 0.04. In this case, holding the liability ratio steady will require a primary structural surplus of 1 percent of GDP.

Suppose now that a tax cut or increase in program expenditures moves the primary structural balance toward deficit, say from its initial value of 0.01 to 0. As a result, the liability ratio will begin to increase, and as it does so, PSB* will also increase. As time goes by, rather than converging, the gap between actual value and the steady state value of the primary structural deficit increases. The wider the gap, the more rapid the increase in the liability ratio. As shown by the upper curve in Figure 7.4, liabilities will grow without limit unless there is a new change in policy that will raise taxes or cut program spending.

Similarly, when the interest rate is greater than the growth rate, a policy change that raises taxes or cuts program spending will cause a decrease in the liability ratio. Liabilities will eventually fall to zero, after which, assuming there are no further policy changes, the ongoing budget surplus can be invested in a sovereign wealth fund that increases in value at an ever-increasing rate.

It appears, then, that the much-feared scenario in which taxes are so low or spending so high that government liabilities increase without limit is a real possibility only when the interest rate on government liabilities is greater than the rate of growth of GDP, when both parameters are averaged over the business cycle. If the growth rate is higher than the interest rate, any fixed target for the primary structural balance, whether surplus or deficit, will be sufficient to prevent unlimited increase or decrease in the liability ratio.

FIGURE 7.4

Evolution of liability ratio following a change in primary structural balance

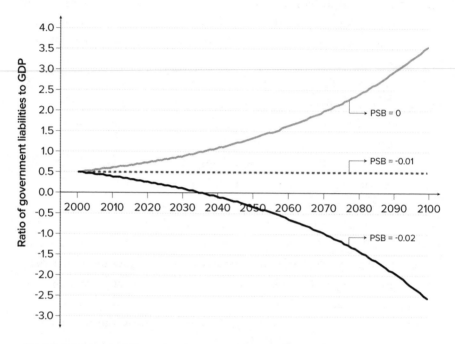

Source: Author's calculations.
Note: GDP = gross domestic product; PSB = primary structural balance, G = low growth, R = high interest rate; Assumptions: R = 0.04 and G = 0.02.

On the other hand, if the long-term value of the interest rate exceeds that of the growth rate, a primary structural balance target becomes more problematic. Yes, there will always be some value of the primary structural balance that is just right to keep the liability ratio at its current value, but the stability of the deficit ratio in that case would be less like that of a table and more like that of a unicycle. Any deviation from the initial conditions, unless corrected, would send the liability ratio toward unlimited increase or decrease. True, unless the disturbance were very large, the initial rate of change of the liability ratio would be small, but it would not be self-correcting.

Which case, then, is more likely? Figure 7.5 shows the relationship between interest rates and growth rates for the United States from 1970

FIGURE 7.5

Interest rates vs. growth rates (nominal), 1970–2017

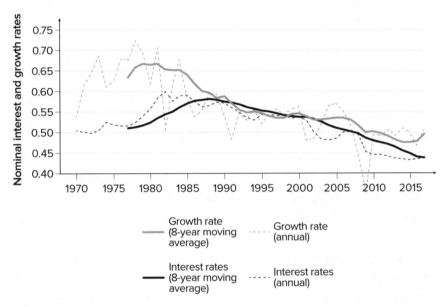

Source: Author's calculations.

Note: Dotted lines = annual data; solid lines = 8-year moving average; R = interest rate; G = growth rate.

to 2017. The growth rate is the rate of increase in nominal GDP. The interest rate shown is federal interest expenses divided by debt held by the public plus the monetary base—an approximation of the variable R in our model.[3] The dotted lines show annual data, while the solid lines show moving averages over an eight-year period, which is the average peak-to-peak duration of business cycles over this time span.

Over the entire period from 1970 to 2017, the average nominal interest rate on federal liabilities was 4.7 percent and the average growth rate of nominal GDP was 6.7 percent. During the 1970s, rapid inflation raised the rate of growth of nominal GDP and also, with a lag, raised nominal interest rates. Inflation rates fell during the 1980s, but interest expenses did not fall as rapidly as inflation, partly because fear that inflation might return kept rates high on newly issued securities and partly because of the need to continue paying high interest rates on fixed-rate securities issued during the high inflation years. As a result, there was a period in the 1990s when interest expenses per dollar of liabilities exceeded the rate of nominal GDP growth by a small amount. In the 2000s, investor expectations adjusted to continued low inflation. As they did so, interest rates fell, and interest expenses again dropped below the rate of nominal GDP growth.

On the whole, then, experience with growth and interest rates over the past half century has been consistent with scenarios in which a fixed target for the primary structural deficit would result in a finite steady-state value for the liability ratio. Looking forward, informed by historical values, we might reasonably assume a long-term nominal GDP growth rate of 4 percent (2 percent real plus 2 percent inflation) and an average nominal interest expenses on total liabilities of 1.5 percent. If so, then a primary structural deficit of 2.5 percent of GDP, equivalent to an overall structural deficit of 4 percent of GDP, would be sufficient to stabilize the liability ratio at 100 percent of GDP, including net debt of 80 percent of GDP and a monetary base of 20 percent of GDP.

Those figures are not greatly different from projections for 2019, as of this writing, but they give little margin for error. In particular, they do allow for the possibility that maintaining a liability ratio of 100 percent in the long run might put upward pressure on interest rates or slow the rate of growth. If so, the liability ratio might begin to grow unsustainably.

A more cautious approach, then, might reasonably set a tighter target for the primary structural balance than expected for fiscal year 2020, and aim for a steady-state liability ratio of well under 100 percent of GDP. If that were done soon, while interest rates and growth rates remain close to those recently observed, then the steady-state level of debt could be brought down by a primary structural balance target that was still in deficit, but not by so much as it is at present. An even more cautious approach that wanted to guard against the possibility of near-term rise in interest rates relative to the growth rate could aim for a structural surplus. Ultimately, the choice among these alternatives would depend not only on static forecasts of interest rates and growth, but also on estimates of the degree to which an elevated liability ratio has the potential to affect both variables.

FUNCTIONAL SUSTAINABILITY

That brings us to our third perspective on sustainability, that of "functional sustainability." A country's fiscal policy can be said to be functionally sustainable if it imposes a set of rules and decisionmaking procedures that adjust fiscal parameters over time to serve some rational public purpose.

Unfortunately, the United States does not have a fiscal policy that is functionally sustainable in this sense. Little has changed in the decades since Herbert Stein, Chairman of the Council of Economic Advisers under Presidents Nixon and Ford, wrote that

> we have no long-run budget policy—no policy for the size of deficits and for the rate of growth of the public debt over a period of years. Annually we make decisions about the size of the deficit that are entirely inconsistent with our professed long-run goals, with the explanation or hope that something will happen or be done before the long-run arises, but not yet.[4]

In his article, Stein goes on to argue for rules and procedures that would ensure that annual decisions regarding taxes and spending are constrained by explicit, long-term fiscal policy goals. Little progress toward that ideal has been made since he wrote. On the contrary, the traditional process of orderly budgeting and appropriation has broken down and been replaced by ad hoc measures such as continuing resolutions, sequestrations, and debt ceiling suspensions. This section will not attempt to establish a full set of sustainable fiscal rules, but rather will propose some metarules with which any more specific rules should be consistent.

METARULE NO. 1

Metarule no. 1 is that fiscal rules should be at least cyclically neutral and permit countercyclical measures depending upon political maturity and cross-party consensus.

This proposition is universally accepted in the serious literature on fiscal policy rules. It would hardly be worth mentioning were it not for the perennial political popularity, in the United States at least, of rules calling for annual balance of the federal budget. Over the past 80 years, such rules have been proposed again and again as constitutional amendments. These balanced budget amendments, some of which have come frighteningly close to passage, would be profoundly procyclical, since they would require tax increases or spending cuts during downturns and would allow spending increases or tax cuts or both when the economy was at or above full employment.

In contrast, a cyclically neutral rule, such as a fixed target for the primary structural balance, would take full advantage of automatic stabilizers to moderate the business cycle. As explained in the previous section, the specific target could be chosen to maintain a desired ratio of total government liabilities to GDP or to ensure that the liability ratio would converge toward the desired level over time.

In theory, a rule that mandated a target value for the primary structural deficit on average over the business cycle, but that allowed temporary countercyclical tax and spending measures on a discretionary basis, would be even better. However, practical considerations might make such a rule unfeasible. For one thing, it is possible that lags and forecasting errors might be such that attempts to pursue discretionary fiscal stimulus or restraint would turn out to be counterproductive. There could also be political difficulties. The procedures and institutions necessary to implement a rule allowing for active countercyclical policies would be considerably more complicated than those for a cyclically neutral rule. That complexity could make it easier for the party in power to game the rule for short-term political advantage and harder to penalize attempts to do so.

Accordingly, countries like the United States that lack sufficient political maturity and cross-party consensus might do best to stick with a simple, cyclically neutral rule. At most, such a rule could include narrowly defined exceptions, for example, an allowance for added fiscal stimulus during periods in which interest rates fell to the zero bound, rendering monetary stimulus ineffective.

METARULE NO. 2
Metarule no. 2 is that microeconomic aspects of fiscal policy should be subordinate to macroeconomic fiscal policy rules.

As specified by Metarule no. 1, a functionally sustainable fiscal rule should hold budget balances to a path that is at least cyclically neutral and consistent with a sustainable steady-state liability ratio. Doing so should serve the macroeconomic purposes of promoting stability and growth. However, such a rule should not constrain microeconomic details of fiscal policy such as the structure of taxes and the composition of spending.

Even with a sustainable fiscal rule in place, tax reform would remain an important issue. However, specific initiatives, for example, reduction in distortionary payroll or corporate income taxes, should be proposed in a form that is revenue neutral over the business cycle. They should be offset by increases in taxes thought to be less distortionary, say, consumption or carbon taxes, or by spending decreases. Similarly, spending increases—even putatively growth enhancing ones such as infrastructure spending—should be accompanied by cuts in other spending programs or appropriate tax increases.

Some would object that this metarule could hamper the introduction of appropriate countercyclical stimulus, such as a cut in personal tax rates, during a deep slump. That is true, just as it would also discourage reckless procyclical tax cuts or spending increases during good times when GDP at or above the potential level temporarily pushes the annual budget toward surplus. Even so, this objection misses the point. If we suppose that the country's political system is sufficiently mature and disciplined, then room for countercyclical fiscal stimulus or constraint could be built into the basic fiscal rule itself. If not, as is arguably the case in the United States today, then it would be better to forego the benefits of active countercyclical policy than to give free rein to the opportunistic impulses of whatever party happens momentarily to control of the levers of public finance.

METARULE NO. 3

Metarule no. 3 says that a functionally sustainable fiscal rule should target sustainable paths for deficits and liability ratios, but it should not attempt to constrain the overall fiscal size of government.

This metarule would disallow measures such as a 2011 version of a balanced budget amendment that would have placed a ceiling on federal expenditures of 18 percent of GDP.[5] Instead, it would require neutrality as to whether a given target, such as a 1 percent primary structural surplus, is, say, achieved with expenditures of 18 percent of GDP and taxes of 19 percent, or expenditures of 38 percent of GDP and taxes of 39 percent.

This rule is open to the objection that a smaller size of government could enhance economic growth and is therefore an appropriate part of a rule for fiscal policy. Without getting into the complex debate over the empirical validity of the relationship between growth and size of government, let us stipulate for the sake of discussion that it is true. Even so, there are at least three arguments for why a rule for fiscal sustainability should not attempt to constrain the size of government.

The first argument is that maximizing the growth of GDP is not the only objective of economic policy. The size of government that maximizes the growth rate is not necessarily the same as that which maximizes other aspects of freedom and prosperity. On the contrary, my own research indicates that the size of government is negatively correlated with broad measures of prosperity such as the Social Progress Index or the Legatum Prosperity Index or various sets of their subcomponents.[6] Size of government, defined narrowly, is also negatively related to popular indexes of freedom, such as the Fraser Institute's *Economic Freedom of the World*[7] and the Cato Institute's *Human Freedom Index*.[8] Instead, quality of government, as measured by indicators of rule of law, protection of property rights, government integrity, and so on is more important for freedom and prosperity than the size of government. These are robust results that hold across subsamples of governments rich and poor, with a variety of different measures of size, freedom, and prosperity, and with a variety of different controls and statistical specifications.

The second argument for maintaining flexibility with regard to the size of government is that spending and taxes of a certain minimum size may be necessary for maintaining the political sustainability of a market economy, even if that is, arguably, greater than the size that maximizes growth. In a long essay on what he calls the "free market welfare state," the Niskanen Center's Sam Hammond calls attention to Joseph Schumpeter's belief that capitalism would become the ultimate victim of its own success, inspiring reactionary and populist movements against its destructive side that would inadvertently strangle any potential for future creativity. Hammond argues that "the countries that have eluded Schumpeter's dreary prediction have done so by combining free markets with robust systems of universal social insurance."[9]

The third argument for fiscal rules that do not constrain the size of government does not depend on whether the first two are true or false, but only on whether substantial political factions believe one or the other of them is. The most successful attempts to establish rules for fiscal sustainability, such as those in Sweden or Chile, have worked as well as they have because they have commanded broad support across political parties and coalitions. Without such support, no rule can survive a change of government. There is a much greater likelihood of finding cross-party political support for rules that say, "avoid insolvency," or "don't allow limitless growth of liabilities," or "moderate the business cycle, don't exacerbate it," than to seek broad support for a quantitative cap on the size of government.

In short, even if the growth-maximizing size of government is very small (itself a debatable proposition), growth is not everything. Maximum growth is not necessarily consistent with maximum freedom, and any rule for long-term fiscal sustainability needs to be able to survive regular changes in government.

COMBINING THE PERSPECTIVES

This chapter began with the assertion that a sustainable fiscal policy is one that sets rules for government expenditures, taxes, deficits, and debt that allow an economy to meet current needs without compromising the ability of future generations to do likewise. It then introduced three perspectives on this broad concept of fiscal sustainability.

The first perspective frames sustainability as a matter of maintaining equitable solvency—the ability to pay all financial obligations in full and on time. A country that issues its own currency, never contracts debts in any other currency, and does not subject itself to extraneous self-imposed limits can unconditionally maintain equitable solvency.

However, following such a rule does not protect a country from policy mistakes that cause harms that fall short of outright insolvency—austerity, high unemployment, slow growth, cycles of booms and busts, inflation, or even hyperinflation.

The second perspective frames sustainability as a matter of avoiding the unconstrained growth of liabilities. The mathematical conditions for avoiding unconstrained growth of liabilities are fairly straightforward. The section shows that a rule that sets an appropriate target value for the primary structural balance of the government budget is sufficient to avoid the unconstrained growth of liabilities.

The third perspective frames sustainability in terms of rules for fiscal policy that serve a rational public purpose by establishing macroeconomic conditions conducive to the flourishing of freedom and prosperity. It notes that to be successful, fiscal rules must be sustainable, not just in terms of accounting or debt dynamics, but also politically sustainable under a democratic government.

Economics is not the only discipline that is concerned with sustainability. Environmentalists, for example, often invoke the so-called Brundtland definition, according to which environmentally sustainable development is development that meets the needs of the present without compromising the ability of future generations to meet their own needs. Similarly, we could define sustainable fiscal policy as a set of rules for taxes, expenditures, budget balances, and liabilities that allows the present generation to meet its economic needs without compromising the ability of future generations to do the same. Working within the three complementary perspectives discussed in this chapter, it should be possible to devise specific rules to ensure real fiscal sustainability.

BIBLIOGRAPHY

Alesina, Alberto, and Guido Tabellini. "Bureaucrats or Politicians? Part I: A Single Policy Task." *American Economic Review* 97, no. 1 (2007): 169–79.

Barro, Robert J., and David B. Gordon. 1983. "A Positive Theory of Monetary Policy in a Natural Rate Model," *Journal of Political Economy* 91, no. 4 (1983): 589–610.

Basso, Henrique S., and James S. Costain. 2017. "Fiscal Delegation in a Monetary Union: Instrument Assignment and Stabilization Properties." Banco de España Working Paper, No 1710, March 28, 2017, https://papers.ssrn.com/sol3/papers.cfm?abstract_id=2942118.

Beetsma, Roel M. W. J., and Xavier Debrun. "The New Stability and Growth Pact: A First Assessment." *European Economic Review* 51 (2007): 453–77.

————. *Independent Fiscal Councils: Watchdogs or Lapdogs?* CEPR Ebook, London: Center for Economic Policy Research, 2018.

Beetsma, Roel, Xavier Debrun, and Randolf Sloof. "The Political Economy of Fiscal Transparency and Independent Fiscal Councils." ECB Working Paper, No 2091. European Central Bank, Frankfurt am Main, Germany, 2017.

Beetsma, Roel, Xavier Debrun, Xiangming Fang, Young Kim, Victor Duarte Lledo, Samba Mbaye, and Xiaoxiao Zhang. "Independent Fiscal Councils: Recent Trends and Performance." IMF Working Paper, No 18/68. International Monetary Fund, Washington, 2018.

Bénassy-Quéré, Agnès, Markus K. Brunnemeier, Henrik Enderlein, Emmanuel Farhi, Marcel Fratzscher, Clemens Fuest, Pierre-Olivier Gourinchas, Philippe Martin, Florence Pisani, Hélène Rey, Nicolas Véron, Beatrice Weder di Mauro, and Jeromin Zettelmeyer. "Reconciling Risk Sharing with Market Discipline: A Constructive Approach to Euro Area Reform." CEPR Policy Insight 91. Centre for Economic Policy Research, London, 2018.

Bergman, U. Michael, Michael M. Hutchinson, and Svend E. Hougaard Jensen. "Promoting Sustainable Public Finances in the European Union: The Role of Fiscal Rules and Government Efficiency." *European Journal of Political Economy* 44 (2016): 1–19.

Bernanke, Ben. "The Taylor Rule: A Benchmark for Monetary Policy?" Ben Bernanke's Blog, Brookings Institution, April 28, 20015, https://www.brookings.edu/blog/ben-bernanke/2015/04/28/the-taylor-rule-a-benchmark-for-monetary-policy/.

Bi, Huixin. "Sovereign Default Risk Premia, Fiscal Limits, and Fiscal Policy." *European Economic Review* 56, no. 3 (2012): 389–410.

Blanchard, Olivier, Giovanni Dell'Arriccia, and Paolo Mauro. "Rethinking Macroeconomic Policy." IMF Staff Position Note No. 2010/3. International Monetary Fund, Washington, 2010.

Bohn, Henning. "The Behaviour of US Public Debt and Deficits." *Quarterly Journal of Economics* 113, no. 3 (1998): 949–63.

Budina, Nina T., Andrea Schaechter, Anke Weber, and Tidiane Kinda. "Fiscal Rules in Response to the Crisis—Toward the 'Next-Generation' Rules: A New Dataset." IMF Working Paper No. 12/187, International Monetary Fund, Washington, 2012.

Buiter, Willem H. "Ten Commandments for a Fiscal Rule in the E(M)U." *Oxford Review of Economic Policy* 19, no. 1 (2004): 84–99.

Calmfors, Lars. "What Remains of the Stability and Growth Pact?" SIEPS Report No. 9. Swedish Institute for European Policy Studies, Stockholm, 2005.

Carnot, Nicolas. "Evaluating Fiscal Policy: A Rule of Thumb." European Economy, Economic Papers No. 526. European Commission, Brussels, 2014.

Chadi, Adrian, and Matthias Krapf. "Religious Confessions and Euro Skepticism in Germany." Working paper. Département d'économétrie et d'économie politique (DEEP), Faculté des Hautes Études Commerciales (HEC), Université de Lausanne, 2015.

Combes, Jean-Louis, Xavier Debrun, Alexandru Minea, and René Tapsoba. "Inflation Targeting, Fiscal Rules and the Policy Mix: Cross-effects and Interactions." *Economic Journal* 123, no. 615 (2018): 2755–2784.

Debrun, Xavier and Tidiane Kinda. "That Squeezing Feeling: The Interest Burden and Public Debt Stabilization." *International Finance* 19, no. 2 (2016): 147–178.

Debrun, Xavier, Tidiane Kinda, Luc Eyraud, Teresa Curristine, Jason Harris, and Johann Seiwald. "The Functions and Impact of Fiscal Councils." IMF Policy Paper, July. International Monetary Fund, Washington, 2013.

Eyraud, Luc, and Tao Wu. "Playing by the Rules: Reforming Fiscal Governances in Europe." IMF Working Paper No. 15/67. International Monetary Fund, Washington, 2015.

Eyraud, Luc, Xavier Debrun, Andrew Hodge, Victor Lledo, and Catherine Pattillo. 2018a. "Second-Generation Fiscal Rules: Balancing Simplicity, Flexibility and Enforceability." IMF Staff Discussion Note No. 18/04. International Monetary Fund, Washington, 2018.

Eyraud, Luc, Anja Baum, Andrew Hodge, Mariusz Jarmuzek, Young Kim, Samba Mbaye, and Elif Ture. "Fiscal Policy, How to Calibrate Fiscal Rules: A Primer." IMF How To Notes, March, International Monetary Fund, Washington, 2018.

Ghosh, Atish R., Jun I. Kim, Enrique G. Mendoza, Jonathan D. Ostry, and Majvasj S. Qureshi. "Fiscal Fatigue, Fiscal Space and Debt Sustainability in Advanced Economies." *Economic Journal* 123, no. 566 (2013): F4–F30.

Gonçalves, Carlos Eduado S., and Alexandre Carvalho. "Inflation Targeting Matters: Evidence from OECD Economies' Sacrifice Ratios." *Journal of Money, Credit and Banking* 41, no. 1 (2009): 233–243.

Grigoli, Francesco, Alexander Herman, Andrew J. Switson, and Gabriel Di Bella. "Output Gap Uncertainty and Real-Time Monetary Policy." IMF Working Paper No. 15/14. International Monetary Fund, Washington, 2015.

Gruen, Nicholas. "Making Fiscal Policy Flexibly Independent of Government." *Agenda* 4, no. 3 (1997): 297–307.

Halac, Marina, and Pierre Yared. "Fiscal Rules and Discretion in a World Economy." *American Economic Review* 108, no. 8 (2018): 2305–2334.

Heinemann, Friedrich, Marc-Daniel Moessinger, and Mustaga Yeter. "Do Fiscal Rules Constrain Fiscal Policy? A Meta-Regression-Analysis." *European Journal of Political Economy* 51, C (2018): 69–92.

Hofstede, Geert, Gert Jan Hofstede, and Michael Minkov. *Cultures and Organizations: Software of the Mind.* 3rd ed. New York: McGraw-Hill, 2010.

Holston, Kathryn, Thomas Laubach, and John C. Williams. "Measuring the Natural Rate of Interest: International Trends and Determinants." *Journal of International Economics* 108, S1 (May 2017): S59–S75.

International Monetary Fund. "Fiscal Rules: Anchoring Expectations for Sustainable Public Finances." IMF Policy Paper. IMF, Washington, 2009, https://www.imf.org/external/np/pp/eng/2009/121609.pdf.

———. "Fiscal Exit: From Strategy to Implementation." *Fiscal Monitor.* IMF, Washington, November 2010.

———. "Now Is the Time: Fiscal Policies for Sustainable Growth." *Fiscal Monitor.* IMF, Washington, April 2015.

———. "Analyzing and Managing Fiscal Risks: Best Practices." IMF Policy Paper. IMF, Washington, 2016.

Jonung, Lars. "Looking Ahead Through the Rear-View Mirror: Swedish Stabilization Policy as a Learning Process 1975–1995. A Summary." Ministry of Finance, Stockholm, 2000.

———. "Reforming the Fiscal Framework: The Case of Sweden 1973–2013." Chapter 8 in *Reform Capacity and Macroeconomic Performance in the Nordic Countries,* edited by Torben M. Andersen, Michael Bergman, and Svend E. Hougard Jensen. Oxford, UK: Oxford University Press, 2015.

King, Mervyn. Changes in UK Monetary Policy: Rules and Discretion in Practice." *Journal of Monetary Economics* 39, no. 1 (1997): 81–97.

Kliem, Martin, and Alexander Kriwolusky. "Toward a Taylor Rule for Fiscal Policy." *Review of Economic Dynamics* 17, no. 2 (2014): 294–302.

Kopits, George. "Independent Fiscal Institutions: Developing Good Practices." *OECD Journal on Budgeting* 3 (2011): 35–52.

Kopits, George, and Steven A. Symansky. "Fiscal Policy Rules." IMF Occasional Paper No 162. International Monetary Fund, Washington, 1998.

Kumhof, Michael, and Douglas Laxton. "Simple Fiscal Policy Rules for Small Open Economies." *Journal of International Economics* 91, no. 1 (2013): 113–127.

Kydland, Finn E., and Edward C. Prescott. "Rules Rather than Discretion: The Inconsistency of Optimal Plans." *Journal of Political Economy* 85, no. 3 (1977): 473–492.

Larch, Martin, Paul van den Noord, and Lars Jonung. "The Stability and Growth Pact. Lessons from the Great Recession." European Economy, Economic Papers 429, December 2010. European Commission, Brussels.

Larch, Martin, and Thomas Braendle. "Independent Fiscal Councils: Neglected Siblings of Independent Central Banks? An EU Perspective." *Journal of Common Market Studies* 56, no. 2 (2018): 267–283.

Leeper, Eric M. "Equilibria Under 'Active' and 'Passive' Monetary and Fiscal Policies." *Journal of Monetary Economics* 27, no. 1 (1991): 129–147.

———. "Monetary Science, Fiscal Alchemy," *Proceedings—Economic Policy Symposium—Jackson Hole.* Federal Reserve Bank of Kansas City, 2010, pp. 361–434.

Leijonhufvud, Axel. "The Long Swings in Economic Understanding." In *Macroeconomic Theory and Economic Policy: Essays in Honour of Jean-Paul Fitoussi*, edited by K. Vela Velupillai. London: Routledge, 2004.

Lukkezen, Jasper, and Coen Teulings. "A Fiscal Taylor Rule." CPB background document. CPB Netherlands Bureau for Economic Policy Analysis, The Hague, Netherlands, April 23, 2013.

Mauro, Paolo, Rafael Romeu, Ariel Binder, and Asad Zaman. "A Modern History of Fiscal Prudence and Profligacy." *Journal of Monetary Economics* 76 (November 2015): 55–70.

Ostry, Jonathan D., Atish R. Ghosh, Jun I. Kim, and Mahvash S. Qureshi. "Fiscal Space." IMF Staff Position Note No. 10/11, International Monetary Fund, Washington, 2010.

Peletier, Ben, Robert A. J. Dur, and Otto H. Swank. "Voting on the Budget Deficit: Comment," *American Economic Review* 89, no. 5 (1999): 1377–1381.

Portes, Jonathan, and Simon Wren-Lewis (2015), "Issues in the Design of Fiscal Rules." *The Manchester School* 83, no. S3 (2015): 56–86.

Reuter, Wolf Heinrich. "National Numerical Fiscal Rules: Not Complied With, But Still Effective?" *European Journal of Political Economy* 39 (September 2015): 67–81.

Rose, Richard. *Lesson-drawing in Public Policy. A Guide to Learning Across Time and Space*, Chatham, NJ: Chatham House Publishers Inc, 1993.

Roth, Felix. "Political Economy of EMU: Rebuilding Systemic Trust in the Euro Area in Times of Crisis." European Economy Discussion Paper No 016, September 2015. European Commission, Brussels.

Summers, Lawrence. "Secular Stagnation and Monetary Policy." *Federal Reserve Bank of St. Louis Review*, Second Quarter 2016, 98, no. 2 (2016): 93–110.

Tabellini, Guido, and Alberto Alesina. 1990. "Voting on the Budget Deficit." *American Economic Review* 80, no. 1 (1990): 37–49.

Taylor, John B. "Discretion Versus Policy Rules in Practice." *Carnegie-Rochester Conference Series on Public Policy* 39 (1993): 195–214.

———. A Historical Analysis of Monetary Policy Rules, in *Monetary Policy Rules*, edited by John B. Taylor. Chicago: University of Chicago Press, 1999.

———. "Reassessing Discretionary Fiscal Policy," *Journal of Economic Perspectives* 14, no. 3 (2000): 21–36.

———. "Swings and the Rules-Discretion Balance." Chapter 12 in *Rethinking Expectations: The Way Forward for Macroeconomics*, edited by Roman Frydman and Edmund Phelps. Princeton, NJ: Princeton University Press, 2013.

Turner, David, Maria Chiara Cavalleri, Yvan Guillemette, Alexandra Kopoin, Patrice Ollivaud, and Elena Rusticelli. "An Investigation into Improving the Real-Time Reliability of OECD Output Gap Estimates." OECD Economics Department Working Papers No. 1294. OECD Publishing, Paris, 2016.

van der Ploeg, Frederick. "Back to Keynes?" *CESifo Economic Studies* 51 no. 4 (2005): 777–822.

Walsh, Carl E. "Inflation Targeting: What Have We Learned?" *International Finance* 12, no. 2 (2009): 195–233.

Woodford, Michael. "The Taylor Rule and Optimal Monetary Policy." *American Economic Review* 91 (2001): 232–237.

Wren Lewis, Simon. "Comparing the Delegation of Monetary and Fiscal Policy." In *Restoring Public Debt Sustainability—The Role of Independent Fiscal institutions*, edited by George Kopits. Oxford, UK: Oxford University Press, 2013.

Wyplosz, Charles. "Fiscal Policy: Institutions versus Rules." *National Institute Economic Review* 191, no. 1 (2005): 70–84.

CHAPTER EIGHT

EFFECTIVE FISCAL RULES BUILD ON CONSENSUS

KURT COUCHMAN

THE PURPOSE OF FISCAL RULES

Fiscal rules are not simply for accounting, nor only to meet budget targets. They should facilitate responsible governing. That includes avoiding the overuse of "common-pool resources,"[1] such as the wallets of American taxpayers.

Unfortunately, that ideal bears little resemblance to the irresponsible "governing" practiced lately. Congress repeatedly chooses the short-term path of least resistance while pushing challenging trade-offs into the future. America's debt didn't appear suddenly. It grew, month by month and year by year, one crisis or failure of leadership at a time.[2] The longer Congress waits to address imbalances, the harder it becomes.[3] Catching up on deferred maintenance while keeping up with day-to-day matters is difficult. Eventually it will become insurmountable.

The past cannot be undone, but we can recover. Better fiscal rules can facilitate real governance and the practice of politics. In other words, public agents—primarily members of Congress—would collectively make choices and set priorities under constraints from enforceable fiscal goals. Reaching consensus on fiscal goals, constraints, and enforcement among those who will be bound by them is, needless to say, a challenge.

Setting and enforcing targets has other benefits, such as reducing the prospect of a fiscal crisis. Maintaining lenders' faith in the credit of the American sovereign is crucial to the stability of and support for our system of government. Retaining the ability to borrow during emergencies requires prudence during times of plenty.

Fiscal responsibility gives policymakers and the public ongoing reasons to search for and eliminate waste. Waste, fraud, and abuse squander taxpayer resources, invite corruption, and undermine the public's trust in our institutions.

The objective of fiscal rules is sound governance. The character of those rules matters immensely.

PRINCIPLES FOR EFFECTIVE FISCAL RULES

Sound governance does not belong to any particular political party or political philosophy. It is the institutionalization of the classical virtues of prudence, justice, courage, and temperance. Prudence to maintain the polity for the long term with a margin for the unexpected. Justice for future generations not to be robbed by their elders. Courage to resist demands of powerful interests against the unorganized public. And temperance to accept limits on what government can reasonably take from the people or achieve on their behalf.

Both Republicans and Democrats can either display civic virtue or practice vice. The rules that structure their incentives tip the balance one way or the other, depending on external circumstances as well as individual knowledge and characters.

The best rules guide interest into socially productive functions. Albert Hirschman's *doux commerce* thesis—that market systems make serving our fellow man through mutual exchange more appealing than plundering him—has parallels in the public sphere.[4] Self-interest is hardly the exclusive motivation of policymakers, but it matters.

Ideally then, effective fiscal rules would encourage informed trade-offs between priorities. They would promote learning and knowledge so legislators have sound reasons for their preferences and the ability to explain them to the people they represent.

CONSTITUTIONS PROMULGATE PRINCIPLES

Constitutional fiscal rules have been sought without success since the beginning of the republic. Observing ruinous debt in Europe, Thomas Jefferson wished it were possible to amend the Constitution "taking from the federal government the power of borrowing."[5] Nonetheless, he and all other responsible statesmen have recognized the need to borrow for emergencies, especially war.

Popular support is high for amending the Constitution to end chronic borrowing through balanced budgets. A 2011 poll found that 74 percent of respondents favored "a constitutional amendment to require a balanced federal budget."[6] The people know that Congress cannot control itself without external discipline. When crafting a balanced budget amendment (BBA), however, several considerations are crucial.

First, constitutional provisions are principles. They are not legislation. They are not self-enforcing. They are not detailed. They do not usually specify who is to do what, when, or how.

Constitutional provisions are broad statements of consensus. Putting them into practice depends on the normal legislative process and what can be enacted and sustained. Generality fosters consensus at the constitutional stage. The American system requires two-thirds of both houses of Congress and three-fourths of state legislatures to ratify a new constitutional amendment, but no president or governor.

Second, the process for approving constitutional amendments needs to be kept in mind. Under rules of the Senate[7] and the House of Representatives,[8] the Committee on the Judiciary of each body has jurisdiction over all proposed amendments to the Constitution, no matter the subject. Jurisdiction over "implementing legislation" for an enacted constitutional amendment, however, varies by subject matter. For a BBA, the Budget Committees would take the lead.

Third, the specific language of BBA proposals has prevented prior passage. General support for binding fiscal rules exists in the public and perhaps even among members of Congress. As always, the devil is in the details, and some versions are positively possessed.

These three elements—politics, process, and policy—determine prospects. Views on implementing legislation options and policies to reach balance factor in as well. The remainder of this chapter will be divided between a specific discussion of constitutional fiscal rules and a more general discussion of statutory implementing legislation. Statutes' general treatment is partly due to space and partly because some details are still being developed. This chapter's legislative appendix details several options.

MOST BBAs HAVE MANY PROBLEMS

The "traditional" BBA approach is represented by H.J. Res. 22 (116th Congress),[9] introduced by Rep. Steve Chabot (R–OH). If it could succeed, this chapter would not be needed.

Amending the Constitution isn't easy. It requires two-thirds support in both houses: 67 votes in the Senate and 290 in the House, assuming no vacancies or absences.

In April 2018, an earlier version failed in the House, 233 to 184 (55.9 percent) with six Republicans opposed and only seven Democrats supporting.[10] In November 2011, it failed 261 to 165 (61.3 percent) with four Republicans opposed and 25 Democrats supporting.[11] In December 2011, 67 senators voted for one of two BBAs, 47 to 53[12] for the "conservative" version and 21 to 79[13] for the "center-left" version. One Republican backed both.

The balance requirement is the most basic element. Nearly all BBAs, including H.J. Res. 22, would require annual balance. That's a mistake.[14]

U.S. revenue policies in a dynamic economy yield a volatile revenue stream. Binding revenue and spending tightly together each year would force considerable policy instability into both sides. Planning beyond the short term would challenge both recipients of federal funding and those who pay for it, as well as Congress. This instability would introduce policy-based risk premiums into planning, reducing investment and undermining prosperity.

Federal policies naturally include what Keynesian economists call "automatic stabilizers." Recessions depress revenue and boost spending. The result is (greater) deficits.

During recessions, revenue falls below trend growth largely because business profits decline and lower employment reduces personal income and payroll taxes. On the spending side, increased joblessness boosts demand for safety net programs like health, nutrition, and income support programs such as Medicaid, the Supplemental Nutrition Access Program, and unemployment compensation.

Annual balance, strictly enforced, would interfere with these automatic adjustments. Whether or not these countercyclical policies stabilize the economy in the Keynesian sense, their fiscal impacts are clear. This creates formidable political and policy headwinds for annual balance.

It gets worse. These proposals define balance between receipts and outlays. Outlays occur when federal agencies pay out to individuals and contractors. Congress does not directly control outlays. Congress controls budget authority, which is the authority for agencies to spend. Budget authority is like the agencies getting a paycheck. Outlays are when agencies cut checks for goods and services, so outlay timing is irregular.

Further, these BBAs confuse broad constitutional language with specific statutory drafting. For example, they invoke the "fiscal year." Such a definition belongs in implementing legislation. Simple "year" is appropriate for the Constitution.

Many BBAs would change the balance of powers between Congress and the president. They would require the president to submit an annual budget proposal that balances and meets other stipulations. Under the Constitution, the president's main budget-related jobs are to sign (or veto) appropriations legislation and to take care that the laws are faithfully executed. Statute already requires the president to submit a budget proposal,[15] and that's where it belongs, not in the Constitution. Giving the president an explicit budget-related function in the Constitution could be the unintended foundation for further confusion about presidential powers.

The next element is the "safety valve," which allows exceptions to the balance rule. H.J. Res. 22 has three. First, three-fifths of the whole number (every current member, whether voting or not) of each house could deficit spend for any reason. Second, a majority of the whole number of each house could do so during a military conflict. Third, a declaration of war would automatically suspend balance.

A safety valve is vital. Emergencies happen, and without a usable exception from balance, the political will to sustain balance would crumble. But do different circumstances require different thresholds, and what is appropriate for thresholds?

Emergencies take many forms. The political question is whether the emergency justifies an exemption from balance. The threshold should be uniform. Looking to history, Congress has overwhelmingly supported the vast majority of emergency circumstances. And if a supposed emergency or the proposed response to it can't get broad support, that's a sign that something about it is ill-advised.

The appropriate threshold is a compromise among competing factors. It must be low enough to be useful for emergencies and to prevent a small, cohesive group from leveraging it for something else. It must be high enough to discourage frivolous use and to preserve the norm of balance. Three-fifths—the effective threshold for Senate approval—is clearly too low to serve as an effective check. This topic is discussed further in the sections that follow.

The initial transition to balance is the last vital element of a BBA. The federal deficit is nearly $1 trillion per year and rising.[16] Congress needs a realistic period to make the substantial changes to reach balance.

It isn't easy, and it would take time. The fiscal year 2019 budget resolution from the House Budget Committee included assumptions to balance within 10 years, but no one expected them to be enacted. It assumed $8.1 trillion in deficit reduction over the 10-year window, yet only $302 billion would have been cut with the fast-track deficit-reduction "reconciliation" process.[17] Even that 3.7 percent of the total would require the House and the Senate to agree on a budget resolution, for both to approve reconciliation legislation, and for the president to sign it. None of these steps occurred for FY 19.

Republican budget resolutions do not generally include revenue increases for deficit reduction, except through economic growth. Democrats will make more revenue the price of support for a budget deal. The challenge is finding the least anti-growth policies to satisfy that demand.

Even putting all spending and revenue options on the table doesn't mean that rapid balance is politically viable. Most policy changes must be phased in. Proposals that would require balance in two, three, or even five years (as in H.J. Res. 22) after ratification are not realistic. These are the most universal problems. Many others exist.

Some BBAs demand supermajorities for raising the debt limit—another statutory construct that doesn't belong in the Constitution. In addition, the Constitution grants Congress the power to borrow,[18] so the debt limit may already be excessive delegation. Further, a well-crafted BBA and implementing legislation would control the debt, making a debt limit redundant at best. Finally, constitutional provisions should be principles that are kept as simple as possible.

Many Republicans would limit spending as a percentage of gross domestic product (GDP) or establish supermajorities to increase revenues. Democrats oppose both, and their support is needed to establish and sustain fiscal rules.

A constitutional rule must accommodate a range of policy options and governance visions. Otherwise there is no consensus, and no BBA is possible. The size, scope, and content of government must remain the domain of normal politics within the constitutional framework, even with a requirement for balance.

Some would exclude certain programs from balance. Certainly, some programs should be insulated from *enforcement* under implementing legislation, but all must be included for balance to be meaningful.

Most BBAs have serious political and policy shortcomings. Two have a chance.

CRAFTING A BASIC, PRINCIPLES-BASED BBA

Constitutional language should be simple, establish broad principles, and leave the details to legislation. Budget process is complicated, but at the constitutional level, only three elements are needed: (a) the balance requirement, (b) an exception, and (c) a transition to balance.

THE RULE FOR BALANCE

In theory, a BBA could be as simple as "The budget shall be balanced," and statute could do the rest. In practice, slightly more specificity makes sense. The most recent BBA I wrote for a House member begins,

"Expenditures and receipts shall be balanced, which may occur over more than one year to accommodate economic conditions."[19]

Another version I previously wrote for another House member is more precise: "Total expenditures for a year shall not exceed the average annual revenue collected in the three prior years, adjusted in proportion to changes in population and inflation."[20]

If the Constitution must detail the mechanics of balance, the latter is an excellent choice. It would make spending and revenue policies far more stable and predictable than annual balance. It would establish a countercyclical budget rule to accommodate adjustments during recessions.

Yet balance need not be precisely defined in the Constitution. A general principle is enough to create the expectation of balance and the flexibility to adapt to business cycles. On language, "expenditures" and "receipts" are the general terms that already appear in the Constitution.[21]

EMERGENCY SPENDING

A fiscal rule's survival depends on a careful exception. Emergencies happen, and sometimes strict balance doesn't make sense. The statutory challenge is to offset the emergency over a reasonable period thereafter. Otherwise it could become an often-used loophole.

Many BBAs would set aside balance more easily for military contingencies than for other emergencies. Sometimes extra funds would be limited to the conflict. Sometimes the contingency would suspend balance for everything, which could subtly encourage wars to escape fiscal discipline.

Deviating from balance should happen under a single, uniform threshold. Some emergencies are more important than others, and those are most likely to have broad support. Simple language minimizes games and creative definitions.

The appropriate threshold requires careful weighing. Following Buchanan and Tullock, political externalities—like excessive debt—must be balanced with workable transaction costs, such as providing appropriately for emergencies.[22]

The traditional BBA threshold of three-fifths is too low. Under current practice, the Senate effectively requires three-fifths to pass ordinary legislation. Following ratification of a BBA, it might matter more, but perhaps not.

Higher levels are possible, such as the two that already appear in the Constitution: three-fourths and two-thirds.

Three-fourths would tend to reserve emergency spending for real emergencies. It's also low enough to impede the organization of enough members—109 members is one-fourth of the House—for them to have leverage over the measure, especially in the face of an emergency.

Three-fourths would, however, affect the dynamics of the presidential veto.[23] After congressional majorities pass legislation, the president may veto if he disapproves. Congress must then attempt to override the veto with a two-thirds vote in both houses. Creating a three-fourths standard for emergency spending would establish a novel relationship with the veto-override threshold.

A lower threshold of two-thirds would also bring discipline, especially combined with public expectations and implementing legislation. Organizing small groups to hold it hostage would be even more difficult while also ensuring broad bipartisan consensus. It preserves the normal veto process. Finally, it is already by far the most common constitutional supermajority.

A two-thirds supermajority for exceptions to balance has strong constitutional and economic foundations. In U.S. history, major emergency situations have generally obtained at least two-thirds support in both Houses. When they haven't, some responses were intentionally drafted to pass more narrowly, such as the 2009 stimulus bill. Others may not have been worth doing in any case. Unfortunately, a more complete discussion of marginal cases belongs in another venue.

TRANSITION TO BALANCE

The last crucial element is moving from the profligate status quo to initial balance. The BBA paradox is that public demand and congressional interest are highest when a politically viable path to balance is hardest to imagine. When deficits are lower and less threatening, binding fiscal rules seem less necessary.

A well-crafted BBA must accept and accommodate this reality. Despite the short-term incentives created by frequent elections to the House of Representatives, members are capable of thinking longer term and sometimes do so.

Even if a BBA with a short transition were somehow ratified, it would either create unnecessary adjustment pain or encourage Congress to reach excessively for the emergency spending valve. Either outcome—or both—would corrode public support and congressional norms to faithfully practice fiscal responsibility.

Reaching balance would occur over the period specified in the BBA plus the time it takes for three-fourths of state legislatures to ratify it. Ratification would likely take one to four years, in accordance with prior constitutional amendments.[24] If the amendment allowed a 10-year transition, Congress would probably have 11 to 14 years to reach balance after sending a BBA to the states.

It's a long time, but not that much longer than the assumptions embedded in budget proposals. The FY 19 budget resolution from House Budget Committee Republicans assumes balance in nine years. Comparable budget resolutions would normally have the support of a majority of the House. As a Republican vision document, however, it attracts no Democrats' votes and includes more spending cut assumptions than are likely to be possible.

Enacted reforms to reach balance would therefore take at least a decade. Working out these bipartisan deals will be difficult. They can only be done with enough time and with rules that do not presuppose policy outcomes other than ending chronic deficits.

However, the time to reach balance cannot be too great, or it will seem like more empty promises. The momentum from enacting a BBA must immediately transfer to implementing legislation and policy reforms. Even a quickly adopted comprehensive deal would take most of a decade to fully phase in. A 10-year transition following a few years for ratification seems to be about as fast as can realistically be expected.

A PRINCIPLES-BASED BBA CAN SUCCEED

The last BBA proposal I wrote for a member of Congress[25] meets these criteria and has had more than 60 bipartisan cosponsors:

> Section 1. Expenditures and receipts shall be balanced, which may occur over more than one year to accommodate economic conditions. Expenditures shall include all expenditures of the United States except those for payment of debt, and receipts shall include all receipts of the United States except those derived from borrowing.
>
> Section 2. For emergency situations two-thirds of the House of Representatives and the Senate may for limited times authorize expenditures exceeding those pursuant to rules established under section 1. Debts incurred from such expenditures shall be paid as soon as practicable.
>
> Section 3. Congress shall have power to enforce this article by appropriate legislation, which shall allow not more than ten years after ratification to comply with section 1.

In summary, constitutional language differs from statutory language. It establishes principles, which are given life by implementing legislation. If the aforementioned proposal approaches the ideal BBA language, the statutes defining, tracking, and enforcing these principles are at least as important.

That ongoing project will comprise the rest of the chapter. Deeper discussion of BBA design and implementing legislation will, I hope, eventually receive book-length treatment.

STATUTES IMPLEMENT PRINCIPLES BY NAVIGATING EFFECTIVENESS AND SUSTAINABILITY

Statutes turn constitutional principles into governing instructions. They define terms, establish procedures, create accountability, and otherwise guide executive and legislative processes. They give the public—and sometimes the courts—the details needed to judge whether the principles are being faithfully followed.

Defining balance and keeping track is the first objective. Enforcing it and encouraging politicians to comply is the greater challenge. Many of these options can be enacted without a balanced budget amendment in place, although the public consensus for balance wouldn't be as strong, and supermajorities for emergency spending that were established by mere legislation would not be enforceable.

SETTING FISCAL GOALS

Fortunately, Switzerland provides a model for defining and tracking balance. Article 126 of the Swiss Constitution provides the principle,[26] and implementing legislation is codified in the Federal Law for the Confederation's Budget. Upon my request in 2016, the Law Library of Congress produced a report explaining and translating these provisions.[27]

The Swiss generally require balance over the business cycle. A "compensation account" tracks adherence to an annual spending cap. The revenue-based cap accommodates the business cycle to be mildly countercyclical. A post-fiscal-year review determines whether spending has exceeded the limit, and if so, the subsequent spending cap must compensate.

Emergency spending is tracked with an "amortization account." This is available only if the necessary spending exceeds a certain amount, thus encouraging the government to seek offsets for relatively small unanticipated needs. Crucially for continued consensus, the rule leaves choices about the mix of spending reductions and revenue enhancements to the regular political process. Emergency spending above a nominal amount must be repaid within three or six years, depending on the size, and this window can be extended in the case of ongoing or recurring needs.

The United States cannot immediately adopt a business-cycle-balanced-budget rule, of course, without a specified statutory transition. It would be possible to allow spending to exceed a revenue-based spending cap by gradually declining amounts each year until balance is reached. Congress would have full flexibility to choose fewer services and less revenue or more services and greater revenue. As an aside, a benefit of keeping specifics in statute is that they can be more easily altered as circumstances change.

Another approach could also reach the same goal. Suppose that spending doesn't grow faster than GDP, and spending growth slows if the debt burden increases. Both parts are needed because a spending rule may not reach balance if it is disconnected from revenue. A debt brake eventually ensures that the gap between spending and revenue closes, the budget balances, and Congress lives within its means.

Simply limiting federal spending growth to GDP growth would begin to stabilize the budget, mostly by making spending binges less frequent. To curb debt growth, the spending growth rate could be reduced a small amount—a fraction of a percentage point—each year that the debt grew as a percentage of GDP.

An additional rule should address long-term, unfunded liabilities, which annual cash-flow accounting does not. Promised pension and health care spending without commensurate funding has become a serious challenge in both the public sector and some parts of the private sector. We are finding that today is yesterday's distant future, and the past's easy promises are coming due.

One such option would state that the fiscal gap cannot expand, or perhaps must be reduced over time by at least a specified rate. The fiscal gap is the difference between projected spending and projected revenue, all discounted to current dollars.

Adapting the Swiss framework to American laws and institutions is not technically complicated (see the specific proposed legislation in the appendix). The challenge is enforcement. Switzerland lacks specific enforcement provisions, yet it has faithfully maintained fiscal discipline, even during the 2008 financial crisis and its aftermath. Yet the political system, culture, and geopolitical position of Switzerland differ substantially from the United States.

Consider the political dynamics of rule compliance in the presence or absence of explicit enforcement mechanisms. As mentioned previously, fiscal rules are meant to constrain political externalities that well-organized factions would impose on the body politic and taxpayers.

In the classic problem of concentrated beneficiaries imposing small, diffuse costs on the many, the many are unjustly burdened, but the imposition isn't enough to motivate most to take political action. The relatively few beneficiaries each get big benefits, so the benefits of political participation outweigh the costs.

Dividing legislative power between a differently constituted House and Senate has often checked majoritarian impulses. It has been less effective checking concentrated beneficiaries. Proliferating special programs and exemptions in spending accounts, revenue policies, and regulatory structures bear witness to the ability of special interests to prevail over regular taxpayers.

Fiscal rules make it harder for Congress to play Santa Claus. Deficits are nearly $1 trillion and rising. With outlays of nearly $4.5 trillion in FY 2019, 22 percent of federal spending is going on the credit card.[28] There's little discipline. Politicians don't have a ready excuse for not doing what a powerful interest wants. A balance rule changes those dynamics.

CAVEATS ON AUTOMATIC BUDGET ENFORCEMENT

Enforcement mechanisms should ensure that missing the agreed-upon targets has consequences. Yet there are grounds for caution.

First, politicians may rely on the rules too much. The path of least resistance is often to avoid action. If the rules address a problem tolerably well, politicians are less likely to seek better ways of reaching fiscal goals. They may prefer to focus on other things when they and the public think fiscal discipline is being addressed. Of course, the perfect can't be the enemy of the good, and "mostly responsible" is better than not at all, so rules-based discipline may still be reasonable.

Second, the rules get blamed for constituent impacts. Following the Budget Control Act of 2011, many politicians didn't believe—or claimed not to believe—that the sequester cuts and subsequent caps would happen. The caps became a lightning rod for criticism, even though majorities of the House and Senate voted for them.

These two risks are connected. Political durability requires maintaining consensus that the approach taken was a reasonable outcome. When rules operate mechanically and few politicians have a stake in defending outcomes, the public dialogue shifts to the rules. This can unravel the consensus that established the rules in the first place.

It is possible, at least sometimes, that following the rules without explicit enforcement mechanisms may be more politically effective and durable. In Switzerland, each budget and its associated policy choices require the legislature's consent. The shared experience of affirming the package provides credibility and staying power that automatic enforcement may not.

ENFORCEMENT OF BUDGET GOALS

With that significant caveat, automatic enforcement is probably needed in the United States. The budget should involve all spending—direct and discretionary, domestic and foreign, "on-budget" and "off-budget"—and all revenue policies. Enforcement must touch each category.

Enforcement has multiple purposes. Some aspects would automatically enact fiscal consolidation. Others would encourage policymakers to act. Some would do both.

DISCRETIONARY ENFORCEMENT

Annual appropriations—"discretionary spending"—include programs generally considered to be core government activities: defense, foreign affairs, homeland security, the courts, and so on. It includes some federal components of transportation, housing, education, health care, veteran programs, agriculture, and others.

These accounts were the main target of the Balanced Budget and Emergency Deficit Control Act of 1985 and the Budget Control Act of 2011 (BCA). Both imposed caps on separate "security" and "nonsecurity" discretionary categories, enforced by across-the-board sequestration of "nonexempt" spending if total spending would otherwise breach the caps. Under the BCA, sequestration happened only in 2013. Since then, Congress has been free to reallocate funding under the caps.

Discretionary spending is a small and declining fraction of total spending, but it is politically sensitive. Much direct spending is made up of transfer payments to individuals, but recipients of direct spending are relatively poorly organized politically. Recipients of discretionary spending, however, are highly organized and politically active. Tightly constraining these accounts has not been durable.

Lesser limits may be possible within a comprehensive framework. The defense and nondefense discretionary caps could return at the current, most recently enacted levels, if spending exceeds one or more targets described previously. No nominal cuts would be needed. Congress could prioritize within the limits. Related options include (a) "breaking the firewall" between defense and nondefense, so trade-offs can take place across all appropriated programs, and (b) allowing discretionary increases if properly offset.[29]

Another discretionary option is to automatically continue current funding if Congress fails to pass appropriations legislation. An automatic continuing resolution would prevent an impasse from causing a shutdown. This need not involve periodic cuts, as often proposed, but could simply freeze current funding. As I explain elsewhere,[30] this would narrow the decision set and reduce the scope of conflict. New spending deals would have to improve on the status quo, as judged by congressional majorities, instead of merely being better than a shutdown, which is an outcome no one really wants.

The incentive to appropriate would remain. Changing priorities require funds to be reallocated. Moreover, an automatic continuing resolution that freezes spending would require new appropriations to adjust for population growth and inflation, at least. Combined with tempered views on the scope of the possible, the appropriations process would likely run smoother.

Enforcement could also distinguish between authorized and unauthorized appropriations. Some $318 billion of 2018 discretionary spending, almost entirely in nondefense accounts, does not have an active authorization of appropriations from the committees of jurisdiction.[31] In the State and Foreign Operations Appropriations Act accounts, for example, about 98 percent of spending lacks a current authorization.[32] A 1 to 2 percent increase to authorized programs under an automatic continuing resolution could let them keep up with inflation while encouraging authorizing committees to update and reauthorize other programs.

Discretionary spending is not driving our deficit and debt trajectory. It is, however, what Congress spends the most time considering. Automatic enforcement must address other budget factors, but it cannot ignore Congress's primary focus.

DIRECT SPENDING ENFORCEMENT

Direct spending programs don't require recurring congressional authorization to spend funds. They are the primary fiscal challenge, making up 70 percent of spending and growing faster than the economy. That cannot be sustained indefinitely. These programs include Social Security, Medicare, Medicaid, many veterans' benefits, federal civilian and military retirement, Supplemental Security Income, agriculture programs, food stamps, and others.

Many recipients depend on them due to old age, illness, or other challenges they cannot easily address, if at all. Others have employment-based eligibility, like pensions and veterans' benefits. The financial security of individual Americans is at stake, so reforms must be done carefully. Nonetheless, options for automatic enforcement while protecting the vulnerable are available.

Some programs have been subject to automatic enforcement under statutes that apply across-the-board cuts to "nonexempt" programs. This approach is relatively easy to negotiate and draft. If implemented, it would reduce expenditures and perhaps nudge Congress to grapple with fiscal imbalances to avoid these specific mechanisms.

In practice, however, such across-the-board cuts are politically unsustainable. Programs are diverse, but one rule for all makes organizing their beneficiaries relatively easy. This approach also avoids the vital question of protecting the most vulnerable or providing adequate time for those who can adjust their expectations to do so.

The key is to identify parameters that can be adjusted incrementally, repeatedly, and perhaps with some delay. Those who are least able to adapt should be affected least. Even those who can adjust will often need time.

For example, Social Security (Old Age and Survivors Insurance) is the largest federal program at nearly $900 billion in FY 19.[33] Focusing on old age benefits, at least five incremental, repeatable options exist for targeted benefit reductions and two for revenue increases. The size of each option and whether to include it is a political question more than it is a technical matter.

On the spending side, the normal retirement age (currently increasing from age 65 to 67 by two months per birth year) could be increased further, as could the early retirement age, currently 62 years. A worker becomes a "fully insured individual" after 40 quarters (10 years) of qualifying work, and benefits are based on 35 years of work history. One or both could be extended. Finally, the "bend points" for calculating initial benefits could be reduced or the thresholds at which each applies could be changed, thus preserving full benefits for lower lifetime earners while reducing them for higher earners who generally have other retirement income.

On revenue, the Social Security payroll tax rate or the contribution base could increase. Many other options exist to save and strengthen Social Security.[34] Automatic budget enforcement, however, favors changes that can occur incrementally, repeatedly, and possibly with timing lags.

A similar approach could be taken for many other programs. Not every possible tweak should necessarily be included, but this approach is a credible alternative to clunky, politically unsustainable, across-the-board cuts to direct spending programs.

REVENUE ENFORCEMENT

Revenue options must also be considered, even for those disinclined to shift more resources from the private to the public sector. The United States has a spending problem that tax hikes alone cannot solve. Some revenue increases may be politically necessary, however.

Both Republicans and Democrats need to support a durable deal for fiscal consolidation. Both sides will have to accept tough choices to prevent fiscal calamity, and all need to be able to claim "wins."

In addition, government already burdens the productive sector with borrowing. Debt finance is a hidden cost with pernicious effects. Reducing borrowing by necessary spending reductions and relatively small revenue increases is still a large net reduction in government burden.

As with spending, revenue-focused enforcement can happen incrementally and repeatedly. The precise composition should give strong weight to the least harmful ways of revenue raising. In the language of economics, the ideal options would impose the least deadweight loss, that is, they would minimize the excess burden of taxation.[35] By this standard, income taxes—corporate and individual—are less attractive.

More attractive may be tax expenditures relative to a consumption base, rather than the Haig-Simons comprehensive income base, which characterizes deductions for cost recovery, savings, and investment similar to corporate welfare and social engineering provisions.[36]

POLITICAL ENFORCEMENT

Political enforcement mechanisms may also be useful. Identifying those that are both effective and appropriate is challenging, however.

"No budget, no pay" has been a popular idea. Yet passing a budget resolution—which has limited policy effects—is only one aspect of Congress's job. Why should that determine when and whether they get paid? It puts more pressure on members who need their salary compared to their wealthy colleagues. Doing a budget resolution doesn't mean that it's a good one. Far from clearly helping, "no budget, no pay" may also lead to accusations that members selfishly supported the budget resolution to get paid, not because it was any good.

Other political enforcement options have similar dynamics. That doesn't necessarily disqualify them, but more consideration of the future political and policy impacts is needed to decide if, on balance, each advances the public good.

A few political enforcement options stand out. First, if Congress meets responsible fiscal targets, they shouldn't have to vote on increasing the debt limit. It could be automatically suspended until a target is breached, after which "extraordinary measures" would give Congress several months to get back on track or face that vote.

Another option is a fast-track process that would become available several times per year for popular, major deficit reduction legislation. An implementation of this concept that I've developed would apply to legislation scored as reducing the 10-year deficit by 5 percent. Among such bills, the bill with the most cosponsors would be voted on first. The second and third would be those with the most cosponsors that had *not* cosponsored a bill considered this way earlier in the year.

It would be like reconciliation but could include any combination of spending cuts, revenue increases, and regulatory reforms. It would bypass the committees of jurisdiction, injecting competition into the system and encouraging authorizing committees to manage programs under their responsibility. If this process is only available when deficits are projected every year for the next decade, it would help normalize deficit reduction until balance is in sight. Finally, it would encourage diverse coalitions to come up with feasible approaches to fiscal responsibility.

Like everyone else, politicians follow incentives. Effective budget enforcement must reflect their diverse motivations for spending, revenue, and political dynamics. A constitutional rule strengthens public accountability, but it is insufficient without careful implementing legislation.

CONCLUSION

A well-crafted balanced budget amendment[37] to the Constitution can succeed politically and as policy. Its congressional passage and ratification in state legislatures would establish a national consensus that getting to balance in a reasonable period is the appropriate fiscal goal. It would also create an enforceable supermajority standard for emergency spending.

The definition of "emergency spending" and much more would belong in implementing legislation. Such a statute is not a single rule, but a bundle of mutually reinforcing rules that set expectations and encourage legislators to follow them.

Further reforms may be useful or even needed for the statutory budget process, for the rules of the House and the Senate, for the rules of the Senate and House Republican and Democratic conference rules, and perhaps for campaign and electoral rules.[38]

No single rule can adequately address America's fiscal management or other governance challenges. Every new rule or rule change affects a complex structure of rewards and punishments for policymakers, their staff, advocacy organizations, administration officials, state and local officials, the American public, and even officials of other countries. Attempting to understand and coordinate them all may be beyond the scope of any mind.

We cannot hope for a silver bullet. Neither can we hope to fix everything all at once. We can, however, focus on a limited set of rule changes with the best prospects for improving our governance as it exists, not as we wish it were. As we observe and learn, as spectators or participants, other opportunities or mistakes to correct will come into focus.

No system of government has ever been perfect. With humility, hard work, and perseverance, however, we can make it work better than it has before.

APPENDIX

HIGHLIGHTS OF GENUINE REFORMS EARN AMERICANS' TRUST AGAIN ACT LEGISLATIVE PROPOSAL[†]

I. Spending cap is prior year's cap, increased by average GDP growth over last five years. [Sec. 101(a)]

Spending cap (budget authority: BA) = $\text{Spending}_{(T-1)}$ * $(1 + \text{AVG\%} \Delta\text{GDP}\{T - 6{:}T - 1\})$

Example: FY 19 BA = FY2018 Spending ($4.108) * (1 + AVG %ΔGDP [2013 − 2018] [.0401]) = $4.272 in T [= current year]

II. If debt burden grew, spending growth incrementally reduced by 0.1 percentage point (PP). [Sec. 101(a)(2)]

If debt-to-GDP ratio increased during fiscal year 2, then FY cap is 0.1 PP less than otherwise.

Example 1: FY 17 debt-to-GDP > FY 16 debt-to-GDP, FY 19 BA = $4.108 * (1 + 0.0401 − 0.001) = $4.269.

Example 2: If FY 18 debt-to-GDP > FY 17 debt-to-GDP, FY 20 BA = FY 19 BA * (1 + AVG%ΔGDP − [2 * 0.001]) = $4.269 T * (1 + 0.0416 − 0.002) = $4.438

III. Emergency spending must be offset later but effects excluded from above [Sec. 102].

IV. If actual spending "breached" cap, then [Title II, Subtitle A] automatic adjustments.

1. *Discretionary:* frozen at current year levels (year following breach year) for next budget year [Sec. 202]

2. *Direct/mandatory spending:* various incremental adjustments, some delayed [Sec. 203]

3. *Revenue policies:* various incremental adjustments, generally for next tax year [Sec. 204]

V.   If deficits projected for next 10 years, then expedited consideration of major deficit reduction [Title II, Subtitle B]

VI. If Congress fails to appropriate or enact a continuing resolution, then automatic continuing resolutions fund programs [Title II, Subtitle C]

1. Two percent inflation adjustment for authorized programs like defense, intelligence.
2. Two-year limit on Army appropriations required by U.S. Constitution Art. I, Sec. 8, cl. 12.

VII. Incentives and opportunities to enact reforms

1. Require president's budget to propose deficit reduction options [Sec. 403].
2. Suspend debt ceiling until and unless total spending cap breached [Sec. 404].

VIII. Vote on a Balanced Budget Amendment [Title V]

†Most elements can be enacted independently or with other budget reforms.

LEGISLATIVE PROPOSAL OF GENUINE REFORMS EARN AMERICANS' TRUST AGAIN ACT

[Author's note: *Portions of this appendix are derived from existing statutes or from legislative proposals drafted with the assistance of the House Office of the Legislative Counsel. I am not an attorney and make no representation that the proposal is optimally drafted. Consultation with qualified legal counsel on any provision of interest is recommended.*

Elements of this proposal have varying degrees of independence. Some could be adopted in isolation. Others could be combined with aspects of existing law. Each component may be considered a module for accomplishing a particular objective and may be substitutable with other approaches to the same goal.]

SEC 1. SHORT TITLE: This Act may be cited as the "Genuine Reforms Earn Americans' Trust (GREAT) Again Act of 2019."

SEC. 2. DEFINITIONS. Unless otherwise specified, the definitions of terms shall be consistent with those in section 3 of the Congressional Budget and Impoundment Control Act of 1974 (2 U.S.C. 622) and section 250 of the Balanced Budget and Emergency Deficit Control Act of 1985 (2 U.S.C. 900).

TITLE I—SETTING OBJECTIVES FOR A SUSTAINABLE FEDERAL BUDGET

SEC. 101. SETTING AN ANNUAL SPENDING TARGET

(a) ESTABLISHMENT OF A SPENDING CEILING.—The ceiling for the estimated authorized total budget authority for the fiscal year beginning on October 1 shall equal the total budget authority for the prior fiscal year increased by the spending growth factor. The calculation of the total budget authority for the prior fiscal year shall exclude adjustments under paragraph (b) (1), paragraph (b)(3), and section 102. [Note: *To minimize potential for gaming, emergency spending should not affect the baseline in either direction, although it should be incorporated into the debt burden reduction factor (below).*]

    (1) SPENDING GROWTH FACTOR.—The spending growth factor for a fiscal year equals—

        (A) The average of the growth in gross domestic product (GDP) over the five fiscal years immediately prior to the budget year

        (B) Less the cumulative debt burden factor.

    (2) DEBT BURDEN FACTOR.—The debt burden factor specified in paragraph (1)(ii) shall begin at zero (0) and shall:

        (A) Increase by one-tenth of one percentage point, cumulatively, [Note: *increasing this parameter would slow spending growth more quickly and reach balance sooner; decreasing it would slow spending growth more slowly and reach balance later.*] for each fiscal year during which the debt held by the public increased as a percentage of gross domestic product between the beginning and the end of the second prior fiscal year; and

        (B) Decrease by one-tenth of one percentage point, cumulatively but not below zero, for each fiscal year during which the debt held by the public decreased as a percentage of gross domestic product between the beginning and the end of the second prior fiscal year.

    (3) The House of Representatives, the Senate, and the President shall adhere to the spending ceiling when considering legislation and executive proposals with fiscal implications.

(b) INCREASING THE SPENDING CEILING.—When adopting a budget resolution, supplemental appropriations, and other amendments to the budget resolution, Congress may increase the ceiling to reflect—

    (1) An emergency, as defined in section 250(c)(20) of the Balanced Budget and Emergency Deficit Control Act of 1985 (2 U.S.C. 900(c)(20));

(2)   Revisions in GDP estimates; or

(3)   Timing shifts of expenditures or revenues due.

An increase in the ceiling shall not be permitted unless the additional amount equals or exceeds 0.5 percent of the initial ceiling announced under paragraph (c)(1).

(c)   CALCULATION.—The Congressional Budget Office (CBO) and the Office of Management and Budget (OMB) shall provide independent estimates of the spending ceiling for the upcoming fiscal year to the Committees on the Budget.

(1)   CBO shall submit such estimate in the report required by section 202(e) of the Congressional Budget Act of 1974.

(2)   OMB shall submit such estimate with the submission of the president's budget proposal under section 1105 of Title 31, United States Code.

(3)   The chairs of the Budget Committees shall jointly announce the initial spending ceiling for the upcoming fiscal year within seven (7) calendar days of the later of the CBO and OMB estimates.

(A)   The chairs of the Budget Committees shall adopt the lower estimate of the CBO and OMB estimates for the initial spending ceiling, unless both houses of Congress approve the other estimate.

(B)   If only one estimate from CBO or OMB for the initial spending ceiling is available by the third Monday in February, the chairs of the Budget Committees shall announce it as the initial spending ceiling.

(C)   If neither CBO nor OMB has provided an estimated ceiling by the third Monday in February, the chairs of the Budget Committee shall announce a provisional initial spending ceiling within seven (7) days of that date, which in no case shall exceed the most recent CBO estimate of the current law baseline of budget authority for the fiscal year.

(4)   CBO and OMB shall provide updated estimates by the end of each month to the Budget Committees. The chairs of the Budget Committee shall jointly announce each revised spending ceiling within seven (7) calendar days of receiving the first revised estimate from CBO or OMB, based on the lower estimate, unless both houses of Congress have approved the other estimate, or the sole estimate, as applicable, or if no revised estimate is available, maintaining the most recently announced estimate.

SEC. 102. EMERGENCY SPENDING ACCOUNT ESTABLISHED.

(a)   ESTABLISHMENT OF EMERGENCY SPENDING ACCOUNT.—Spending for an emergency under section 101(b)(1) shall be charged against an emergency spending account that is separate from the spending ceiling. When OMB finds that the spending ceiling exceeds actual authorized spending in a fiscal year, the difference shall be credited to the emergency spending account. The term emergency shall be defined as in section 250(c)(20) of the Balanced Budget and Emergency Deficit Control Act of 1985 (2 U.S.C. 900(c)(20)).

(b)   SHORTFALLS OF THE EMERGENCY SPENDING ACCOUNT.—A shortfall of the emergency spending account in the prior fiscal year will be offset within the next six fiscal years by equal proportionate reductions to the spending ceiling in section 101. This provision shall not be construed as precluding more rapid reductions in the shortfall.

(1)   The period under the prior sentence starts again if the shortfall of the emergency spending account increases by more than 0.5 percent of the spending ceiling.

(2)   In the case of an ongoing emergency, Congress may extend this period by statute.

SEC. 103. REPORTS.

CBO shall include in the report required to be provided in section 202(e) of the Congressional Budget Act of 1974 (2 U.S.C. 602(e))—

(a)   Such information as is necessary and proper to determine compliance with the provisions of this title.

(b)   Estimates of the fiscal gap of the United States Government.

(1)   The fiscal gap shall equal the difference between

(A)   The net present value of future spending by the United States government, including to pay interest and principle on outstanding debt and

(B)   The net present value of all future revenue of the federal government.

(2)   The applicable range shall be the infinite horizon.

(3)   Estimates incorporating projections of current policy and of current law shall be provided.

(4)   To the extent practicable, contingent liabilities of federal insurance, loan, loan guarantee, and similar programs shall be provided using both Federal Credit Reform Act of 1990 and fair-value accounting methodologies.

Discussion of the fiscal gap shall include but not be limited to its growth through legislative, demographic, and other factors, and an overview of options to reduce it. [Note: *It may be premature to include the fiscal gap in budget enforcement until policymakers understand what it measures and why it matters.*]

TITLE II—ENSURING PRUDENTIAL FISCAL MANAGEMENT

SUBTITLE A—AUTOMATIC DEFICIT REDUCTION

SEC. 201. DEFINITION OF BUDGET BREACH. Not later than 90 days following the conclusion of a fiscal year, OMB shall re-estimate the final spending ceiling for the recently concluded fiscal year using updated GDP estimates and any adjustments under section 101(b). [Note: *Treasury produces a Monthly Treasury Statement eight business days after the end of a reporting month. Aggregates for a full prior fiscal year would be available by mid-October. GDP "advance" estimates come out a month after the end of a quarter, "2nd" within two months, and "final" within three months. When a budget resolution is produced, only 3 of 20 quarters are uncertain. When a fiscal year ends, however, only 1 quarter in 20 is uncertain. When sequestration happens (in January), final data is available for all quarters. https://www.bea.gov/newsreleases /national/gdp/gdpnewsrelease.htm.*] OMB shall determine whether and to what extent the budget authority for a fiscal year has exceeded the ceiling established in section 101 of this Act.

(a) If the actual budget authority provided for a fiscal year exceeded the ceiling established under section 101, OMB shall undertake the adjustments in sections 202, 203, and 204.

(b) If the actual budget authority provided for a fiscal year did not exceed the ceiling established under section 101, OMB shall not make the adjustments in sections 202, 203, and 204, and the difference shall be credited to the emergency spending account.

SEC. 202. FREEZE OF DISCRETIONARY SPENDING AMOUNTS. Upon a finding described in subsection 201(a), OMB shall announce discretionary spending caps for the following fiscal year consistent with the Balanced Budget and Emergency Deficit Control Act of 1985 (2 U.S.C. 900 et. seq.). Such caps shall equal the rate of budget authority for the revised security category and the revised nonsecurity category, respectively, existing at the time that such a finding is announced. If total budget authority for either category or both exceeds the limit(s) in a year for which discretionary caps are in place, the excess shall be subject to a sequester order under the Balanced Budget and Emergency Deficit Control Act of 1985.

SEC. 203. ADJUSTMENTS TO DIRECT SPENDING PROGRAMS.

[Note: *These options merely illustrate an "incremental enforcement" approach. This is not necessarily a recommendation for the precise amendments mentioned. Incremental reforms that can build on each other should be developed by committees of jurisdiction under the guidance and direction of congressional leadership.*] Upon a finding described in subsection 201(a), the Director of the Office of Management and Budget shall order the following actions:

(a) CHAINED CPI.—Notwithstanding any other provision of law, any infla-tion adjustment announced within the year shall be calculated using the Chained Consumer Price Index for All Urban Consumers.

(b) OLD AGE, SURVIVORS, AND DISABILITY INSURANCE.—

　　(1) BEND POINT REDUCTION.—For persons who become eligible for Old Age benefits after thirty-six (36) months or thereafter, reduce the primary insurance amount (42 U.S.C. 415(a)(1)(A) attributable to the top (initially 15 percent) bracket by two (2) percentage points. When such percentage equals zero (0), subsequent reductions shall be applied to the next bracket (initially 38 percent).

　　(2) BEND POINT FREEZE.—For persons who become eligible for Old Age benefits in thirty-six (36) months or thereafter, the inflation adjust-ments to the brackets for primary insurance amounts (42 U.S.C. 415) shall be suspended.

　　(3) ELIGIBILITY AGE INCREASE.—Increase by one (1) month per birth year for three birth year cohorts the normal and early retirement ages (42 U.S.C. 416(l)) for persons who become eligible for Old Age benefits in thirty-six (36) months and thereafter.

　　(4) LENGTHEN TERM TO BE FULLY INSURED INDIVIDUAL.—Increase the period (42 U.S.C. 414(a)(2)) by one-quarter of a year, for persons eligible for Old Age benefits not earlier than thirty-six (36) months and thereafter.

　　(5) LENGTHEN PERIOD FOR CALCULATING PRIMARY INSURANCE AMOUNT.— Increase the initial 35-year period (42 U.S.C. 415(b)) by three (3) months for persons eligible for Old Age benefits not earlier than thirty-six (36) months and thereafter.

(c) MEDICARE.—

　　(1) MEANS-TESTING IN PART B.—

　　　　(A) INCREASE THE REDUCTION IN PREMIUM SUBSIDY BASED ON INCOME.—Increase the applicable percentage in subclause 1395r(i)(3)(C)(i)(III) of this law by two (2) percentage points for persons becoming eligible for Part B benefits beginning thirty-six (36) months and thereafter following the finding of a budget breach. Requirements for Part B premiums to equal one-half or fifty percent of the actuarial rate of such coverage shall be calculated without regard to the effects of this provision.

(B) SUSPENSION OF INFLATION ADJUSTMENT.—No inflation adjustment for amounts related to Medicare Part B premiums shall be provided under 42 U.S.C. 1395r(i)(5) shall be made in the year following a budget breach. Requirements for Part B premiums to equal one-half or fifty percent of the actuarial rate of such coverage shall be calculated without regard to the effects of this provision.

(2) MEANS-TESTING IN PART D.—Adjustments specified in paragraph (a) shall apply to Part D premium calculations at 42 U.S.C. 1395w-113(a)(7).

(3) ELIGIBILITY AGE INCREASE.—Increase the age-based eligibility for Medicare (initially age 65) for persons who become eligible for benefits in the third year or thereafter by two (2) months per birth year for three birth year cohorts. (42 U.S.C. 1395c)

(d) MEDICAID.—

(1) REDUCTION IN FMAP.—Reduce by one (1) percentage point the Federal medical assistance percentage for each State, territory, or other entity below what such entity would otherwise be eligible under 42 U.S.C. 1396d(b).

(e) ET CETERA.—[Note: *Many, perhaps most, direct spending programs have one or more elements that are conducive to incremental, repeated adjustments. Whether to include them in enforcement, of what magnitude, and with what delay, is primarily a political question.*]

SEC. 204. ADJUSTMENTS TO REVENUE PROVISIONS.

Upon each finding described in subsection 201(a), the Secretary of the Treasury shall take the following cumulative actions, which shall be effective for the tax year beginning not earlier than thirty (30) days prior. Except for subsection (a), each adjustment shall be in addition to any prior adjustments under such subsection. [Note: *Some may prefer fiscal consolidation to occur entirely on the spending side. As a practical political matter, however, revenue increases will occur. The objective becomes minimizing damage (dead weight losses) to voluntary society.*]

(a) FICA PAYROLL TAXES.—

(1) Increase by 0.05 percentage points the 6.2 percent Old Age, Survivors and Disability Insurance (OASDI) tax on employees in 26 U.S.C. 3101(a).

(2) Increase by 0.05 percentage points the 1.45 percent Hospital Insurance tax on employees in 26 U.S.C. 3101(b)(1).

(3) Increase by 0.05 percentage points the 6.2 percent OASDI tax on employers (26 U.S.C. 3111(a)).

(4) Increase by 0.05 percentage points the 1.45 percent Hospital Insurance tax on employers (26 U.S.C. 3111(b)).

(5) Increase by 0.10 percentage points the 12.4 percent OASDI tax on self-employed persons (26 U.S.C. 1401(a)) and increase by 0.10 percentage points the 2.9 percent Hospital Insurance tax on self-employed persons (26 U.S.C. 1401(b)).

(6) Increase by an additional five (5) percent the applicable dollar threshold for income subject to the OASDI tax (26 U.S.C. 3121(x)), not to exceed 90 percent of covered income.

(b) SUBSIDIES FOR HEALTH INSURANCE.—Increase by 0.25 percentage points each initial and final premium percentage in the table under 26 U.S.C. 36B(b)(3)(A)(i).

(c) EXCISE TAXES ON ALCOHOL.—Increase by five (5) percent each rate of taxation on alcohol (26 U.S.C. Ch. 51), not to exceed $16.00 per proof gallon.

(d) EXCISE TAXES ON TOBACCO.—Increase by five (5) percent each rate of taxation on tobacco products (26 U.S.C.), not to exceed $20.00 per pound of dry weight.

(e) EXCISE TAX ON FUEL FOR INLAND WATERWAYS TRUST FUND.—Increase by one (1) cent per gallon the Inland Waterways Trust Fund financing rate (26 U.S.C. 4042(b)(2)(A)).

(f) PRIVATE ACTIVITY BONDS.—Increase by five (5) percent the interest on State and local bonds included in gross income (26 U.S.C. 103).

SEC. 205. ANNUAL PROPOSAL ON CODIFYING ADJUSTMENTS.

Not later than 30 days following a finding in section 201(a), the President shall recommend to Congress' consideration a proposal to update the statutes to incorporate all policy changes enacted pursuant to this title.

SUBTITLE B—EXPEDITED DEFICIT REDUCTION PROCEDURES

SEC. 201. This subtitle may be cited as the "Expedited Deficit Reduction Procedures Act of 2019."

SEC. 210. PROCEDURE IN THE HOUSE OF REPRESENTATIVES TO REDUCE DEFICITS.

(a) APPLICABILITY OF EXPEDITED PROCESS.—The procedures set forth in this Act are available in any calendar year in which the report required to be published under section 202(e) of the Congressional Budget Act of

1974 (2 U.S.C. 602(e)) by the Congressional Budget Office published during that calendar year projects a deficit for each of the ten (10) fiscal years following the fiscal year in which it is published.

(b) DETERMINATION OF ELIGIBLE BILL.—On the date that is 15 calendar days before the end of the committee review period, the chair of the Committee on the Budget of the House of Representatives shall publish in the Congressional Record the bill number, estimate of net deficit reduction, and cosponsors of the eligible bill, noting with appropriate typographical devices the cosponsors, if any, who have cosponsored another measure previously considered under this Act in that calendar year.

(c) DEFINITIONS.—As used in this Act—

(1) the term "eligible bill" means a bill with the appropriate title, with the greatest number of eligible cosponsors, and that meets or exceeds the deficit reduction threshold, but if more than one otherwise eligible bill has an equal number of eligible cosponsors, then the chair of the Committee on the Budget of the House of Representatives shall enter into the Congressional Record the bill that was introduced first;

(2) the term "appropriate title" means a bill titled "An Act to provide for deficit reduction under the Expedited Deficit Reduction Procedures Act of 2019";

(3) the term "eligible cosponsors" means Members of the House of Representatives cosponsoring a bill under this Act in any calendar year who have not cosponsored such a bill that has already been considered in the House under this Act in that calendar year;

(4) the term "deficit reduction threshold" means not less than 5 percent of the total deficit projected in the CBO baseline budget projections for the 10 fiscal years following the one in which the report referred to in subsection (a) is published;

(5) the term "deficit" means, notwithstanding section 3(6) of the Congressional Budget Act of 1974 (2 U.S.C. 622(6)), with respect to a fiscal year, the amount by which total outlays, both on budget and off-budget, exceed all receipts both on budget and off-budget during that year;

(6) the term "committee review period" means the period that begins when a bill is referred to a committee of jurisdiction and ends on the applicable discharge date; and

(7) the term "discharge date" means the legislative day of May 1, July 1, or September 15 of each calendar year, or, if such date is not a legislative day, the first legislative day after any such date.

(d) LEGISLATIVE PROCEDURE.—

(1) IN GENERAL.—Before the applicable discharge date, each committee of the House of Representatives to which an eligible bill is referred shall

report that bill, either favorably, unfavorably, or without recommendation, and without any substantive revision. Nothing in this Act shall be construed as preventing any committee from reporting or either house of Congress from considering one or more bills containing technical corrections or substantive amendments to eligible bills as defined by this Act.

(2) FAILURE TO REPORT.—If any committee fails to report a bill referred to in paragraph (1) prior to the discharge date, that committee shall be immediately discharged from further consideration of that bill.

(e) EXPEDITED CONSIDERATION IN THE HOUSE OF REPRESENTATIVES.—

(1) IN GENERAL.—Not later than five legislative days after an eligible bill is reported or the committees of referral have been discharged from further consideration thereof, it shall be in order to move to proceed to consider the bill in the House. Such a motion shall be in order only at a time designated by the Speaker in the legislative schedule within two legislative days after the day on which the proponent announces an intention to the House to offer the motion. Such a motion shall not be in order after the House has disposed of a motion to proceed with respect to that bill. The previous question shall be considered as ordered on the motion to its adoption without intervening motion.

(2) CONSIDERATION.—Except as provided in paragraph (3), if the motion to proceed is agreed to, the House shall immediately proceed to consider the bill referred to in paragraph (1) in the House without intervening motion. Such bill shall be considered as read. Except as provided in paragraph (3), all points of order against such bill and against its consideration are waived. The previous question shall be considered as ordered on such bill to its passage without intervening motion except two (2) hours of debate equally divided and controlled by the proponent and an opponent and one motion to limit debate on the bill.

(3) PUBLICATION.—As soon as practicable after an eligible bill is reported or discharged from any committee of jurisdiction, the chair of the Committee on Rules shall place the bill on the website of the committee.

(4) EXTRANEOUS MATTER.—When the House is considering a bill pursuant to paragraph (2), if a point of order is made by any Member against any change made by a committee to the introduced bill other than a technical or conforming amendment and the point of order is sustained by the Chair, that matter shall be deemed stricken from the bill.

SEC. 211. EXPEDITED PROCEDURES IN THE SENATE.

(a) COMMITTEE CONSIDERATION.—In the Senate, upon receipt of a bill passed in the House of Representatives pursuant to this Act, it shall be jointly referred to the committee or committees of jurisdiction, which shall report the bill without any revision and with a favorable recommendation, an unfavorable recommendation, or without recommendation, not later than 5 legislative days after receipt in the Senate. If any committee fails to report the bill within that period, that committee shall be automatically discharged from consideration of the bill, and the bill shall be placed on the appropriate calendar.

(b) MOTION TO PROCEED.—Notwithstanding Rule XXII of the Standing Rules of the Senate, it is in order, not later than 2 days of session after the date on which a bill under paragraph (1) is reported or discharged from all committees to which it was referred, for the majority leader of the Senate or the majority leader's designee to move to proceed to the consideration of the bill. It shall also be in order for any Member of the Senate to move to proceed to the consideration of such bill at any time after the conclusion of such 2-day period. A motion to proceed is in order even though a previous motion to the same effect has been disagreed to. All points of order against the motion to proceed to the bill are waived. The motion to proceed is not debatable. The motion is not subject to a motion to postpone. If a motion to proceed to the consideration of the bill is agreed to, the bill shall remain the unfinished business until disposed of.

(c) CONSIDERATION.—All points of order against the bill and against consideration of the bill are waived. Consideration of the bill and of all debatable motions and appeals in connection therewith shall not exceed a total of 30 hours which shall be divided equally between the Majority and Minority Leaders or their designees. A motion further to limit debate on the bill is in order, shall require an affirmative vote of three-fifths of the Members duly chosen and sworn, and is not debatable. Any debatable motion or appeal is debatable for not to exceed 1 hour, to be divided equally between those favoring and those opposing the motion or appeal. All time used for consideration of the bill, including time used for quorum calls and voting, shall be counted against the total 30 hours of consideration.

(d) VOTE ON PASSAGE.—If the Senate has voted to proceed to the bill, the vote on passage of the bill shall occur immediately following the conclusion of the debate on the bill, and a single quorum call at the conclusion of the debate if requested.

(e) RULINGS OF THE CHAIR ON PROCEDURE.—Appeals from the decisions of the Chair relating to the application of the rules of the Senate to the procedure relating to the bill shall be decided without debate.

SEC. 212. EFFECTIVE DATE.

This Act shall take effect immediately upon the publication of the next report required to be published under section 202(e) of the Congressional Budget Act of 1974 (2 U.S.C. 602(e)).

SUBTITLE C—ENDING GOVERNMENT SHUTDOWNS

SEC. 221. AUTOMATIC CONTINUING APPROPRIATIONS

(a) IN GENERAL.—Chapter 13 of title 31, United States Code, is amended by inserting after section 1310 the following new section:

"SEC. 1311. CONTINUING APPROPRIATIONS.

"(a)(1) If any appropriations measure for a fiscal year is not enacted before the beginning of such fiscal year or a joint resolution making continuing appropriations is not in effect, there are appropriated such sums as may be necessary to continue any program, project, or activity for which funds were provided in the preceding fiscal year—

"(A) in the corresponding appropriations Act for such preceding fiscal year; or

"(B) if the corresponding appropriations bill for such preceding fiscal year did not become law, then in a joint resolution making continuing appropriations for such preceding fiscal year.

"(2) (A) Appropriations and funds made available, and authority granted, for a program, project, or activity for any fiscal year pursuant to this section shall be at a rate of operations not in excess of the lower of—

"(i) the rate of operations provided for in the regular appropriations Act providing for such program, project, or activity for the preceding fiscal year;

"(ii) in the absence of such an Act, the rate of operations provided for such program, project, or activity pursuant to a joint resolution making continuing appropriations for such preceding fiscal year; or

"(iii) the annualized rate of operations provided for in the most recently enacted joint resolution making continuing appropriations for part of that fiscal year or any funding levels established under the provisions of this Act.

"(B) If this section is in effect at the end of a fiscal year, funding levels shall continue as provided in this section for the next fiscal year, except that such levels shall increase by two (2) percent for programs with a program-specific, current authorization of appropriations. This provision shall not be construed to preclude the sequestration of budgetary authority exceeding any caps established under the Balanced Budget and Emergency Deficit Control Act of 1985.

"(3) Appropriations and funds made available, and authority granted, for any fiscal year pursuant to this section for a program, project, or activity shall be available for the period beginning with the first day of a lapse in appropriations and ending with the date on which the applicable regular appropriations bill for such fiscal year becomes law (whether or not such law provides for such program, project, or activity) or a continuing resolution making appropriations becomes law, as the case may be.

"(4) Pursuant to Article I, Section 8, clause 12 of the Constitution, appropriations for the Army shall not exceed two years from the enactment of the most recent appropriations Act or continuing resolution enacted into law providing appropriations for the Army.

"(b)   An appropriation or funds made available, or authority granted, for a program, project, or activity for any fiscal year pursuant to this section shall be subject to the terms and conditions imposed with respect to the appropriation made or funds made available for the preceding fiscal year, or authority granted for such program, project, or activity under current law.

"(c)   Expenditures made for a program, project, or activity for any fiscal year pursuant to this section shall be charged to the applicable appropriation, fund, or authorization whenever a regular appropriations bill or a joint resolution making continuing appropriations until the end of a fiscal year providing for such program, project, or activity for such period becomes law.

"(d)   This section shall not apply to a program, project, or activity during a fiscal year if any other provision of law (other than an authorization of appropriations)—

"(1) makes an appropriation, makes funds available, or grants authority for such program, project, or activity to continue for such period; or

"(2) specifically provides that no appropriation shall be made, no funds shall be made available, or no authority shall be granted for such program, project, or activity to continue for such period."

(b)   CLERICAL AMENDMENT.—The table of sections of chapter 13 of title 31, United States Code, is amended by inserting after the item relating to section 1310 the following new item:

"1311. Continuing appropriations."

TITLE III—ADDITIONAL PROVISIONS

SEC. 301. CBO AND JCT ESTIMATES TO INCLUDE DEBT SERVICING COSTS.

(a)   IN GENERAL.—The Congressional Budget and Impoundment Control Act of 1974 (2 U.S.C. 621 et seq.) is amended by inserting after section 402 the following:

"ESTIMATES TO INCLUDE DEBT SERVICING COSTS

"SEC. 403. Any estimate prepared by the Congressional Budget Office under section 402, and any estimate prepared by the Joint Committee on Taxation, shall include, to the extent practicable, the costs (if any) of servicing the public debt."

(b) CLERICAL AMENDMENT.—The table of contents of such Act is amended by inserting after the item relating to section 402 the following:

"403. Estimates to include debt servicing costs."

TITLE IV—AMENDMENTS TO PRESIDENT'S BUDGET PROPOSAL AND DEBT CEILING

SEC. 401. REPEAL OF REDUNDANT SENSE OF CONGRESS. Section 1103 of Title 31, United States Code, is repealed.

SEC. 402. PRESIDENT'S BUDGET PROPOSAL TO RESPECT SPENDING CEILING. Subsection 1105(a) of Title 31, United States Code, is amended by inserting before the period of the first sentence "consistent with the requirements of the Genuine Reforms Earn Americans' Trust Again Act of 2019."

SEC. 403. PRESIDENT'S BUDGET PROPOSAL TO INCLUDE OPTIONS TO REDUCE DEFICITS. Subsection (c) of section 1105 of Title 31, United States Code, is amended to read:

"(c)(1) Deficit—

"(A) The President shall recommend in the budget appropriate action to meet an estimated deficiency when the estimated receipts for the fiscal year for which the budget is submitted (under laws in effect when the budget is submitted) and the estimated amounts in the Treasury at the end of the current fiscal year available for expenditure in the fiscal year for which the budget is submitted, are less than the estimated expenditures for that year.

"(B) If estimated expenditures are projected to exceed estimated receipts during the budget year for which the budget is submitted and each of the subsequent nine (9) fiscal years, the President shall recommend legislative options to eliminate not less than 150% of the estimated excess of expenditures over receipts in the ninth year following the budget year. Such options shall begin to reduce the excess during intervening years as soon as practicable.

"(2) Surplus—The President shall make recommendations required by the public interest when the estimated receipts and estimated amounts in the Treasury are more than the estimated expenditures."

SEC. 404. MODIFICATION OF DEBT CEILING.

(a) The debt ceiling established by 31 U.S.C. 3101 shall be suspended except in the case of subsection (b).

(b) Upon the date that is 30 days following a finding described in subsection 201(a), the suspension of the debt ceiling in paragraph (a) will terminate. The limitation in effect under section 3101(b) of title 31, United States Code, shall be increased to the extent that—

    (1) the face amount of obligations issued under chapter 31 of such title and the face amount of obligations whose principal and interest are guaranteed by the United States Government (except guaranteed obligations held by the Secretary of the Treasury) outstanding on such date, exceeds

    (2) the face amount of such obligations outstanding on the date of a suspension under subsection (a) or (c).

(c) Suspension of the debt ceiling may resume after a subsequent finding under subsection 201(b) that no breach of budget authority occurred for the preceding year.

TITLE V—VOTE ON THE BALANCED BUDGET AMENDMENT

SEC. 501. VOTE ON THE BALANCED BUDGET AMENDMENT.
[Note: *adapted from Title II of the Budget Control Act of 2011.*]

After [date] and not later than [date] the House of Representatives and Senate, respectively, shall vote on passage of a joint resolution, the title of which is as follows: "Joint Resolution Proposing a Balanced Budget Amendment to the Constitution of the United States." To the extent practicable, preference shall be given to a joint resolution with at least one sponsor or cosponsor from each major party caucus or to a joint resolution that differs substantially from proposals already considered by Congress, or to a joint resolution with both attributes.

SEC. 502. CONSIDERATION BY THE OTHER HOUSE.

    (a) HOUSE CONSIDERATION.—

        (1) REFERRAL.—If the House receives a joint resolution described in section 501 from the Senate, such joint resolution shall be referred to the Committee on the Judiciary. If the committee fails to report the joint resolution within five legislative days, it shall be in order to move that the House discharge the committee from further consideration of the joint resolution. Such a motion shall not be in order after the House has disposed of a motion to discharge the joint resolution. The previous question shall be considered as ordered on the motion to

its adoption without intervening motion except 20 minutes of debate equally divided and controlled by the proponent and an opponent. If such a motion is adopted, the House shall proceed immediately to consider the joint resolution in accordance with paragraph (3). A motion to reconsider the vote by which the motion is disposed of shall not be in order.

(2) PROCEEDING TO CONSIDERATION.—After the joint resolution has been referred to the appropriate calendar or the committee has been discharged (other than by motion) from its consideration, it shall be in order to move to proceed to consider the joint resolution in the House. Such a motion shall not be in order after the House has disposed of a motion to proceed with respect to the joint resolution. The previous question shall be considered as ordered on the motion to its adoption without intervening motion. A motion to reconsider the vote by which the motion is disposed of shall not be in order.

(3) CONSIDERATION.—The joint resolution shall be considered as read. All points of order against the joint resolution and against its consideration are waived. The previous question shall be considered as ordered on the joint resolution to its passage without intervening motion except two hours of debate equally divided and controlled by the proponent and an opponent and one motion to limit debate on the joint resolution. A motion to reconsider the vote on passage of the joint resolution shall not be in order.

(b) SENATE CONSIDERATION.—

(1) If the Senate receives a joint resolution described in section 501 from the House of Representatives, such joint resolution shall be referred to the appropriate committee of the Senate. If such committee has not reported the joint resolution at the close of the fifth session day after its receipt by the Senate, such committee shall be automatically discharged from further consideration of the joint resolution and it shall be placed on the appropriate calendar.

(2) Consideration of the joint resolution and on all debatable motions and appeals in connection therewith, shall be limited to not more than 20 hours, which shall be divided equally between the majority and minority leaders or their designees. A motion further to limit debate is in order and not debatable. An amendment to, or a motion to postpone, or a motion to proceed to the consideration of other business, or a motion to recommit the joint resolution is not in order. Any debatable motion or appeal is debatable for not to exceed 1 hour, to be divided equally between those favoring and those opposing

the motion or appeal. All time used for consideration of the joint resolution, including time used for quorum calls and voting, shall be counted against the total 20 hours of consideration.

(3) If the Senate has voted to proceed to a joint resolution, the vote on passage of the joint resolution shall be taken on or before the close of the seventh session day after such joint resolution has been reported or discharged or immediately following the conclusion of consideration of the joint resolution, and a single quorum call at the conclusion of the debate if requested in accordance with the rules of the Senate.

TITLE VI—GENERAL PROVISIONS

SEC. 601. RULE OF CONSTRUCTION. This Act is enacted in part pursuant to the rulemaking power of each house of Congress. Either house, with or without the consent of the other, shall retain the power to amend or repeal provisions governing the Rules of its Proceedings. Nothing in this Act shall be construed to supersede the proper powers of any officer or body of the United States Government under the Constitution.

SEC. 602. SEVERABILITY. If any provision of this Act or an amendment made by this Act, or the application of a provision or amendment to any person or circumstance, is held to be invalid for any reason in any court of competent jurisdiction, the remainder of this Act and amendments made by this Act, and the application of the provisions and amendment to any other person or circumstance, shall not be affected.

CHAPTER NINE

MINUTES FROM MIDNIGHT: GROWING PRESSURE ON THE TREASURY MARKET COULD LEAD TO DEFAULT

BAKER SPRING

According to the Compact for America Debt Default Clock, we are only minutes from midnight—that ominous hour when the federal government will face an impending sequence of fiscal crisis, insolvency, and ultimately default. This chapter explores the 12 factors related to the Treasury securities market that are looming over the federal government and examines possible solutions to move it away from the brink of fiscal disaster.

The federal government's gross debt, which includes both debt held by the public and debt held by federal government trust funds, now exceeds $22 trillion.[1] The Congressional Budget Office (CBO) projects this debt will grow to almost $34 trillion in fiscal year 2028.[2] The CBO also projects that gross interest costs in the same year will exceed $1.1 trillion.[3] What's more, then-CBO Director Keith Hall testified in an April 2018 hearing before the Senate Budget Committee that:

> The likelihood of a fiscal crisis in the United States [given the projected debt held by the public] would increase. There would be a greater risk that investors would become unwilling to finance the government's borrowing unless they were compensated with very high interest rates; if that happened, interest rates on federal debt would rise suddenly and sharply.[4]

Hall is correct that the projected debt will be the single most important factor leading to intense pressure on the Treasury securities market in a way that could lead to a fiscal crisis. If anything, Hall underestimates the risk both because his observation focuses on only the portion of the federal debt held by the public, as opposed to the larger gross debt, and because it is likely that a fiscal crisis, should it occur, will be followed rapidly by federal government insolvency and ultimately default. For the purposes of this chapter, default is defined as the failure by the federal government to make timely payment on a debt obligation.

Beyond the projected growth in the federal debt, myriad factors contribute to the growing pressure on the Treasury securities market. Chief among them is the concomitant growth in gross federal interest costs. The Debt Default Clock initiative of the Compact for America Educational Foundation asserts that 12 factors are the most important.[5] It is the objective of the initiative to bring to the attention of the federal government's fiscal policymakers the dangers of the growing pressure on the Treasury securities market and the likelihood it will lead to a sequence of fiscal crisis, insolvency, and default by the federal government if it remains on its current fiscal path. In essence, the Debt Default Clock is a flexible instrument for predicting both the time and the circumstances of the sequence of federal fiscal crisis, insolvency, and default. It is anchored in the observation made by Keith Hall described earlier that at some point investors will be unwilling to finance the federal debt any further. The clock depicts these emerging Treasury market conditions in minutes away from midnight, where midnight is the initiation of the sequence of federal fiscal crisis, insolvency, and default.

This is not to say that the Debt Default Clock implies that the sequence is inevitable. It will happen only if the federal government remains on its projected fiscal path. A review committee updates the clock periodically to account for either positive or negative developments regarding the health of the Treasury securities market. Avoiding a crisis starts with the federal government's adoption of a combination of substantive fiscal policy and budget process changes that specifically serve to lessen the growing pressure on the Treasury securities market.

GROWING PRESSURE ON THE TREASURY SECURITIES MARKET

As a result of a June 26, 2018, forum in Washington, DC, involving a group of experts from both the investment and the fiscal policy communities, the Debt Default Clock now points to 12 important factors that contribute to growing pressure on the Treasury securities market. They are as follows:

1. *There is too much debt.* This is most basic factor driving pressure on the Treasury securities market. Under the Debt Default Clock set at the time of the review committee's fall 2018 update, the debt held by the public is forecast to grow to over 96 percent of gross domestic product (GDP) in the final year of the budget period (2028), and the gross debt will also peak in 2028 at over 113 percent of GDP.[6]

2. *There is no dollar-denominated debt ceiling in place.* Currently, there is no dollar-denominated debt ceiling in place because the debt ceiling law has been suspended.[7] This maneuver imposes psychological pressure on the Treasury securities market because it codifies the assumptions by federal fiscal policymakers that there is no practical limit on the level of federal debt, and that it can be financed by the market essentially indefinitely.

3. *Gross federal interest costs will eat up too much revenue.* Under current projections, gross federal interest costs exceeded 15 percent of federal revenues in 2018.[8] Further, they will remain above this threshold thereafter. Investors will at some point find it disturbing that the federal government is being forced to allocate such a large share of its income to paying interest on its debt.

4. *The federal government could enter an interest-cost death spiral.* Bankers will tell you that they will discontinue lending money to a debtor when large amounts of the money the debtor would otherwise obtain by taking on new debt is going to pay interest on the existing debt. In the same way, factor 4 is a strong indicator of the lack of fiscal health by the federal government. Investors will not fail to account for this lack of fiscal health in the Treasury securities market because it signifies the extent to

which the Treasury is increasing its debt to cover the growing interest costs on the preexisting debt. On this basis, gross interest costs are projected to consume over 90 percent of money raised by the issuance of new debt in 2027.[9]

5. *There is too much spending.* According to historical data regarding revenues (more about revenues later), it is reasonable to expect that the federal government could balance its budget if outlays were held to 17.5 percent of GDP. The problem is that in none of the years from 2000 to 2017 have outlays been at or below 17.5 percent of GDP.[10] This problem is projected to get worse. Projections are that federal outlays will be at 23.6 percent of GDP in 2028, which is the final year of the applicable 10-year budget period.[11] Investors already recognize that excessive federal spending is more the source of the growing fiscal problem than are insufficient revenues.

6. *In relative terms, federal government resources available to finance the debt will shrink.* On a consistent basis, the federal government has used its own trust fund balances to help finance the debt. The largest of these are the Medicare and Social Security trust funds. Demographic projections will cause these two fund balances to decline in the future. This means the trust funds will have less money to make available for financing the debt, and a greater share of this financing will depend on the debt held by the public. The Debt Default Clock projects that the debt held by the public will exceed 80 percent of the gross debt in 2025.[12]

7. *Foreign-held debt may make the Treasury vulnerable to manipulation.* This factor assesses the exposure of the Treasury to manipulation of its position as a debtor by foreign entities for political reasons. Such manipulations could be intended to increase the risk of default, particularly following a successful attempt to remove the U.S. dollar as the world reserve currency. Such a manipulation is all but certain to spook private investors in the Treasury securities market. This factor is calculated on the basis of the share of the debt held by the public that is in foreign hands. The Debt Default Clock shows that foreign-held

debt will exceed 50 percent of the debt held by the public in 2021.[13]

8. *The current structure of the debt, from the Treasury's perspective, may be financially imprudent.* Currently, the combination of debt instruments in Treasury inflation-protected securities (TIPS), Treasury Floating Rate Bills, and other debt instruments that mature in five years or less is a bit higher than 67 percent of the debt held by the public.[14] The Treasury's financial position is put at risk by inflation in the future because the principal of TIPS is automatically adjusted with inflation. Treasury's financial position is put at risk by higher interest rates because the floating rate and early-maturing securities will incur higher interest costs and require refinancing at higher rates. Accordingly, the proportion of the debt in these three categories of securities is too high.

9. *Federal revenues could fall too low.* Obviously, factor 9 is the flip side of factor 5 on outlays. The circumstance for revenues, however, differs from that of outlays. Federal revenues in 2017 were at 17.3 percent of GDP.[15] As a practical matter, this is below the level necessary to achieve a balanced budget. On the one hand, the level for achieving a balanced budget, based on outlays, is 17.5 percent of GDP. Revenues will recover to 17.5 percent of GDP in the not too distant future and exceed 18 percent before the end of the applicable budget period.[16] This projection reflects the enactment of The Tax Cut and Jobs Act of 2017 (Public Law 115-97).

10. *Real economic growth may be too slow to contribute to improving the fiscal position of the federal government.* While not sufficient to stabilize the fiscal position of the federal government, robust economic growth is an essential part of the solution to the fiscal problem. The reason is that a larger economy, all other things being equal, will generate more revenue for the government and reduce the demand for some portions of government spending. At a minimum, 3 percent annual real rate of growth in terms of GDP is necessary to reach a balanced budget. Earlier, government projections were that the real annual rate of growth

would be 3.3 percent in 2018.[17] These projections turned out to be overly optimistic by a small increment. The Debt Default Clock Review Committee will take this into account when it conducts its upcoming review.

11. *Congress has set a bad precedent regarding federal default by permitting the Treasury to pursue "extraordinary measures" in the course of past budget impasses.* In the past, the Treasury has resorted to these "extraordinary measures" to delay for uncertain limited times the point at which it reaches the debt ceiling and risks defaulting on a portion of its debt obligations during times of budget impasses.[18] This was the case for much of 2019. Generally speaking, these measures involve suspending the issuances of securities by the Treasury to certain entities, such as state and local governments, Civil Service Retirement and Disability Fund, Postal Service Retiree Health Benefits Fund, Federal Employees Retirement System, and Exchange Stabilization Fund. In general terms, the Treasury acknowledges these entities are "made whole" following the budget impasses. Typically, this involves making interest payments on the securities that otherwise would have been issued. The Debt Default Clock defines default as a failure by the Treasury to make a timely payment on a debt obligation. Thus, the admission that the entities involved have to be made whole is also an admission of a failure to make timely payments—default according to the standards set by the Debt Default Clock.

12. *Congress needs to scale back programmatic "mandatory spending" and eventually phase it out.* Mandatory programmatic spending, which sets aside net interest payments, does not require the annual appropriation of money by Congress. Effectively, these spending programs are on autopilot. According to a CBO report, programmatic mandatory spending was more than $2.5 trillion in 2017.[19] The CBO projected this spending to grow to more than $4.5 trillion in 2028.[20]

Applying these factors, the Debt Default Clock Review Committee determined in the fall of 2018 that the clock's minute hand rested at four minutes from the midnight hour that initiates the sequence of federal fiscal crisis, insolvency, and default. More specifically, the committee has assessed that where things currently stand, factors 1, 2, 5, 8, 10, 11, and 12 buy no minutes away from midnight. Factors 3, 4, 6, and 7 buy one minute each away from midnight. The review committee retains the discretion to discount up to two of the factors in the course of any review. For example, in May 2018, the Committee chose to discount factor 9 on revenues because this factor was projected to move in a positive direction over the course of the budget period. The Committee's assessment is based on its fundamental belief that the sequence of fiscal crisis, insolvency, and default will stem from a breakdown in the Treasury securities market.

BUYING TIME

Following the logic behind the factors underlying the Debt Default Clock, federal fiscal policymakers can start now to relieve the growing pressure on the Treasury securities market. In general, this means taking the specific steps necessary to move the clock's minute hand away from midnight.

SOLUTION 1: PUT THE FEDERAL BUDGET ON THE PATH TO BALANCE

Relieving the growing pressure on the Treasury securities market starts with the core component of a responsible fiscal policy, which is to put the federal government on the path to balancing the budget before the 10-year budget period ends. Continual deficits and ever-growing debt impose a heavy burden on the Treasury to attract investment dollars to finance this debt. If the federal government stays on the currently projected path regarding the debt, it is inevitable that it will find it difficult to attract these dollars. More specifically, the goals for the factors covering outlays and revenues relative to GDP set the terms for bringing the federal budget into balance. The twin goals of these two factors are to elevate federal revenues to 17.5 percent of GDP and bring spending to the same 17.5 percent of GDP. Fortunately, revenues are projected to exceed this level well before the end of the budget period. This projection comes after accounting for the tax reform law enacted in 2017.[21] This is why the review committee has exercised its discretion to discount the revenue factor at this time.

Spending, on the other hand, has been well above the 17.5 percent level for a long time and is projected to outstrip overall economic growth in the years to come. By any objective standard, the bulk of the federal government's deficit problem rests on the spending side of the ledger. If the federal government is able to constrain projected outlays to 17.5 percent of GDP by the end of the budget period, it will buy one minute away from midnight. If it achieves an actual level of outlays that is at or below 17.5 percent of GDP, that action will buy two minutes from midnight. By meeting the applicable goals for outlays and revenues, the federal government will also advance its position with regard to the size of the debt held by the public and the gross debt as a share of GDP. The benchmarks of the Debt Default Clock are debt held by the public below 70 percent of GDP and gross debt below 100 percent of GDP. These factors currently buy zero minutes from midnight. Prospectively, if both the debt held by the public is forecasted to fall below 70 percent of GDP and the gross debt is forecasted to fall below 100 percent of GDP during the budget period, these changes will then buy one minute from midnight. If both actually fall below the applicable thresholds, it will then buy two minutes from midnight. By definition, it will reduce the financing burden facing the Treasury under current projections. This cannot but help stabilize the Treasury securities market.

SOLUTION 2: ARREST THE FEDERAL GOVERNMENT'S GROWING INTEREST COSTS

As alarming as the continuing deficits are, the federal government's spiraling interest costs are even worse. Two remedies are found in relation to the two factors covering the projected growth in gross interest costs. The first of these factors accounts for the fact that it is simply inadequate to assert that the government can carry its interest costs on the basis of those costs as a share of GDP. The government does not and should not count the entire national economy as the resource it can draw on to accommodate its interest costs. The much more relevant measure of the government's capacity to carry interest costs is its level of revenue. Accordingly, the relevant factor establishes the goal of reducing gross interest costs to 15 percent of federal revenues. That factor currently buys one minute from midnight on the Debt Default Clock because it is below the 15 percent threshold now and will exceed the threshold only later. "Later," however, currently means "later this year." At that point, the factor is likely to buy zero minutes from midnight because the threshold will be exceeded. If, by contrast, there is a change in fiscal policy that results in a projection that assesses that gross interest costs will stay below 15 percent of federal revenues during the budget period, this factor will buy two minutes from midnight.

The second of the two relevant factors uses a different measure for determining the federal government's capacity to carry interest costs: the ratio of interest costs to the amount of money brought in by the issuance of new debt. This is the appropriate way to determine whether the federal government is entering into an interest-cost death spiral because too large a share of the money raised by issuance of new debt is being allocated, at least by implication, to covering the interest on the preexisting debt. The Debt Default Clock establishes the goal of keeping gross interest costs under 70 percent of the money raised through the issuance of new debt. The current estimate is that the level of gross interest costs will exceed 70 percent of the money brought in by the issuance of new debt (in net terms) in 2023. Thus, the relevant factor now buys one minute from midnight. On the other hand, this factor will buy two minutes from midnight if the federal government is able to project that it will stay under the threshold during the budget period. In terms of both these factors related to gross interest costs, investors in the Treasury securities market cannot but help notice the spiraling interest costs and become uncomfortable with them. By the same token, meeting the two goals established by both these factors cannot but help reassure those investing in Treasury securities in terms of keeping their investments safe.

SOLUTION 3: RESTRUCTURE THE FEDERAL DEBT

A less apparent problem to policymakers is that the debt is currently structured in a way that provides insufficient protection against both rising inflation and interest rates. In short, too much of the debt is in TIPS, Treasury Floating Rate Bills, and other securities that mature in five years or less. The factor related to the structure of the debt also points to the solution to this problem. The Treasury should move to restructure the debt by auctioning more long-term securities and scaling back on TIPS, Floating Rate Treasury Bills, and securities that mature quickly, at least in relative terms. Ideally, this change will take place ahead of the anticipated increases in inflation and interest rates. Specifically, the goal should be for the Treasury to scale back the combined total of TIPS, Floating Rate Treasury Bills, and other securities that mature in less than five years to less than 50 percent of all the debt held by the public. Regarding the Debt Default Clock, the relevant factor currently buys no minutes away from midnight. If in the future the holdings of TIPS, Floating Rate Treasury Bills, and near-term maturing debt come down, this factor will buy one minute from midnight for every five-point reduction in the percentage of the total debt held by the public represented by these categories of securities.

SOLUTION 4: GUARD AGAINST FOREIGN MANIPULATION OF THE TREASURY SECURITIES MARKET

The goal following from the factor related to foreign-held debt is to limit such debt to 50 percent or less of the debt held by the public. As noted earlier, the Debt Clock shows that foreign-held debt will exceed 50 percent of the debt held by the public in 2021. This is the point at which this factor will buy zero minutes from midnight. Until then, it buys one minute from midnight. If things improve such that the foreign-held debt falls to less than 50 percent of the debt held by the public and projections show it will remain below this threshold for the budget period, this factor will buy two minutes from midnight.

SOLUTION 5: SUSTAIN REAL ECONOMIC GROWTH AT 3 PERCENT ANNUALLY OR HIGHER

It is axiomatic that financing the currently projected federal debt will at some point become impossible if there is a stagnating economy. The goal here is to get real economic growth to at least 3 percent annually. If the real annual growth rate reaches 3 percent in a single year, it will buy one minute away from midnight. When coupled with the same average annualized rate of growth forecast for the entire 10-year budget period, it will buy two minutes away from midnight. The Debt Default Clock Review Committee will determine whether current and projected real annual growth rates warrant any minutes away from midnight in its next review.

SOLUTION 6: RESTORE THE DEBT CEILING LAW, AND PROHIBIT THE TREASURY FROM ENGAGING IN "EXTRAORDINARY MEASURES"

The goal in the Debt Clock's factor 2 is to restore a dollar-denominated debt ceiling in law and keep the actual debt below that level during the budget period. This factor currently buys zero minutes from midnight because the debt ceiling law is currently suspended. In the future, it will buy one minute from midnight if a dollar-denominated debt ceiling is reestablished by law. It will buy two minutes away from midnight if the dollar-denominated debt ceiling is reestablished and is accompanied by a budget projection that shows that the debt will stay below this ceiling in the course of the 10-year budget period.

Regarding the second of the two relevant factors, Congress should enact a law that prohibits the Treasury from resorting to the use of "extraordinary measures" in the future. Specifically, if either house of Congress has passed such a bill during the then-current Congress at the time of a review committee assessment, it will buy one minute away from midnight. If such a law is fully enacted and remains on the books at the time of the applicable review by the review committee, it will buy two minutes away from midnight. At this point, this factor buys no minutes away from midnight.

SOLUTION 7: UNIFY THE PROGRAMMATIC BUDGET ACCOUNTS

The Debt Default Clock's criteria call for curtailing, and eventually eliminating, programmatic mandatory spending. Contributing to excessive federal spending is the fact that large portions of that spending are procedurally separated from other accounts; therefore, all federal programmatic spending accounts need to be brought under the same stringent standard for control. This means transferring all mandatory spending accounts back to the annual appropriations process and reviewing such spending on an annual basis. Congress, by starting to take such steps now, should be able to reduce this category of spending dramatically. In fact, it should phase it out altogether. If Congress returns enough of this autopilot spending to the appropriated category so that by the end of the 10-year budget period the mandatory category is less in dollar terms than what it was in 2017, it will buy one minute away from midnight on the Debt Default Clock. If the mandatory category is projected to be phased out altogether by the end of the budget period, it will buy two minutes away from midnight. This factor currently buys no minutes away from midnight.

THE COMPACT FOR AMERICA PROPOSES FUNDAMENTAL BUDGET PROCESS REFORM

The solutions detailed previously will not be easy; indeed, recent history teaches us that under the current budget process, taking these steps is essentially a political impossibility. The budget process must be reformed in a way that is intended to make taking the steps outlined previously politically possible. This means fundamental reform, which requires amending the Constitution. Essentially, an amendment needs to facilitate limitations on the size of the federal debt in a way that does not itself lead to default. Further, there needs to be a viable vehicle for advancing such an amendment. Both the substantive amendment and the vehicle for advancing it have been created by the Compact for America.[22]

THE COMPACT FOR AMERICA PROPOSES A VIABLE VEHICLE

The Compact for America vehicle for advancing a budget process reform amendment to the Constitution uses an alternative means for amending the Constitution that fully organizes the states in the process. Organized as we propose, the states can hold an Article V convention for amending the Constitution that will not spiral out of control and that will be effectively bound to serve only one purpose.

At the outset, the Compact for America recognized that Congress will not and, politically speaking, cannot propose an effective budget process reform amendment. The primary reason for this impasse is that Article V requires a two-thirds majority in both houses of Congress to propose amendments. The votes for this are simply not there. This was demonstrated again in early 2018, when a balanced budget amendment acquired majority support in the House of Representatives, but not the two-thirds required.[23] The reason Congress, politically speaking, cannot muster the votes needed for an amendment requiring fundamental budget process reform—one that staves off default—is that such an amendment will at some point in the not-too-distant future require Congress to admit that it has made spending commitments to the American people it cannot keep. Breaking these promises is tantamount to political suicide. The problem is that keeping them, of course, is tantamount to financial suicide. In short, the American people cannot rely on Congress to take the lead in this area.

This is why the Compact for America is using the alternative means for amendment provided in the Constitution when Congress is either unable or unwilling to propose what must be done: The states, rather than Congress, both propose and ratify the necessary amendment. To date, the states have never used this option, primarily because of the legitimate concern that such an amendment process could become either a "runaway" or "do nothing" effort if not properly organized. Thus organizing and unifying the states in such an effort has been the goal of the Compact for America approach.

The Compact for America approach resolves these concerns and improves the chance of success by organizing the participating states into a Compact by having each state enact a substantively identical law to join the Compact. Five states are already members.[24] The Compact serves to demonstrate that the states are taking a responsible approach to amending the Constitution by making public the text of the amendment up front and locking down the rules of procedure at the amendment convention. The Compact makes for a safe, effective, and timely procedure for achieving fundamental budget process reform and staving off federal default.

The text of the proposed amendment is as follows:

ARTICLE __

Section 1. Total outlays of the government of the United States shall not exceed total receipts of the government of the United States at any point in time unless the excess of outlays over receipts is financed exclusively by debt issued in strict conformity with this article.

Section 2. Outstanding debt shall not exceed authorized debt, which initially shall be an amount equal to 105 percent of the outstanding debt on the effective date of this article. Authorized debt shall not be increased above its aforesaid initial amount unless such increase is first approved by the legislatures of the several states as provided in Section 3.

Section 3. From time to time, Congress may increase authorized debt to an amount in excess of its initial amount set by Section 2 only if it first publicly refers to the legislatures of the several states an unconditional, single subject measure proposing the amount of such increase, in such form as provided by law, and the measure is thereafter publicly and unconditionally approved by a simple majority of the legislatures of the several states, in such form as provided respectively by state law; provided that no inducement requiring an expenditure or tax levy shall be demanded, offered, or accepted as a quid pro quo for such approval. If such approval is not obtained within sixty (60) calendar days after referral then the measure shall be deemed disapproved and the authorized debt shall thereby remain unchanged.

Section 4. Whenever the outstanding debt exceeds 98 percent of the debt limit set by Section 2, the President shall enforce said limit by publicly designating specific expenditures for impoundment in an amount sufficient to ensure outstanding debt shall not exceed the authorized debt. Said impoundment shall become effective thirty (30) days thereafter, unless Congress first designates an alternate impoundment of the same or greater amount by concurrent resolution, which shall become immediately effective. The failure of the President to designate or enforce the required impoundment is an impeachable misdemeanor. Any purported issuance or incurrence of any debt in excess of the debt limit set by Section 2 is void.

Section 5. No bill that provides for a new or increased general revenue tax shall become law unless approved by a two-thirds roll call vote of the whole number of each House of Congress. However, this requirement shall not apply to any bill that provides for a new end user sales tax that would completely replace every existing income tax levied by the government of the United States; or for the reduction or elimination of an exemption, deduction, or credit allowed under an existing general revenue tax.

Section 6. For purposes of this article, "debt" means any obligation backed by the full faith and credit of the government of the United States; "outstanding debt" means all debt held in any account and by any entity at a given point in time; "authorized debt" means the maximum total amount of debt that may be lawfully issued and outstanding at any single point in time under this article; "total outlays of the government of the United States" means all expenditures of the government of the United States from any source; "total receipts of the government of the United States" means all tax receipts and other income of the government of the United States, excluding proceeds from its issuance or incurrence of debt or any type of liability; "impoundment" means a proposal not to spend all or part of a sum of money appropriated by Congress; and "general revenue tax" means any income tax, sales tax, or value-added tax levied by the government of the United States excluding imposts and duties.

Section 7. This article is immediately operative upon ratification, self-enforcing, and Congress may enact conforming legislation to facilitate enforcement.

FOCUS ON RESTRAINING DEBT GROWTH

The Compact for America's balanced budget amendment focuses on restraining the growth in debt as the means for arriving at a balanced budget prior to a fiscal crisis and default by the federal government. The proposed amendment serves to limit the ability of the federal government to exercise an unlimited borrowing power while not denying it altogether. It does not require the federal government to balance the budget immediately or even to balance the budget every year, barring certain exceptions. Rather, it caps the debt at 105 percent of the level that exists on the date of ratification and requires the federal government to obtain the approval of the states to raise this cap in the future.

This is not only a viable approach, it will also serve to reassure investors in Treasury securities. First, it puts the federal government on

a glide path to balance following its ratification. Second, the amendment is carefully structured not to generate a fiscal crisis through its
own requirements. The statutory debt ceiling is currently under suspension, which sends a signal to the Treasury securities market that the
federal government believes there is no such thing as excessive debt. The
amendment recognizes that in historical terms the federal government
got on the wrong path regarding fiscal responsibility when it sharply
curtailed presidential impoundment authority through the enactment
of The Congressional Budget and Impoundment Control Act of 1974.[25]
This virtual prohibition on impoundment has caused the debt ceiling
itself to increase the risk of default. A prominent example of this is the
confrontation between President Barack Obama and Congress in 2011
over the matter of raising the debt ceiling.[26] The Compact for America's
amendment avoids this problem by giving the president the authority to
impound spending to the degree necessary to avoid breaching the debt
ceiling absent an approval by the states to raise it. Thus, investors in
Treasury securities can rest assured that the government will not default
under the debt ceiling established by amendment.

Some may argue that the instrument already in statutory law called
sequestration exists as a means to avoid the problem of default under the
debt ceiling. Sequestration imposes across-the-board spending reductions at calculated percentages in broad categories of accounts. The central problem with sequestration is that it is too blunt an instrument. All
spending subject to sequestration is treated equally by it because all the
applicable accounts are reduced by the same percent. Clearly, not all such
spending is of equal value. Using a more discriminating mechanism,
namely expanded presidential impoundment authority, is the better approach. On the other hand, large swaths of the federal budget, mainly
the entitlement programs, are not subject to sequestration at all. This has
adverse effect of forcing a choice of imposing unacceptable reductions in
the accounts subject to sequestration to control overall spending in order
to achieve a balanced budget or failing to achieve a balanced budget.
Impoundment, a much more precise instrument, permits the president
to focus on narrow accounts that represent less worthy spending and to
apply unequal levels of reductions. Further, the Compact for America's

amendment leaves no programmatic spending outside the coverage of its impoundment power.

BUDGET UNIFICATION

Over the last several decades, the federal budget has been balkanized. Some accounts, such as Social Security, have been put off-budget entirely.[27] Other spending programs, such as Medicare, have been put on autopilot by exempting them from the annual appropriations process. Still others—"emergency" spending, for example—have been exempted from sequestration. The result has been that decreasing portions of the federal budget have been subject to annual review and the application of spending restraint. In reality, this balkanization has been an abuse by Congress of the appropriations power granted to it by Article I of the Constitution. That power was granted with the intention of restraining spending, not expanding it. It is not lost on investors that the federal government cannot adopt policies consistent with fiscal responsibility when large swaths of the budget are not subject to the instruments of fiscal discipline.

The Compact's balanced budget amendment restores a unified federal budget by defining outlays that are subject to the fiscal restraints provided by the amendment, including the application of impoundment, as coming from any source. Accordingly, no accounts are left off the table in terms of their eligibility for making contributions toward advancing the federal budget toward balance. This will send a powerful message to the investment community that the federal government has put itself back in the position of achieving a balanced budget by making such a process mathematically plausible.

TAX FAIRNESS

The Compact for America's balanced budget amendment will establish procedures for the enactment of tax laws that serve to make raising revenue the primary purpose of the tax system. The Compact's balanced budget amendment includes a provision that requires a two-thirds vote in both houses of Congress to enact bills that enact a new or increased general revenue tax. However, it also maintains a simple majority requirement in both houses for bills that replace the existing income taxes with an end-user sales tax, or that serve to eliminate existing exemptions, deductions, and credits, and raise revenues through new or additional tariffs or fees.

A purpose of this provision is to focus the federal government's tax system more on raising revenue and less on providing special advantages to select purposes. It will serve to raise revenues in two ways: (a) it will reduce the loss of revenue brought about by specialized exemptions, deductions, and credits in the current system; and (b) it will generate greater economic growth, and therefore higher revenues, by strengthening the supply side of the economy relative the demand side.

Ultimately, this portion of the amendment is designed to reinforce investor confidence in the Treasury securities market by raising revenue without dampening economic growth. The amendment improves the likelihood of shifting the federal tax system away from taxes on income and production and toward taxes on consumption, which should spur greater economic growth. Accordingly, it will make a significant contribution toward avoiding the cycle of fiscal crisis, insolvency, and default growing out of the loss of investor confidence in Treasury securities.

CONCLUSION: FOUR MINUTES TO MIDNIGHT

The makers of federal fiscal policy must recognize that the Treasury securities market is just that—a market. Financing the federal debt necessarily involves attracting capital from investors. When the federal government fails to attract the necessary capital, it will be forced to operate the government on a cash-flow basis thereafter to avoid default. The fact is that investor tolerance for a fiscal policy that incurs ever-growing deficits, debt, and interest costs is not unlimited. The current fiscal trajectory for the federal government, if it continues, will necessarily exhaust investor patience and break the Treasury securities market. When and under what circumstances this will occur are the questions that the Debt Default Clock is designed to answer. The clock is an invaluable tool for educating fiscal policymakers on how to avoid breaking the market and how much time they have to take the necessary steps.

It is also essential to observe, however, that the Treasury securities market operates in a political environment. Politicians can, and from time to time do, make political calculations that run contrary to market requirements. Accordingly, some in the policy community may be tempted to stiff the investors in Treasury securities by refusing to make payments as promised. That is, they may actively pursue default, perceiving it be the least harmful option for the federal government. Such a perception represents a false hope. The immediate relief achieved through default will be followed in short order by a lack of access to capital; this also forces the government back to running on a cash-flow basis. By way of foreign examples, the governments of Greece and Argentina have made this unwise choice in recent years. Closer to home, the government of Puerto Rico has gone down this path. Much to their dismay, these governments have found attempts to battle the forces of the sovereign debt markets a fool's errand. Clearly the U.S. government should not follow their examples.

The minute hand of Debt Default Clock currently stands at four minutes to midnight. This means the federal government may have little time to get off the fiscal path it is currently on. On the other hand, default is not yet inevitable. What the U.S. government needs to do now is take the steps necessary to move the clock's minute hand in a counterclockwise direction. If it takes these steps on a gradual but comprehensive and sustained basis, it will avoid default. History demonstrates, however, that the federal government is unlikely to take these steps absent outside assistance. This is why the states need to step in to force the fundamental changes in the federal government's budget process by proposing and ratifying the balanced budget amendment now being advanced by the Compact for America.

CHAPTER TEN

FISCAL RULES, FISCAL POLICY, AND DEBT: A DYNAMIC SIMULATION ANALYSIS

JOHN MERRIFIELD AND BARRY POULSON

Perhaps the most enduring legacy of the Reagan administration has been the growth-promoting impact of reducing tax burdens on U.S. citizens. The tax cuts enacted during the Reagan years set the stage for two decades of rapid economic growth.

During the late 1980s and 1990s the lower tax burdens were part of the so-called "Great Moderation" in monetary and fiscal policy, not in the sense that formal rules governed these policies, but rather in the convergence of monetary and fiscal policies toward benchmarks consistent with rules that were articulated thereafter. John Taylor[1] documented the convergence of monetary policy toward the benchmarks of a Taylor rule in these years.[2] We documented the convergence of fiscal policies toward the benchmarks set in fiscal rules.[3] The formal fiscal rules enacted in the 1980s and 1990s mandated that the federal government bring expenditures in line with revenues and balance the budget. There is continuing controversy regarding the effectiveness of these fiscal rules. Nonetheless, as the economy grew in the 1990s, expenditures converged with revenues, and the government balanced the federal budget.

The Reagan legacy of reducing tax burdens on U.S. citizens continued with the tax cuts enacted during the Bush administration, and over the past two years, the Trump administration. However, in contrast to the Reagan tax cuts, these tax cuts have been accompanied by retardation in economic growth. The average annual rate of economic growth over the past two decades is approximately 1 percent below the long run average annual rate of growth of 3 percent in the United States. There has been some recovery of the growth rate during the Trump administration, but long-term forecasts project a return to the lower growth rates experienced over the past two decades.

There is growing evidence that retardation in economic growth is linked to the abandonment of the rules-based monetary and fiscal policies pursued during the Great Moderation. In the two papers cited just previously, John Taylor documents how the shift toward discretionary monetary policies contributed to economic instability over the past two decades,[4] and we document how circumvention of fiscal rules resulted in unprecedented increases in deficits and unsustainable growth in debt.

There is perhaps no more controversial issue in this literature than the impact of tax cuts on economic growth. The Tax Cut and Jobs Act of 2017 was the largest tax cut since the Reagan tax cuts enacted in the 1980s. The Trump administration has proposed a new round of tax cuts, including reductions in payroll taxes. The Trump administration maintains that tax cuts enacted over the past two years will stimulate significantly higher rates of economic growth. Indeed, tax cuts are the centerpiece of a wide range of reforms enacted by the administration to promote economic growth.[5]

The Office of Management and Budget (OMB) published the president's fiscal year 2019 budget, projecting a 3 percent growth rate and claiming that debt as a share of gross domestic product (GDP) will decline over the next decade.[6] This forecast of a 3 percent growth rate is at odds with most public and private forecasts of economic growth.

The Congressional Budget Office (CBO) (2018, 2019)[7] estimates that the tax cuts will stimulate economic growth in the short term, but in the long term, growth will fall back to the lower rates experienced over the past two decades. The CBO estimates a growth rate less than 2 percent over the next three decades.[8]

The CBO (2019) projects that under current law the debt held by the public will roughly double to about 150 percent of GDP in 2049.[9] This is a significant increase in the debt burden compared to earlier CBO forecasts. Most of the increased debt burden is due to the recent legislation enacted by Congress, including the Tax Cuts and Jobs Act, and spending increases in the Bipartisan Budget Act of 2018. Because large parts of this legislation would expire under current law, the increased debt burden projected by the CBO occurs primarily over the next decade. If current policies are extended beyond the next decade rather than expiring, the CBO projects that the debt burden will be significantly worse.

The CBO (2019) concludes that under current law the debt to GDP ratio will increase at an unsustainable rate and that higher debt to GDP ratios will result in retardation and stagnation in economic growth.[10] Because of this increased debt burden, the United States is increasingly vulnerable to recessions and other economic shocks that could trigger a debt crisis.

In this controversy there is a growing consensus that these fiscal policies are not sustainable in the long run, and that fiscal reforms must be enacted to address the debt crisis. There is also growing agreement that current fiscal rules have proved to be ineffective, and that new rules are needed to solve the debt crisis.

In this study we explore the controversy regarding fiscal rules, fiscal policy, and debt. The study begins with a discussion of the search for a fiscal Taylor rule (FTR), which prescribes the fiscal stance as a function of past government debt, past output gap, and the past structural primary balance.[11] It then explores second generation fiscal rules designed for U.S. fiscal institutions. Dynamic simulation of the second generation fiscal rules reveals how difficult it will be for the United States to solve the debt crisis in coming decades even with new fiscal rules in place. Solving the debt crisis will in fact require some fundamental reforms in fiscal policy. Since tax policy is at the center of this controversy, the dynamic simulation model is used to estimate the impact of alternative tax policies with new fiscal rules in place.

IN SEARCH OF A FISCAL TAYLOR RULE

In his analysis of the Great Moderation, John Taylor poses a counterfactual hypothesis.[12] What if the rules-based approach to monetary policy that emerged in the late 1980s and 1990s had continued over the past two decades? He and his coauthors simulate the impact of a Taylor rule on monetary policy. They conclude that a rules-based monetary policy could have avoided the destabilizing effects of the discretionary monetary policies pursued in this period. Taylor and others argue that we can no longer rely on the Federal Reserve to pursue discretionary monetary policies that approximate a rules-based policy and that formal monetary rules, such as the Taylor rule, should guide it instead.[13]

Taylor also advocates a rules-based approach to fiscal policy.[14] The fiscal Taylor rule is a rule providing benchmarks to guide discretionary fiscal policy. The objective of the FTR is to promote economic stability over the business cycle while maintaining debt sustainability in the long run.[15]

The FTR requires that a structural surplus is maintained over the business cycle. Application of the FTR means that fiscal policy is anchored in the sense that debt converges to a sustainable level in the long run. The nominal budget balance allows automatic stabilizers to support aggregate demand when actual output is below potential output, and for reductions in expenditures when actual output exceeds potential output. Taylor maintains that this FTR provides a good fit for the fiscal balance in the United States in the long run. He fits the FTR to U.S. fiscal data for 1960 to 1999.

A number of studies have built upon the original Taylor design for an FTR.[16] Debrun and Jonung recently generalized the Taylor FTR in a model that they also fit to U.S. data.[17] Their model provides benchmarks for the nominal budget balance to provide for economic stabilization over the business cycle and convergence of the debt-to-GDP ratio to a given target. They assume the 60 percent target for the debt-to-GDP ratio adopted by the European Union and the Organisation for Economic Co-operation and Development (OECD). They fit the model to U.S. fiscal data for the period 1990 to 2017.

Debrun and Jonung find that in the United States the actual budget balance in the 1990s exceeded the benchmark budget balance.[18] In other words, the fiscal policies pursued during the Great Moderation were actually more prudent than those consistent with their FTR benchmarks. However, over the past two decades the actual budget balance was significantly below that consistent with the benchmarks. This suggests that over the past two decades fiscal policy no longer approximates the rules-based fiscal policy pursued during the Great Moderation.

Debrun and Jonung are somewhat sanguine regarding the prospects for a rules-based approach to fiscal policy in the United States.[19] They argue that while the actual budget balance has been below the benchmark budget balance over the past two decades, there is evidence of convergence toward the benchmark after the financial crisis. They conclude that as the output gap closes, deficits will move back to levels consistent with long-term debt objectives. They seem to suggest that we should expect a return to a rules-based fiscal policy similar to that pursued during the Great Moderation. The authors are also supportive of discretionary fiscal policy to stabilize the economy over the business cycle. The benchmarks in their FTR model provide for discretionary fiscal policy as well as automatic stabilizers. Taylor and other monetary economists are more skeptical of the effectiveness of discretionary fiscal policy in stabilizing the economy over the business cycle.

As Debrun and Jonung note, the simulations of FTRs that they and Taylor conducted are sensitive to data vintage. They have both chosen time periods that include the fiscal policies pursued during the Great Moderation. Their 2018 simulations end in 2017, prior to the impact of fiscal policies pursued by the Trump administration.[20] As the budget balance returns to trillion-dollar deficits we must question their sanguine view of the prospects for U.S fiscal policy. The long-term forecasts of the CBO reveal that at least under current law the United States will incur greater deficits that will further deviate from benchmark budget balances in their FTR. The debt-to-GDP level is projected to increase well above current levels and diverge even further from the 60 percent target considered the sustainable level in their analysis. In short, the

United States does not appear to be returning to the rules-based fiscal policies pursued during the Great Moderation.[21]

We agree with Taylor that over the past two decades the United States has abandoned the rules-based fiscal policies pursued during the Great Moderation. If elected officials had continued to pursue those more prudent fiscal policies, the country could have avoided a debt crisis. But hoping that elected officials will again be guided by an FTR to stabilize the economy over the business cycle and reduce the debt-to-GDP ratio to a sustainable level is wishful thinking. Because the United States has abandoned a rules-based fiscal policy, it will be even more difficult to solve the debt crisis. We maintain that the United States must now enact the more stringent fiscal rules that have proved to be effective in addressing the debt crisis in Switzerland, Sweden, and other OECD countries. This second generation of fiscal rules for the United States is explored in the following section.

SECOND-GENERATION FISCAL RULES FOR THE UNITED STATES

THE SIMULATION MODEL

There has been a dramatic increase in the number of countries enacting a new type of fiscal rules. In 1990, only a handful of countries had enacted these new fiscal rules; by 2015, 92 countries had them in place.[22]

There is an extensive literature on the design of optimal fiscal rules.[23] A fundamental trade-off is between commitment and flexibility in rule design. Rules may commit elected officials to follow a constrained fiscal policy to achieve a specific target, such as a spending limit or revenue limit designed to achieve a desired debt or deficit target. But the more stringent the rule, the less flexibility elected officials have in responding to economic shocks from recessions or emergencies.[24] The next generation of fiscal rules that we propose, the Merrifield-Poulson (MP) rules, incorporate features that are viewed as optimal from the standpoint of fiscal rules design.[25]

The theoretical and empirical literature on second-generation fiscal rules supports a hybrid approach to rule design. In a hybrid approach a threshold is set for target levels of debt-to-GDP and deficit-to-GDP ratios that trigger fiscal policy responses. The optimal target thresholds must be tight enough to achieve a sustainable fiscal policy, but not so tight that policymakers cannot respond to economic shocks. This hybrid approach can resolve the trade-off between commitment and flexibility in fiscal rule design.

Our proposed rules introduce flexibility in a number of ways. For example, if the policy instrument is an expenditure limit, elected officials have discretion in determining how stringently to apply the limit. In the long term a spending limit is gradually increased to meet the increased demand for government services, such as pension and health benefits for an aging population. Elected officials can set a spending limit multiplier at unity in the medium term, and then adjust the multiplier upward in the long term.

Flexibility is also introduced in the form of debt and deficit brakes. Debt and deficit brakes are designed to give elected officials flexibility in constraining fiscal policy in the medium term. When debt and deficits reach threshold levels, this triggers debt and deficit brakes that impose a more stringent spending limit. The debt and deficit brakes provide flexibility to elected officials in the form of multipliers. A multiplier set at unity would apply a debt brake or deficit brake gradually at threshold levels. A multiplier greater than unity would apply the debt brake and deficit brake more stringently above the threshold levels.

Our proposed deficit/debt brake is complemented by other fiscal rules. An emergency fund provides for stabilization over the business cycle and for other emergencies such as natural disasters and military conflict.[26] The MP rules allow for deficits in the emergency fund in periods of financial crisis and recession.[27] The MP rule addresses countercyclical government services demand growth with a higher spending cap equal to half the amount of revenue declines. However, like the Swiss debt brake, these deficits in the emergency fund must be offset by surpluses in the primary budget in the near term. As in the Swiss case, deficits in the emergency fund must be balanced by surpluses within a fixed time frame. The emergency fund is similar to the notional account used in Switzerland to achieve budget balance in the near term. The rules constraining the emergency fund could be suspended in the case of a war.[28]

Some countries have enacted fiscal rules with a "golden rule" which exempts government capital expenditures from the spending limits.[29]

We propose a version of the golden rule that would retain the integrity of the fiscal rule. Investment spending spurs economic growth, so some countries exempt it from spending caps and also allow debt financing. But even with a clear formal definition of investment, an exemption creates a loophole we want to avoid. So, the MP rule creates regular saving to fund investment beyond what the ex ante fiscal limits allow.

The capital investment fund proposed in the MP rule is patterned after the Swiss model.[30] The capital investment fund is designed to fund infrastructure investments. In periods when economic growth is above the long-term average rate of economic growth, a portion of revenue is set aside in the capital investment fund. In periods of slower economic growth, money is transferred from the capital fund to help finance infrastructure investments. This method of allocating the capital funds in accordance with the rate of economic growth assures a steady growth in infrastructure investment in the long run.

Implementing the MP rule will require a number of reforms in fiscal policy. Since taxes are at the center of the debate, we focus on the impact of the new rules with different tax policies. Specifically, we combine the fiscal rules with a 1 percent tax cut and a 1 percent tax increase.

Our deficit/debt brake is designed for the unique institutions in the U.S. economy. The proposed fiscal rules are simulated for the United States over the forecast period 2019–2042, according to parameters unique to the U.S. economy over this time period.

It is important to contrast the proposed MP fiscal rules with other fiscal rules proposed for the United States. We propose a combination of interrelated fiscal rules designed to achieve multiple targets, including a deficit-to-GDP ratio and a debt-to-GDP ratio. The long-term goal is a sustainable debt-to-GDP ratio. Once a sustainable debt level is reached, the proposed rules approximate a cyclically balanced budget, with surpluses in periods of economic expansion offsetting deficits in periods of economic contraction.

The concept of debt sustainability is controversial, and for that reason we use different measures of sustainability.[31] The most commonly used measure is the fiscal gap, that is, stabilizing the debt-to-GDP ratio at current levels. For highly indebted countries such as the United

States, with total debt in excess of national income, this is a low bar to reach. Debt levels in excess of national income are not considered sustainable in the long run. At a minimum, highly indebted countries should attempt to reduce debt levels to at least equal national income. The consensus estimate of sustainable debt, the measures adopted by the European Union and the OECD, is a debt-to-GDP ratio of 60 percent. For the United States and other highly indebted countries, achieving this sustainable debt level will be a high bar indeed.

If the debt-to-GDP ratio is falling, then eventually the country will close the fiscal gap and achieve a sustainable fiscal policy. How rapidly the country achieves these goals is important, so we analyze the trajectory of debt over the forecast period.

Because a structural deficit has emerged, the fiscal rules must constrain all expenditures. In the medium term, budgets must conform to the targets imposed by the new fiscal rules, and budget processes must be adapted to this rules-based approach to fiscal policy.

The flaw in current U.S. fiscal policy is the failure to set long-term goals and to incorporate those goals into the budget process. Some have argued that it is unrealistic to set long-term goals and impose fiscal rules to achieve them. They argue that Congress already struggles with short-term budgets, and that Congress is not able to hold to long-term goals. But this is an argument for continuing a budget process relying on discretionary fiscal policies that created the debt crisis. Continuing to muddle along with current discretionary fiscal policies is no longer a viable option in the long run.

Critics will argue that such a complex set of rules will be difficult to enact and to implement. We simulate the proposed fiscal rules to show how they can be implemented to achieve the multiple targets. We maintain that a combination of fiscal rules is a prerequisite for fiscal stabilization in the United States over the long term.

DYNAMIC SIMULATION OF THE MODEL

We use dynamic simulation analysis to measure the impact of the proposed rules combined with tax reforms on the budget and on the U.S. economy over the forecast period 2019–2042.[32] The simulation results provide insight into the role that fiscal rules can play in achieving debt sustainability. Details of the dynamic simulation model are provided in the appendix.[33]

Our GDP, personal income, population, inflation, and fiscal data are from standard sources, including the CBO, OMB, Department of Commerce, and Department of Labor. The National Bureau of Economic Research (NBER) produced our income elasticity of federal revenue data. Lacking an official source for "emergency spending," and faced with the inability to cobble together reliably complete annual emergency spending estimates from separate sources, we estimated emergency spending data as the Troubled Asset Relief Program revenue-adjusted difference between the planned deficit, or surplus, and the typically much larger change in the national debt. Simulation results and sensitivity analysis of the major parameters on the model are available at the website vetfiscalrules.net.

The following discussion summarizes the results of the simulation analysis. The simulation analysis focuses on three specifications of the MP rule. The first specification, which simulates applying the MP rule without additional tax policy changes, assumes the tax policies currently incorporated in the CBO *Long Term Budget Outlook*.[34] The second specification assumes that the MP rule is combined with a 1 percent tax cut. The third specification assumes that the MP rule is combined with a 1 percent tax increase.

THE DEBT-TO-GDP RATIO

In Figure 10.1, the debt-to-GDP ratio is simulated over the forecast period. Because the MP rule simulation is based on CBO data for revenue and expenditures, it captures the impact of recent tax cuts; however, the simulation assumes no further tax cuts.

In the MP simulation with otherwise status quo tax rates, total debt increases continuously throughout the forecast period, reaching $57 trillion by the end of the period. The debt-to-GDP ratio increases to a peak of 129 percent in 2028, and then decreases to 110 percent by the end of the period.

In the simulation with the MP rule and a 1 percent tax cut, debt increases to a peak of $39 trillion in 2038, and then falls to $38 trillion

FIGURE 10.1
Debt-to-GDP ratio scenarios

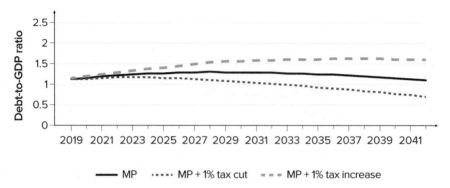

Source: Authors' simulation model.
Note: GDP = gross domestic product; MP = Merrifield-Poulson rule.

at the end of the period. The debt–to–GDP ratio increases to a peak of 117 percent in 2024, and then falls to 69 percent at the end of the period.

In the simulation with the MP rule and a 1 percent tax increase, total debt increases very rapidly throughout the forecast period, reaching $77 trillion at the end of the period. The debt to GDP ratio increases throughout the forecast period, reaching 159 percent by the end of the period.

THE DEFICIT-TO-GDP RATIO

In Figure 10.2, the deficit–to–GDP ratio is simulated over the forecast period. In the simulation with the MP rule, deficits increase in the first few years and then decrease over the remaining years of the forecast period. The deficit–to–GDP ratio increases to a peak of 7.4 percent in 2022, and then falls to 1.9 percent at the end of the period.

In the simulation with the MP rule and a 1 percent tax cut, deficits increase in the first few years and then decrease. The government is able to balance the budget in 2038 and then generate surplus revenue in the remaining years of the forecast period. In the final year the government generates a surplus equal to 1 percent of GDP.

FIGURE 10.2
Deficit-to-GDP ratio scenarios

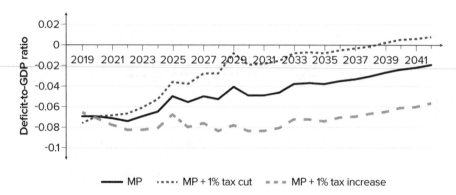

Source: Authors' simulation model.
Note: GDP = gross domestic product; MP = Merrifield-Poulson rule.

In the simulation with the MP rule and a 1 percent tax increase, deficits increase throughout the forecast period. The deficit–to–GDP ratio fluctuates at around 7 percent.

THE GENERAL FUND SPENDING-TO-GDP RATIO

In Figure 10.3, the general fund spending-to-GDP ratio is simulated over the forecast period. In the simulation with the MP rule and no tax rate changes, general fund spending as a share of GDP falls throughout the forecast period, from 11 percent in the initial year to 4 percent in the final year.

With the MP rule and a 1 percent tax cut, general fund spending as a share of GDP falls a little more rapidly throughout the forecast period, also reaching 4 percent in the final year.

With the MP rule and a 1 percent tax increase, general fund spending as a share of GDP falls less rapidly throughout the forecast period, reaching 5 percent in the final year.

THE TOTAL SPENDING-TO-GDP RATIO

In Figure 10.4, the total spending-to-GDP ratio is simulated over the forecast period. In the simulation with the MP rule and no other change,

FIGURE 10.3

General fund spending-to-GDP ratio scenarios

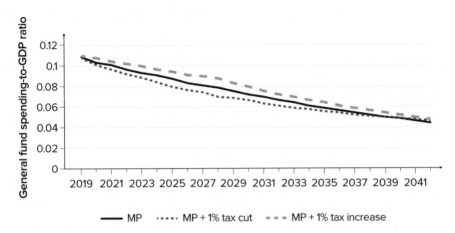

Source: Authors' simulation model.
Note: GDP = gross domestic product; MP = Merrifield-Poulson rule.

FIGURE 10.4

Total spending-to-GDP ratio scenarios

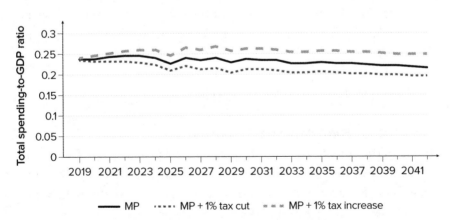

Source: Authors' simulation model.
Note: GDP = gross domestic product; MP = Merrifield-Poulson rule.

FIGURE 10.5

General fund revenue-to-GDP ratio with MP

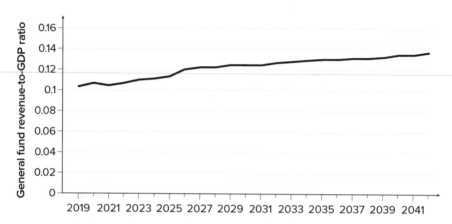

Source: Authors' simulation model.

Note: GDP = gross domestic product; MP = Merrifield-Poulson rule.

total spending as a share of GDP increases to a peak of 24 percent in 2022 and then decreases over the forecast period to 22 percent in the final year.

With the MP rule and a 1 percent tax cut, total spending as a share of GDP decreases throughout the forecast period, reaching 19 percent in the final year.

With the MP rule and a 1 percent tax increase, total spending as a share of GDP fluctuates about 25 percent.

THE GENERAL FUND REVENUE-TO-GDP RATIO

In Figures 10.5, 10.6, and 10.7, the general fund revenue-to-GDP ratio is simulated over the forecast period. In the simulation with the MP rule alone, general fund revenue as a share of GDP increases throughout the period, reaching 14 percent in the final year.

With the MP rule and a 1 percent tax cut, general fund revenue as a share of GDP also increases to 14 percent in the final year.

With the MP rule and a 1 percent tax increase, general fund revenue as a share of GDP increases to 13 percent in the final year.

FIGURE 10.6
General fund revenue/GDP ratio with MP + 1% tax cut

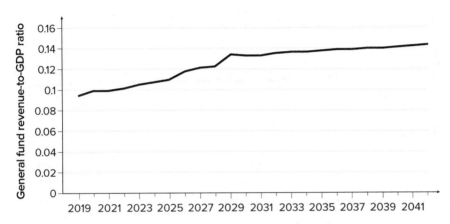

Source: Authors' simulation model.
Note: GDP = gross domestic product; MP = Merrifield-Poulson rule.

FIGURE 10.7
General fund revenue-to-GDP ratio with MP + 1% tax increase

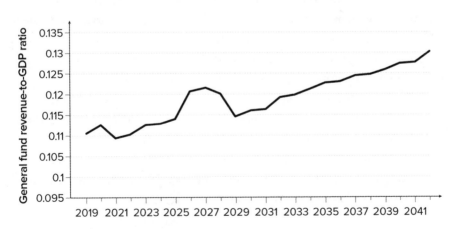

Source: Authors' simulation model.
Note: GDP = gross domestic product; MP = Merrifield-Poulson rule.

FIGURE 10.8

Interest-to-general fund revenue ratio scenarios

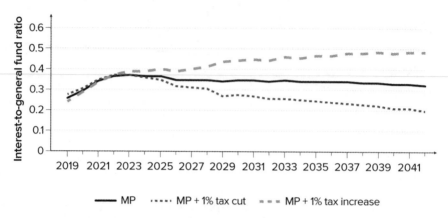

Source: Authors' simulation model.
Note: MP = Merrifield-Poulson rule.

INTEREST EXPENDITURE-TO-GENERAL FUND REVENUE RATIO

In Figure 10.8, interest expenditure as a share of the general fund revenue is simulated over the forecast period. In the simulation with the MP rule alone, interest expenditure as a share of general fund revenue increases to a peak of 37 percent in 2023, and it decreases to 32 percent at the end of the forecast period.

With the MP rule and a 1 percent tax cut, interest expenditure as a share of general fund revenue increases to a peak of 37 percent in 2023, and it decreases to 20 percent at the end of the period.

With the MP rule and a 1 percent tax increase, interest expenditure as a share of general fund revenue increases rapidly throughout the forecast period, reaching 48 percent in the final year.

THE REVISED GDP-TO-ACTUAL GDP RATIO

In Figure 10.9, the revised GDP to actual GDP ratio is simulated over the forecast period. In this context, the term "revised GDP" refers to estimated GDP in the simulation analysis, and the term "actual GDP" refers to GDP projected in the CBO *Long-Term Budget Outlook*.

FIGURE 10.9

Revised GDP-to-actual GDP ratio scenarios

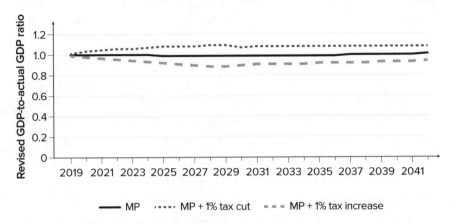

Source: Authors' simulation model.

Note: GDP = gross domestic product; MP = Merrifield-Poulson rule.

In the simulation with the MP rule alone, revised GDP relative to actual GDP remains roughly constant over the forecast period. With the MP rule and a 1 percent tax cut, revised GDP relative to actual GDP increases throughout the period, reaching 108 percent at the end of the period. With the MP rule and a 1 percent tax increase, revised GDP relative to actual GDP falls throughout the forecast period, reaching 94 percent in the final year.

ANALYSIS OF FISCAL RULES, TAX REFORM, AND DEBT SUSTAINABILITY

The dynamic simulation analysis reveals that combining the MP fiscal rules with a tax cut is a superior strategy in achieving debt sustainability. The impact of expenditure caps and tax cuts on economic growth is crucial in understanding how these policies reduce debt.

The combination of expenditure caps and tax cuts significantly increases economic growth compared to the other simulations. The dynamic simulation analysis captures the positive impact of reductions in the marginal tax rate on economic growth. The dynamic simulation model assumes a relationship between tax cuts and economic growth that is based on research by NBER.[36] The NBER estimates that historically, GDP increased by 1.21 percent per 1 percent decrease in the tax burden. This estimate is consistent with our estimate of the historical relationship between growth rates and changes in income tax rates at the state level.[37]

Thus, much of the higher growth rate simulated with the MP rule and a 1 percent tax cut is based on this historical relationship. Because the simulation is based on dynamic analysis rather than static analysis, the simulations capture the positive impact of tax cuts on economic growth. The forecast period provides sufficient time for the simulation analysis to capture the full positive impact of these cuts. The increased revenue that accompanies the growth offsets the static revenue loss due to lower marginal tax rates.

It is important to emphasize how expenditure caps are combined with tax cuts to constrain government spending in the simulation analysis. The expenditure limits imposed by the fiscal rules directly constrain general fund expenditures. The rules limit the amount of debt that can be issued to fund total expenditures. When total debt exceeds the debt tolerance level, a debt brake is applied. Since total debt exceeds the debt tolerance level throughout the forecast period, the debt brake impacts total spending each year. Thus, other expenditures, including Social Security and Medicare spending, are indirectly constrained by the debt brake.

The dynamic simulation analysis also captures the positive impact on economic growth of changes in government expenditures.[38] The dynamic simulation model assumes an opportunity cost rate of 6 percent when resources are shifted from the private to the public sector, a rate based on historical evidence over the past half century. Thus every dollar that remains in the private sector boosts economic growth.

The combination of fiscal rules and a 1 percent tax cut results in fewer resources shifted from the private to the public sector compared to the alternative simulations. There is a modest reduction in the share of general fund spending in GDP with the tax cut. However, there is a significantly lower ratio of total spending in GDP with the tax cut. With the fiscal rules and a 1 percent tax cut, total spending as a share of GDP is reduced to 17 percent, well below the share of total spending in GDP in recent years.

The simulation analysis probably underestimates the positive impact of this combination of expenditure caps and tax cuts on economic growth because of changes in the composition of spending over the forecast period. The assumption is that the 6 percent opportunity cost in shifting resources from the private to the public sector applies to all federal spending. The growth in other expenditures increases income transfers, such as spending for the entitlement programs Social Security and Medicare, which have a negative impact on economic growth. Because the combination of fiscal rules and a 1 percent tax cut constrains other expenditures more effectively, these policies limit income transfers.

The simulation analysis does capture the negative impact of interest expenditures on economic growth. Interest payments increase with higher levels of debt over the forecast period. The combination of expenditure caps and tax cuts reduces total debt and interest payments on the debt compared to the other simulations.

One could argue that using a portion of the debt to finance capital investment expenditures could have a positive impact on economic growth, as with the so-called golden rule. But using debt to finance increases in other expenditures, and especially transfer payments, has a significant negative impact on growth. The simulation analysis reveals that without the proposed fiscal rules, by the end of the forecast period the government is borrowing to finance interest payments on the debt. If debt is used to finance interest payments on the debt in the private sector, it is called a Ponzi scheme.

CONCLUSION: HOW WE LEARNED TO STOP WORRYING AND LOVE DEBT

The combination of expenditure caps and tax cuts reduces the debt-to-GDP ratio significantly compared to the CBO forecast for debt under current law. The dynamic simulation analysis lends support to the Trump administration argument for tax cuts to promote economic growth, and a growth strategy based on tax cuts can also be consistent with a sustainable debt level in the long run. However, tax cuts must be combined with stringent fiscal rules to constrain spending, and the government must generate hundreds of billions of dollars in savings earmarked for debt reduction each year over the next three decades. Generating that savings would require fundamental reform in all expenditure programs, including the major drivers of debt: entitlement programs. Savings must also be generated through federal asset sales and privatization.

In short, solving the debt crisis will require considerable downsizing of the federal government. Neither the president nor Congress are discussing the reforms in fiscal rules and fiscal policies needed to solve the debt crisis. Indeed, it appears that citizens as well as elected officials have become complacent about the debt. A recent *Wall Street Journal* article concludes that "repeated false alarms about debt-related crises in advanced countries such as Japan, the U.S., and the UK have left many investors and analysts increasingly skeptical of the idea that burgeoning sovereign-debt piles in those nations pose a major threat to markets."[39] President Trump is skeptical of those who predict a debt crisis; he is quoted as saying about the day of debt reckoning, "yeah, but I won't be here." Trump defends his sanguine attitude toward debt by arguing that if you grow the economy you don't have a debt problem.[40]

This sanguine attitude can be attributed to Keynesian views that continue to dominate discussion about public debt. For example, Paul Krugman argues for complacency toward public debt. He criticized President Barack Obama for not pursuing more fiscal stimulus during the financial crisis, despite trillion-dollar deficits and a doubling of the national debt.[41]

Krugman and other Keynesians argue that the United States is experiencing *secular stagnation*, an idea that can be traced back to John Maynard Keynes and his disciples during the Great Depression. Keynesians maintain that fiscal stimulus is now needed to restore long-term economic growth. Krugman argues that because of secular stagnation there is "even less reason than before to obsess over government debt:" He suggests that "Debt is way-way down on the list of things to worry about, absolutely trivial compared with, say, crumbling infrastructure, which should be fixed without worrying about paying as you go.'"[42]

Keynesians argue that because the economy is experiencing secular stagnation, expansionary fiscal policies are needed to boost the rate of economic growth.[43] Recently, Krugman and other Keynesians defended elected officials who advocate higher taxes on the wealthy to finance this expanded role for government in the economy.[44]

Our simulation analysis turns this Keynesian argument on its head. To boost economic growth the government should combine fiscal rules to constrain government spending with tax cuts. With these policies in place, the government could reduce debt to sustainable levels over the next three decades. The Keynesian policy prescription to increase government spending and increase taxes would have a negative impact on economic growth and exacerbate the debt crisis.

The major flaw in the Keynesian view is to focus on the impact of fiscal policy in the near term and defer consideration of the impact of fiscal policy in the long term. As the simulation analysis reveals, the negative impact of increased government spending and higher taxes on economic growth in the near term is quite limited. It is only after the first few years of the forecast period that these policies have a major impact on the rate of economic growth.

Conversely, the positive impact of reduced government spending and lower taxes on economic growth in the near term is quite modest. But after the first few years of the forecast period, the economic growth rate with these policies in place accelerates.

The short-term bias in the Keynesian view is evident in the simulation of government revenue and spending with these alternative fiscal policies. The tax increase generates higher revenues over the first few years of the forecast period; the static revenue gains from higher taxes offsets the negative effects of the higher taxes on economic growth and revenue. It is only in the last decades of the forecast period that higher taxes are accompanied by significantly lower economic growth and revenue growth.

In the simulation analysis there is not a great divergence in total spending over the first decade of the forecast period with the different policies in place. However, after the first decade there is greater divergence; the total spending-to-GDP ratio with the tax increase rises, while that with the tax cut falls.

These biases in Keynesian fiscal policies are then reflected in the trend of deficits and debt over the forecast period. With the tax increase, deficits as a share of GDP fluctuate around current levels over the first decade. It is only in the last decades of the period that higher taxes are accompanied by a discontinuous rise in deficits and debt as a share of GDP. With the tax cut, in the long term the budget is balanced, and debt is reduced to a sustainable level.[45]

It is not surprising that Keynesians want us to focus on the impact of fiscal policy in the near term and defer considerations of debt to the long term. But if Keynesians are truly interested in boosting economic growth, they would not advocate increased taxes and more deficit-financed government spending. Retardation in economic growth is due not to secular stagnation as the Keynesians argue, but rather to unconstrained growth in deficit financed government spending and the accumulation of an unsustainable debt burden.

To test the vulnerability of the economy to economic shocks, we estimated the impact of a mild recession.[46] Assuming that our proposed fiscal rules are in place, the government could use nondiscretionary fiscal policy, that is, automatic stabilizers, to respond to recessions, and still close the fiscal gap by the end of the forecast period. Using nondiscretionary fiscal policy to respond to recessions is the fiscal policy Milton Friedman advocated a half century ago.[47]

Our research reveals that the United States is now extremely vulnerable to major economic shocks, such as a financial crisis. Even with our proposed fiscal rules in place, the federal government does not have the space to use fiscal stimulus the way that President Obama did during the last financial crisis. Pursuing such Keynesian policies now would make it impossible to close the fiscal gap and would expose the economy to the kind of debt spiral that Paul Krugman and other Keynesians dismiss.

The dynamic simulation analysis reveals that we are not doomed to retardation in economic growth. We can restore long-term economic growth and reduce debt to sustainable levels by constraining the growth in federal spending. The combination of expenditure caps and tax cuts is the optimum policy to achieve these objectives.

The United States cannot muddle along with current fiscal policies and postpone addressing the debt crisis indefinitely.[48] The economy is now vulnerable to recessions and economic crises, and the people of the United States can't assume that economic growth will make the debt crisis go away. President Trump and Congress will probably have to address the debt crisis sooner than they think.

APPENDIX: THE DYNAMIC SIMULATION MODEL

This appendix summarizes the main components of the dynamic simulation model (more detailed equations are available at the website vetfiscalrules.net).

The central element of the MP rule is an ex ante cap on discretionary spending growth. The two best approximations of a general basis for increased demand for discretionary federal spending are personal income growth and population plus inflation. Since our studies of state fiscal stress indicated that personal income growth is too volatile a basis for capping spending growth, the MP rule caps spending growth at a multiple of the sum of population growth and inflation.

A discretionary spending limit (DSP) rises, annually, at a multiple of population growth plus inflation (AFAF) unless the proximity of the deficit or debt to the MP rule's designated deficit and debt threshold levels triggers braking. Countercyclical supplementary spending occurs when revenue declines from one year to the next.

$$
DSP_t = IF \begin{pmatrix} \left(1 + \left((1 - DEBTBADJ_t - DEFBADJ_t) \times AFAF_t\right)\right) > 1, \\ \left((DSP_{t-1} - CCYCSP_{t-1}) \times \left(1 + \left((1 - DEBTBADJ_t - DEFBADJ_t) \times AFAF_t\right)\right)\right) \\ + CCYCSP_t, DSP_{t-1} \end{pmatrix}
$$

$$(10.A.1)$$

Where:

DSP = simulation-revised discretionary spending

AFAF = allowed fiscal adjustment factor, ((population + inflation) × MULT).

CCYCSP = countercyclical general fund spending

DEBTBADJ = debt brake–based adjustment of AFAF

$$
DEBTBADJ_t = IF \begin{pmatrix} DEBTGDP_{t-1} < (0.8 \times DEBTTOL), 0, \\ \left((DEBTGDP_{t-1} \div DEBTTOL) \times \left(DEBTGDP_{t-1} - (DEBTTOL \times 0.8)\right)\right) \\ \times DEBTBRATE \end{pmatrix}
$$

Where:

DEBTGDP = national debt divided by GDP
DEBTTOL = "tolerance" level for debt/GDP ratio
DEBTBRATE = DEBTBADJ adjustment factor/rate

$$\text{DEFBADJ}_t = \text{IF}\left(\begin{array}{l} \text{DEFGDP}_{t-1} < (0.8 \times \text{DEFTOL}), 0, \\ ((\text{DEFGDP}_{t-1}/\text{DEFTOL}) \times (\text{DEFGDP}_{t-1} - (\text{DEFTOL} \times 0.8))) \\ \times \text{DEFBRATE}) \end{array}\right)$$

Where:

DEFBADJ = deficit brake-based adjustment of FAF
DEFGDP = deficit divided by GDP
DEFTOL = "tolerance" level for deficit/GDP ratio
DEFBRATE = DEFBADJ adjustment factor/rate

The 0.8 in some of these equations is there to initiate braking, gradually, as the debt or deficit approaches the threshold levels (80 percent × .60 = .48 for debt); (80 percent × .03 = .024 for the deficit). The not-shown other part of the IF in Equation (10.A.1) bars spending reduction so that zero is the lowest possible growth rate; a constraint not present in each simulation. The braking criteria—capping spending growth below AFAF—are the debt and deficit measures that arise from comparing all revenue to all spending, including interest payments, entitlements, emergency fund and capital fund deposits, and countercyclical spending.

$$\text{RTOTSP}_t = \text{DSP}_t + \text{SSSP}_t + \text{MEDSPA}_t + \text{RINT}_t + \text{KDEP}_t + \text{NEDEP}_t \qquad (10.\text{A}.2)$$

Where:

RTOTSP = simulation-revised total spending
INT = simulation-revised interest on the national debt
SSSP = Social Security spending
MEDSPA = Medicare Part A spending
KDEP = deposit into investment fund

$$\text{NEDEP} = \text{IF}\left(\begin{array}{l} ((\text{EDEPR}_t \times \text{DSP}_t) + \text{EBAL}_{t-1} - \text{EMERG}_t) > \text{ECAP}_t, \\ \text{ECAP}_t - \text{EBAL}_t + \text{EMERG}_t - \text{EINT}_t, (\text{EDEPR}_t \times \text{DSP}_t) \\ + \text{EINT}_t \end{array}\right)$$

EDEPR = cap on emergency fund deposit rate
EDEPR = emergency fund deposit rate (percent of general fund spending)
EMERG = emergency fund spending
ECAP = emergency fund account balance cap
EINT = interest paid to/by emergency fund

$$RGDP_t = ((RGDP_{t-1} + GDPA_t - GDPA_{t-1}) \times (RMTR \times (FEDTBURD_{t-1}$$
$$- FEDTBURD_{t-2}))) + (OCR \times (RREV_{t-1} - TOTSP_{t-1})) \qquad (10.A.3)$$

Where:

RGDP = Simulation-revised GDP

GDPA = Actual GDP

RMTR = Growth Acceleration Coefficient for Federal Tax Burden

FEDTBURD = federal tax burden, measured as revenue/GDP.

OCR = growth opportunity cost rate for diversion of resources from private-sector to public-sector use.

$RREV = RGFREV_t + RSSMEDREV_t$

RGFREV = Simulation-revised General Fund Revenue

RSSMEDREV = Simulation-revised Medicare Part A Revenue

DEBT REDUCTION WITHOUT HIGHER TAXES: GRADUAL PRIVATIZATION OF FEDERAL MINERAL ASSETS

NICK LORIS

Policymakers will not solve America's fiscal crisis without meaningful structural reforms that address the major contributors to the federal government's unsustainable spending. Reining in excessive spending and fixing entitlement programs are essential to getting the country's fiscal house in order. However, policy reforms in other areas could generate revenue to help pay down the debt without raising taxes. One example is the sale of mineral assets beneath U.S.-owned lands and waters.

Increasing production on federal lands and in America's territorial waters on the Outer Continental Shelf would raise revenues from bonus bids for new leases, royalties, and rents. Most of the natural resource value on federal lands and waters consists of coal, oil, natural gas, and natural gas liquids. The money collected from onshore and offshore mineral leasing is already one of the largest sources of nontax revenue for the federal government. According to the Government Accountability Office, the federal government has collected royalties from leasing the rights to extract more than 70 different minerals.[1] Renewable energy projects on federal lands also generate revenue for the Treasury. The royalties collected from mineral production on federal land and offshore are split among the general Treasury, state governments, and other federal programs like the Reclamation Fund and the Land and Water Conservation Fund.[2]

With plentiful reserves of coal, natural gas, uranium, and oil, the United States is literally the land of opportunity. America has an abundance of natural resources, including sufficient energy reserves to provide Americans with affordable, reliable energy for several centuries. Pundits and energy experts sometimes call America "the Saudi Arabia of coal."

In effect the United States is also the Saudi Arabia of oil and the Russia of natural gas. For more than a decade, the United States has been the world's largest natural gas producer. Last year, energy companies operating in America produced more natural gas than did the entire Middle East.[3] In a few short years, the United States will likely become the world's largest exporter of liquefied natural gas.

And, according to a report from the federal government's Energy Information Administration in September 2018, U.S. crude oil production surpassed that of Saudi Arabia and Russia.[4] Human ingenuity, technological innovation, and the power of the free market have proved the predictors of imminent resource exhaustion to be dead wrong.

The energy boom has produced astounding economic benefits and put money back into the wallets of American families.[5] It has created more opportunities for people directly associated with extraction, including data scientists, engineers, and geologists. Moreover, it has provided more employment opportunities for local businesses near extraction sites, such as hardware stores, hotels, laundromats, and restaurants. Even for businesses not directly or indirectly associated with energy production, cheaper energy has lowered the cost of doing business. Nearly every business in the United States uses energy as an input cost for its product, even if it is as simple as paying the electricity bill or filling up a vehicle with gasoline or diesel to transport goods. Cheaper energy means companies across the country incur lower operational costs and therefore have more resources to invest in labor and capital. Chemical companies are investing heavily in the United States, citing the affordable and abundant natural gas as their motivation. The American Chemistry Council reports that, as of September 2018, the industry is cumulatively investing over $200 billion on 333 projects in the United States.[6]

The story of America's energy renaissance is even more amazing given that federal energy policy actively hindered it as it was taking place. U.S. energy companies and energy consumers are fortunate that much of the shale oil and shale gas deposits in the United States lie beneath state and privately owned lands. Federally owned lands are also full of energy potential, but a bureaucratic regulatory regime has mismanaged land use for decades.

Not only has this regulatory regime led to lost economic opportunity, but federal and state governments are missing a significant revenue generator as well. Providing access for exploration and creating an efficient regulatory process that allows energy projects to move forward in a timely manner will increase revenue through more royalties, leases, and rent; and it will create jobs and help lower energy prices. More economic activity in these areas—for instance, through higher demand for hotel space, restaurants, or trips to Walmart—will generate additional revenues.

The goal for policymakers for energy production on federal lands and waters should not be maximizing revenue but instead creating a framework that relies on price signals. The ever-changing dynamics of energy markets and energy prices make it difficult to know just how much money the Treasury could collect from mineral extraction on federal lands and waters. Nevertheless, estimating the amount of natural resources that lie beneath federal soil and off America's coasts and examining trends in production will present a better picture. Knowing these resources exist is only a small part of the story. Overcoming policy, regulatory, and economic obstacles is the bigger battle. Winning in the court of public opinion will also be critical. Ultimately, creating a framework that minimizes the federal government's role in energy production will help the federal government generate the most revenue.

AN ESTIMATE OF RESOURCES AND HISTORICAL TRENDS

The federal estate is massive, consisting of some 635–640 million acres and hundreds of millions of subsurface and offshore mineral rights.

Within the Department of the Interior (DOI), the Bureau of Land Management manages about 700 million subsurface acres located primarily in 12 western states.[7] Offshore, the U.S. Outer Continental Shelf (OCS) is 2.3 billion acres.[8]

Onshore and offshore, these areas are incredibly resource rich. The DOI's Bureau of Ocean Energy Management estimates OCS resources to include 89.82 billion barrels of oil and 327.42 trillion cubic feet of natural gas.[9] And according to the Institute for Energy Research highlights, other federal assets beneath the ground include 10.4 billion barrels of oil and 8.6 trillion cubic feet of natural gas in the Arctic National Wildlife Refuge; 896 million barrels of oil and 53 trillion cubic feet of natural gas in the National Petroleum Reserve–Alaska; 982 billion barrels of oil shale in the Green River Formation in Colorado, Utah, and Wyoming; and 957 billion short tons of coal in the lower 48 states.[10] As indicated in Figure 11.1, most resources on federal lands are in the western United States.

A 2012 study from the Congressional Budget Office (CBO) estimates that immediately opening federal areas to oil and gas leasing could generate $150 billion in government proceeds over a 10-year period.[11] Other economic analyses look at the dynamic effects of increased energy production for coal, oil, and natural gas on federal lands, which would add revenues from royalties, bonus bids, and rents, as well as higher tax revenues from increased economic activity. A study commissioned by the Institute for Energy Research in 2015 projects that the federal government would collect $3.9 trillion in proceeds over a 37-year period.[12] A 2017 study by the Committee to Unleash Prosperity projects $3 trillion in government revenues over the next 25 years.[13]

Of course these estimates should be taken with a grain of salt. Estimating the amount of money the federal government would generate from maximizing energy extraction on federal lands is tricky business. Royalties make up a large percentage of the revenue collected by the federal government. In fiscal year (FY) 2016, royalties made up 86 percent of the revenue collected from energy production on federal land. Over half of the total revenue came from crude oil royalties alone. Because the royalty revenue changes depending on the amount of the resource

FIGURE 11.1

Public lands, onshore federal and Indian minerals in lands of the United States (responsibilities of Bureau of Land Management [BLM], lower 48 states)

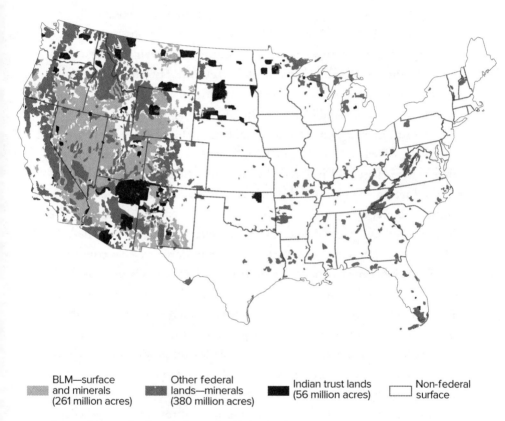

BLM—surface and minerals (261 million acres)

Other federal lands—minerals (380 million acres)

Indian trust lands (56 million acres)

Non-federal surface

Source: Institute for Energy Research, "Federal Assets above and below Ground," January 17, 2013.

Notes: Of the approximately 700 million acres of federal mineral estate, about 166 million acres have been withdrawn from mineral entry, leasing, and sale, except for valid existing rights. Salable minerals such as sand and gravel basically are the responsibility of each federal surface management agency. The map depicts only Indian reservations at least 23,000 acres in size, not all Indian trust lands.

produced and the value of the resource, the money collected by federal and state governments can change rapidly and unpredictably.

For instance, the revenues generated from coal, oil, natural gas, and hydrocarbon gas liquids and renewables was nearly $6 billion in FY 16.[14] When oil prices were higher, in FY 13, the federal government collected more than $14 billion. One could look at price projections and resource production 10, 20, or 50 years into the future. But given the unpredictability of the supply and demand of energy, the fast-changing nature of technological innovation, and the uncertainty of global economic growth, any results would be exceedingly unreliable.

Examining energy production trends over the past decade provides a snapshot of where we are today and, if the status quo remains the same, where we could be headed in the near future. Several trends in the production of coal, oil, and natural gas on federal lands are worth noting. Production of coal decreased by a little over 161 million tons, for a decrease of 33.1 percent since 2008. A slight uptick occurred in 2017 as U.S. coal exports made up for the decline in domestic coal consumption.[15] Production of natural gas (measured in thousands of cubic feet, or Mcf) decreased by about 2 billion Mcf, for a decrease of 31.6 percent. However, production of oil on federal lands increased by 261 million barrels, for a robust increase of 47.4 percent. Although the Trump administration has made more areas available for oil production, much of the increase over the past few years has been a response to changes in price, not policy.[16]

Since 2008, revenue from extracting natural resources from federal lands has declined steadily (See Figure 11.2). Revenue from coal decreased by almost $584 million, or 51.1 percent. Revenue from natural gas liquids decreased by about $320 million, or 58.4 percent. Despite increases in production, low oil prices caused revenues to decline in recent years before climbing back to 2008 levels in 2018. And revenue from gas on federal lands dropped by about $1.5 billion, or 27.3 percent.

Price alone does not dictate energy production on federal lands. A number of policy-based and regulatory obstacles prevent energy producers from leveraging America's energy abundance. These obstacles include the

FIGURE 11.2

Revenues for energy sources

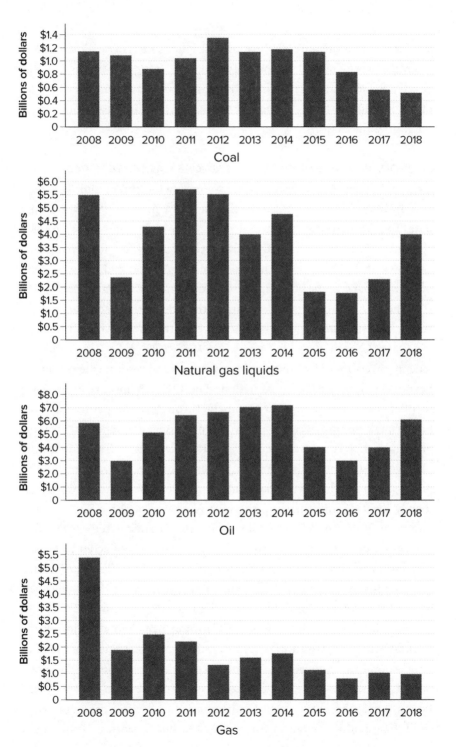

Source: U.S. Department of Interior, "Natural Resources Revenue Data," www.revenuedata
.doi.gov/explore/#federal-revenue.

laws that guide offshore drilling, which ignore market realities; federal micromanagement and inflexibility; treating energy as if it is a public good; a federal bureaucracy that adds costs and delays; and the difficulty of predicting the future of energy markets. I examine each of these in the following sections.

LAWS GUIDING OFFSHORE DRILLING IGNORE MARKET REALITIES

Extracting energy in U.S. territorial waters is a multistep, multiyear process. In 1953, Congress passed the Submerged Lands Act (SLA), granting states the rights to certain natural resources—including oil, gas, minerals, and seafood, as well as other marine and plant life—for three nautical miles off the coast.[17] For historical reasons, Texas and the west coast of Florida have ownership rights extending nine nautical miles.[18] Title II of the SLA not only grants the states the title to the resources but also authorizes the states to manage and develop them. Also passed in 1953, the Outer Continental Shelf Lands Act (OCSLA) (Title III) established federal government jurisdiction over minerals and resource development beyond the limit of state jurisdiction. The OCSLA authorizes the DOI to offer leases for energy development through a competitive auction process, taking into account environmental concerns, state and local input, and other "national needs."[19] DOI implements a five-year leasing plan which stipulates which areas are open to resource development. The process is comprehensive and includes multiple public comment periods; merely drafting and finalizing the plan is a two- or three-year process. Passed in 2006, the Gulf of Mexico Energy Security Act (GOMESA) allocates a portion of the offshore royalty revenues collected to coastal restoration and protection and stipulates that Louisiana, Texas, Alabama, and Mississippi receive 37.5 percent of all qualified offshore revenues. The GOMESA also prohibits oil and gas leasing within 125 miles of the Florida coastline in the Eastern Planning Area and a section of the Central Planning Area until 2022. Because the development of the five-year program is comprehensive and includes multiple public comment periods, merely drafting and finalizing the plan takes two to three years. For instance, the most recent finalized offshore leasing program under the Obama administration for 2017–2022 began with a Request for

Information in June 2014; former Interior Secretary Sally Jewell approved the program in January 2017.[20] Mineral and natural resource extraction is a time-consuming and capital-intensive operation. A company must win the lease sale or acquire the mineral rights, obtain the permits, conduct seismic surveys, build the necessary infrastructure, and drill and case the well. The entire process can take multiple years, and the oil and gas industry makes investments considering multiple time horizons. The current five-year planning process is not set up to match the way commercial energy investments should be (let alone *are*) determined.

The federal government's current policy disregards how markets function; it takes a static approach to dynamic energy markets. These markets are exceedingly complex, and prices play a critical role by efficiently allocating resources to their highest-valued use. Investment decisions change as prices change. Oil prices can fluctuate significantly from one month to the next, and still more over a five-year window. For example, after adjusting for inflation:

- In 2007–2008, the price of oil increased from $66 per barrel to $94 per barrel.
- In 2008–2009, the price dropped to $56 dollars per barrel, then increased to $74 per barrel in 2009–2010.
- In 2011–2013, the price rose above $94 per barrel.
- In 2014–2015, the price decreased from $87 per barrel to $44 per barrel.
- By 2016, significant increases in supply and less-than-projected demand pushed the price down to $38 per barrel.[21]

Energy companies need to plan for both the near and the long term. They should be allowed to respond more efficiently to price fluctuations rather than waiting on a lengthy planning process and specific lease-sale schedule. The federal government should conduct lease sales if commercial interest exists and the sales do not jeopardize national security.

Productively, the Trump administration is acting to open areas previously off-limits to oil and gas exploration, which could generate significant revenues for the Treasury. In January 2018, the Department of

Interior issued its draft National Outer Continental Shelf Oil and Gas Leasing Program for 2019–2024.[22]

The proposal lists 47 potential lease sales off the coasts of Alaska and in the Pacific, the Atlantic, and the Gulf of Mexico. It would make more than 90 percent of the total federal acreage available for exploration and development.[23] As Katherine MacGregor, principal deputy assistant secretary for Land and Minerals Management, said at the time, "This proposed plan shows our commitment to a vibrant offshore energy economy that supports the thousands of men and women working in the offshore energy industry, from supply vessels to rig crews."[24] While not all areas will be in the final plan, opening new areas to offshore development will result in more energy, more jobs, and consequently more revenues for the federal government.

COLORADO ILLUSTRATES FEDERAL MICROMANAGEMENT AND INFLEXIBILITY

On land, federal ownership and control result in the same static approach to dynamic energy markets that occur offshore. A recent oil and natural gas discovery in Colorado illustrates the inflexibility and other problems due to federal management.

In June 2015, the U.S. Geological Survey (USGS) discovered that Colorado has 40 times more technically recoverable natural gas resources than previously estimated. The discovery makes Colorado's Mancos Shale in the Piceance Basin the second-largest known shale reserve in the country (after Pennsylvania), assessed by the USGS with more than 66 trillion cubic feet of gas, 74 million barrels of shale oil, and 45 million barrels of natural gas liquids.[25] Previously, the USGS had estimated that the area held only 1.6 trillion cubic feet of technically recoverable natural gas and provided no estimates for oil.[26] Yet these vast resources are not reflected in recent federal land-management plans for the region, which could be in effect for over a decade.

Though the economic potential for Colorado's natural resources is great, federal bureaucracy stifles development by drastically curtailing where and how companies can access oil and gas resources in the Colorado Mancos Shale region. Much of the Mancos Shale falls under lands managed by the U.S. Forest Service (FS, under the Department of Agriculture), which collaborates with the Bureau of Land Management (BLM, under the DOI) to manage oil and gas resources. The FS defines the lands available and the conditions for oil and gas development (among other uses) in management plans. The BLM then conducts and administers leases. Such plans generally govern resource management for 15 to 20 years.

In December 2015, the FS finalized its resource management plan for new leases in the White River National Forest, one of several in the Mancos Shale region. The plan significantly restricts the land that is available for resource development. Of the 2.3 million acres, the FS makes only 194,100 acres accessible for oil and gas extraction.[27] This acreage is half the amount that was available under the previous plan, finalized in 1993, and just over 8 percent of the total available acreage. On the basis of this plan, the BLM published a final environmental impact statement in August 2016, canceling 25 of the 65 already-existing leases on that land; the remaining leases will be modified to meet the FS's requirements for new leases.[28]

In the December 2015 plan, Forest Manager Scott Fitzwilliams wrote, "If new information or technological advances show the need to revisit this decision, I have the authority to do so. But at this time, I have decided to take a more conservation-minded approach to future gas leasing in the White River National Forest."[29] Since then, the USGS has announced its discovery of 40 times more technically recoverable natural gas than previously estimated. Taking that second look is exactly what some members of Congress are asking the BLM to do for existing leases there.[30] The same should be done elsewhere. There are 69 trillion cubic feet of proved natural gas reserves on federal (onshore) lands and 5.3 billion barrels of proved oil reserves on federal (onshore) lands.[31] Yet the Obama administration restricted access to these resources both directly (as in the case of the White River National Forest) and indirectly (via lease auction, moratoriums, and permit delays).[32]

Because land owned by the federal government is abundant and diverse, grazers, farmers, tourists, hunters, and other individuals and groups have an interest in how federal agencies manage the White River National

Forest and other federal lands like it. For that reason, Congress passed multiple land-use laws to guide federal agencies. The Multiple Use and Sustained Yield Act, the National Forest Management Act for the FS, and the Federal Land Policy and Management Act (FLPMA) for BLM are some of the principal guides for agencies on multiple land use. In practice, however, political agendas and bureaucratic priorities often cast interested parties to the side, limiting (in some instances prohibiting) certain economic activity, such as energy development.

For example, the parameters established in the FLPMA for multiuse land, sustained yield, and environmental protection guide the BLM's approach to land management.[33] Though these parameters may sound accommodating to all interested parties, each entails value choices that communities might prioritize and define differently than the federal government. The federal government is not in a good position to discern how these parameters ought to be applied on the ground and in a variety of communities. Nor should that be its role.

The Colorado example is just one of many that illustrate the federal government's ill-fitting management. The FS's White River resource management plan is a static approach to an otherwise dynamic environment and industry, as the USGS discovery months later showed. It offers a misguided notion of environmental stewardship, presuming that no management is good management and "keeping it in the ground" is the best way to protect the environment. Rather than accommodating multiple uses, the primary vision guiding the decision—what Fitzwilliams and the FS called "environmentally preferable"—was one allowing "no new leasing."[34] Management alternatives seem to have been measured according to how closely they aligned with this standard of "no use" rather than a standard of multiuse.

Hardly an isolated problem, this particular debate over multiuse land in this area of Colorado has been brewing at least since 2010 when the FS first began publicly reviewing the White Forest management plan.[35] A particularly controversial area is the Thompson Divide, where various groups have protested against further oil and gas leasing, though wells have been operating there since 1947.[36] Executive director of the Thompson Divide Coalition, Zane Kessler, says that "this is about local control and a community's desire to determine its own future" rather than out-right opposition to the oil and gas industry.[37] But federal management of the land neither meaningfully fosters local and state control nor encour-ages more creative solutions at the local level between apparently compet-ing uses for the land. Instead, Sen. Michael Bennet (D-CO) has taken up the issue by introducing the Thompson Divide Withdrawal and Protec-tion Act to prohibit oil and gas resource development.

Similar debates have surfaced around other issues too, such as the Department of the Interior's regulatory scheme for habitat for the greater sage grouse. In this instance, the DOI did not seek meaningful or timely participation from local commissioners in nearby Garfield County, de-spite the extensive local efforts to restore habitat and grouse populations while also accommodating multiuse purposes.[38] Apparently, though, national environmental groups that agreed with the DOI's approach did receive greater access to federal decisionmakers.

These examples illustrate the larger systemic problem of federal land management and multiuse land strategy. Local land-use issues, and un-doubtedly highly contentious ones, should not need to wait for the U.S. Congress or a federal agency to weigh multiple choices. Federalizing land management instantly politicizes decisions on a national level. Col-orado has 9 representatives and senators, and yet 526 other members of Congress and the Department of the Interior have a say in how federal land is used there. Unsurprisingly, larger political battles muddy local is-sues and concerns. Too often, Congress forces decisions through "must pass" legislation, such as omnibus spending bills, rather than considering land-use issues on their own merits.[39] And the president can unilaterally designate land as a national monument without input from Congress or states, adding more land-use restrictions in the process.[40]

This Washington-centric approach to management stifles creative, collaborative solutions to competing interests that could be resolved at local, state, or regional levels without the baggage of national po-litical battles and federal regulatory processes. While states and local communities may not always make perfect decisions, the best envi-ronmental policies are site-specific and situation-specific and emanate from liberty.[41]

THE PROBLEM WITH TREATING ENERGY AS IF IT IS A PUBLIC GOOD

Oil and gas production are booming in some regions of the United States, while the rate of production in others has slowed or even decreased. The divergent trajectories in production primarily boil down to one word: ownership. Much of the growth is occurring on private and state-owned lands. Despite the abundance of oil and gas beneath federal lands and off America's coasts, oil and gas output on federally owned lands has been mostly stagnant or declining. Companies operating in the United States have been the world's largest producers of oil and natural gas for six years; as a result, the nation is reaping the tremendous economic benefits that such large-scale production generates. This success emerged organically from innovation in the private marketplace to unlock energy resources formerly thought inaccessible rather than from any specific government policy to promote these technologies and processes.

The OCSLA, Congress's declaration of policy, states that the Outer Continental Shelf is a "vital national resource reserve held by the Federal Government for the public, which should be made available for expeditious and orderly development, subject to environmental safeguards, in a manner which is consistent with the maintenance of competition and other national needs."[42] The phrase "held by the Federal Government for the public" is the crux of the matter: The federal government should not hold mineral rights for the public.

The establishment of national needs, national interest, or public interest determinations is broadly problematic for energy development and projects. Decisions that should be left to the private sector and guided by price signals are instead left to the federal government. For instance, national and public interest determinations have been manipulated into pretexts to obstruct energy development and energy infrastructure.[43]

Unlike air or national security, minerals are not a public good. Public goods are nonrival and nonexcludable. A nonrival good can be consumed by an additional consumer at extremely low rates of marginal cost. Nonexcludable goods are goods that people cannot be easily prevented from consuming. The energy that people use to light their schools, heat their homes, and move their vehicles is rival and excludable. For example, Katie cannot have access to gasoline unless she pays for it.

Moreover, when Katie purchases a gallon of gas, that gallon cannot be simultaneously consumed by another consumer. Natural resources like oil and natural gas are privately produced and privately consumed.[44] Just as the federal government does not make public or national interest determinations for the clothes its citizens purchase, neither should it do so for the energy they produce and consume.

Another serious problem with public interest and national interest determinations is that they concentrate decisions in the hands of government officials and regulators. No concrete definitions exist for national or public interest determinations, so these determinations are inherently subjective. As free-market environmentalist Jane S. Shaw writes in discussing public choice theory, "Although people acting in the political marketplace have some concern for others, their main motive, whether they are voters, politicians, lobbyists, or bureaucrats, is self-interest."[45] In other words, government officials are people, too.

For example, the Natural Gas Act empowers the federal government to reject the export or import of natural gas to or from non–free trade agreement countries if that import or export is not "consistent with the public interest."[46] However, the law never specifies what criteria should be considered when addressing the public interest. The U.S. Department of State contends with similar opaqueness for the national interest determination when deciding on cross-border pipelines. Moreover, the OCSLA gives no outline or detail for what the DOI should consider as "national needs."

The vagueness of these considerations allows government officials to make decisions that properly belong to companies in the private sector. Rather than meeting objective criteria, these determinations empower regulators to arbitrarily make determinations for the rest of the nation. Government officials will not always make determinations on whether to develop resources in accordance with the public interest or even objective, transparent science; instead, they may base them on their own subjective values.

The Obama administration's revised 2017–2022 leasing plan is evidence of such subjectivity. Private actors incentivized by the profit motive will know much better than regulators in Washington where, when, and why drilling should take place. That does not preclude the need for an environmental review and permitting process, or consideration of national security impacts, but the permitting process should not be embedded in a five-year planning process that outlines where companies may produce energy in accord with a subjective, extremely vague public interest determination.[47]

A FEDERAL BUREAUCRACY THAT ADDS COSTS AND DELAYS

The fundamental issue is that federal ownership and control of minerals offshore (and onshore) has taken decision rights away from states. Both economically and environmentally, states have proved they can manage energy development prudently. For example, where states have authority over applications for permits to drill and conduct environmental reviews, oil and gas production has soared.[48] Energy companies have capitalized on the wealth of resources on private- and state-owned lands.[49] Most shale oil and shale gas—from which much of the domestic production is coming—is not under federal control, and the energy industry and consumers alike have benefited as a result.[50]

However, federal regulations and federal landownership have rendered vast quantities of recoverable oil and natural gas onshore and offshore either inaccessible or more costly to extract.[51] Permitting energy extraction on federally owned land will result in more oil and gas extraction and create jobs in areas that may not otherwise see such economic growth. On average, the federal processing of an application for a permit to drill (APD) in FY 16 was 257 days, while state processing is typically 30 days or less.[52] The statute actually requires the Bureau of Land Management to process APDs in 30 days, but that requirement has been routinely ignored, and the process bogs down with regulatory red tape.

In response to President Trump's Executive Order 13783, Promoting Energy Independence and Economic Growth, the Department of the Interior published a report that analyzes the regulations that burden domestic energy.[53] DOI Secretarial Order no. 3354 calls for solutions to streamline the process for onshore and offshore permitting. Former DOI secretary Ryan Zinke said in July 2017, "Oil and gas production on federal lands is an important source of revenue and job growth in rural America, but it is hard to envision increased investment on federal lands when a federal permit can take the better part of a year or more in some cases. This is why I'm directing the BLM to conduct quarterly lease sales and address these permitting issues. We are also looking at opportunities to bring support to our front line offices who are facing the brunt of this workload."[54]

In January 2017, the BLM had more than 2,800 APDs pending. The DOI's commitment to streamlining the process and permitting new projects while maintaining strong environmental protections will produce more oil and gas on federal lands. A better process will incentivize more companies to take interest in energy production on federal lands, which will likely result in higher bonus bids and more royalty revenues coming into federal coffers.

THE DIFFICULTY OF PREDICTING THE FUTURE OF ENERGY MARKETS

Trying to predict the future value of minerals beneath federal lands and in the Outer Continental Shelf is a fool's errand. Prices and policies change. What could be a valuable untapped resource today may be relatively worthless 30 years from now. Or the resource could be even more valuable. Coal is a good example. With more than 480 billion short tons of coal recoverable with today's technology, the United States can provide electricity for more than 500 years at current consumption rates. How much of that coal will eventually be consumed is anyone's guess. Cheap natural gas and cheaper, subsidized renewables are replacing coal as an electricity-generating source. Environmental and climate regulations have forced several coal-fired power plants into early retirement. However, as we've seen in the energy sector throughout history, prices change, businesses innovate, and technology improves.

New, cleaner-burning coal-fired power plants and innovative smaller coal plants could compete with other energy sources in the future. Coal exports have grown and could continue to do so as both developed and developing countries around the world are continuing to consume coal and planning to use much more in the future. State and local opposition to new coal export terminals could thwart some of that growth. So, in the short term, we don't know what's going to happen. Policymakers should not implement policy based on what well-experienced lobbyists and so-called experts predict. That's how we end up with market-distorting energy policies that hurt Americans—as energy consumers and as tax-payers. Many of the harmful energy policies we have today were built on predictions about running out of oil or some new technology that would emerge with help from the American taxpayer. We have energy conser-vation mandates on cars and appliances. We mandate blending corn into our fuel supply even though it is costly and has unintended consequences for the environment and food prices. We've spent billions of dollars try-ing to push uneconomical technologies into the market.

The economic pain cuts deeper than just wasted taxpayer money because government interventions distort free enterprise, create govern-ment dependence, and allow Washington to direct the flow of private-sector investments. The number of investment opportunities is broad and expansive, but the available capital is limited. Of course investors must choose among the different projects, but government favoritism diverts limited capital. It dictates who should receive the capital by extending the confidence of the government through a subsidy to a politically favored technology or company. For instance, private investors sank $1.1 billion into Solyndra, a solar energy start-up. Much of the private financing came after the Department of Energy announced that Solyndra was one of 16 companies eligible for a loan guarantee in 2007. That $1.1 billion could have been invested elsewhere in the economy. Solyndra's well-known bankruptcy indicates that it certainly should have been.[55]

Conventional resources such as coal, oil, and natural gas currently provide about 80 percent of America's energy needs and 80 percent of the world's energy needs. That could change as nuclear and renewables outcompete these fuels, or conventional resources could continue to supply around 75 percent of our energy for the next half century. Price signals should determine what sources provide households and busi-nesses with the most dependable energy at the most competitive price.

Prices, after all, communicate information to energy producers and to energy users. Higher prices for oil incentivize companies to extract and supply more. They also incentivize entrepreneurs to invest in innovative alternatives to oil, whether batteries, natural gas vehicles, or biofuels. Drivers will examine their consumption options as well, whether carpooling, finding alternative modes of transportation, or, over time, purchasing a more fuel-efficient vehicle. The role of policymakers should be to open access to these resources, eliminate regulations that are devoid of any meaningful benefit, and establish a permitting process that allows energy producers to respond to the price signals in the marketplace.

SOLUTIONS

Simply having a fire sale of the minerals on federal estates is unrealistic and unlikely to produce the desired outcome of generating substantial revenues. Doing so could significantly reduce the price of the minerals or, conversely, might not produce much interest at all. Some areas might generate significant value, for example, any of the federal holdings in the Permian Basin in western Texas and southeastern New Mexico. Others might generate little or no interest, as with the DOI's offshore lease sale in the Gulf of Mexico. In March 2018, the DOI offered up the largest offshore lease sale in history with discounted royalties to attract bidders. Though the auction produced $124.76 million in winning bids, companies bid on only 1 percent of the acreage, far less than what the DOI had envisioned.[56] An outright fire sale of minerals would generate less interest if a minimum bid was set. Removing the minimum bid and allowing companies to buy the minerals outright would do little in terms of generating serious revenues. It would be a one-time, underpriced injection into the Treasury.

Instead, Congress and the executive branch should take a number of actions to maximize the potential value of energy resources on federal lands and waters. Several important steps are involved.

COLLECT BETTER ESTIMATES OF RESOURCE POTENTIAL ON FEDERAL LANDS AND WATERS

One way to boost interest in mineral production is with up-to-date information on the resource potential beneath federal soil and U.S. territorial waters. Many resource estimates are long out of date. More accurate information will better inform companies as to whether it makes sense to drill exploratory wells and commit labor and capital to certain geographic areas.

Myron Ebell, a director at the Competitive Enterprise Institute, testified before the House Natural Resources Committee and underscored the need to have accurate estimates of resource potential:

> Much of the data comes from geologic studies that are one, two, or even three decades old, and the assessment is thus based on outdated technology and scientific understanding that has been superseded by subsequent research. A comprehensive survey based on current geological knowledge and using up-to-date techniques, including seismic testing, is long overdue.
>
> When similar geological surveys have been proposed in the past, they have never gotten started in the face of objections that they will cost too much and take too long. Undoubtedly, the same objections will be raised again in an effort to remove this provision from the bill. In my view, the objections of time and money are real, but are far outweighed by the value of having much better information about the extent and location of America's offshore energy resources. Incomplete and inadequate knowledge of federally-controlled resources is not of course restricted to offshore resource[s] and regularly contributes to poor management decisions by the federal land agencies on a wide variety of issues.[57]

As with energy production on private and state-owned lands, knowledge of resource estimates can change quickly. Many of the past and even current estimates likely underestimate America's energy wealth because they fail to keep up with technological advancements that have led to the discovery of new resources. In fact, innovative companies have squashed exaggerated claims of looming resource exhaustion.

Allen Gilmer, cofounder and executive chair of Drillinginfo (an oil and gas analytics firm now called Enverus), recently called the Permian Basin "a permanent resource." Gilmer remarked, "The research we've done indicates that we have at least half a trillion barrels in the Permian at reasonable economics, and it could be as high as 2 trillion barrels. That is, as a practical matter, an infinite amount of resource."[58] The

Bureau of Land Management's September 2018 Permian Basin oil and gas lease auction in New Mexico fetched nearly $1 billion in bonus bids, and unexplored parcels of land went for more than $95,000 an acre.[59] This sale set a record for BLM in part because the resource quantities that exist in the Permian Basin are known. Better access to information and a streamlined environmental review and permitting process that empowers industry to respond more efficiently to market signals could yield similar benefits elsewhere onshore and offshore.

EMPOWER STATE GOVERNMENTS, AND CREATE EFFICIENT REGULATORY PROCESSES

Proposed legislation, the Federal Lands Freedom Act, would give states the authority to administer leasing, permitting, and regulatory programs for development of all energy resources on federal lands. (The bill excludes Indian lands, national parks, and congressionally designated wilderness areas.) States are already well-positioned to help transition to better management of these resources. Under the Federal Lands Freedom Act, states would be able to develop a regulatory program for energy development on federal lands and submit the program to the departments of the Interior, Energy, and Agriculture. This provision would replace redundant federal requirements, such as the National Environmental Policy Act.

State control, local governance, and private-sector participation would result in more accountable, effective management. While the federal government can simply shift the costs of mismanagement to federal taxpayers, states have powerful incentives to better manage resources on federal lands. State governments can be more accountable to the people who will directly benefit from wise management decisions, especially as they pertain to natural resource management.

Much of the shale oil and shale gas deposits in the United States lie beneath state and privately owned lands, and an important reason for the rapid increase in production has been an efficient permitting process in those settings. Ohio requires that permits be processed within 21 days and expedited permits within 7 days. Other states have similarly short time frames: Texas's average is 4 days (and for expedited permits, 2 days).

Even in California, a permit must be processed within 10 days; if it is not, it is automatically approved.

According to a 2015 Property and Environment Research Council report, "On average, states generate more revenue per dollar spent than the federal government on a variety of land management activities, including timber, grazing, minerals, and recreation."[60]

Moreover, incentives to invest in and steward the environment are stronger when people have direct ownership and responsibility.[61] BLM and FS lands lost $4.38 per acre from 2009–2013, while trust lands in four western states earned $34.60 per acre. Simply in terms of recreation, states do a better job of making a return on their investment. Idaho and Montana averaged $6.86 per dollar spent on recreation on state trust lands; in contrast, the BLM earned $0.20 and the FS $0.28 per dollar spent, resulting in a net loss.[62]

Transferring decision rights to states and the private sector could make the energy industry more responsive to price changes. According to a working paper from Utah State University economists:

> Even though 99% of federal drilling permits are eventually approved, bureaucratic delay imposes costs through delay and dampening. Drilling response is slower, and thus wells on federal lands do not respond to high oil and gas prices as quickly as private lands. These delays also lead to lower overall price responses—fewer overall wells drilled in response to price increases. Our findings indicate that the potential for improving the responsiveness of federal lands to price signals could be achieved through a reduction in delay in the BLM permitting process.[63]

While the study examines federal lands, similar logic could apply to federal waters as well. Remedying this situation could compensate states appropriately through expanded royalty revenue collection. With the exception of Alaska, states receive 50 percent of the revenues generated by onshore oil and natural gas production on federal lands.[64] Congress should apply this allocation offshore as well, including current operations in the Gulf of Mexico. If Congress successfully transfers the permitting and environmental review to the states, the states should receive an even larger share of the royalty revenue collected.

Drilling off states' coasts and allowing them a larger share of the royalty revenue would encourage more state involvement in drilling decisions. Offshore drilling would also promote state and local government participation in allocating funds, helping close deficits, enabling coastal restoration and conservation, and providing funds for schools.

Congress should eliminate the five-year plans and authorize the DOI to conduct lease sales if interest for development exists. Lease sales should be offered in consultation with the affected states and would need to meet any Department of Defense requirements. Such a reform would allow the safe development of energy off America's coasts while empowering state stakeholders. Removing the lengthy and unnecessary planning process would create a system that is more responsive to price changes and flexible to the needs and interests of states.

After eliminating the five-year planning process, Congress should overhaul the offshore leasing process by amending the OCSLA and SLA and transferring the environmental review and permitting process to the states. The state regulatory program would replace federal requirements (e.g., from the Clean Air Act and the National Environmental Policy Act). To support their reviews, state regulators could request technical or safety expertise from the Bureau of Ocean Energy Management and the Bureau of Safety and Environmental Enforcement and use previous DOI environmental assessments as a framework. In addition, state regulators could work in conjunction with the Environmental Protection Agency and the U.S. Coast Guard to assess environmental impact and maritime safety and security.

OPEN ENERGY AUCTIONS TO ALL PARTIES

Currently, only energy companies can bid on lease auctions, and the federal government requires leaseholders to demonstrate intent to develop the resources. Restricting who bids and requiring the winner to develop the parcels eliminates competition and fails to assess the relative value of the land. Conservationists, recreationists, alternative energy companies, ranchers, or environmentalists may value the land more for their intended use than do oil and gas developers. As economist Michael Giberson and research fellow Shawn Regan write in their public comment on federal oil and gas royalties, "No method reliably integrates the variety of diverse, predominantly subjective, and sometimes conflicting values into a single, uncontroversial auction reserve price."[65] Opening the leasing process to all interested parties would not only create more competition but also potentially more cooperation. An environmental organization could partner with a grazer to bid on a block of land. An energy company could coordinate with conservationist groups to use the land in ways that ensure both parties benefit. Natural resource extraction would likely still occur, but oil and gas production would occur because the energy companies value the land and resources more than other contending interests do. As values change (e.g., if oil prices rise), buyout programs and lease re-offerings would ensure that competing interests remain involved in current and future land-use decisions. One challenge would be establishing a mechanism to compensate taxpayers for lost royalty revenues; one solution would be for the BLM to assess grazing, recreation, or other land-use fees. Giberson and Regan write:

> In a number of cases private conservation groups have negotiated with parties over specific grazing rights or oil and gas leases on federal lands in an effort to protect environmental values. As long ago as 1992 the Conservation Fund purchased grazing rights in the Glen Canyon National Recreation Area in southern Utah. By 2003, at least a half-dozen conservation and sportsmen organizations had grazing permit buyout programs. In 2012 the Trust for Public Land, a conservation group, worked with a variety of other groups and donors to purchase and retire oil and gas leases representing 58,000 acres in Wyoming's Hoback Basin from Plains Exploration and Production Co.[66]

ANOTHER SOURCE OF FEDERAL REVENUE:
THE STRATEGIC PETROLEUM RESERVE

After the Arab oil embargo and the formation of the Organization of the Petroleum Exporting Countries (OPEC) in the 1970s, the United States and countries around the world felt a need to hold more oil inventories for emergency purposes. The United States joined the International Energy Agency in 1974 to coordinate a multilateral response to oil supply shocks. As part of that commitment, Congress created the Strategic Petroleum Reserve (SPR) the following year. The SPR holds nearly 700 million barrels of crude oil that serve as an emergency stockpile in case of supply shocks that cause price spikes. The intent was to mitigate U.S. economic vulnerability from supply disruptions, not to be a national defense stockpile. However, the SPR has not been used as an effective response to oil price spikes.

The Energy Policy and Conservation Act of 1975 (EPCA), the SPR's enabling legislation, constrains the president's authority to release the reserves; the problem, however, is that the limitations and conditions for SPR drawdowns are not credible justifications for the reserve's existence. Furthermore, the executive branch can interpret the conditions vaguely, making an SPR release more about domestic party politics than policy. For instance, even if drawing down SPR reserves has little market effect, it may help a president politically by creating the perception that the administration is "doing something" about a crisis.

The EPCA requires a presidential finding that a "severe energy supply interruption" exists, and the following conditions must be met:

- "An emergency situation exists and there is a significant reduction in supply which is of significant scope and duration;
- "A severe increase in the price of petroleum products has resulted from such emergency situation; and
- "Such price increase is likely to cause a major adverse impact on the national economy."[67]

Supply disruptions are not reason enough for government stockpiling; they can be addressed through market forces with an abundance of private inventory, not government-controlled resources. Even so, the empirical benefits associated with the government's use of reserves during an alleged emergency are dubious and difficult to accurately assess. Isolating the release's effect on the global oil market is difficult given all the other variables involved.

Some studies have found that SPR releases could lower oil prices as much as 32 percent; however, those studies estimate price impacts from optimal SPR management, not actual effects of SPR releases on global oil prices or SPR releases in practice.[68] Obtaining the optimal price effect would be difficult, argue economists Timothy Considine and Kevin Dowd, because "a more fundamental problem arises from vesting a political entity with the inherently complex task of allocating oil across time and space—a task that is probably best left to market forces."[69]

Considine estimates that a drawdown during a supply shock would have much less impact, lowering prices only 3.5 percent.[70] This is in large part because other countries or private companies holding inventories could increase their own reserves and also because the amount released is marginal compared to the global supply and demand for oil.

University of California, Berkeley economist Reid Stevens drew similar conclusions on SPR's futility using econometric modeling to show that SPR releases have no impact on lowering prices. Stevens measured oil price effects of SPR purchases and withdrawals, testing effects of anticipated and unanticipated purchases of oil for the SPR and sales to the market. Reid found that no matter the certainty, SPR sales did not lower oil prices; however, unanticipated purchases to build up SPR inventory increased oil prices 1.5 percent.[71]

The historical use of reserves in times of unanticipated supply shocks proves this to be true. During the Gulf War, Iraq's invasion of Kuwait took 6.5 percent of the world's oil supply offline, causing prices to jump from $15 per barrel in July of 1990 to $30 in October. As Considine and Dowd outline[s], the lost supply was offset by increases from OPEC, not drawdowns from SPR. President George H. W. Bush did not release reserves from the SPR until the United States' strike on Iraq in January 1991. The price dropped more than $10 per barrel before any SPR crude reached the market.[72]

While some analysts attribute drops in prices to public announcements signaling that more supplies will reach the market, this was not likely the case during the Gulf War. The Congressional Research Service reports that the decreasing crude price was due to other factors:

> Oil analysts attributed the price drop to optimistic reports about the allied forces' crippling Iraqi air power and the diminished likelihood,

despite the outbreak of war, of further jeopardy to world oil supply. There appeared to be no need for the IEA plan and the SPR drawdown to help settle markets, and there was some criticism of it. DOE offered more than 30 million barrels of SPR oil for bid, but only accepted bids on 17.3 million barrels.[73]

One problem for optimal SPR use is the federal government's inability to predict future events and consequently having a slow or late response. If concerns exist, for instance, that conflict overseas will exacerbate supply disruption, the government may hold onto the reserves. If the conflict does not worsen, The Department of Energy (DOE) may not sell SPR reserves quickly enough to mitigate the supply shock. President George W. Bush ordered a quick SPR release during Hurricane Katrina, but the release was ineffective in mitigating price shocks because the refineries and pipelines also closed as a result of the hurricane.

In other instances, the emergency situations in which the executive branch released oil from the SPR have been questionable and controversial. In 2000, in the midst of an election year, the Clinton administration used the SPR for personal political gain. As gas and home heating oil prices rose, Vice President Al Gore, running for president at the time, urged President Bill Clinton to draw down reserves to lower prices.[74] Clinton's own Treasury secretary, Lawrence Summers, criticized the release, saying the SPR should not be used to manipulate market prices and using SPR to do so would "set a dangerous precedent."[75]

President Barack Obama's coordinated release with the International Energy Agency (IEA) in 2011 is another instance when releasing reserves from the SPR did not pass rational or economic muster set by the conditions for drawdowns. Libyan production—which supplies only 2 percent of the world's oil—had been offline for almost three months when the administration released reserves from the SPR. Oil prices were high at the time for reasons that had nothing to do with Libya. Market forces were responding to other factors, in particular, steadily rising global demand, especially from China and India, for the better part of a year. No emergency situation existed, no supply shock occurred, and therefore there was no need for an SPR drawdown.

The ineffective and political manner with which the executive branch has used the SPR should be reason enough for Congress to liquidate the asset. Policymakers should also reconsider why the United States has international commitments to hold reserves given the ability of the private sector to respond to price spikes and the diversity of global energy markets.

America has access to oil for commercial use and national security, through both domestic production and acquisitions abroad. Even if the oil market becomes fractured in the event of a security crisis or a major war, both the global market of suppliers and the channels to distribute oil are highly diversified. Oil reaches its final destination with great fluidity. And if the market becomes segmented because one or more channel is disrupted, the United States will still be in a position to import oil. The route by which that oil reaches its final destination may not be the most efficient if multiple shipping lanes or pipelines are unavailable, but sources much greater and more sustainable than the SPR will still get the oil to U.S. ports.

Liquidation of the SPR would follow the same procedure as other federal sales do now. The DOE issues a Notice of Sale outlining the conditions for the sale, including the quantity available for sale, delivery modes, minimum quantity to be purchased, the federal government's crude oil base reference price and delivery price indexing process, delivery periods, letter-of-credit requirements, and the means of ensuring compliance with existing statutory requirements for selling and transporting petroleum products.[76] DOE establishes a sale price based on the sale of similar crudes in the region; offers have to be at or above 95 percent of the sales price estimate.[77] DOE then takes the highest-priced offers until the entire amount offered is sold. The actual payment to the government is made on an index-price basis.

For example, in a test sale in March 2014, DOE offered 5 million barrels and received 37 bids from 12 companies.[78] DOE's report to Congress notes:

> Under the SPR Standard Sales Provisions (SSPs), SPR oil is sold on an indexed price basis to minimize oil markets risks. A base reference

price of $101.4020 was established by the Government using the average five-day price of Southern Green Canyon (SGC) crude traded prior to the Notice of Sale. The differential between the Offeror's bid price and the Government's base reference price was then used to adjust the buyer's price at the time of delivery. The buyer's final price was computed by applying this differential to the average five day traded SGC price surrounding the buyer's delivery date.[79]

Receipts upward of $468.5 million were deposited into the Treasury with the delivery price of $93.75 per barrel, and DOE completed the delivery over a 47-day period.[80]

Congress should authorize DOE to auction 10 percent of the country's previous month's total crude production. Basing the sales on the previous month's U.S. production would allow Congress to drain the SPR over a two- to three-year time frame and do so without disrupting markets.[81] Congress should then decommission the salt caverns currently used to store the SPR or sell them to the private sector if a commercial interest exists to use the caverns for private inventory.

Congress should explicitly stipulate that all revenues collected from SPR sales go exclusively toward deficit reduction, without reciprocating increased spending. Congress has proposed using temporary SPR sales to pay for increases in other areas, such as funding for the Highway Trust Fund. The recognition that DOE should eliminate the reserve is not an invitation to find ways to spend the revenue.

The U.S. government should also remove itself from any commitment with the IEA to hold reserves, implement demand constraints, coordinate response measures, reduce dependence on foreign oil, and transition to alternative sources of energy. The United States could simply withdraw from the agreement, or it could end its participation in the International Energy Program altogether.[82] Getting rid of the SPR would allow markets to respond to price increases more efficiently than the government can. Government-controlled reserves only distort the actions of the private sector. Private inventories, which may be even higher in the absence of a government-owned stockpile, or which may not respond to a price shock in anticipation of a government release of SPR, would act more efficiently.

CONCLUSION

Simply put, the federal government owns too much land and mineral wealth. Americans would benefit tremendously from greater access to the energy resources on federal lands through lower prices, a healthier economy, and tax revenues to pay down the national debt. In addition, our Strategic Petroleum Reserve should be sold, as it has little economic or national security value. The goal of selling these resources should not be to maximize revenue for the federal government but to empower markets to work efficiently. These policies are best for Americans as energy consumers. Higher proceeds coming into the federal government will be a welcome bonus.

CHAPTER TWELVE

SOCIAL SECURITY AND MEDICARE SPENDING GROWTH: IS IT JUST MORE SENIORS OR MORE PER SENIOR?

JOHN GAREN

Most long-term projections indicate a large increase in the size of federal government spending. For example, in 2018, the Congressional Budget Office projected that federal spending as a share of gross domestic product (GDP) will rise from 20.6 percent in 2018 to 26.9 percent by 2040.[1] This is greatly concerning to many people who worry that the increased role of government in the economy—and the consequent reduction of the private sector—inevitably comes with diminished work and investment incentives, reduced productivity, limited economic growth, and lessened opportunities for individuals to improve their lives.

Over half of the projected increase in federal spending is due to increased spending on Social Security and Medicare.[2] Thus, any discussion of limiting federal spending should address these two programs. This chapter examines two aspects of the projected increases in Social Security and Medicare. One is purely demographic. The baby boom generation has begun to retire and will do so in increasing numbers over the next two decades—thereby driving up spending. The other is the generosity of the benefits paid by the two programs. If benefits are expanding, that also adds to the growth in spending.

The two aspects have different implications for efforts to limit spending. If all of the increase were due to growth in the senior population, setting limits on spending would be more difficult because that would require reducing benefits. However, if a good deal of the increase in spending were due to benefit increases, limiting spending could be accomplished by slowing the growth in benefits or capping benefits at current levels. As described later, both aspects contribute to the growth in spending, so there is room for limiting this growth without actually cutting benefits. Indeed, capping real spending per beneficiary at 2017 levels has substantial effects on the expected path of future spending. Instead of rising to about 12 percent of GDP, it rises to about 9 percent and falls thereafter to a share no larger than today's. However, the methods used to limit spending growth are important. For example, using price controls on services and mandating limits on types of coverage would likely generate shortages, nonprice rationing, and political infighting over what is covered and who is served. These methods of limiting spending growth are highly undesirable.

The rest of this chapter is organized as follows. First, I provide more background and details on the expected spending growth of these programs and on the magnitude of the issue. Second, I describe how spending and spending growth on Social Security and Medicare can be broken into components. These components are the number of seniors—the primary beneficiaries of the spending—as a share of the population, spending per senior, and GDP per capita. Spending per senior is denoted as *absolute generosity* and spending per senior relative to GDP per capita is denoted as *relative generosity*. The latter indicates benefits per senior relative to per capita national income.

Third, I present the data on the forecasted time path of these components. Seniors' share of the population will grow by about one-third by 2040. Additionally, real Social Security and Medicare benefits per senior are forecast to grow as well. However, real GDP per capita is expected to grow a little faster than real Social Security benefits per senior, but slower than real per-senior Medicare benefits. Fourth, I show

FIGURE 12.1

Social Security and Medicare spending as a percentage of GDP

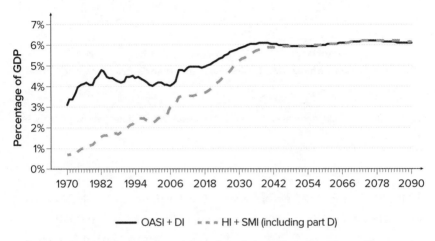

Source: Social Security and Medicare Boards of Trustees, "Status of the Social Security and Medicare Programs: A Summary of the 2018 Annual Reports," 2018, p. 4.

Note: DI = Disability Insurance; GDP = gross domestic product; HI = Hospital Insurance; OASI = Old Age Survivors Insurance; SMI = Supplemental Medical Insurance.

the results of exercises that simulate capping real Social Security and Medicare benefits per senior. Growth in simulated spending still rises for some period because of the growth in the senior population—though by much less than current projections—and spending as a share of GDP eventually declines. Finally, I discuss issues regarding limiting spending on these programs, as well as the pitfalls of price controls and mandated limits on coverage, and then I offer a conclusion.

BACKGROUND

To illustrate the issues addressed in this chapter, Figure 12.1 shows past and forecasted spending on Social Security and Medicare, as percentages of GDP, from 1970 to 2090.[3] Social Security spending, though it rose and fell somewhat erratically until the mid-2000s, has risen substantially over the past 10 years and is forecasted to continue to do so until about

TABLE 12.1

Some federal spending categories as a percentage of GDP, fiscal year 2017

Defense	Nondefense discretionary	Medicaid	Other means-tested	Other mandatory	Net interest	Total
3.1	3.2	2.0	1.7	2.0	1.4	20.8

Source: Office of Management and Budget, "Historical Tables," https://www.whitehouse.gov/omb/historical-tables/.
Note: GDP = gross domestic product.

2040. Medicare spending has been on a sharp, upward trajectory since its inception, and this trajectory is predicted to continue to 2040.

In fiscal years 2017–2040, total Social Security and Medicare spending is expected to rise by roughly 3.5 percent of GDP—from about 8.5 percent to around 12 percent. In raw terms, nominal GDP is predicted to increase by 173 percent between 2017 and 2040. Over the same period, the forecasted growth in nominal Social Security spending is 237 percent and for Medicare it is 338 percent.[4]

The increase in spending of 3.5 percent of GDP for these two programs is quite large. Table 12.1 helps put this in perspective. The table displays several other categories of federal spending as shares of GDP for FY 17.[5] During that year, federal spending on national defense was 3.1 percent of GDP. Spending on nondefense discretionary programs was 3.2 percent of GDP. The increases in Social Security and Medicare just noted are equivalent to adding another Department of Defense or doubling nondefense discretionary expenditures, plus more. Moreover, as shown in Table 12.1, the other major categories of spending fall well short of the 3.5 percent increase for Social Security and Medicare.

The magnitude of the issue is clear. Before considering possible solutions, it is useful to diagnosis sources of the problem. In particular, how much of the predicted increase in Social Security and Medicare spending is simply due to the aging of the population and how much is due to the generosity of the programs?

COMPONENTS OF SPENDING GROWTH

Breaking down into component parts the changes in Social Security and Medicare spending as a share of GDP is a straightforward matter. These parts are the growth in the senior citizen population share, the growth in spending per senior, and the growth in GDP. Equation (12.1) does so formally for Social Security:

$$SS/GDP = [(\text{pop } 65+) / (\text{total pop})]\ ^* \ [(SS/\text{pop } 65+)] / \\ [GDP / (\text{total pop})], \tag{12.1}$$

where SS = Social Security spending; pop 65+ = the population of people age 65 and older; and total pop = total national population.

The first term in square brackets is the share of the nation's population that is age 65 and older, that is, "seniors." The next term in square brackets is Social Security spending per senior. The final square-bracketed term is GDP per capita. The generosity of Social Security can be thought of in two ways. One is the second term: Social Security spending per senior. This translates approximately to Social Security benefits per beneficiary, though not exactly.[6] A second measure is spending per beneficiary relative to GDP per capita. This method measures per senior benefits relative to per person national income. In Equation (12.1), this is the second and third terms combined. The first measure is absolute generosity; the second measure is relative generosity.

Changes in SS/GDP can be written as in Equation (12.2):

$$\%\Delta(SS/GDP) = \%\Delta(\text{senior pop share}) + \%\Delta(\text{benefits per senior}) \\ - \%\Delta(GDP \text{ per capita}), \tag{12.2}$$

where %Δ denotes percent change.

Thus, the percent change in Social Security spending as a share of GDP is the percent change in the senior share of the population plus the percent change in absolute generosity less the percent change in GDP per capita. Alternatively, the percent change in SS/GDP can be broken down into just two components: the percent change in the senior share

FIGURE 12.2

Share of population age 65 and older, 1970–2050

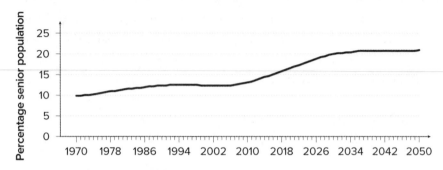

Source: Social Security Administration, "2018 OASDI Trustees Report," Social Security Area Population, Table V.A3, Intermediate Years, 2018.

of the population plus the percent change in relative generosity. This is possible because the change in relative generosity is the final two terms of Equation (12.2). Medicare spending and its growth can be broken down in an analogous way.

MORE SENIORS OR MORE PER SENIOR?

Equation (12.2) makes clear that increases in spending as a share of GDP may arise simply because of the aging of the baby boom generation. Figure 12.2 illustrates the past and forecasted share of the U.S. population age 65 and older.[7] From the mid-1980s to the mid-2000s, this share was fairly stable at just over 12 percent. It then began to grow, and by 2017 it was over 15 percent. It is expected to continue to grow and then stabilize at just under 21 percent by the late 2030s. Thus a great deal of growth in the population age 65 and older is yet to come. Accordingly, at least some part of the growth in Social Security and Medicare results from the simple demographic fact of the aging baby boom.

Now consider the relative generosity of Social Security and Medicare, that is, the benefit per senior relative to GDP per capita: compute real Social Security spending per senior and real Medicare spending per

FIGURE 12.3

Relative generosity: Social Security per senior and Medicare per senior as percentage of GDP per capita

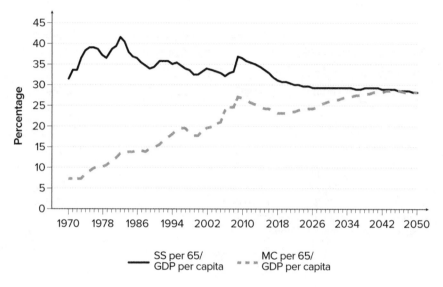

Source: Author's calculations.

Note: GDP = gross domestic product; MC = Medicare; SS = Social Security.

senior, then divide each by real GDP per capita.[8] These computations are made using the GDP price deflator.[9] For values beyond 2017, the computations rely on the Social Security Administration's spending, GDP, and GDP deflator intermediate forecasts. Figure 12.3 depicts the findings. Social Security benefits are the solid black line, and Medicare is in dashed gray.

The relative generosity of Social Security benefits was high and rising in the 1970s and much of the 1980s, then settled into a fairly stable value of just over 30 percent of GDP per capita. That number rose after the Great Recession, largely because of slow growth in GDP per capita at the time. It is forecasted to fall somewhat from the 2017 value of 32 percent and stabilize at around 29 percent of GDP per capita.[10] Thus, relative generosity of Social Security is clearly falling slightly. However, as Table 12.2 shows, absolute generosity is forecast to rise.

TABLE 12.2

Absolute generosity: Social Security and Medicare spending per senior, 2017 and 2040

	2017 (actual)	2040 (estimated)	% change
Social Security spending per senior	$18,715	$24,267	29.66%
Medicare spending per senior	$13,940	$23,443	68.18%
GDP per capita	$58,544	84,094	41.39%
Senior (age 65+) population share	15.36%	20.69%	34.70%

Sources: Social Security Administration, "2018 OASDI Trustees Report," Table VI.G10, 2018; Boards of Trustees, Federal Hospital Insurance and Federal Supplemental Medical Insurance Trust Funds, "2018 Annual Report," 2018.
Note: GDP = gross domestic product.

The situation regarding Medicare is different. From 1970, the program's relative generosity rose substantially from 7.33 percent of per capita GDP to about 24 percent just before the Great Recession. In the years following the Great Recession, these values were elevated due to slow GDP growth. In 2017, relative generosity had returned to its prerecession level of about 24 percent. It is predicted to rise to 28.32 percent by 2040 and stabilize at that level. Thus, increased relative generosity matters a good deal in the expected growth of Medicare spending as a share of GDP.

Regarding absolute generosity, forecasts indicate large increases for both programs. Table 12.2 displays a summary, with real spending per senior in 2017 and estimated real spending in 2040. Although Social Security relative generosity is expected to fall slightly before stabilizing, absolute generosity is expected to rise. As shown in the first row of Table 12.2, spending per senior will rise from $18,715 to $24,257, an increase of nearly 30 percent. The second row shows that Medicare absolute generosity is expected to rise from $13,940 per senior to $23,443, a 68 percent increase. GDP per capita, shown in the third row, is predicted to rise faster than Social Security spending per senior but slower than Medicare spending per senior. This is consistent with the earlier discussion regarding the relative generosity of the programs.

To illustrate each of the components of spending changes, the fourth row of Table 12.2 adds the values for the share of seniors in the population. This share is expected to rise by 35 percent. To summarize, spending on both Social Security and Medicare is driven to some extent by the growth of the population over age 65. For Social Security, higher levels of future spending also are driven by increasing spending per senior. Though Social Security spending per senior is growing, it is growing somewhat slower than the growth of GDP per capita thus reducing its share of GDP. For Medicare, spending per senior is expected to rise and to rise faster than GDP per capita, thus adding to its increase as a share of GDP.

SIMULATIONS: WHAT HAPPENS WITH CAPS ON RELATIVE AND ABSOLUTE GENEROSITY?

This section considers two exercises related to limiting spending on Social Security and Medicare. In particular, one simulates the outcome of capping the relative generosity of the programs at their 2017 levels and the other simulates the outcome of capping absolute generosity. Note that neither involves spending cuts to the beneficiary population. Capping relative generosity implies that per-senior spending relative to GDP per capita remains the same. In fact, this exercise entails increases in spending per senior as it will grow at the same pace as GDP per capita.[11] Capping absolute generosity implies no cuts below (or increases above) the 2017 levels of real spending per senior.

First consider capping relative generosity. For Social Security, this has little effect. Under the status quo, relative generosity falls slightly from now into the future. For this reason, I have not included Social Security in this simulation.

Figure 12.4 shows the simulation for Medicare, with spending per senior fixed at 23.81 percent of GDP per capita—its 2017 value. The solid line in Figure 12.4 shows the forecasted values of Medicare spending as a

FIGURE 12.4

Simulation of Medicare spending as share of GDP: relative generosity capped at 2017 level

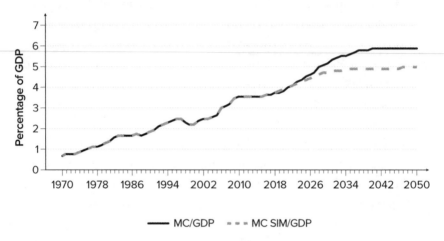

Source: Author's calculations.
Note: GDP = gross domestic product; MC = Medicare; SIM = simulated.

share of GDP, and the dashed line shows the simulated shares. Simulated values begin to diverge from the forecast in a few years. These values stabilize at around 4.9 percent of GDP, which is about one percentage point below the forecast values.

Next consider capping absolute generosity. Figure 12.5 shows the simulations for both Social Security and Medicare, with spending per senior capped, in real terms, at their 2017 levels. For Social Security this is $18,715 per senior, and for Medicare it is $13,940 per senior. As in Figure 12.4, the simulations show the resulting spending as shares of GDP.

In this scenario, substantial effects emerge. Simulated Social Security spending peaks at just over 5 percent of GDP and then falls below 5 percent. This result is in contrast to the Social Security Administration forecast of spending rising to and stabilizing at 6 percent of GDP. Simulated Medicare spending grows but peaks at 3.9 percent of GDP, then begins to fall. The forecast, in contrast, has Medicare spending growing to almost 6 percent of GDP and remaining at that level.

FIGURE 12.5

Simulation of Social Security and Medicare spending as shares of GDP: absolute generosity capped at 2017 levels

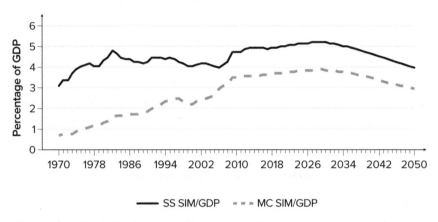

Source: Author's calculations.
Note: GDP = gross domestic product; MC = Medicare; SIM = simulated; SS = Social Security.

FIGURE 12.6

Forecasted and simulated total spending, Social Security and Medicare, as share of GDP: simulated spending with capped absolute generosity at 2017

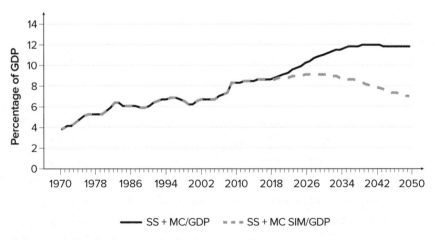

Source: Author's calculations.
Note: GDP = gross domestic product; MC = Medicare; SIM = simulated; SS = Social Security.

Figure 12.6 illustrates the total effect of simulated spending relative to forecasted spending, plotting the total of Social Security and Medicare spending as a share of GDP. The solid black line shows the forecast, and the dashed gray line gives the simulated values with capped real absolute generosity. The differences are rather striking. The forecast is for spending to rise fairly rapidly above the current 8.5 percent to nearly 12 percent of GDP, then to stabilize there. For the simulation, spending rises somewhat to over 9 percent of GDP, then begins to steadily decline. By 2040, the simulated value is 8.2 percent. This is lower than current spending and well below the 2040 forecasted spending of 11.9 percent.

COMMENTS ON IMPLEMENTATION

Implementing any major program of spending limitations is always difficult, particularly with strong interest groups involved. This is certainly the case with Social Security and Medicare. I do not offer specifics in this respect. Rather, the following comments address some of the issues that have been raised regarding Social Security and Medicare spending and pitfalls to be avoided. Regarding pitfalls, it is particularly important to avoid, as much as possible, the political determination of specific program benefits and nonprice rationing, both of which lead inevitably to conflict and discord.

With respect to Social Security, a number of ideas have been put forth to limit spending. One is raising the retirement age. A gradual increase in the age of full retirement to 67 is already in place. Obviously this reduces somewhat the share of the elderly population that receive funds. Any additional increase in the retirement age would have the most effect on those younger than the baby boom generation, and it is the baby boom that causes much of the spending surge. So I do not consider this point further.

Another idea for limiting Social Security spending is to change the benefit formula to make it even less favorable to high-income individuals. This is implicit means testing of benefits, and it moves Social Security more toward being a safety net program. Limiting the benefits of high-income individuals naturally reduces the generosity for that group. If the limitations are substantial enough, then average generosity is effectively capped. Although total spending per senior may be capped in this way, spending increases for some individuals and falls for others.

Turning to Medicare, raising the age of eligibility has not yet been considered. One reason is that it makes early retirement infeasible. Early retirement is straightforward with respect to Social Security. People can support themselves with their own retirement funds until they reach Social Security eligibility age. For health insurance, there are scant insurance options, aside from Medicare, once one retires and exits employer coverage. Thus, raising Medicare's age of eligibility would force many people to retire later than desired.

With respect to limiting Medicare spending growth, there are important pitfalls to avoid. One is limiting payments to providers. Payments to providers should be at market-determined rates. Any attempt to pay less causes shortages of the supply of medical services and nonprice rationing. Both are to be avoided. Shortages are frustrating for program recipients and also lead to nonprice rationing. With insufficient supply to satisfy demand, the short supply is allocated on a nonprice basis. This often means that those who have the best connections or political influence are the ones who obtain the service. This is not a desirable way to allocate goods.

Another undesirable way to limit spending growth is to cap the availability of various services and procedures. Procedure quotas may also lead to guidelines regarding who qualifies for the limited number of procedures. This too creates nonprice rationing and invites political influence. People with political clout will have the loudest voices regarding what services are covered and who obtains them. Those without such clout will lose out and receive insufficient care. This method encourages unproductive rent seeking.

Moving Medicare to a premium support program alleviates these problems. Seniors would receive a voucher to purchase a health insurance plan of their choice. If the plan costs more than the support amount, individuals could add their own funds to purchase the plan. Spending growth could be limited simply by limiting the growth in the dollar amount that individuals receive. This method avoids the negative consequences of limiting provider reimbursement rates or limiting procedures.

Reimbursements to providers would be at market rates, so no shortages or nonprice rationing would result. Individuals could choose plan coverage on their own without government mandates. They could economize on the coverages that are least valuable to them. There would be no unsavory political determination of what is covered. And a premium support program saves on the wasteful costs of rent seeking and eliminates the social discord from political infighting.

CONCLUSION

With forecasts indicating that Social Security and Medicare will take another 3.5 percent of GDP, many analysts are concerned. As noted previously, this is the spending equivalent of adding another Department of Defense to the budget, plus a little more. A good deal of this increase is clearly due to the rising population of seniors who are becoming eligible for these programs. However, a good deal also is due to forecasted rising real benefits per senior. The latter provides an opportunity for limiting the growth of spending without cutting benefits. Simulations indicate that limiting benefits to their real, 2017, per-senior value can have substantial effects. Instead of rising to 12 percent of GDP and stabilizing there, spending would rise to only 9 percent of GDP and then fall. However, efforts to limit spending should avoid price controls, nonprice rationing, and politically determined coverages. Adopting a premium support program for Medicare, with a cap on spending, is a good solution.

CHAPTER THIRTEEN

CURB RISING DISASTER AND EMERGENCY SPENDING

JUSTIN BOGIE

Over the past 30 years the number of declared disasters and emergencies and the amount of money spent in response have been on the rise. While disaster relief was once used as a legitimate response to natural disasters and other emergencies, it has turned into a way for Congress to evade spending caps and increase spending. Adding to that problem, almost none of this new spending is being paid for but instead adds to the federal deficit.

The federal disaster and emergency process is broken, leaving the government unprepared when unforeseen events strike and costing taxpayers tens of billions of dollars in deficit spending. Congress must take steps to reform disaster and emergency spending so that it not only can function more effectively but also do so without exacerbating federal budget shortfalls.

THE ORIGIN OF DISASTER AND EMERGENCY SPENDING

The Robert T. Stafford Emergency Relief and Disaster Assistance Act of 1988 gave the president the authority to issue disaster declarations for a variety of events. These can range from widespread national disasters to smaller localized events.[1]

Typically disaster spending is provided in one of three ways. The first is through annual appropriations. Most disaster declarations are funded through the Federal Emergency Management Agency's (FEMA) Disaster Relief Fund (DRF). These funds are unique in that they are classified as "no-year" money, meaning they do not expire and can be carried over from year to year. The DRF is intended to be used for noncatastrophic disasters, meaning costs do not exceed $500 million per occurrence.[2]

DRF funds can be distributed from three categories of disaster aid: individual assistance, public assistance, and hazard mitigation. Decisions on how to distribute the funds are left up to FEMA officials onsite. FEMA and the president also have the authority to issue a disaster declaration for Fire Management Assistance Grants and to make funding available for that purpose.[3] In fiscal year (FY) 2018, the DRF received a regular appropriation of $535 million.[4]

The second type of disaster spending is a product of the Budget Control Act of 2011 (BCA). While the BCA created caps on discretionary spending for 2012–2021, it created categorical adjustments that could be made each year to increase spending. One of those adjustments is for additional disaster relief spending. Money designated for a disaster spending cap adjustment can be used for purposes that would be carried out pursuant to the Stafford Act. To determine the amount of the annual cap adjustment, the Office of Management and Budget (OMB) calculates the average level of disaster funding over the previous 10 years.[5] In FY 18, disaster adjustment totaled $7.4 billion.[6]

Third, Congress has the ability to provide additional funding through an emergency supplemental appropriation. Whereas the DRF is used for noncatastrophic disasters, supplemental appropriations are intended to be used for events that breach the $500 million per incident threshold.

Unlike the first and second types of disaster funding, which must adhere to the provisions of the Stafford Act, emergency designated spending can be authorized for much broader uses. In addition to disaster response, Congress and the president can request emergency funding for any need determined to be too urgent to be postponed until the next regular enactment of appropriations.[7] In recent years, emergency funds have been used to respond to hurricanes, increase security on America's southwest border, and address the Ebola virus outbreak of 2014.[8]

These emergency funds are added to any other previously provided appropriations; and they are not subject to the BCA caps or the Statutory Pay-As-You-Go Act of 2010 (PAYGO). PAYGO requires that any law changing taxes, fees, or mandatory spending must not increase projected deficits over 5- and 10-year periods; it is enforced through automatic mandatory cuts known as sequestration.[9] There is virtually no limit to how much money Congress can appropriate under an emergency designation.[10] In FY 18, Congress enacted $125.6 billion in emergency spending, mainly in response to three major hurricanes that impacted the southeastern United States and Puerto Rico as well as a small portion to fight wildfires on federal lands. However, much of the hurricane funding went to programs that are not equipped to, and do not provide, disaster aid.

DISASTER AND EMERGENCY SPENDING GROWS STEADILY

Since the passage of the Stafford Act in 1988, the number of annual disaster declarations has risen steadily. In 1988 FEMA reported only 16 declared disasters.[11] Over the eight-year term of President Ronald Reagan there were an average of 28 disaster declarations per year.[12] Under Presidents George W. Bush and Barack Obama the average number of annual disaster declarations rose to 130 per year.[13] In calendar year 2017 there were 137 declared disasters,[14] and through September of 2018 there had been 110.[15]

The scale of those declarations has also been on the rise. In FY 89, supplemental emergency appropriations totaled $1.2 billion, or about one-half of 1 percent of the entire federal budget.[16] Throughout the 1990s, supplemental appropriations continued to rise, with the discretionary portion totaling more than $129 billion over the decade. Approximately $76 billion of that total went toward the Gulf War, while the remaining $53 billion was used for nondefense purposes.[17] The trend has continued over the past 20 years, with $497 billion in nondefense supplemental appropriations and nearly $2 trillion for fighting the global war on terrorism.[18]

Though the levels of spending are smaller, a similar pattern has developed in supplemental disaster appropriations to the DRF. In 2000–2011, additional appropriations to the DRF averaged $1.8 billion annually.[19] Since the passage of the BCA, that average has risen to $6.7 billion per year, an increase of 272 percent.[20]

While the rapid growth of emergency appropriations is concerning, another trend is equally troublesome. During the 1990s Congress paid for 40 percent of total supplemental spending by rescinding unspent funding from programs and agencies across the federal government.[21] Since 2000, efforts to pay for emergency appropriations have been almost nonexistent, with the exception of FY 06 when approximately one-third of emergency appropriations were offset through rescissions.[22]

In 2017, President Trump put forth a $44 billion emergency request in response to several hurricanes. The request included $59 billion in offsets that would have more than paid for the entire package, but Congress ignored the request.[23]

If all of the money being authorized for disaster and emergency spending was being used for life-saving efforts and immediate response and recovery needs, then one could argue that the designation is justified. Unfortunately, numerous examples from past events make clear that a large amount of the funding designated for disasters and emergencies is not meeting those criteria. Moreover, Congress should find ways to pay for the new spending, regardless of its designation or use.

Out of $125 billion in FY 18 emergency funding, most of which was appropriated in direct response to three hurricanes, the DRF received less than $50 billion. The Department of Housing and Urban Development's Community Development Block Grant (CDBG) fund received over $35 billion[24] (about 10 times its regular appropriation); the long-troubled National Flood Insurance Program (NFIP) received a taxpayer-funded bailout of $16 billion;[25] and the Small Business Administration's disaster loan program received $1.8 billion in emergency disaster relief funding.[26]

The disaster loan program is a government subsidy for private businesses. The program has a history of poor management and falls outside the proper scope of the federal government. Giving it the authority to provide grants to whomever it sees fit is an improper use of emergency funding and fails to prioritize aid to those who need it most.

The inclusion of emergency funding for the CDBG is inappropriate. It gives broad grant authority to the Department of Housing and Urban Development to determine who is most deserving of the billions of dollars in federal aid. The program is not well-targeted to low-income communities and is not transparent, making it difficult to assess whether it is meeting its stated goals.

The Army Corps of Engineers received more than $15 billion in emergency funding in response to 2017 storms.[27] This amount is in contrast to its annual appropriation of less than $7 billion in 2018.[28] The influx of Army Corps of Engineers funding is less a response to natural disasters and more an effect of the congressional earmark moratorium that has been in place for the past eight years. Lawmakers are upset with the lack of progress on water infrastructure projects since the moratorium went into effect. Emergency funding provides a way to get around the earmark ban and send federal taxpayer dollars for infrastructure projects to lawmakers' districts.[29]

Recent natural disasters are not the only examples of the abuse of the emergency spending designation. Of the $50 billion in emergency Hurricane Sandy relief, $16 billion went to Housing and Urban Development's CDBG fund. It received $4.5 billion more in emergency funding than FEMA's DRF.[30]

In response to hurricanes Katrina, Rita, and Wilma in 2005, Congress provided nearly $95 billion in emergency appropriations as well as a $17 billion bailout to the NFIP. About half of that money went to FEMA's response efforts, and 92 percent was spent within two years of the storms.[31]

However, there was also much waste and abuse. The Louisiana Road Home program received a $1 billion CDBG program grant. A Government Accountability Office report issued a year after the storms estimated that between $600 million and $1.4 billion in emergency funding was paid improperly or to fraudulent individuals. In one case, $20,000 was paid to an inmate who listed a post office box as his damaged property.[32] In 2013, an inspector general's report found that $700 million of the money could not be accounted for.[33]

TENSIONS WITH THE BUDGET CONTROL ACT

Perhaps the biggest reason for the recent rise in disaster and emergency spending is the enactment of the BCA. Among other provisions, the act implemented discretionary spending caps for 2012–2021. And although the act was intended to reduce spending, it also allowed for certain annual adjustments to be made. The categories eligible for adjustment include disasters, emergencies, Overseas Contingency Operations (OCO, formerly designated as emergency spending), and program integrity initiatives.

In addition to amending the caps to increase spending, Congress has also exploited these cap adjustments to circumvent the limits. Since the enactment of the BCA, the average annual amount of supplemental disaster funding has more than quadrupled. Supplemental emergency funding has been on an upswing as well. In the five years prior to the enactment of the BCA, emergency funding averaged $22.5 billion per year. In 2012–2018, that annual average increased to $29 billion.

Finally, there's the issue of OCO funding. This category of uncapped funding was originally used to respond to the 9/11 attacks. It was intended to serve as temporary funding to fight the spread of terrorism.[34] Instead it has become a slush fund that allows Congress to evade the BCA caps and increase spending.

In FY 18 Congress appropriated $65.2 billion for OCO for national defense and an additional $12 billion for state and foreign operations. Seventeen years after 9/11, instead of serving to fight terrorism, this money is increasingly going toward propping up the base Department of Defense and State Department budgets. The Pentagon has already put forth plans to transfer as much as $49 billion in OCO funding to its base budget in FY 20.

The BCA caps created an uncomfortable situation for lawmakers. They forced Congress to prioritize spending which, under normal circumstances, would mean that to increase spending in one area, such as defense, another area has to be cut. But that constraint creates tension for lawmakers who want to neither raise taxes nor cut spending. Emergency spending and other cap adjustments provide a way out. They allow Congress to increase spending without worrying about offsetting it through cuts to other programs or new taxes.

RECOMMENDATIONS TO REFORM DISASTER AND EMERGENCY SPENDING

In an effort to make the disaster and emergency spending more effective and more fiscally responsible, Congress should pursue a series of reforms.

CODIFY THE DEFINITION OF DISASTER AND EMERGENCY SPENDING AND ENFORCE IT

One of the problems with the emergency designation is the lack of a clear definition of "emergency" in the law. Congress and the president are left with considerable latitude about what qualifies as an emergency. As described previously, emergency spending has grown and lawmakers have been able to evade spending restraints.

To add accountability and transparency to emergency spending, Congress should by statute define what qualifies as an emergency. To ensure that Congress cannot simply waive the statute as is done with some budget enforcement rules, this one should be enforced through a point of order that requires a two-thirds majority vote to waive.

In 1991 the OMB issued guidance on emergency spending that included a definition. The definition stated that to qualify as emergency spending, a provision must meet five criteria:

1. Necessary (essential or vital, not merely useful or beneficial)
2. Sudden (coming into being quickly, not building up over time)
3. Urgent (requiring immediate action)
4. Unforeseen
5. Not permanent[35]

Formalizing this definition would help ensure that emergency funding is being used for legitimate purposes. The end result could mean not only better responses but also more cost-effective methods.

LIMIT THE TIME FRAME FOR SPENDING EMERGENCY DESIGNATED FUNDS

Currently, disaster and emergency funds are appropriated as no-year money, meaning the money is "available for obligation for an indefinite period."[36] For example, of the $50 billion in emergency appropriations approved by Congress after Hurricane Sandy, only $17 billion was allocated to "meet immediate and critical needs."[37] The remaining $33 million was for long-term recovery efforts and infrastructure improvements to help prevent damage in future disasters.[38]

An emergency is defined as an event that requires immediate action. Six years after Hurricane Sandy, some of the emergency funding has still not been spent. Moving forward, Congress should adopt time limits and other more specific limitations for how the funds can be used. If money is left unspent, it should be automatically rescinded and returned to the Treasury. These measures would ensure that the funds are going toward true emergencies.

BUDGET FOR RECURRING DISASTERS WITHIN FEMA'S BASE BUDGET

When tested according to the five criteria laid out in the OMB guidance, FEMA's DRF budget-cap adjustment would not meet the standard to qualify as disaster funding. Over the past five years the fund has, on average, received $6.7 billion in additional funding through the disaster designation, money which is not subject to the BCA caps. Before enactment of the BCA, the five-year average was $1.6 billion per year.

The disaster-cap adjustment has become a means for Congress to evade the BCA spending caps and supplement FEMA's base budget. While Mother Nature is inherently unpredictable, history shows that some flooding, severe weather, and wildfires, among other disasters, will occur each year in the United States. The consistency with which Congress provides additional disaster funding every year proves this true. And because of the sharp increase in disaster declarations over the past 30 years, the DRF's base budget of $535 million is no longer sufficient to handle even a low-end storm season.[39]

Congress should stop providing a budget-cap adjustment for disaster-designated spending and budget for recurring expenses within regular agency budgets.

CLARIFY AND LIMIT THE SITUATIONS IN WHICH
FEMA CAN ISSUE DECLARATIONS

The growth in the DRF is largely due to the spike in the number of federal disaster declarations; and the growth in declarations is a direct result of changes in policy and regulation under the Stafford Act. The act increased the share of disaster-response costs covered by the federal government. In the event of a disaster, states normally have to pay for the costs of responding. But if the president declares a major disaster worthy of federal assistance, then the federal government covers at least 75 percent of response costs. The result has been that states now request federal help whenever they can because of the significant federal dollars that come with a disaster declaration. This creates a vicious cycle as states respond to increased federalization of disasters by preparing less than they should: states are less prepared for disasters, they request more federal help, and the downward cycle is perpetuated.

To mitigate this problem, the Department of Homeland Security should reduce the number of disasters to which FEMA responds, leaving many smaller disasters fully in the hands of states and local governments.

REDUCE THE FEDERAL SHARE FOR DISASTER
DECLARATIONS TO 25 PERCENT

The Stafford Act made it much easier for states to request disaster assistance, leading to the spike in the number of declarations and the amount of money spent. The act requires that damages top $1.50 per capita for states to receive aid. In 16 states that amounts to less than $5 million.[40] Setting the bar to acquire federal assistance so low puts FEMA in high demand. And that leaves FEMA's budget and readiness spent when truly catastrophic disasters strike.

Congress should reduce the federal share of disaster costs so that only truly large disasters receive a 75 percent federal cost share. For most medium-severity disasters, FEMA should cover closer to 25 percent of disaster costs. By limiting disaster declarations and limiting cost sharing, FEMA will be able to put more money aside for catastrophic disasters, which is when federal disaster funding is most needed.

Such reform is better for disaster response: more prepared and invested state and local governments will improve overall disaster preparedness and response. And it is more fair: taxpayers in states that do not have many disasters, or that do a better job preparing for disasters, currently subsidize high-risk and low-preparedness states through the current federal model.

END THE RELIANCE ON OVERSEAS CONTINGENCY OPERATIONS FUNDING TO PAY FOR BASE DEFENSE REQUIREMENTS

As with disaster and emergency spending, OCO funds are a category of spending that was explicitly exempted from BCA caps. Since 2001, an estimated $1.8 trillion has been appropriated to the Department of Defense, State Department, and U.S. Agency for International Development for activities and operations in response to the 9/11 attacks and the continuing war on terrorism.[41] There is no statutory limit to the amount of OCO funds that can be appropriated in a given year.

Unfortunately, rather than fulfilling their intended purpose, more and more OCO funds are being used to prop up the base budgets of all three agencies. Since 2014, the Pentagon has been shifting funding from base accounts into the OCO account. This provides a mechanism to increase base defense spending without violating the BCA caps.[42]

Congress and the president should work together to phase out the use of OCO funding entirely. Instead, they should fully fund national defense through the base budget at the level needed to protect the nation from increasing threats across the globe and save additional spending for true emergencies and unforeseen threats.

PHASE OUT THE NATIONAL FLOOD INSURANCE PROGRAM

The NFIP was established in 1968 to provide flood insurance for at-risk properties and to mitigate flood risks through land-use regulation.[43] Congress noted at the time that ad hoc disaster relief was placing "an increasing burden on the nation's resources," which could be alleviated by insurance coverage.[44]

Some 5 million properties are currently insured under the program. Property owners are eligible if their community adopts and enforces floodplain-management regulations that meet or exceed federal standards.[45] FEMA has little discretion in issuing policies regardless of the degree of flood risk or repetitive claims.[46] Unsustainably low premiums have crowded out the private insurance market and have led to the NFIP being perpetually in debt. In 2018, the program's most recent bailout totaled $16 billion.[47]

Congress should release aggregated claims data necessary for private insurers to price private insurance and eliminate the subsidies and other giveaways that secure the government's flood insurance monopoly.

CONCLUSION

Disaster and emergency spending and response in their current form are broken. Too much of the funding is going toward purposes that do not represent true emergencies, and too little of the spending is being offset. Taxpayers are left holding the bag to pay for events that do not impact many of them.

Congress must take steps to ensure that disaster and emergency funding targets the direct response and recovery needs of impacted individuals and communities. The country as a whole must do a better job of preparing for the unforeseen before it happens instead of relying on government bailouts afterward. By putting reforms in place now, Congress can ensure a better and more cost-effective response next time a disaster strikes.

CHAPTER FOURTEEN

IMPROVING TRANSPARENCY AND ACCOUNTABILITY IN FEDERAL BUDGETING

ROMINA BOCCIA

Budgeting—that is, establishing spending priorities and identifying the revenue to pay for this spending—is a fundamental act of governing. Congress has a responsibility to the American people to exercise its constitutionally granted power of the purse with prudence and deliberation. Congress is failing the American people in this duty by delegating vast authority to the executive branch and neglecting to engage in the budgeting process actively and with discipline.

This chapter offers ways for Congress to reengage in the federal budget process—to review federal spending, prioritize among federal programs and activities, and improve fiscal sustainability today and in the future. It suggests reforms to the budget process to strengthen the congressional exercise of the power of the purse, improve incentives to follow the budget process, and enhance accountability and transparency in federal budgeting.

THE ROLE OF THE BUDGET PROCESS

The U.S. Constitution specifies in Article I, Section 9, clause 7, that "no Money shall be drawn from the Treasury, but in Consequence of Appropriations made by Law; and a regular Statement and Account of the

Receipts and Expenditures of all public Money shall be published from time to time."[1]

Congress adopted the Budget and Accounting Act of 1921 and the Congressional Budget and Impoundment Control Act of 1974 (1974 Budget Act) to establish the framework for an orderly budget process and the regular and deliberate debate of fiscal issues.[2] The 1974 Budget Act establishes a timeline to guide completion of the congressional budget process, including specific deadlines for the enactment of all appropriations bills before October 1 of each fiscal year. The purpose behind the budget process is to ensure that Congress evaluates national priorities carefully, establishes appropriate spending levels and sources of revenue, and performs critical oversight over how the executive branch is spending taxpayer dollars, in accordance with statutory intent.

Congress routinely ignores the law and neglects to pass a budget resolution and appropriations bills in an orderly and timely fashion. In the most recent 21 fiscal years, from 1999 through 2019, Congress completed a budget resolution in only 10 years, or 48 percent of the time. The budget resolution included reconciliation instructions in only 8 of those years, or 38 percent of the time. Of the associated reconciliation bills, 7 were enacted into law.[3]

A better functioning budget process is needed to reestablish fiscal control and to increase public transparency and accountability.

BUDGET ACCOUNTING REFORMS

IMPLEMENT FAIR-VALUE ESTIMATES TO MEASURE THE COST OF FEDERAL CREDIT PROGRAMS

Government estimates understate the cost of federal credit programs because they fail to account for market risk. To provide more accurate budgetary information, Congress should adopt fair-value estimates for the cost of federal credit programs. The cost of most federal activities is recorded in the budget on a cash basis, in accordance with recommendations made by the 1967 Budget Concepts Commission.[4] However, the lifetime costs of federal credit programs, including both direct loans and loan guarantees, are recorded up front on an accrual basis, pursuant to the requirements of the Federal Credit Reform Act of 1990 (FCRA).[5]

Under the FCRA, the estimated net subsidy cost of a direct loan or a loan guarantee is recorded at the time of loan origination in accordance with the present value of all future financial flows from the transaction. Present value calculations use discount rates to assign a value in today's terms to a receipt or payment that is scheduled to occur in a future year.[6]

The FCRA requires that the government use Treasury interest rates when discounting the value of future financial flows. The U.S. government pays low interest rates on the money it borrows because investors view these debt obligations as effectively free of default risk. However, a risk-free interest rate is the wrong one to use when discounting the financial flows of federal credit programs.[7]

When the federal government makes loans or loan guarantees, such as to homeowners and students, it is taking on the risk associated with broad macroeconomic shifts that might affect the ability of borrowers to meet their payment obligations. For example, a prolonged recession and high unemployment would raise the number of loans in default. This risk—called market risk—is not included in the rates the federal government pays when it borrows in public markets.

Fair-value estimates, an alternative to FCRA estimates, incorporate market risk by using market interest rates to discount the cash flows of federal credit programs. The Congressional Budget Office (CBO) determined that fair-value estimates provide a more comprehensive measure than FCRA estimates of the cost of federal credit programs.[8]

The estimated overall budgetary impact of federal credit programs varies between savings and costs under these two procedures. Under FCRA procedures, the CBO estimates that $1.5 trillion in new loans and loan guarantees issued by the federal government in 2019 would generate budgetary savings of $37.4 billion over their lifetime—thereby reducing the deficit. Under fair-value procedures, the CBO estimates that those loans and guarantees would have a lifetime cost of $37.9 billion—thereby adding to the deficit.[9]

To implement fair-value estimates for federal credit programs, the FCRA should be amended to require that market interest rates be used to estimate the net subsidy cost of those programs. Adopting fair-value estimates for federal credit programs would provide more accurate information to Congress and the public on the true cost to taxpayers of federal credit programs.

ADD DEBT SERVICE IN COST ESTIMATES OF PROPOSED LEGISLATION

Congress should have information on the full cost or savings of proposed legislation at the time of its consideration. With ongoing deficits, high levels of debt, and rising interest rates, debt service spending is becoming more important to the federal budget outlook. However, the debt service effects of proposed legislation are not currently reflected in the methodology for producing cost estimates. As a result, Congress is generally not informed of the total cost or savings of legislation at the time of its consideration. Estimates of proposed legislation should therefore include debt service costs. Debt service can have a significant effect on the deficit impact of legislation, particularly in the case of major legislation. For example, in its April 2018 baseline report, the CBO estimated that the combined effect of new laws enacted since June 2017, such as the Tax Cuts and Jobs Act, the Bipartisan Budget Act of 2018, and the Consolidated Appropriations Act in 2018, will increase the deficit over 10 years by $2.7 trillion, including $515 billion in debt service spending.[10]

Adding debt service to cost estimates for proposed legislation whose fiscal impact is currently measured relative to the current-law baseline would be straightforward.[11] However, doing this for individual appropriations measures is less straightforward. The debt service effects of proposed individual appropriations bills could be measured relative to the most recently enacted appropriations bill with an adjustment for inflation or, in the case of an omnibus appropriations bill, relative to the CBO baseline projection of discretionary spending for the applicable year.

Including the costs of debt service in cost estimates would better inform Congress and the public of the total fiscal impact of proposed legislation at the time of its consideration. Therefore, debt service cost estimates should be added to proposed legislation to better characterize the full budgetary cost or savings of proposed legislation.

INTEGRATE RECURRING PROGRAMS INTO BASELINE BUDGET

Congress should end the longstanding budget gimmick of scoring savings for short-term extensions of certain revenue-generating programs that Congress has no intention of ending. Under current procedures, certain programs that generate revenue (such as customs user fees) are assumed to fall out of the current law baseline when their authorization expires. Congress, which generally has no intention of allowing such programs to expire, has a history of enacting short-term extensions of these programs to generate the appearance of mandatory spending savings relative to the baseline. These scored savings are generally used to offset the cost of new mandatory spending over the 10-year budget window. But because Congress has no intention of allowing such programs to expire, their short-term extensions fail to produce actual mandatory spending savings.

Thus, after a limited number of short-term extensions (say two or three), the baseline should be changed to assume that such programs continue permanently. Once added to the baseline, the enactment of future extensions of such programs would no longer generate spending savings. This proposal would increase accountability by ending a longstanding budget gimmick.

DEFINE AND NARROW WHAT COUNTS AS MANDATORY SPENDING

Congress should initiate a budget concepts review to properly assess what should count as mandatory spending and establish a legal definition that is sufficiently narrow. For decades, spending on mandatory programs has been growing more rapidly than spending on programs and agencies funded by annually appropriated discretionary spending. Appropriations committees must allocate funding for discretionary programs subject to an overall cap on discretionary spending. In recent years, most discretionary funding has been limited by caps that were originally specified in the Budget Control Act of 2011 and were modified by subsequent legislation.[12]

As a result, most individual discretionary programs must compete with each other for funding. In contrast, most mandatory spending programs do not have to compete for funding. They are not generally subject to spending caps. Instead, mandatory spending is largely determined by eligibility criteria and funding formulas, some of which were enacted several decades ago.

This special treatment is encouraging Congress and various administrations to designate more and more funding as mandatory, including grant programs that until recently were subject to annual appropriations. Circumventing budget caps in this way is an abuse of fiscal responsibility. Moreover, the CBO current-law baseline, in accordance with statutory requirements, generally assumes that most mandatory spending programs continue after their authorizations lapse, further shielding spending from scrutiny.

Congress should explicitly define and narrow the designation for mandatory spending programs. Unless a program meets the narrow definition, it should be categorized as a discretionary spending program. This proposal could increase fiscal discipline by taking programs off autopilot and making them compete for annually appropriated discretionary funding. Increased competition for funding should help prioritize funding among programs. Lower priority or less effective programs would more likely be curtailed.

CODIFY THE DEFINITION OF DISASTER AND EMERGENCY SPENDING

Lawmakers have shown a greater tendency in recent years to abuse disaster and emergency spending designations to circumvent fiscal restraints like the Budget Control Act spending caps. Emergency and disaster spending is intended to be used to respond to major, unpredictable, sudden, and urgent crisis situations that call for a national response. In total, Congress drove up deficit spending by an additional trillion dollars over the past five years by declaring spending to be for emergency purposes.[13]

One driving force behind this abuse of the emergency designation is the lack of a clear definition of what is allowable. Congress and the president are left with too much latitude regarding what qualifies as an emergency.[14]

To enhance accountability and transparency in emergency spending, Congress should define by statute what qualifies as an emergency. To ensure that Congress cannot simply waive the statute, as happens with many budget enforcement rules by a simple-majority vote, the statute should be enforced through a point of order that requires a two-thirds majority vote to waive it.

In 1991, the Office of Management and Budget (OMB) issued guidance on emergency spending that included one possible definition. The definition stated that to qualify as emergency spending, a provision must meet five criteria: an expenditure that is necessary (essential, not merely useful), sudden (arising quickly, not building up over time), urgent (requiring immediate action), unforeseen, and temporary in nature.[15] Codifying this definition would help ensure that emergency funding is used for legitimate purposes. Disaster responses should be appropriate, targeted, and cost-effective.

ADOPT A TRANSPARENT SPENDING BASELINE

Congress should adopt a transparent spending baseline to clearly distinguish a spending increase from a spending cut or a freeze. The government has a responsibility to present its budget to the people in an intelligible manner that enables average Americans to easily determine whether their representatives are increasing, decreasing, or keeping spending flat.

One reason people have lost trust in their elected representatives is that they play so-called baseline games. These games obscure fiscal developments and have earned the federal government a dubious reputation: only in Washington can limiting the growth in spending be called a spending cut.[16]

To restore public trust in federal accounting, federal budget reports should clearly identify all the sources of change in outlays between one year and the next. A fully transparent baseline would begin with the current fiscal year's spending levels and clearly indicate all sources of increases or decreases, be they adjustments for inflation, population, or current law. Proposed legislative changes should then be estimated against this new baseline. This change would allow the press, interested citizens, and independent watchdogs to assess the consequences of fiscal action and inaction, equipping the public with relevant, straightforward information to hold their representatives accountable.

MEASURES TO STRENGTHEN ENFORCEMENT

SUNSET UNAUTHORIZED PROGRAMS

To increase the transparency and oversight of federal programs and activities, Congress should sunset programs that have not been authorized. Historically, Congress has passed enabling legislation—known as authorizations of appropriations—to authorize the appropriation of funds (generally discretionary funding) to carry out a program or function. The appropriations committees rarely provided funding for unauthorized programs or functions. In recent years, however, appropriations for programs that were never explicitly authorized, or whose authorizations have expired, have become more common. Senate rules explicitly prohibit unauthorized appropriations, but the point of order against them is usually waived by a simple-majority vote. In fiscal year 2018, the CBO identified 1,035 authorizations that expired before the beginning of the fiscal year. The CBO estimates that $318 billion was appropriated for those agencies, programs, or functions that year.[17]

Unauthorized appropriations lack transparency and oversight. Funding programs and activities that are not regularly evaluated through the authorization process allows them to grow unchecked whether or not they are serving a legitimate purpose or accomplishing their goals effectively.

Congress should put unauthorized appropriations on a gradual sunset path, beginning with a 5 percent spending reduction the first year, growing to a 10 percent reduction the second year, and ending all funding if Congress fails to reauthorize the program for a third year. This proposal would encourage a review of the large array of unauthorized programs that continue to receive annual appropriations. And it would likely lead to a reduction in spending on programs that are wasteful or redundant.

PLACE A TIME LIMIT ON EMERGENCY DESIGNATED FUNDING

Currently, disaster and emergency funds are appropriated as "no-year" money, meaning that the money is "available for obligation for an indefinite period."[18] However, for emergency spending to respond effectively to sudden, urgent, and temporary needs, it must provide an immediate and direct response to crisis situations. Once the crisis has abated, money designated for immediate emergency response should be withdrawn.

Allowing agencies to spend emergency money over an indefinite period of time encourages abuse. Emergency appropriations that provide for multiyear or no-year funding can result in large unobligated balances that persist for years. This creates opportunity for such funds to be used for purposes beyond their original intent and causes spending to be higher than would otherwise be the case.

REQUIRE PASSAGE OF BUDGET RESOLUTION
BEFORE SPENDING OR TAX BILLS

This proposal would require that each chamber of Congress pass the budget resolution—establishing its blueprint for fiscal policy—before it considers individual spending and tax bills. Section 303 of the 1974 Budget Act already generally prohibits House or Senate floor consideration of spending or tax legislation until a chamber has approved the budget resolution.[19] The rationale is that the budget resolution is intended to establish broad fiscal policy and that without it, Congress has no context to guide individual spending and tax bills. However, Section 303 contains major exceptions to this general prohibition, and it is one of the few budget rules that the Senate can waive with a simple-majority vote. These features greatly weaken the provision.

Some attempts have been made to strengthen the injunction. For example, in 2011, Sens. Ben Cardin (D–MD) and Kelly Ayotte (R–NH) cosponsored an amendment that would make it out of order in the House or Senate to consider any legislation after April 15 unless Congress had adopted the concurrent resolution on the budget for the forthcoming fiscal year.[20] Unfortunately, no action was taken on the measure.

This proposal would strengthen Section 303 of the Budget Act to more significantly restrict floor action on spending and tax legislation until a budget resolution is adopted. And, compared with the current budget process, it would provide both the House and the Senate with more incentive to pass a budget resolution.

A related, less targeted proposal is the No Budget, No Pay Act, introduced by Sen. Mike Braun (R–IN), which would discontinue paying lawmakers' salaries after October 1 if they failed to pass a budget resolution and spending bills by that deadline. The last time lawmakers passed all 12 spending bills on time was in 1996. This proposal is promising because it would give lawmakers a greater stake in completing a successful budget process cycle. The legislation would take effect after February 21, 2021, in compliance with the 27th Amendment to the Constitution, which limits Congress from changing compensation during a current session of Congress.[21]

TRANSPARENT, ACCOUNTABLE BUDGETING

Budgeting is a fundamental act of governing. Congress must reengage in the federal budget process to regularly review federal spending, prioritize among federal programs and activities, and ensure fiscal sustainability today and into the future. Congress must also ensure that the federal budget is presented to the public in a way that is transparent and intelligible to enable constituents, journalists, and outside watchdogs to hold legislators accountable for fiscal action and inaction. Budget process reforms should focus on ways to strengthen the congressional exercise of the power of the purse, improve incentives to follow the budget process, and enhance accountability and transparency in federal budgeting.

CHAPTER FIFTEEN

FEDERAL BUDGET PROCESS REFORM: ADDING A RESOURCE CONSTRAINT AND IMPROVING COST MEASUREMENT

MARVIN PHAUP

Reform of the federal budget process is a perennial topic of interest to analysts and policymakers. This interest is driven by a consensus that the current budget process performs poorly in terms of its economic objectives of stability, efficiency, and equity. Specifically, under the current process, policymakers have chosen an unsustainable debt trajectory that threatens both long-term stability and the ability of government to adopt short-term stabilization initiatives. In addition, policymakers often adopt legislation that is suboptimal in terms of both efficiency and equity. To determine how the budget process might contribute to those poor policy choices, it is necessary to identify the function of budgeting, the essential information needs of those carrying out this activity (user needs), and the performance of the current process in meeting those needs.

The practice of budgeting is a natural response to universal scarcity: the condition that beneficial uses to which available resources may be allocated vastly exceed the available limited supply of resources. This limit applies to governments as strongly as it does to individuals and private institutions. Every unit of resources that government uses must be given up by someone. For all, scarcity implies the necessity of choice and a potential gain from systematically choosing an allocative path for resources that maximizes benefits from those resources. This is the essence of budgeting.

Recognizing that the function of budgeting is constrained optimization also reveals its essential information requirements: budget makers must know the resource constraint (how much is available), the opportunity cost (value of scarce resources consumed) for each considered alternative use, and the expected social benefit from each. Although this observation may seem utterly unexceptional and commonplace, the current federal budget process fails to provide this requisite information in salient form to elected policymakers. Just as oddly, proposals to provide this information in recent years have aimed almost exclusively at improving the measurement of benefits, as though the requirements for a well-defined constraint and relevant cost measures had already been addressed fully. This chapter aims to rebalance reform efforts toward adding a salient resource constraint and improving cost measurement by demonstrating their absence from and inadequacy in the current federal budget process. It also suggests how those essential features might be added to the existing process.

NO CONSTRAINT

Advancing the claim that the current federal budget process lacks an effective budget constraint risks running afoul of the admonition to "avoid statements with which no one would disagree." Nonetheless, the failure of most budget reform proposals to include this feature implies either that such a constraint already exists or—more baffling—that it is unneeded.

One bit of evidence on this issue is the Congressional Budget Office's (CBO) annual long-term (30-year) projection of budget revenues, outlays, deficits, and debt, which assumes the indefinite continuation of current law and budget policy. The projections indicate that under those assumptions, debt grows as a share of GDP without identifiable limit. Figure 15.1 renders the 2018 projection.

FIGURE 15.1

Federal debt, spending, and revenues

Federal debt held by public rises

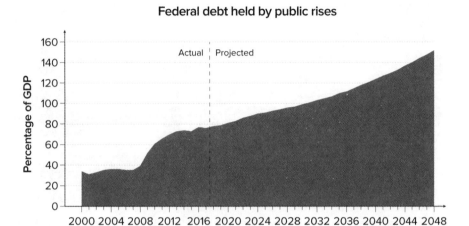

Growth in total spending outpaces growth in total revenues

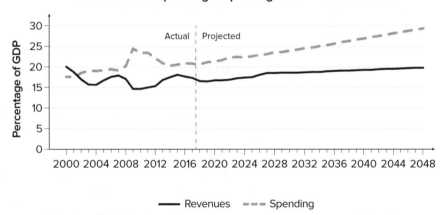

— Revenues   ▪▪▪ Spending

Source: Congressional Budget Office, "The 2018 Long-Term Budget Outlook," June 2018, https://www.cbo.gov/publication/53919.

Note: GDP = gross domestic product. The extended baseline generally reflects current law, following CBO's 10-year baseline budget projections through 2028 and then extending most of the concepts underlying those baseline projections for the rest of the long-term projection period.

FIGURE 15.2

Federal debt held by the public

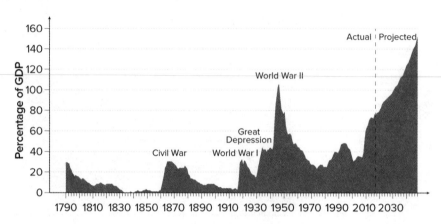

Source: Congressional Budget Office, "The 2018 Long-Term Budget Outlook," June 2018, https://www.cbo.gov/publication/53919.
Note: GDP = gross domestic product.

It was not always so. As indicated in Figure 15.2, for many decades the balanced budget norm was a dominant feature of federal budget policy. Deficits were permitted, but only during wars and other extraordinary emergencies. Once the crisis had passed, deficits were replaced by surpluses and the debt was paid down. Since the early 1970s, however, federal debt has been on a long-term upward trend. Debt has become the favored means of financing increases in government spending and reductions in taxes in good times and bad.

The balanced budget norm imposed a constraining fiscal discipline on the federal budget process by limiting spending to amounts that constituents were willing to pay in taxes. Both intellectual and political factors played a role in the abandonment of that constraint.

The Keynesian Revolution in fiscal policy—embraced by the U.S. government during the presidencies of John F. Kennedy, Lyndon Johnson, and Richard Nixon—added a new, major function to budgeting by sovereign governments, namely to "balance the economy" at high rates of employment and economic growth. Thus, spending and the size of the deficit were to be determined primarily by policymakers' assessment of the needs of the economy for fiscal stimulus to maintain high employment and growth. The elevated importance of this function relegated balancing the budget and restricting spending to amounts collected in taxes to secondary status at best.

An important contribution to the ascent of Keynesian macroeconomic policy was economist Abba Lerner's 1943 essay "Functional Finance and the Federal Debt."[1] Lerner proposed that lawmakers pursue the goal of macroeconomic stabilization through highly active budget policies; specifically, he recommended that aggregate demand should be managed by frequent changes in federal spending and taxes to maintain high employment and price stability. One implication of the proposed policy was that deficits and debt would be determined by prevailing economic conditions rather than considerations of long-term fiscal balance. To the extent that the ratio of debt to national income required stabilization, this could be accomplished by central bank control of the interest rate relative to the rate of growth of the economy: an interest rate lower than the rate of economic growth would reduce the ratio.[2] Further, to allay the concerns of traditional, conventional analysts, Lerner emphasized an essential difference between sovereign governments and other institutions: in a fiat money system, government debt is usually denominated in the currency of the issuer, so the government can never be forced into an involuntary default on its debt, which it can always redeem with newly created money. Thus, government debt does not pose a threat to government's solvency in the way that private debt can threaten private issuers. Government is not subject to a conventional budget constraint.

Lerner's vision of functional finance and its implications for sustainable fiscal policies is now regarded as an artifact of a highly simplified model, unsuited to the politics of democratic decisionmaking.[3] It ignores the long lags that hamper effective fiscal management of the economy and the harm to economic and political stability from a policy of repaying debt with an inflationary issue of newly created money. Lerner's postulated escape from a long-term debt constraint likely leads to a catastrophic loss of living standards and shock to social stability.[4]

Nonetheless, the ghost of "functional finance" continues to haunt the fiscal and budget policy process, and it provides a basis of the so-called

Modern Monetary Theory. Policy choice continues to honor the thesis that the principal function of federal budgeting is to maintain the economy at full employment and promote economic growth. With rare exceptions, the economy is seen as persistently falling short or in danger of doing so. And the political imperative is to attend to the current need rather than to a distant future problem with federal debt, conveniently denominated in the currency of the realm.

A strategic political decision also played an important role in the abandonment of the balanced budget norm. In 1976, Jude Wanniski published "Taxes and a Two-Santa Theory" in the *National Observer*.[5] Wanniski described the Democrats as the spending-Santa party and argued that, to survive as a competitive political entity, the Republicans would have to return to their 1920s Harding-Coolidge Era role as the tax reduction–Santa. Wanniski's argument—that the Republicans had become the politically untenable dispensers of pain in raising taxes to pay for free spending enacted by the Democrats—resonated among Republicans and sharply reduced the influence of GOP fiscal conservatives. This reasoning appears to have swept away the last effective voice for a balanced budget norm. Deficits and debt now command bipartisan support as the preferred means of financing an increasing flow of gifts to constituents from the cornucopia of the federal coffers. However, as Eugene Steuerle has noted, the downside is that these benefits are loans to be repaid, not gifts.[6]

The current federal budget process lacks an effective budget constraint. A budget process without a constraint is not a budget process because scarcity is no longer an issue. Without scarcity, cost becomes meaningless because nothing has to be sacrificed to obtain desired benefits. Choice is necessary only because of the scarcity of legislative time, and it concerns only the sequencing of the provision of benefits. But, in time, constituents can have it all.

THE WIDE WORLD OF CASH-BASIS BUDGETARY ACCOUNTING

Seemingly every government has a set of procedures that it describes as a budget process. In the United States that process consists largely of a system inherited from historical practice, overlaid with modest changes in form and content.[7]

The core of that process is cash-basis accounting, initially adopted in the earliest days of the republic, when the role of government was much smaller and simpler than today. This accounting method measures inflows and outflows of cash to and from the government when those flows occur. It recognizes changes in one asset, cash, and one liability, Treasury debt held by and owed to nonfederal entities. All other assets and liabilities are excluded from the accounting. The accounting period is one fiscal year, supplemented with future year projections of annual cash flows.

The summary of the annual budget aggregate flows under this accounting consist of tax revenues collected by the government, outlays disbursed,[8] and the deficit or surplus, which is revenues less outlays. That deficit also articulates the change in net position for a balance sheet consisting of holdings of cash assets and Treasury debt liabilities held by owners that are not part of the federal government. Cost estimates for proposed legislative changes in federal spending or taxes consist of the net effect of those changes on federal revenues, outlays, and the deficit by fiscal year.

Even though the budget aggregates are not subject to procedural constraint—other than majority agreement—policymakers exhibit a pronounced preference for lower costs and deficits, all else equal. As is well known, cash accounting systems are well suited to strategic management of reported costs, and especially to deferring cost recognition to future fiscal years. For example, asset sales conducted concurrently with increases in spending can offset the net effect of increases in outlays and the deficit.[9] Shifting payments from the last day of a fiscal year to the first day of the next effectively lowers the deficit of the current year. Collecting fees or taxes for benefits to be delivered later can mask the reported cost of spending increases in the year the collections are received.

Widespread use of such budget maneuvers to "manage" the salient costs of legislation means that the current federal budget process often lacks meaningful and relevant estimates of the opportunity cost of enacted policies.

ILLUSTRATIVE CASES OF "MANAGED" BUDGET COST

Here I offer three cases of strategically mis-measured budget costs whose accounting remedies are well defined: a more comprehensive measurement focus (what is measured); basis of accounting (when measured); and consistent application of the current, functionally derived "matching principle" for budgetary accounting.

FEDERAL ASSUMPTION OF THE DISTRICT OF COLUMBIA'S DEFINED BENEFIT PENSION PLANS

Although this bailout example is about 20 years old, it provides a likely irresistible precedent for the many states and large cities with deeply underfunded defined benefit plans. It is also a case where the true, fiscal cost of a policy action is not apparent on inspection of the legislation.

In the late 1990s, the government of the District of Columbia (DC) was under great financial stress, such that the prospect of default of its public debt was a significant risk. DC's financial condition was inextricably related to past federal policies affecting the local government, especially before home rule. This linkage was a major factor creating a sense of implied responsibility by the federal government for DC's dire condition. An obvious point of fiscal stress was the significantly underfunded pension plans for police, firefighters, and teachers; the plans held assets of $3.2 billion against about $9 billion in earned retirement benefits, leaving a shortfall of $5.8 billion.

The most transparent option for federal assistance would have been for the federal government to provide a grant of $5.8 billion to the pension plan. However, cash payment of that amount would have had a cash-basis budget cost estimate of $5.8 billion. Sponsors were interested in framing legislation to provide the same assistance but at a much lower reported budget cost.

In the Federal Assumption of DC Pension Plans (Title XI, Balanced Budget Act of 1997, P.L. 105-33), Congress found such an approach. Under that act, the federal government assumed responsibility for paying all pension benefits earned to date. No further benefits could be earned in the transferred plans.

The 10-year CBO cost estimate for this legislation reported zero net effect on mandatory spending for the first 8 years of federal payments, fiscal years 1998–2005, because new pension outlays were expected to be offset by the proceeds from annual sales of the $3.2 billion marketable securities acquired by the federal government. The pension portfolio of assets was projected to be fully liquidated after eight years. The absence of a further offset to pension benefit payments resulted in a projected total of $1 billion in federal outlays for fiscal years 2006 and 2007 combined.

The legislation was also credited with savings of $50 million per year in discretionary spending for seven years in payments the federal government was to pay to the pension plans under previous law. Thus, the total 10-year outlay and deficit cost of the assumption of the underfunded plans was $1 billion for years 9 and 10, less $350 million in discretionary savings, rather than the $5.8 billion federal loss from accepting $9 billion in pension liabilities in exchange for $3.2 billion in assets.

Note that the actual subsequent timing of security sales by the Treasury would be of no consequence. A cost estimate is not a law, but rather a projection of intent conveyed to budget analysts by policy officials. Further, for subsequent budgets, outlays for the assumed DC pension plans were included in the current law baseline and no longer salient to future budget allocative decisions.

COMMUNITY LIVING ASSISTANCE SERVICES AND SUPPORTS ACT

Title VIII of the Affordable Care Act of 2010 established the Community Living Assistance Services and Supports Act—the so-called CLASS Act.[10] It created a home care health insurance program, including a crucial requirement that the secretary of Health and Human Services develop and adopt a premium and benefit structure that would produce revenues sufficient to cover claims. Further, if such a benefit-premium structure could not be identified, the secretary was prohibited from initiating the program. Subsequently, in October 2011, owing to the anticipated effects of adverse selection, the secretary, Kathleen Sebelius, announced that she was unable to offer assurances that the program could be structured to be entirely self-supporting. Accordingly, the effort to establish the program was abandoned.

In preparing a cost estimate for the legislation, however, the CBO assumed that actuarial premiums and benefits could be developed and successfully administered. It therefore prepared projections of equal value cash inflows from premium collections, beginning with the assumed initiation of the program and deferred outflows for claims payments spread over three decades.

Eligibility for benefits under the insurance required five-year vesting, employment for three of those years, and payment of premiums through payroll deduction. Accordingly, the 10-year cost estimate projected net collections from the CLASS Act of $72 billion.[11] It thus provided a salient but fundamentally false indication that the legislation would produce a new and usable inflow of resources to the government.

This cost estimate also flies in the face of the clear legislative logic that the budgetary resource cost of this program was expected to be zero: either premium collections would fully offset the cost of projected claims or the program would not be adopted. It reflects a commitment by budget staff to a historical method of budgetary accounting that ignores the principle that the budget should recognize the full cost or gain, if any, at the time the decisions is made to incur costs. That accounting principle derives from the purpose of public budgeting, which is to allocate scarce resources across alternative beneficial uses to obtain maximum social benefits.

Within a year of enactment of the legislation, policymakers learned that the projected $72 billion in gains was illusory and not to be collected. But cost estimates are salient and used in decisions at the point of enactment, not when actual costs and collections are known.

MANDATORY SPENDING

About 70 percent of federal spending is mandatory, meaning that it is not subject to annual control through the appropriations process. Instead, this spending is controlled by provisions in authorization laws that specify eligibility and benefits. Social Security and Medicare account for the largest share of this spending, most of which provides benefits to people who for reasons of age, disability, disease, unemployment, or lack of marketable skills are unable to provide for themselves or their families. Funding for the largest of these programs comes from taxes levied on those who are working. Payment of taxes creates an expectation—encouraged by political authorities—that benefits will be available to those paying taxes when or if they themselves become eligible. This expectation promotes a willingness to pay and a planned reliance on future benefits by the current generation of workers.

Cash-basis accounting for these transfer programs defers recognition of cost until benefits are paid to beneficiaries. That is, to a time when it would be socially and politically unthinkable to withhold payments to those in a condition of need. Deferral of cost recognition for benefits being earned in expectation today also suggests that the government on behalf of taxpayers may be facing a future, but not a present, financing shortfall. The absence of a salient, current-period cost of accumulating benefits increases the difficulty of managing those costs—until they are paid and it is too late to withhold payment. Mandatory spending under current law is projected to rise relative to national income without identifiable limit.

Cash-basis accounting renders the costs of mandatory spending virtually unmanageable. Accelerating the budgetary recognition of mandatory costs from the time when cash is paid to beneficiaries to the time when it is earned is feasible, but that would require replacing the current cash-basis system with an accrual system.[12] Accruals are presently used in the budget to recognize the current-period cost of such activities as the payment of interest on the public debt, federal direct loans and loan guarantees, and lease purchases of assets. Extending accruals to mandatory spending is likely a necessary condition for including the cost of this use of scarce budgetary resources in budget decisions.

In light of the absence of both a resource constraint and relevant measures of the opportunity cost of considered alternatives, the unresolved issue is not why the budget process performs badly, but rather how policymakers manage to credibly describe this activity as the socially important function of budgeting. A related question is whether the public should allow them to do so.

REMEDY: ADDING A CONSTRAINT

Proposals to add the requisite information are already at hand. Many forms of a constraint could be integrated into the existing process, including annual balance rules, intermediate and long-term debt targets, and fiscal gap rules. Each has advantages and disadvantages, but if enforced, they could improve budget outcomes compared with current policy. The existential question for democratic governments, however, is whether elected authorities can enact and enforce limitations on themselves.

An annual balanced budget rule and its close relative, the Tax and Expenditure Limitation, are frequently proposed as simple, widely understood means of forcing federal budget makers to limit resource use. However, these proposals have also been dismissed as unworkable at the national level because of the implied restriction on the ability of fiscal policy to stabilize the economy. In fact, an annual rule is more restrictive than necessary, as demonstrated by the success of the balanced budget norm, under which deficits were permitted during defense or economic emergencies, with debt pay-down in the postcrisis period.

One means of reconciling annual restrictive rules with active macro-stabilization is to require funding of budget contingency or "rainy day" funds. A key to successful use of this practice is for the government to estimate the annual long-term expected amount of fiscal stimulus needed and to reserve those sums, without requiring a politically unsustainable budget surplus. One applicable precedent for achieving this objective is the current accounting for interest on the public debt, which is recognized in budget outlays when earned rather than when paid. Payments to the interest payable account, which is treated as nonbudgetary, are reported in budget outlays and the deficit when dollars are transferred to the interest payable fund, rather than when payment is made later to the government's creditors. Similarly, stimulus spending could be scored as outlays in good times prior to actual spending during economic downturns.

To increase the probability for success in reserving resources in good times, the process could be governed by a rule as automatic as spending now is for mandatory programs: no congressional action would be required for the annual transfer of funds to the rainy day reserve account or for the disbursement of stimulus. Rather, spending from the fund would be triggered by an index, such as the unemployment rate or a specified period of weak growth in real GDP. Outlays could be earmarked in advance, for example, for grants to state and local governments, which are usually forced to reduce spending during national recessions.

A related constraining rule would aim at stabilizing the federal debt as a share of GDP. Several studies have recommended this approach to adding a resource constraint to the budget process. One is the 2018 proposal from the Committee for a Responsible Federal Budget (CRFB). The basic idea is that by limiting debt as a share of GDP, increases in outstanding debt would be permitted, but only consistent with higher income and growth in demand for low-risk Treasury debt. A limit on the growth of debt would constrain the growth in spending by requiring an increase in taxes if spending rose by more than the permitted growth in debt.[13]

Debt limits are usually expressed in terms of a long-term target with an intermediate target path to the long-term level. The dual challenge of this approach is the desire to permit some short-term budget flexibility to deal with unexpected fiscal events while maintaining a strong commitment to the long-term target. The CRFB proposal attempts to deal with this tension by making the congressional budget resolution a law, which would require a presidential signature and, presumably, prior political commitment from both the executive and the legislative branches of government. Either automatic execution or an unwavering commitment to fiscal discipline and restraint by policymakers is likely to be required if fiscal policies are to be constrained.

A third approach would establish a fixed target value for the long-term—say, 25-year—fiscal gap, which measures the present value of the difference between projected annual revenues and outlays as a share of GDP. This approach could have the advantage of promoting simultaneous enactment of offsets to short-term departures from long-term debt targets. If, for example, the present value of the shortfall over 25 years is currently 2 percent of GDP, Congress and the president might be able to agree to adopt policies, to be phased in over 25 years, that would reduce the gap to a lower level, perhaps zero. In subsequent years, the gap would be reestimated, and the time path of the policy adjusted to maintain the target value. The gain from the use of the fiscal gap measure is that policies to raise taxes and reduce spending would become effective in the future when they would have been anticipated and prepared for by taxpayers and beneficiaries. The risk is that when the time arrives for those measures to take effect, elected officials would yield to political pressure to repeal them. One means that might make reversing course more difficult would be to require that policies to reduce the gap in the future would have to begin their phase-in at some minimal level immediately on enactment.

REMEDY: RECOGNIZING THE TOTAL RESOURCE COST OF A BUDGET DECISION WHEN THE DECISION IS MADE TO INCUR THAT COST

This remedy is not original to this chapter. It has been hiding in plain sight in every president's budget proposal for more than two decades. The following is an oft-repeated principle, sometimes referred to as the "matching principle for public budgetary accounting," accompanied by an explanation of its critical importance to effective budget choice and decisions:

> The budget needs to measure costs accurately so that decision makers can compare the cost of a program with its benefits, the cost of one program with another, and the cost of one method of reaching a specified goal with another. These costs need to be fully included in the budget up front, when the spending decision is made, so that executive and congressional decision makers have the information and the incentive to take the total costs into account when setting priorities.[14]

The only modification that needs to be made to current practice is to increase the comprehensiveness of the cost measure beyond net cash outflow in the year the cash is expected to be paid out by the government. Broadening the focus to include the total value of inflows and outflows that are attributed to a decision will help limit the scope of legislation in the strategic-design phase and improve the relevance and contents of cost estimates.

CHAPTER SIXTEEN

THE GOLDEN RULE OF PUBLIC FINANCE AND PROSPECTS FOR ITS REVIVAL

RICHARD M. SALSMAN

The golden rule of public finance (GRPF) holds that if governments borrow, they should do so primarily for productive, not consumptive purposes. A principle of fiscal prudence, the GRPF condones net borrowing by sovereigns, over the course of a cycle, only to create capital goods that yield a return and foster private-sector productivity, not to fund ordinary expenses or redistributive transfers that undermine prosperity, curb tax revenues, and jeopardize debt servicing. Public debt is justifiable, serviceable, and sustainable if it is issued mainly to fund durable, income-producing assets, not if its proceeds fund ephemeral or wasteful consumption; it is warranted only to the extent it helps *create wealth* over future decades, not to the extent it *redistributes or destroys wealth* in the present.[1]

As a fiscal norm, the GRPF has faded over the past century or so, in both theory and practice. As an informal institution, it still has its defenders, but its defense remains a minority view in public finance scholarship.[2] A norm of fiscal prudence has given way to a passive resignation to the "inevitability" of fiscal profligacy. Once a key aspect of 19th-century Victorian-Gladstonian principles of public finance,[3] the GRPF was abandoned piecemeal beginning in the 1930s, amid the financial turmoil and fiscal profligacy of the Great Depression, and thereafter, amid the vast public financing requirements of World War II. As a reputable rule, the GRPF faded further in the decades after the last vestiges of the international gold standard were jettisoned in the early 1970s. In recent decades only a handful of sovereigns (including Germany and the UK) clung to some form of GRPF; but they abandoned the rule when they succumbed to the avalanche of public debt and monetization that accompanied and followed the 2008–2010 financial crisis and global recession.[4] Debt finance is barely mentioned in today's top-selling public finance textbook, and the GRPF is ignored entirely.[5] Faint calls for a diluted GRPF now come only from those who fear that "austerity" budgets and the successive diminution of "fiscal space" globally will deter public investment and prevent a full resort to deficit spending in future recessions.

The erosion of long-held golden norms in fiscal and monetary affairs alike is neither random nor inexplicable; it reflects a deeper erosion in the golden rule of morality, which holds that as individuals we should treat others as we wish others to treat us in turn. This reciprocal ethical norm undergirds fair dealing, nondiscrimination, and the equal protection of the law; its erosion, in contrast, permits unequal, unjust treatment, which typically becomes codified in law, politics, policymaking, and public finance.

FOUNDATIONS OF THE GRPF

Two justifications are typically offered for the GRPF, the first primarily economic, the second moral. The *economic* justification for a golden rule in public finance echoes the corporate finance principle that debt is more likely to be fully serviced (via payments of principal and interest) if its proceeds are deployed to create the future income streams upon which debt service crucially depends. Loan proceeds should finance capital assets that yield a return (or make the economy more productive than it might otherwise be), not consumable goods or services that yield little or nothing. Even in household finance, debts incurred to buy homes, autos, appliances, diplomas, and vacations are not serviceable without an adequate income earned from productive activity. Nothing inherent in public finance exempts governments from the need to abide by these principles; and failing to abide by them, nothing prevents governments from suffering fiscal, monetary, and economic failure.

The second justification for a golden rule in public finance is mainly *moral* and holds that it is only fair that citizens pay for what they get and use; current generations should not have to shoulder (by taxes) the entire cost of durable public goods created today, which will benefit future generations; the latter should pay most of today's cost via future taxes, to help service previously incurred public debt.[6] Nor should future generations be burdened by public debts conveyed to them by ancestors, unaccompanied by productive and remunerative assets that help service the debt.[7] This justice-oriented benefits principle is as applicable to debt-financed public spending as it is to tax-financed outlays. Its counterpart, which has become dominant in recent decades, is the ability-to-pay principle, which severs the link between cost (payment) and benefit (use) and requires, in essentially socialist terms, that the state secure funds "from each according to his ability" and transfer them "to each according to his need."[8] This is most clearly seen when future generations are burdened with current welfare spending on the assumption that because they will probably be wealthier, they will better be able to pay for it.

The GRPF has rarely been codified in law, nor has it been strictly stipulated as doctrine in the constitution of any nation.[9] Some governments in recent decades have adopted deficit limits, debt caps, and spending "brakes," both constitutionally and statutorily. But during recessions and financial crises these legal boundaries have been readily breached, without much official concern to effect a remedy.[10] The best example is the European Union's Stability and Growth Pact, in place since 1998.[11] The pact has never embodied a GRPF, however. Yet for at least a century prior to the 1930s, before the spread of Keynesian notions, the GRPF was a widely recognized and broadly practiced *informal* fiscal norm.[12]

Although the GRPF has been abandoned, no widely accepted alternative fiscal norm has replaced it. More than a half century ago, James Buchanan discerned and critiqued what he called "fiscal nihilism"—the rejection of any and all fiscal rules per se.[13] In the past decade, Keynesian premises and principles, widely discredited in the 1970s, have seen a revival. In place of a fading GRPF, a nearly opposite norm presumes that federal spending for consumption is acceptable—indeed indispensable, reflecting the persistent Keynesian fear of inadequate aggregate demand—and that this spending should be financed not by higher taxes (which might reduce aggregate demand) but by the issuance of vast new sums of public debt, even if the debt is not likely to be fully serviced.[14] An alternative approach, using the doctrine of "Ricardian equivalence," denies any material difference between tax and debt finance, and it therefore sees no problem with borrowing to consume.[15] As for unsustainable public debt and default risk, some argue that public bondholders' astute and heightened expectation of default provides ethical cover for sovereigns to default deliberately.[16] This idea could become the new norm in future decades: publicly consume by borrowing, then default *on principle.* A recent work, reversing causality, insists that defaults on public debt can rectify an alleged harm inflicted by private creditors. This presumes that public over-indebtedness is due not to predatory borrowing by a profligate state, but to predatory lending by bondholders who could have lent elsewhere but chose to lend to a state.[17]

EROSION OF THE GRPF

Metaphorically, the GRPF might be pictured as a "finger in the dike" which necessarily fails to stop a flood of fiscal profligacy that originates in unrestrained democratic choice. If the problem is political, not economic, an eroded GRPF is the effect, not the failed preventive, of public debt deluges.

Over the past century, four fiscal phenomena detrimental to the GRPF and to economic prosperity have become the norm in the United States and in other major economies. First, public spending has increased both in real terms and relative to GDP. Second, the composition of public outlays has shifted from traditional capital spending (infrastructure) to spending on consumption (intangibles, including income transfers, health care, higher education, and various "social insurance" schemes). Third, to fund increasing public consumption, governments have come to rely more on debt finance (and unfunded "entitlement" promises) and less on tax finance; in the latter case, some states have become reliant

TABLE 16.1

U.S. federal revenues, spending, and debt, 1819–2018

	Years	Average share of GDP			
		Revenues	Spending	Differential	Debt
Prior 100 years	1819–1918	2%	3%	0%	9%
Past 100 years	1919–2018	14%	17%	–3%	55%
Prior 50 years	1919–1968	11%	14%	–3%	50%
Past 50 years	1969–2018	17%	20%	–3%	59%
Prior 10 years	1999–2008	17%	19%	–1%	62%
Past 10 years	2009–2018	16%	21%	–5%	100%

Source: U.S. Office of Management and Budget, "Historical Tables," Table 1.1., https://www.whitehouse.gov/omb/historical-tables/.
Note: GDP = gross domestic product.

on a narrow subset of (richer) taxpayers, versus less-taxed or untaxed citizens. Finally, public obligations have increased not only in absolute terms but relative to GDP (i.e., public leverage has increased).

Focusing on the United States, Tables 16.1, 16.2, and 16.3 illustrate material shifts in the pattern of U.S. public finance in recent decades. Federal outlays averaged 17 percent of GDP over the past century compared with just 3 percent over the prior century, and they have averaged 20 percent of GDP during the past 50 years compared with 14 percent during the prior 50 years (Table 16.1). Deficit spending outside of wartime was rare in the century prior to 1918, but the budget differential has averaged –3 percent of GDP since then; the differential has averaged –5 percent of GDP over the past decade, causing a rise in federal debt as a share of GDP to an average of 100 percent over the past decade compared with 62 percent over the prior decade (Table 16.1). During these two decades the spending share of GDP has risen, while the revenue share has declined.

As for the composition of federal spending, U.S. public investment has diminished over the past half century relative to increases in social spending and transfers. U.S. budget analysts conveniently distinguish spending

TABLE 16.2

U.S. federal spending by type, 1962–2018

Year	National defense	Human resources	Physical resources	Net interest	Other
	Share of total federal spending				
1962	49.0%	29.6%	8.3%	6.4%	6.7%
1990	23.9%	49.4%	10.1%	14.7%	1.9%
2018	15.4%	72.8%	3.3%	7.4%	1.1%
Year	**Share of nominal GDP**				
1962	8.9%	5.4%	1.5%	1.2%	1.2%
1990	5.1%	10.5%	2.1%	3.1%	0.4%
2018	3.2%	14.7%	1.0%	1.5%	0.4%

Source: U.S. Office of Management and Budget, "Historical Tables," Tables 3.1. and 9.1, https://www.whitehouse.gov/omb/historical-tables/.
Note: GDP = gross domestic product.

on physical resources versus human resources, each of which excludes defense spending.[18] Spending on physical resources has decreased relative to all federal outlays, from 8.3 percent in 1962 to just 3.3 percent in 2018, while outlays on human resources have increased from 29.6 percent of the total in 1962 to 72.8 percent in 2018 (Table 16.2). To accommodate this shift, military expenditures have declined from 49.0 percent of the budget in 1962 to just 15.4 percent in 2018. Interest expense now comprises a budget share (7.4 percent) more than double the share devoted to investment (3.3 percent) and more than it did in 1962 (6.4 percent), albeit less than it did in 1990 (14.7 percent) due not to less debt but to lower interest rates.[19]

Real growth in U.S. federal spending on "major public physical capital, research and development, and education and training," including defense outlays (Table 16.2), has decelerated from 2.5 percent per annum between 1962 and 1990 to just 1.0 percent per annum between 1990 and 2018.[20] As a portion of all spending, such outlays have declined steadily from 32.3 percent in 1962 to 18.2 percent in 1990 and 12 percent in 2018. Growth in nondefense investment spending has decelerated more, from

3.7 percent per annum (1962–1990) to just 1.8 percent per annum (1990–2018), and now comprises just 7.3 percent of all federal spending, down steadily from 9.0 percent in 1962 and 7.7 percent in 1990. Nondefense federal investment spending has never been a large share of total output, but it is now just 1.5 percent of GDP, having averaged 3.0 percent of GDP from 1962 to 1990 and 1.8 percent of GDP from 1991 to 2017. In contrast, gross private domestic investment has averaged 18 percent of GDP since 1962 (in a range of 13–21 percent),[21] and its growth has not decelerated: in real terms it has been steady, at 4 percent per annum from 1962 to 1990 as well as from 1990 to 2018. Whereas the private sector invested $3.4 trillion in 2017, the federal government invested less than a tenth of that ($278 billion), albeit supplemented by another $364 billion spent by state and local governments.[22]

Even if all public investment was value-adding and helped boost the productivity of the private-sector economy, it has undeniably diminished in recent decades, due not to stricter commitments to budget balance or fiscal austerity but to ideological-political commitments to more consumption-oriented social spending and transfers. The shift in spending priorities may partly explain the deceleration in private-sector productivity growth since the 1970s. Real output per hour worked in the U.S. business sector grew by a compounded rate of just 1.9 percent per annum between 1970 and 2018, a pronounced deceleration from the growth of 3.3 percent per annum registered between 1947 and 1970.[23] The shifting composition of public outlays from investment to consumption may explain a large part of the productivity decline, and federal spending can explain even more of the decline to the extent that public capital spending itself has been wasteful.

Even if the GRPF had been strictly followed in recent decades, with the result that far less public debt was incurred (being ineligible to fund social-consumptive outlays), it might not have helped the economy maintain or increase its previously high-productivity growth. Although the GRPF can preclude public borrowing to fund consumption, it cannot preclude a material and sustained shift from productive (investment) spending to consumptive (transfer) spending. Nor can the GRPF ensure that public investment will be productive, or more so than private investment. The GRPF might preserve productivity gains because, to the extent it requires consumption spending to be tax-financed, it might encourage taxpayer resistance to such spending; but likewise, ideological and electoral support for social spending can motivate politicians to fund it by less-painful, less-visible ways, such as debt finance.

Having documented empirically the material shift in U.S. federal spending volumes and patterns over the past century, it's helpful also to consider concomitant changes in money, public debt, and output. Table 16.3 reveals that while federal debt and the money supply have grown more quickly over the past half century (1969–2018) compared with the prior half century (1919–1968), real output has grown less quickly. Faster rates of debt and money creation haven't translated into faster economic growth rates. Real output growth has slowed further over the past decade (2009–2018) compared with the previous one (1999–2008), as debt growth has accelerated from 6.7 percent per annum to 7.2 percent per annum.

SHOEHORNING EVER MORE SPENDING INTO THE GRPF

An erosion of the integrity of the GRPF is also visible today as a result of attempts to rationalize all types of government spending. Historically, besides tangible public capital (infrastructure), there has always been semi-intangible public capital (services), including national defense, the courts, and law enforcement. Government at its best provides justice, and the constitutionally limited, fiscally responsible state does that job best. "Social justice" acolytes, in contrast, command sovereigns to flout principles of plain justice by redistributing income and wealth. Those hoping to preserve and extend the size and scope of government may acknowledge the validity of the GRPF but nevertheless applaud its abandonment. To the extent that careful studies have revealed redistributive "social spending" schemes to be detrimental to productivity and living standards,[24] a temptation has emerged to reclassify public consumption as "public investment." Politicians in recent decades have pledged more public spending not only for traditional, tangible infrastructure (roads, bridges, tunnels, ports, power grids) but also for "investment" in "our

TABLE 16.3

U.S. federal debt, money supply, and output, 1919–2018

	Years	Compounded annual growth rates			
		Debt	Money	IPI	GDP
Prior 50 years	1919–1968	5.5%	4.8%	4.2%	3.8%
Past 50 years	1969–2018	8.6%	8.5%	2.1%	2.8%
Prior 10 years	1999–2008	6.7%	11.9%	0.4%	2.6%
Past 10 years	2009–2018	7.2%	7.7%	1.7%	1.9%

Sources: Historical Statistics of the United States, U.S. Department of Commerce, Federal Reserve; Federal Reserve Bank of St. Louis, Monetary Base (total), FRED Economic Data, https://fred.stlouisfed.org/series/BOGMBASEW; Federal Reserve Bank of St. Louis, Industrial Protection Index, FRED Economic Data, https://fred.stlouisfed.org /series/INDPRO; Federal Reserve Bank of St. Louis, Real Gross Domestic Product, FRED Economic Data, https://fred.stlouisfed.org/series/GDPCA (since 1929); Louis Johnston and Samuel H. Williamson, "What Was the U.S. GDP Then?," MeasuringWorth.com, https:// www.measuringworth.com/datasets/usgdp/# (pre-1929); U.S. Department of Commerce, "Historical Statistics of the United States, Colonial Times to 1970: Bicentenial Edition," U.S. Census Bureau, 1975, https://www.census.gov/library/publications/1975/compendia/hist _stats_colonial-1970.html.
Note: Money=monetary base; IPI=industrial production index; GDP = real gross domestic product.

children," in education, health care, retirement security, the ecosystem, and myriad other purposes, not all productive. Such a reclassification possibly appeals to traditional proponents of investment, but it works to preserve and expand public consumption at the expense of investment. The GRPF becomes a dead letter regardless of whether it is *rejected fallaciously* as a barbaric relic of a bygone era of fiscal rectitude, or whether it is *endorsed erroneously* on the dubious grounds that most public outlays are now akin to capital outlays that can be predominantly and safely debt financed.

Politicians are not alone in rebranding consumption as investment. In public economics, all types of public outlays have been classified as "capital investment," including outlays on public schools (to create human capital); social insurance (to create safety nets); food stamps or unemployment benefits (to provide countercyclical measures mitigating recessions); the prevention of climate change (to preserve natural resources); bailouts of "systemically important" banks and firms (to prevent financial-economic meltdowns); and sports, recreation, entertainment, and the arts (to provide emotional fuel and local pride). Even spending on war, an obvious act of destruction, might be called an investment if it preserves a nation's autonomy, liberty, or security (the preconditions of prosperity). Such spending also entails operational expenses, which some might say deserve to be capitalized. If so, nearly all public spending can be considered capital spending and legitimately debt financed. The real danger now is not so much that an objective rule like the GRPF is breached, but that classifications of public spending become so subjective that most outlays and debts can be designated GRPF-compliant.

Weak-form defenses of the GRPF today aim less at ensuring that public debt is used only to fund public capital investment and more at ensuring that at least *some* material budget allocation remains for such investment, especially when a large and growing portion of public outlays becomes consumptive and crowds out both public and private investment. The worry was heightened as fiscal-austerity plans proliferated post-2008. Forced to choose, politicians more willingly curtailed capital outlays than transfer outlays; the choice was seen as less risky electorally. If public economists now admit any vestigial value in a GRPF, it is only the GRPF's capacity to ensure that public investment survives fiscal stringency. A GRPF can now "safeguard" public investment, which presumably helps in recovery from recession, embodies "growth-friendly properties," and provides "intergenerational equity." According to an International Monetary Fund report:

> Golden rules impose a ceiling on the overall deficit net of capital expenditure (also called current balance). With a zero ceiling, borrowing is permitted to finance investment only; current spending must be covered by revenues. Golden rules are designed to promote and protect capital expenditure, which is seen as more pro-growth and politically easier to cut than other types of spending. These rules are also more consistent with intergenerational equity than other budget balance rules, since they shift the burden of financing public investment projects from current to future generations, which will be the

main beneficiaries of such projects. The growth-friendly properties of golden rules should not be overstated.[25]

Similarly, Achim Truger worries that European sovereigns suffering wide budget deficits will face "fiscal constraints" that might "drive member states into austerity" and make things worse.[26] However, he notes:

> The golden rule of public investment . . . is widely accepted in traditional public finance and would allow financing net public investment by government deficits thus promoting intergenerational fairness as well as economic growth. A pragmatic version focusing on net public investment as defined in the national accounts minus military expenditures plus investment grants for the private sector could quickly be implemented. Net public investment should be deducted from the relevant deficit measures of the Stability and Growth Pact and the fiscal compact. Over time it could be technically and statistically refined and potentially include other—more intangible—types of investment like education expenditures. . . . The golden rule would have to be complemented by expansionary fiscal policy to provide the urgently needed boost to the European economy in the short term.[27]

As discussed, much analysis of the GRPF today presumes that public capital investment is either productive, in the sense of being self-sustaining (through fees), value-adding, or helpful (even necessary) to enhancing private-sector productivity. But the presumption is questionable when a capital project is defended primarily as a job creator (not necessarily a wealth creator, given featherbedding and other corruption) or as a spending multiplier. The premise is also questionable to the extent that public capital analysis excludes or underestimates opportunity costs, or the foregone (private) use of resources deployed publicly. Analysis is partial, as it calculates only the potential return on investment of a public outlay or the productivity of existing public capital; to be truly convincing, analysis must prove that a public outlay or asset is *more* productive, over the long run, than the private alternative (if one exists and is genuinely demanded). Even when some public infrastructure proves to be valuable, in isolation it does not prove that the private sector could not be its superior, more profitable builder and operator. Private options are crowded out if infrastructure is deemed an inevitable monopoly, and therefore necessarily a government undertaking.[28] Not only might public infrastructure be productively *inferior* to similar-purpose private versions, but badly built, underbuilt, or undermaintained (yet monopolized) public assets can *impede* private-sector economic growth and productivity. Even public schools may prove so inferior to private alternatives that they generate not positive but negative externalities, as when they waste or destroy potential human capital.

Even if it is valid to assume that public infrastructure is as productive (or more so) than similar-purpose private infrastructure, two potential problems remain: an insufficient amount of it may be built, and large public debts nonetheless may be incurred to fund not investment but consumption.[29] Even productive public capital may be deficient in aggregate and in its power to service public debt.

THE GOLD STANDARD IN MONEY

The GRPF is but one of a few crucially important public finance rules that have been abandoned over the past century. Monetary rules have been similarly abandoned, most notably the international classical gold standard, which was first diluted a century ago, then jettisoned partially in the 1930s and entirely in 1971. The twin abandonment of fiscal and monetary rules in the past century was no coincidence. State control of money via central banking facilitates deficit spending, provides a ready demand for new public debt through debt monetization, artificially lowers borrowing costs, and helps impose implicit inflationary debt defaults. Nor is it coincidental that debt finance has so materially substituted for tax finance in the past century, unlike the prior one.

Table 16.4 makes clear that U.S. federal deficit spending and debt buildups have become the norm since the gold-based dollar was jettisoned in 1971 and have grown much larger relative to the economy's productive prowess in those years. U.S. spending was more restrained, and fiscal discipline was superior, under the previous two (gold-based) monetary regimes. Since 1971, federal spending has averaged 20.0 percent

TABLE 16.4

U.S. spending, budget gap, and debt under three monetary regimes, 1870–2018

Monetary regime/ years	Spending	Surplus– deficit	Gross debt	% of time with deficit spending
Classical gold standard/1870–1913	2.5%	0.3%	11.9%	28%
Hybrid gold-fiat system/1914–1970	13.3%	–2.6%	45.7%	64%
Inconvertible fiat system/1971–2018	20.0%	–3.0%	60.1%	94%

Source: U.S. Office of Management and Budget, "Historical Statistics of the U.S.": Table 1.1, https://www.whitehouse.gov/omb/historical-tables/; TreasuryDirect, "Monthly Statement of the Public Debt (MSPD) and Downloadable Files," https://www.treasurydirect.gov /govt/reports/pd/mspd/mspd.htm (Gross debt); Federal Reserve Bank of St. Louis, "Gross Federal Dept,", FRED Economic Data, https://fred.stlouisfed.org/series/FYGFD (Gross debt series since 1939).

of GDP, and deficit spending has occurred 94 percent of the time, causing gross federal debt to average 60.1 percent of GDP. During the hybrid (part-gold-based) monetary system of 1914–1970, spending averaged only 13.3 percent of GDP, while deficit spending occurred just 64 percent of the time, and debt averaged 45.7 percent of GDP. Under the classical gold standard (1870–1913), public spending averaged only 2.5 percent of GDP, and deficit spending occurred only 28 percent of the time, with debt averaging a mere 11.9 percent of GDP.

The U.S. Federal Reserve wasn't fully established until 1914 and thus didn't exist (and wasn't needed) under the automaticity of the classical gold standard regime of 1870–1913. In this period there was minimal federal spending and a negligible resort to federal borrowing; from start to finish, thanks to budget surpluses, the gross federal debt was cut in half. Just as there was no need for central banking in this period because public spending was restrained and largely tax-financed, there was also no need for a byzantine system of fiscal rules, because the fiscal norm was budget balance and the GRPF.

Public finance and central banking now work in tandem—thus politically and unscrupulously. Most major central banks now wield near-complete discretion to conduct monetary policy in any manner they choose, without any material accountability. In recent years they've elected to monetize vast new sums of public debt at artificially low interest rates; in so doing, they have abandoned even the pretense of "independence," which seemed so crucial to securing their credibility in the 1990s.

Closely related to the erosion of fiscal and monetary rules and discipline over the past century, the United States has been transformed politically, from a constitutionally limited liberal republic into a relatively unconstrained illiberal democracy. Chronic deficit spending is inevitable whenever politicians win and keep office by satisfying popular preferences; powerful, free-riding majorities expect their public benefits (via spending) to exceed their public burdens (via taxes)—a profligate fiscal combination that politicians can deliver only when free of fiscal or monetary rules.

The current search (by some) for fixed fiscal rules amid widespread fiscal profligacy is not unlike the search (by others) for fixed monetary rules amid arbitrary central bank policymaking.[30] In each case the search is understandable and commendable, at least to those who prize principle and fiscal or monetary integrity. But such searches will prove futile to the extent that politicians and policymakers prefer and enjoy constitution-free discretion, seconded by an apathetic and nescient democratic citizenry. Once politicians removed the golden monetary handcuffs from central bankers in 1971, they removed as well the incentive for those bankers (and finance ministers) to care much about budgetary balance or fiscal rectitude. We now live in a time of near-unlimited policy discretion in fiscal and monetary affairs alike. In each realm democratic rulers now reign—without rules. That is precisely the form of arbitrary governance that constitutional liberals of yore fought so hard to resist and restrain.

THE GOLDEN RULE IN MORALITY

The erosion of golden norms in both fiscal and monetary matters plausibly reflects a deeper erosion in the golden rule of morality, which holds that ethics should be sufficiently objective and consistent as to be universally applicable and practicable; if so, one should treat others as one wishes to be treated by them in turn. This norm of reciprocal respect undergirds fair dealing interpersonally, nondiscrimination socially, and equal treatment before the law and politically.

Like the erosion of fiscal and monetary rules, the golden rule in ethics also has eroded in recent decades. Ethical norms influence social, legal, political, and ultimately fiscal and monetary norms. If one erodes, so does the other, through a long chain of causation. Without the golden rule in ethics, people feel justified in treating others unequally and disrespectfully, not as ends in themselves but as means to their own exploitative ends. A world bereft of the golden rule is one of people seeking dependency and a free ride. Codified in policy, it's a world of graduated tax rates that punish the rich for the unearned benefit of the nonrich; it's a world of financial repression that artificially reduces the cost of public debt at the expense of holders; it's a world of bailouts for financial miscreants, a world of corrupt rent-sellers, and a world of fiscally irresponsible officials deploying schemes to promote consumption, spread dependency, and bequeath both inferior-quality public assets and excessive debts to voiceless future generations.

The GRPF in fiscal affairs and the gold standard in monetary affairs have not been lost to the world because they were inefficient or impractical; if ever-rising living standards are preferred, few public institutions better help achieve such standards than sound money and sound finance. History is illustrative. The Industrial Revolution and Financial Revolution, which fueled and fostered economic prosperity beginning in the 18th century, were made possible by credible, rational, and sustainable systems of sound money and sound finance, especially as practiced in the UK and the United States.

The GRPF and the gold standard have been lost to the contemporary world not for technical or economic reasons, but for moral, legal, and political reasons: these golden rules were fundamentally incompatible with the vast and rapid expansion in the size, scope, power, and cost of government over the past century, and incompatible also with the concomitant shift to more subjective, less rule-bound, and more discriminatory norms of public spending and finance. In money, discretion has displaced rules of any kind; in fiscal affairs the ability-to-pay principle of taxation has displaced the benefits principle, while transfer spending on the needs of consumption has displaced outlays on the needs of production. An erosion of the golden rule of morality has bred discriminatory public governance, necessitating substantially less-sound and less-stable systems of both public money and public debt.

The erosion of sound public finance and public money reflects a diminution in the justice-oriented benefits principle, which links the value one receives from public goods and services to the price (in taxes or fees) one pays for them. This link is severed by the increasingly dominant ability-to-pay principle, which embodies the socialist adage that contributions—whether in taxes paid or loans made—must come "from each according to his ability," with proceeds sent "to each according to his need." Wealth is forcibly transferred from producers to consumers, with deleterious effects on saving, investment, productivity, and living standards. More confiscatory taxes impose injustices and degrade incentives to produce; if instead public debt is incurred to facilitate transfers, its full servicing is ultimately jeopardized by a successively less-dynamic (because capital-starved) economy.

PROSPECTS FOR A REVIVAL

A feasible restoration of rational norms in fiscal-monetary affairs requires a new appreciation of the benefits of the golden rule in ethics, and beyond that, a recognition that moral rectitude requires the respect and protection of equal individual rights for all before the law. Without credible and lasting political constitutionalism, there cannot be credible and lasting fiscal or monetary constitutionalism. Politically, a golden rule manifests in what James Buchanan and Roger Congleton call a "nondiscriminatory democracy," which is roughly equivalent to a constitutionally limited liberal republic.[31] They revive and defend a "generality" standard whereby constitutions and statutes bar sovereigns from enacting or imposing on the citizenry anything other than general rules applied to (and abided by) all equally.[32]

In the nondiscriminatory, constitutional society, public benefits and burdens must match, as far as possible, a policy that prohibits the exploitation of some by others; no individual or group is forced to suffer net burdens so that others may enjoy net benefits. This principle is embodied in the U.S. Constitution, not only in its Bill of Rights (barring invasions of the liberties of all citizens, equally), but in its "general welfare" clause (preamble), its tax uniformity requirement (Article I, Section 8), its "equal protection" clause (Fourteenth Amendment), and its "guarantee" of a "republican form of government" (Article IV, Section 4). These provisions implicitly preclude not only a welfare state but unconstrained majoritarianism and the type of public governance that serves not the general welfare but specific (individual or subgroup) welfares at the expense of other welfares. The result of such disparate treatment, in modern parlance, is rent-selling, rent-seeking, pressure-group warfare, special-interest legislation, intergenerational inequity, unsound money, unsound finance, and unpayable debts.

Fiscal rules like the GRPF are not likely to be adopted—and if adopted, not faithfully executed—if the majority in a democracy rejects the golden rule; prefers free rides; and politically envies, exploits, or dispossesses economic minorities (including those with high income and large wealth).[33] Nor does that context permit strict monetary rules. Populist politicians will always eschew any rules that are unsupported electorally; but even tenured, elite academic economists today largely oppose fiscal and monetary rules that might constrain public debts and monetization, as they have so well in the past.[34]

A citizenry that favors a government of great size, scope, and power necessarily also favors a government of great cost—to frugality, liberty, and prosperity. If that citizenry also wishes to shirk personal responsibility for the high cost of government, it will oppose institutions and rules that tie rulers' hands. Ultimately, qua subjects, citizens will come to favor *rulers without rules*—that is, rulers substantially free of constitutional, fiscal, and monetary restraints, because free also of moral restraints.

A revival of the GRPF, like that of the gold standard, does not face insurmountable technical barriers; it is possible if a majority of citizens favors constitutionally limited government. This becomes more likely if they reject the dominant ability-to-pay principle in favor of the benefits

CHAPTER SEVENTEEN

ADMINISTRATION VS. POLITICS IN THEORIES OF DEMOCRATIC BUDGETING

RICHARD E. WAGNER

All but one American state has some constitutional requirement for a balanced budget, but few of them operate this way. In 1979, the federal government also enacted a public law that required a balanced budget by 1982, known as the Byrd-Grassley Amendment.[1] This law has not been repealed, but neither have budgets become balanced. These observations point toward a dichotomy within the theory of democratic budgeting, which Vincent Ostrom[2] set forth in describing what he regarded as the intellectual crisis in American public administration. One side of this dichotomy treats budgeting as an administrative matter of pursuing rules for rational action. The other side recognizes that democratic budgeting has a political character that cannot be reduced wholly to self-enforcing rules. While personal budgeting is a simple matter of individual rationality, democratic budgeting is not reasonably reducible to individual rationality. To the contrary, democratic budgeting entails interaction among myriad individual rationalities. At this point, democratic budgeting butts against Carl Schmitt's recognition of the autonomy of the political within society.[3]

When treated as a technical or administrative matter, no difference exists between individual and political budgeting. In both settings, budgeting entails projections of anticipated revenues and planned outlays.

Those anticipations and plans are invariably subject to uncertainty in various forms. Actual revenues might fall short of anticipated revenues for any number of reasons: a vendor might have become insolvent and so withholds payment, or an accident might have destroyed inventory, thereby increasing outlays beyond what had been anticipated. Deviations between anticipations and plans can thus result for both individuals and political entities. Such imbalance, however, does not deny the proposition that operating with a balanced budget is a relatively simple matter, administratively speaking. It means only that balance cannot be achieved at every instance in a temporal sequence of activity.

Deficits will be incurred in some periods, whereas surpluses will be incurred in others. Over a sequence of periods, however, deficits and surpluses will offset one another; there will be no tendency toward either surplus or deficit. Any enterprise will be hit by exogenous shocks to its anticipations and plans, but the aggregate impact of those shocks will typically be roughly zero. In modern democratic politics, however, budget deficits seem to have systemic character, which in turn suggests that budgeting is not reducible to public administration because the autonomy of the political will be unavoidably present.[4]

RATIONALITY AND IDEOLOGY IN DEMOCRATIC BUDGETING

Adam Smith famously opined, "What is prudence in the conduct of every private family can scarce be folly in that of a great kingdom."[5] Just as prudent conduct for a family called for modest surpluses during good times, reserving deficits for bad times, so would prudent conduct by a king follow the same principle of sound finance. We should note that in Smith's time, government was controlled by a monarch, whose household (court) is indeed a kind of family; thus both regular families and those of monarchs can be theorized about with regard to the choices they make. Both families and monarchs are thus subject to the principles of rational action, as Smith well knew.

John Maynard Keynes's 1936 publication of *The General Theory of Employment, Interest, and Money* turned the world of economic theory upside down by making spending, not thrift, the road to prosperity. The eminent historian of economic thought Mark Blaug summarized

Keynes's overwhelming impact on economic theory by noting: "Never before had the economics profession been won over so rapidly and so massively to a new economic theory, and nor has it since. Within the space of about a decade, 1936–46, the vast majority of economists throughout the Western world were converted to the Keynesian way of thinking."[6] The Keynesian theory claimed that aggregate misery, not prosperity, would result if all entities in society followed the classical principle of sound finance. Within the Keynesian framework, where aggregate income was identical to aggregate expenditure, an increase in saving by private citizens would cause depression unless government increased its spending to offset the increase in private saving.

This Keynesian theory of fiscal policy faltered in several respects. The simplest respect was recognition that an increase in saving by some people generally entailed an increase in spending by other people. It was rare that increased saving would find people burying cash in their back-yards. Far more common would be an increase in deposit balances in financial institutions, and those increased balances typically would lead to increased lending for commercial purposes. Therefore, the increase in private saving does not typically lower aggregate spending because it finances an increase in commercial spending on business enterprises.

The Keynesian theory of fiscal policy misdirected the attention of economists by treating as a general case what was at most a special case. Classical economic theory explained how free markets generally operated to maintain full employment, giving particular emphasis to explaining how deviations from full employment would set corrective forces in motion. A system of free markets could not sustain a general depression, but a system of governmentally controlled markets could.

The Keynesian theory of fiscal policy started from a condition of general depression and asked whether government spending might aid escape from that depression. In other words, the Keynesian theory was a special theory that pertained to societies already in depression; it was not a general theory of economic activity that explained how societies could get into depression. To be sure, Keynes titled his book a general, not a special, theory, which was surely unfortunate for advancing the cause of economic understanding even though that title probably contributed to the book's success.

The general case of economic understanding remains encapsulated by the classical theory of sound finance where governments are the same types of economizing entities as are families and individuals. Before Keynes, American budgetary practice generally reflected the classical principles of sound finance. Until the 1930s, the federal government normally ran modest surpluses to reduce the debt that had been accumulated during periods of war and depression. What Buchanan and Wagner called the "old-time fiscal religion" died slowly between the 1930s and 1960s, but it did die.[7] We still hear calls for restoring the old-time fiscal religion, but the clamor for restoration is now relatively quiet. Public opinion in the United States seems much like that in the European Union: deficits are fine so long as they are kept within manageable limits. Many U.S. states, moreover, exceed the EU limits, as do many of the EU member nations.

As a formal matter, a monarch and a consumer face the same setting for budgetary choice. It is, however, different for a democratic form of government. Democratic budgeting is not reasonably understood by the same principles that pertain to individual budgeting, either by private citizens or by monarchs. Democratic budgeting entails *interaction* among a collection of individuals, and interaction among the members of a group presents new analytical phenomena that are not present for individual choice, as Munger and Munger explain in their lucid examination of group interaction.[8] Two pertinent phenomena explain a collective process of interaction that is irrelevant for individual choices. The first concerns the set of rules through which a group moves from individual desires to some group outcome. Different rules will typically generate different outcomes within the same set of people, recognition of which lends heightened significance to the processes through which budgetary rules are selected. The second phenomenon is the ideological beliefs and presuppositions people hold. These don't matter for market choices because people pay for their choices in any case. They do matter for collective interaction because people don't pay for their "choices"; indeed, as individuals, they don't make choices at all. As Vilfredo Pareto explained in distinguishing between logical and nonlogical action, collective action in large part resides within the domain of sentiment and public opinion.[9]

A century ago, government was small, with spending being about 10 percent of total output. Furthermore, federal regulation had a narrow range, so commercial interaction was governed largely by private law. These days, public law is ubiquitous in the governance of commercial interaction. What is treated as public opinion would seem to take on even greater significance as a source of political power than it had a century ago, when such theorists as Friedrich Wieser and Bertrand de Jouvenel characterized public opinion as the source of political power.[10]

Public opinion, it should be noted, is not reasonably assimilable to the notion of preferences in economic theory. Economists seem to treat preferences as private matters.[11] This treatment follows from the model of general equilibrium, which enables the reduction of a society of interacting individuals to a representative agent who acts but does not interact with other people. Hence, preferences are data, often genetically formed data, though the Becker-Stigler formulation also provides room for preferences to be learned through practice.[12] The key point about preferences, in any case, is their private character: they are a property of an individual, and any change they undergo is through individual action; that change is then appraised as a private matter by those individuals.

Public opinion has little to do with the preferences with which economists commonly work. Public opinion resembles the Keynesian beauty contest, in which people are not trying to predict who will win the contest but are trying to guess how other voters will vote. This setting gives public opinion a fickle quality compared with the relatively hard-wired aspect that preferences have in economic theory. To be sure, some Italian theorists from almost a century ago, such as Gaetano Mosca and Vilfredo Pareto, recognized this quality of public opinion in their theories about political competition.[13] For them—and in contrast to the public choice tradition of political competition initiated by Duncan Black and Anthony Downs,[14] wherein candidates sought to locate their platforms relative to relatively hard-wired voter preferences—Mosca and Pareto treated candidates as trying to frame images of themselves that resonated with the sentiments of voters.[15] Electoral competition was a competition among the images that candidates were able to create and was not an effort to locate some center of mass within some map of given preferences.

To describe politicians as marketers of self-image is not to deny the possibility of developing plausible theories about democratic budgeting.[16] To the contrary, it is merely to note that ideological formulations must play a large role in any such theory. It is also to note the infirmities of modeling democratic budgeting as rational choice because doing that creates a universalist concept of a rational chooser, meaning that budgetary outcomes can be reasonably explained as the optimizing choice of some representative individual within the polity.

Within the alternative—group interaction setting of democratic budgeting—are significant differences in what participants regard as desirable outcomes, and with budgeting processes entailing a good deal of thrust and parry as participants compete to obtain more of what they desire in a context where there is little by way of a common or universal desire. Sure, one can say that prosperity or well-being are universal desires. But they are formalistic vacuities that lack explicit substantive content. To replace those platitudes with substance, it is necessary to move to the level of individual details through which such universal concepts as prosperity or well-being are constituted. When this is done, it becomes readily apparent that all policy and budgetary actions influence the pattern of prices within society, with changes in those prices changing the pattern of incomes within society. It's no wonder that Webber and Wildavsky organized their history of budgeting in the West around the theme of budgeting as entailing conflict among people over how they were to live together in relatively close geographical confinement.[17]

BUDGETING: PERSONAL VS. DEMOCRATIC

As we have already noted, a monarch was a person, though clearly he was a "Big Player" and not an ordinary player along the lines that Roger Koppl sets forth: While a Big Player faces wider options than an ordinary player, it is reasonable to characterize all players as choosing among the options they confront.[18] For Adam Smith, monarchy was the governing norm, and it was reasonable for people in such positions as his to seek to civilize the monarch by offering instruction regarding the affairs of state. Smith wrote at a time when governance was based largely on status relationships and not the contractual relationships that would come into the foreground during the following century, as Henry Maine explained in his oft-cited remark that progressive societies during the mid-19th century were characterized by movement from status-based to contract-based relationships.[19]

During the feudal period, a landowner could not subdivide his land but had to leave it intact to his eldest son under primogeniture. Similarly, a married woman could not own property under coverture because ownership was vested in the husband by virtue of his status. During the liberal period of the 19th century, these relationships of status morphed into contractual relationships, where patterns of landownership and participation in commerce by women were governed by contract, not by status.

Thus to instruct a monarch in Smith's time was not the same thing as instructing a democratic parliament. It is a categorical mistake to think that meaningful instruction is the same under both types of regimes. A monarch is a person, and people have preferences and face choices. It is reasonable to think of someone like an Adam Smith explaining how a monarch who wanted to govern a prosperous nation would be cautioned to avoid profligacy in conducting his affairs of state. The monarch might listen, or he might not, but conducting the affairs of state would reside in his bailiwick all the same. To be sure, monarchs had to be concerned with their survival in a setting where other people would like to possess the throne.[20] Hence, monarchs faced problems of organizing their courts that bear a family resemblance to the problems business owners face in organizing their firms. Both can be usefully illuminated through models of rational action.

Each member of a parliament will face choices, a continual parade of them. Those members and their choices, however, cannot be reasonably reduced to a single, choosing entity. Sure, we often speak of parliaments making choices, but this is a linguistic convenience that often misleads thought rather than informing it. Democracy entails *interaction* among a variety of participants, and there is no good reason for thinking that those who participate in governance operate with something approaching a consensus that would allow the analytical reduction of the parliament to a single person. A theorist can always posit the presence of consensus among the members of a group, but such consensus would be an analytical convenience, not a necessary fact of existence. Periods of near consensus might manifest from time to time, but the historical record clearly shows that periods rife with antagonism can also manifest within the process of democratic governance.

Without organization, the members of a parliamentary assembly are just a mob that is incapable of action, as Robert Michels sets forth in describing the oligarchic tendencies within parliamentary assemblies.[21] There is almost no way that several hundred people can have a serious discussion among themselves, with consensus arising after discussion. To the contrary, parliamentary organization will provide a subset of members with the power to control the agenda of deliberation, illustrating the oligarchical character of large-scale parliamentary governance. Bertrand de Jouvenel elaborated on this phenomenon in explaining why it would be impossible for a well-meaning parliamentary chair to ensure free and open discussion of all options, because of the scarcity of time, both to allow everyone to air their opinions and, more significantly, to ensure that all presentations of opinions would have an audience.[22]

The case of the renowned Italian public finance theorist Antonio de Viti de Marco is instructive regarding the oligarchic tendencies within large-scale democracies.[23] De Viti initiated what a half century later morphed into the theory of public choice when he set forth an explanatory approach to the theory of public finance.[24] De Viti distinguished between two forms of democratic governance, which he described as cooperative and monopolistic. The cooperative form described a pattern of consensual governance where near-universal agreement existed on the activities that governments undertook and on the methods by which governments were financed. The taxes people paid were reasonable facsimiles of the prices they paid through market transactions. By contrast, the monopolistic form described a setting where parliamentary majorities dominated minorities, leading to a situation where parliamentary losers were forced to support activities that parliamentary winners desired.

While de Viti's academic work as a professor of public finance at the University of Rome centered on this interest to construct theories about fiscal activity within democratic regimes, it is worth noting that he also served for nearly 20 years as a member of the Italian Parliament, elected from his home district near Lecce. Although de Viti's theoretical work was necessarily abstract, he did not think that theoretical work was disconnected from his practical work as an Italian parliamentarian. The worlds of practice and theory are separate but related.

A theory of public finance for de Viti did not offer instruction for parliamentary practice, but rather uncovered some of the underlying and perhaps hidden logic that undergirds parliamentary practice. In this respect, de Viti discerned two categories of parliamentary action. One category pertained to actions that provided universal benefit; the other category pertained to actions that provided benefit to subsets of people, with those benefits made possible by impositions on others. The universal activities corresponded to de Viti's model of the cooperative state; the particularistic activities corresponded to de Viti's model of the monopolistic state. In a compilation of essays written mostly during his parliamentary years, he took a ground-level orientation toward the operation of factional or monopolistic democracy by chronicling his 20 years of struggle.[25] Democratic budgeting was replete with winners and losers, and the task of ideology is twofold: to enable winners to feel good about their predations by enshrouding them in an ideology of public beneficence, and to sooth the feelings of losers by conveying the image that their losses were necessary to achieve a higher good.

De Viti was a contemporary of John Maynard Keynes. Keynes did not believe that the British government was truly democratic despite its nominally democratic form. Keynes's biographer tells us that Keynes believed that the conduct of government in Britain was effectively in the hands of a few wise and well-meaning people who operated through discussion and persuasion.[26] This, incidentally, was Frank Knight's vision of ideal democracy, and it mirrored de Viti's concept of cooperative democracy.[27] Yet de Viti with his parliamentary experience presents us with many instances of factional domination whereby winning coalitions exploit the remainder of society.

A SOCIETAL TOPOGRAPHY: ACTION LEVEL AND SYSTEMS LEVEL

Wagner,[28] following Resnick,[29] advances a biplanar societal architecture that distinguishes between an action level and a system level. The action level is the locus of all human action. By contrast, the system level contains both the results of actions and the ideological images that address menus of desired systemic properties. This distinction recalls the adage "Think globally and act locally." Actually, the only option is local action, for the global (system) level is not an object of direct action.

Observations pertaining to the global level emerge out of interactions among participants at the local level. Resnick illustrates this point about distinct societal levels with a traffic jam.[30] The individual cars that constitute the jam act and interact on the ground level where all action occurs. The traffic jam emerges out of interaction among those cars, and it has properties that differ from those of the cars that constitute the jam. Most significantly, time-lapse photography would show the traffic jam moving backward. Yet every car in the jam moves forward, though slowly, until it clears the jam. The jam has emergent qualities that are not carried by the individual cars but instead emerge through interaction among the cars. It would be a categorical mistake to describe a traffic jam as a gigantic car that moves backward. Backward movement is not a property of the cars that constitute the jam. To the contrary, it is an emergent feature of certain patterns of interaction among them.

Wagner extends Resnick's formulation to distinguish between a micro level where all actors act in economizing fashion and a macro level where no action can occur but has real existence all the same just as a traffic jam has real existence.[31] Sure, people continually speak of doing something to change macro patterns or outcomes, just as they speak of doing something to relieve traffic jams.

Both micro and macro levels of existence are real, but action can take place only on the action level. The macro level can be acted on only indirectly through changing patterns of action and interaction at the micro level. With the relationship between micro and macro levels being emergent and not direct, the standard theory of all kinds of economic policy, including budgeting, calls for rethinking and modification. All action must be local in that it is attached to the ground somewhere, so to speak. Yet actions that set public policy are aimed at or addressed to some global or system quality. The system level encompasses many types of constructions, projections, anticipations, hopes, and ideologies. They are portraits of systemic possibilities, as imagined in a theorist's mind, but they are portraits however they are fashioned.

A politician might favor an increased rate of economic growth. All the same, the measured rate of economic growth is not a direct object of choice. To the contrary, it is a result of interactions among numerous individuals within a society. It is plausible to claim that programs that increase the return to commercial and industrial investment will increase the rate of economic growth. To say this, however, is not to say that the rate of growth is subject directly to choice. It is only to say that some objects at the micro level can be modified in a manner that might reasonably be thought to lead to an increase in measured economic growth. What is being measured are increases in the value of firms in response to programs that increased the profitability of certain commercial and industrial enterprises.

Policy measures influence the returns to particular types of activities, with that pattern of influence aggregating to some increase in a measure of economic growth. That measured growth, however, is not an object of choice but is rather a consequence of ground-level changes in the costs and gains of different patterns of economic activity. An increased rate of growth is not something that can be accomplished through direct action. It can be accomplished only indirectly through local actions that end up having the projected effect.

All action is local, necessarily so. For instance, an appropriation for foreign aid that transfers $1 billion to relatively poor nations will do so through some such device as buying combines from American manufacturers and perhaps transporting them overseas on ships made in America. The macro-level outcome is and must be tied to some micro-level pattern of interaction that generates that macro-level pattern. This distinction between a micro level of action and a macro level of emergent interaction ramifies throughout the domain of political economy, public finance, and budgetary processes. I shall now illustrate this point with respect to budgeting and budgetary processes.

RICARDIAN EQUIVALENCE AND BUDGET DEFICITS:
SEPARATING TRUTH FROM ERROR

Any consideration of public debt must start with Ricardian equivalence, or the idea that debt-financed public spending cannot increase demand. Robert Barro reminds us that Keynesian expositions of fiscal policy neglect or seek to deny this fact.[32] Yet public debt is deferred taxation of an equivalent present value to the tax that would have otherwise been imposed. When this situation is viewed within the framework of orthodox macro theory, fiscal policy vanishes as an instrument of economic policy, because budget deficits can't increase aggregate spending. All budget deficits can do is induce people to decrease private consumption to create a fund to finance the higher future taxes. The debt-financed increase in public spending is offset by increased private saving. Aggregate spending remains unchanged.

Barro's framework reflects the logic of macroeconomics when the system is presumed to reflect rational action. Empirically, Ricardian equivalence has been found to tell only an incomplete story.[33] Within orthodox macro theory, the incompleteness is thought to reflect incomplete rationality within the macro system, as conveyed by notions of debt illusion where people are construed as treating the replacement of taxation with public debt as inducing them to think they are wealthier when they are not. This claim on behalf of debt illusion, moreover, resonates with the growing interest in behavioral economics in recent years with the challenges it offers to orthodox formulation of rational action.

Ignored in the controversy over deficit finance, Ricardian equivalence, and rationality in economic action is recognition that the system level is inert in that it is not and cannot be a locus of action. The system level cannot be acted on directly because all action occurs on the action level. How actions on that level project to the system level, moreover, is a complex matter that depends on patterns of interaction among entities throughout their action-level choices. Figure 17.1 illustrates the point.[34] There, the system level is conveyed by the AS-AD (aggregate supply–aggregate demand) model. System observations are generated through interactions at the level of action. This level is described by a

FIGURE 17.1

Aggregate variables within an ecology of plans

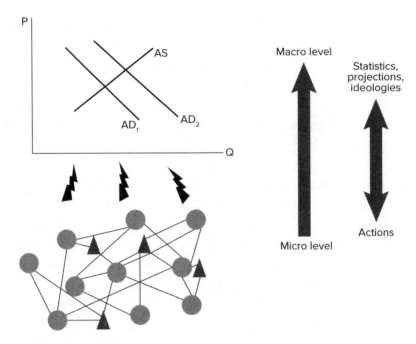

Source: Illustration by author.
Note: AS = aggregate supply; AD = aggregate demand.

combination of circles and triangles to denote that the action economy contains a combination of political and market entities.

Any so-called policy action must start somewhere on the action level. Eventually, that action will project onto the system level, but just how that projection occurs will depend on the pattern of interaction among the entities that interact on the action level. There is no good reason to assume that all those interactions are reducible to that of some representative agent or interaction. To the contrary, we may reasonably anticipate that people will differ in how they react. Suppose the policy action in question is a debt-financed increase in public spending. In standard macroeconomic theory, that increase in spending would be represented by an increase in aggregate demand. In contrast, the arithmetic of Ricardian equivalence would hold that aggregate demand was unchanged because the increase in political demand was offset by a decrease in private demand.

All such formulations treat as factual the ability of economic actors to affect systemic outcomes without constructing some pattern of action and interaction that will generate that outcome. Suppose, instead, that we try to do so. Older expositions of fiscal policy require some identifiable government agency to increase its spending on real activities, which occurs at one of the triangles in Figure 17.1. The means to do that, moreover, come from the Treasury, which places an issue of bonds with some brokerage house, represented by a circle in Figure 17.1. This operation will project as an increase in aggregate demand by the standard exposition of fiscal policy. What is especially notable, however, is that different points of injection for the increased spending will create different patterns of gain within the economy, even if they all yield the same increase in aggregate demand. What happens then is a micro-theoretic, not macro-theoretic, matter. Public debt may have no effect on net worth in the aggregate, and yet it can redistribute wealth within the society, depending both on the way spending is increased and on the way that future taxes will likely be imposed.

Contemporary references to quantitative easing change this analysis not one bit. References to the system level miss the process that generates the observations. Any increase in aggregate demand—should this be the outcome of the program—is causally a secondary outcome of the program. This recognition means that standard, system-theoretic depictions of public policy constitute a form of shell game. A shell game operates by misdirecting the observer's attention. Systems-oriented discussions of budgeting misdirect the spectator's attention from what is really happening, just as happens with a shell game.

The macro scheme of thought converts all individuals into averages with pro-rata shares of any claimed societal outcome, as illustrated by representative agent modeling. Hidden from view in this scheme of thought is the recognition that any policy action entails a choice between options,[35] with those options conferring different patterns of gain and loss within the population. One of the particularly notable illustrations of the macroeconomic policy shell game is the common claim that internally held public debt is something we owe to ourselves. This claim is a piece of ideology that erases any distinction between winners and losers from policy operations.

BUDGETING WITH THE STATE AS A FINANCIAL INTERMEDIARY

When it comes to democratic budgeting, we must acknowledge that the "state" does not pertain to an acting entity that trades on its own account. As previously described, it is a categorical mistake to treat a democratic state as if it were a monarchy. A monarch borrows on his or her own account. A democratic legislature does not. If a democratic state borrows, the legislators who authorized the borrowing do not become indebted. The legislature is but an intermediary that stands between people who have programs for which they seek support and people who have the means to support those programs but who would often rather not provide such support. In other words, public debt can play out differently within democratic polities, depending on the particular institutional and constitutional rules that govern the legislative establishment of public debt.

To illustrate this point about institutional and constitutional rules, imagine a town with 10,000 residents that finances its activities with an equal per capita charge imposed on everyone. This is the simplest tax system imaginable: the annual budget is divided equally among the residents. Let us assume that the charge is $1,000 annually, which yields an annual town budget of $10 million. The budget is distributed among a number of town activities, one of which provides for maintenance of an earthen dam that provides water for drinking, irrigation, and recreation. One year, a rare earthquake created cracks in the dam that a team of engineers asserted would only worsen until the dam burst. Those engineers estimated that construction of a replacement dam made of steel and concrete would require $50 million and could be completed in one year. The town council faces the problem of how to finance the new dam, for which it has two options given its tradition of apportioning taxes equally among residents.

One option is to declare a one-time increase in the town's budget to $60 million to maintain existing services while providing $50 million for the dam. This year, each resident would receive a tax bill of $6,000, of which $5,000 was a one-time charge for the dam. In this manner, the dam would be financed with a balanced budget that contained two elements: one element was the annually recurring appropriation for $10 million; the other element was the extraordinary appropriation for $50 million.

Although public debt would not be involved in financing the dam, many residents would likely borrow to finance some or all of their share of the appropriation for the dam. Private indebtedness would increase as some residents borrowed to finance their share of the special tax assessment. To recognize that some residents would borrow to discharge their obligations also requires the presence of creditors who would effectively discharge the tax obligations for the borrowers in exchange for future amortization payments from the borrowers. Financing the dam in this manner would increase private indebtedness within the town, but the town does not incur public debt.

To be sure, the town council could decide to issue debt in its name to finance the dam. The members of the town council, however, do not trade on their personal accounts. They do not become indebted, other than perhaps for their pro-rata share of the dam's expense. The town council is merely a financial intermediary that oversees a network of borrowing and lending within the town, replacing the private financial transactions that would otherwise have resulted.

At this point, the institutional arrangements governing the discharge of public debt become significant. In this respect, we can use James Buchanan's distinction between explicit liability and contingent liability as alternative approaches to democratic indebtedness.[36] Explicit liability describes an arrangement where public debt is treated as if it were private debt. With this arrangement, each individual is assigned a $5,000 liability that is treated in the same manner as mortgage debt and other forms of consumer debt.[37] That debt remains with the individual until it is discharged or passes into the decedent's estate upon death. With this arrangement, some individuals will surely become insolvent or move away without settling their account. To the extent that happens, the town will not collect enough revenue to pay creditors. With such possible insolvency being a feature of explicit liability, creditors will require higher interest rates to cover the default risk they face.

Public debt, however, is issued under contingent liability, which means that a person's future liabilities depend on various circumstances that are in play in future years, rather than being stipulated at the time the debt is incurred. With contingent liability, the town's ability to pay creditors does not depend on the solvency of residents in future years. If some residents become insolvent, the town can impose higher taxes on other residents to maintain the payments originally promised to creditors.

With ordinary commercial transactions, the burden of default rests on lenders, which in turn makes lenders cautious in extending loans. With contingent liability, by contrast, one borrower's insolvency is met by increasing the liability on other borrowers. With lenders thus facing a lower risk from borrower insolvency, public debt transactions understandably carry lower rates of interest than personal debt transactions.

This lower rate of interest, however, does not represent some form of general social gain. It is not that government is a lower-risk borrower, for to say that is to treat democratic legislatures as if they were monarchs. To the contrary, the lower rate of interest charged on public loans reflects a lower risk to lenders, yes, but only because the risk of personal default is shifted onto other taxpayers. Public debt operations redistribute risk but do not reduce it.

EXIT AND VOICE IN THE RESTRICTION OF FACTION

The Founders of the American constitutional republic recognized that democratic arrangements bred factions wherein successful coalitions could secure benefits for themselves through imposing costs on the remainder of society. Within the preceding illustration of a small town deciding to build a new dam, suppose the town's population was divided between those who wanted to reinforce the earthen dam and those who wanted to build the steel-and-concrete dam. Figure 17.2 illustrates the point, where d_1 illustrates demand for the earthen dam and D_2 illustrates demand for the concrete dam. Further suppose a small majority favors the concrete dam.

FIGURE 17.2

Consensual vs. factual democracy

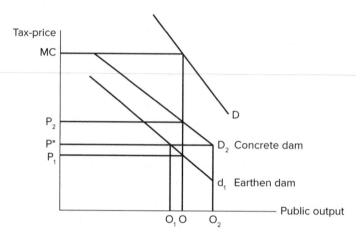

Source: Illustration by author.

Two categories of institutional arrangement exist under which a dam might be provided, and they can be designated as *consensual* and *factional*. Under the consensual arrangement, everyone would agree to provide the same type of dam. Those who have relatively strong demands would make larger payments to finance the dam, as Figure 17.2 illustrates. As shown, everyone agrees to provide the size of dam denoted as O, and with high-demanders paying tax prices of P_2, while low-demanders pay P_1. Under the factional institutional arrangement, the majority of residents dominates the minority, meaning in this case that everyone pays P^* for the dam. The members of the winning coalition are paying P^* for a service they value at P_2, while the members of the losing coalition are paying P^* for what they value at only P_1.

This divergence in values between members of the winning and losing coalitions illustrates a redistribution of cost when a political process replaces market transactions. Yet this redistribution does not conclude the analysis; it is only a point of departure. Beyond redistribution, the factional arrangements also create division among the population, whereas such division did not exist with the consensual arrangements. The price

P* in Figure 17.2 denotes the arrangement where the cost of any budgetary output is apportioned equally among the residents, whereas residents pay different prices according to the strength of their demands under the consensual arrangements.

Under the factional arrangements, no consensus is reached on the size of the dam. The members of the winning coalition prefer the larger dam denoted as O_2 to the size of dam denoted by O. The redistribution of income created by the common price in the face of divergent demands for the dam sets in motion an expansion in the size of the town's budget by an amount denoted by P* $(O_2 - O)$ in Figure 17.2. Factional institutional arrangements both redistribute income and expand the size of the budget compared with consensual arrangements.

Budget deficits emerge out of a fiscal process that enables the members of winning coalitions to shift costs onto the remainder of society. Borrowing can increase support relative to what would happen if tax liabilities were assigned at the time the project was approved. What will be the case if introduction of the option of public debt increases support for the dam? Obviously, more people must regard public debt as beneficial than regard it as harmful.

Replacement of a set of private loans with a public loan reduces the rate of interest charged for those loans. On this account alone, public debt would seem to increase support for the project. This lower interest rate is commonly interpreted as representing the position of government as a lower-cost borrower. Although accurate, this statement is also misleading because no identifiable entity becomes indebted with the public loan. The town does not become indebted; rather, it merely intermediates among the residents. However, that intermediation is not performed explicitly but is folded into the budgetary process where any explicit assignment of liabilities is lost from view.

In an earlier age when frugality was thought to be a quality of good government, we might well imagine some predilection against deficit finance in normal times, as characterized the United States before the 1930s. Once public opinion changes in the direction of thinking that budget deficits can also serve as a tool of economic management, a democratic polity takes on a different default setting with respect to presumptions about good budgeting. Previously, debt was regarded negatively. Now it is regarded neutrally or even positively, increasing the willingness to engage in deficit finance.

Deficit finance lowers the perceived cost of government in two distinct ways. One way entails some lowering of tax burdens for some people. When liabilities are not assigned personally, the perceived cost of collective activity falls for those who possess relatively short time horizons, as well as for those who are largely or wholly exempt from the tax base. Under contingent liability, deficit finance enables people with relatively short time horizons to reduce their anticipated tax burdens. In contrast, under personal liability someone who leaves town or dies does not escape liability. The debt remains with the person despite moving elsewhere, and it transfers to the estate upon death. The analysis of debt under personal liability works as if people operated with infinite horizons, which means in turn that borrowing does not entail a perceived lower cost than taxation.

The second way that public debt increases support for government spending is by its ability to create an organized interest group in support of higher spending. When government is financed under a balanced budget, people must evaluate government programs in two capacities: as payers of tax and as beneficiaries of services. With respect to Figure 17.2, we can divide a population into three groups and designate them as positives, negatives, and neutrals. The neutrals would desire neither increase nor decrease in the size of the budget. The negatives would like the size of the budget to shrink, and the positives would desire an expansion in the size of the budget.

If we suppose that neutrals abstain from voting, whether a project is undertaken with debt financing depends on the relative numbers of net taxpayers and net beneficiaries, with debt being pursued if net beneficiaries outnumber net taxpayers. Left out of this numerical account is recognition of how public debt might transform neutrals or negatives into positives.

Public debt creates a subset of taxpayers who have a special interest in public spending because public spending is the means by which they are compensated for their earlier payment of taxes by buying debt issued by the town. Once we move into the world of factional politics, it is useful to distinguish between willing debtors and forced debtors. Willing debtors are those who would have supported the expenditure program under taxation and supported it more strongly when it was financed by debt. Forced debtors would not have supported the program under tax finance and are forced to bear a burden of debt repayment all the same.

Albert Hirschman distinguishes between exit and voice as ways of influencing the performance of organizations.[38] Hirschman treats these methods as independent, meaning that each exerted independent influence over organizational performance. There is surely merit in treating the two as *inter*dependent, which would mean that the strength of voice would depend on the scope for exit. Voice is necessary to learn about the sources of organizational weakness. But exit is necessary if voice is to do its work because voice without exit lacks muscle. All the same, Hirschman's central interest was in getting economists to think more seriously about voice; it was not to sort through possible forms of interaction between exit and voice.

It is worth noting that hotels and shopping centers are commercial enterprises that provide both public and private goods as they are traditionally defined.[39] For instance, hotels provide public transportation, in the form of "subways" that run vertically, and they do so without direct charge. Hotels likewise provide sanitation and security services free of direct charge. The cost of supplying these publicly available services is incorporated into the price of rooms.

Should a hotel provide levels of such services that do not mesh with the desires of clients, those hotels will typically lose patronage, either because hotel amenities are unsatisfactory or because room prices are too high. The owners of the hotel have the managerial problem of providing bundles of services that tenants desire in a cost-effective manner. Exit and voice work together in promoting this tendency.

The cost of exit generally varies directly with the size of political units, though that cost also depends on other considerations. For instance, the cost of exit is surely lower for a tenant than for a homeowner because the homeowner must incur the expenses associated with buying and selling real estate. For a renter of housing, however, exit is of similar costliness to a client in a hotel. As the cost of exiting a jurisdiction increases, residents may find that they have effectively posted a bond that they must sacrifice if they exit. And as the cost of exit rises, the value of voice surely declines as well because expressions of uneasiness or dissatisfaction become less significant. Those at whom the voice is directed know that individuals won't escalate to exiting unless the cost of staying exceeds the threshold created by the cost of exit.

What does the easiness or difficulty of exit have to do with public debt? When exit is relatively easy, democratic polities will tend to operate consensually, as illustrated by Figure 17.2 when everyone agrees on the public output. What leads to this mode of operation is the need for the supporters of political programs to attract taxpayers to their jurisdictions. With exit, jurisdictions must attract residents who can locate in other jurisdictions. The political process is roughly constrained to operate consensually not so much out of intention as out of necessity when exit costs are low.

The cost of exit surely rises ceteris paribus as one moves up the scale of government from local to national. As exit becomes more costly, voice becomes increasingly a form of cheap, ineffective talk. Where exit is easy, political exchanges are mostly dyadic relationships that capture mutual gains. When exit is costly, political exchanges still operate because the world of democratic political economy is constructed through transactions. With costly exit, however, those transactions take on triadic character.[40]

Triadic exchanges have both winners and losers in any transaction. Figure 17.2 illustrates this situation, which arises when some people prefer the earthen dam while others prefer the concrete dam. The winners receive a net gain from the transaction; the losers lose by paying more in taxes than however much they value the project. With respect to the town and its dam, the winners are net beneficiaries while the losers are net taxpayers. For triadic transactions, the ability of the transactional web to incorporate people who would veto the fiscal operation if they had the ability to do so provides the cost reductions for those who support the project in question.

SOME CLOSING REMARKS ON DEMOCRATIC BUDGETING

Ricardian equivalence holds that public debt is just deferred taxation, with the present value of that deferred taxation being equivalent to the current taxation that would otherwise have been imposed. Public debt alters the timing of nominal tax payments, but that is all it does. Yet Ricardian equivalence is an incomplete and even misleading scheme of analysis because it reduces a society to a single individual, therefore avoiding all phenomena that stem from differences among people.

Ricardian equivalence holds that for any set of debtors and creditors, the sum of what the debtors owe is equal to the sum of what the creditors are owed. Debtors and creditors occupy different sides of a transaction, and the opposition of interests is an integral feature of credit transactions. Public debt is therefore more than a deferment of taxation. It also undermines the principles of contract that are the basis of trust in society.[41]

Ordinary debts follow the contractual logic of promise and commitment.[42] A borrower promises to repay a debt and the lender relies on that promise. Through such private law arrangements, trust builds through experience in societies governed by private law principles.

This situation can change when public law comes into play. Besides a public debt that exceeds $22 trillion, the U.S. federal government has an implicit debt in the form of unfunded liabilities that exceeds $100 trillion by some estimates. Suppose you put unfunded liabilities into the contractual language of promise and commitment. An unfunded liability means that the promises that have been made to beneficiaries exceed the commitments that have been imposed upon taxpayers by something on the order of $100 trillion. This situation surely qualifies as a form of systemic lying.

Public debt corrupts the practice of contract to the extent that promises regarding the future do not vest in the present sponsors who make those promises. With the monarchs of old, their promises to repay creditors in the future vested with the monarchs. By contrast, no such vesting exists with democratic public debt, though it could if liability for future payments were assigned at the time the debt was created. To be sure, if politicians had to assign those future liabilities now, they would surely be less eager to resort to public debt, which in turn would surely lower their desires to spend.

CHAPTER EIGHTEEN

WHY DEFICITS?

DAVID J. HEBERT

The reality of the U.S. fiscal situation is apparent to even the untrained eye. The problem of persistent government debt plagues not only the federal government but all 50 state governments as well. Pointing this out is nothing new. What is new and perhaps noteworthy, however, is the juxtaposition of the public sector's indebtedness with the private sector's profitability. In a time where multiple private companies are now worth over $1 trillion and setting record levels of profit, the U.S. public sector seems to be hemorrhaging money at a faster rate than ever before. This gap between public indebtedness and private profitability is perplexing and worth exploring further.

As Richard Wagner has observed on this subject: "While living within a budget can be difficult, most people manage to do it most of the time. Even elected legislators seem to do this with their personal accounts, as we rarely hear of them having persistent financial difficulties."[1] As Wagner points out, the issue with persistent U.S. debts and deficits arises not because the individual legislators are unable to balance a budget—they routinely do so in their own lives. He goes on to note that even groups of people, such as clubs and churches, can operate within a balanced budget, so the current fiscal problems of the United States cannot merely be the result of group decisions or group dynamics per se.

Finally, this inability to balance the budget cannot simply be the result of the sheer difficulty of the problem of using astronomical numbers in budgeting. If it were, then we would expect errors to be unbiased, causing governments to run deficits in some years and surpluses in others, with the errors canceling one another over a sufficiently long time. The fact that the real world is characterized by deficits every year—and typically larger-than-predicted deficits—means that something inherent in the public system is biasing the fiscal outcome toward deficits and not doing so in the private sector.

To explore this issue, this chapter takes a unique approach to describing the creation and discharge of debt obligations by applying the insights of de Viti,[2] Buchanan,[3] Brennan and Buchanan,[4] Wagner,[5] and Eusepi and Wagner.[6] In doing so, it describes Congress as a polycentric order with somewhat catallactic properties.[7] This catallaxy emerges as a result of the splitting of the fiscal decision.[8]

However, rather than viewing the fiscal decision as being split in two, this chapter builds on some of the author's previous work, which describes a tripartite decision process among appropriations committees, authorization committees, and revenue-generating committees.[9] Where this system (or more accurately, one like it) was initially established to act as a constraint on the behavior of government, today it results in persistent deficits. Understanding how this system works, how it was originally envisioned to work, and the breakdown of the "old-time fiscal religion" generates understanding of the structural and systematic causes of the persistent debt crisis in the United States.[10]

The rest of the chapter will be organized as follows. The next section describes a systems theory approach to understanding the split decision among the three committees: appropriations, authorization, and revenue generation. The second section provides a brief history of the fiscal decision, tracing today's practices to the rise of Keynesianism and the rise of political polarization. The third section grounds this in today's discussion by showing how these forces have morphed into a form of game whereby persistent deficits are created. The chapter ends with concluding remarks.

A SYSTEMS THEORY APPROACH

Members of the U.S. Congress are tasked with making many decisions and casting many votes. For example, "if we suppose that each of the 535 members of the U.S. Congress were given equal speaking time on each of the 10,637 bills considered during the 113th Congress and that Congress spent 80 hours per week only discussing bills and nothing else, each Congressman would receive about five seconds of speaking time per bill."[11] That circumstance would clearly be untenable.

Bertrand de Jouvenel describes the committee system as a practical means of resolving this problem by charging a specific subset of the full assembly with the tasks of the initial discussion of bills pertaining to specific topics—of hammering out the details, as it were—and of presenting the full legislative assembly with a more reasonable bill they can vote on.[12] In a world where each committee is made up of an unbiased, representative sample of the full legislative assembly, the resulting political decision from the committee should be identical to the decision that would have been made by the full legislative assembly, but with the added benefit of requiring fewer members of Congress per bill.

Committees exist for other reasons. For example, the U.S. Congress divides spending and revenue generation into three different types of bills: authorization bills, appropriations bills, and revenue-generating bills. Briefly, an authorization bill describes how much of something the federal government may ultimately purchase. An appropriations bill, by contrast, is what allows the president to actually take the money out of the U.S. Treasury and spend it on what Congress has authorized the president to purchase. The third component of this process is revenue generation, which is typically carried out through tax legislation.

The typology is not chronological; no reason exists for why any one of these bills must come first, second, or last. What it means is that, at least in principle, Congress can authorize the purchase of something and refuse to appropriate any funding for it. In fact, that is partially what happened with the Affordable Care Act in 2010, which was passed into law but was subsequently defunded through the Republicans' blocking the passage of appropriations bills that would have given the president the ability to actually withdraw funds from the Treasury to pay for the Affordable Care Act.

The purpose of this split is to enact a second and deeper layer of a system of checks and balances. In doing so, Congress's decision to spend money is (ideally) constrained not only by how much revenue is brought in each year, but also by Congress's ability to decide that the goal of the policy is laudable and that it can be accomplished at a reasonable cost. We each make these types of decisions in our own lives when deciding whether to purchase something.

For example, in going out to dinner, we are presented with a menu of options and their prices. We then select the option that best satisfies our appetite as well as doing so at the least cost relative to our budget constraints. A $65 steak dinner will certainly satisfy most appetites, but so too might a $12 hamburger. In deciding between the two, we weigh the relative benefits of each against our budget constraints and income earning potential. If we want to indulge our preferences for the steak dinner, we must either make sacrifices elsewhere in our lives or increase our revenue generation lest we incur debts that we cannot pay.

The same cannot be said of governments. The difference is that in the private setting, our spending and revenue-generating decisions are all made by the same individual (in the case of buying and spending) and interdependently (in the sense that we cannot spend money we do not have or otherwise expect to have in the future), whereas in the political setting they are made by different individuals and independently.

Most scholars argue that although such decisions are made separately, they are still interdependent. This notion is most commonly referred to as "Ricardian equivalence," named after the famous economist David Ricardo, who argued essentially that public deficits today are eventually paid off either through higher taxation or reduced future spending.[13] That would mean that the order of the decisions that Congress makes matters. For example, if a spending bill were passed first, it would in effect tie the hands of the revenue-generating committees to pass a bill that would ensure that enough funds were available to pay for the spending. Likewise, the passage of a revenue-generating bill would restrict the total amount of Congress's spending and essentially tie the hands of the spending committees.

In the real world, however, Ricardian equivalence doesn't exist in practice, which is why the order in which the bills are passed is irrelevant. This is not a skeptical or cynical view—currently no document, legislative or otherwise, says that a government must repay its debts. Further, even if such a document were to exist (such as a balanced budget amendment to the Constitution), it is difficult to imagine how, exactly, a balanced budget would result over any sort of time horizon. To understand why, we need to understand government debts as a byproduct of a complex system.

A "system" in this context describes the relationship of the individual parts and how they interact to form the whole. For example, a car can be thought of as a system—it has four tires, an engine (which is itself a system), seats, and various pieces of glass designed to shield the passengers from the outside while providing visibility. We can say with a fair amount of confidence that each of these individual parts contributes toward the overall goal of the system, which is to help convey people from point A to point B safely and comfortably. If any one part were to fail, the ability of the system as a whole would be greatly reduced or even brought to a halt. If an individual tire were to fail, the car would not be 75 percent capable of conveying people between points; the part would need to be repaired or replaced such that the car could be restored to working order.

The same can be said of a legislative assembly. Congress and the decisions that Congress makes can be thought of as the whole, and the individual members, committees, and subcommittees can be thought of as the parts. Although cars and Congress differ in many ways, one that is important in this context lies in the recognition that the individual parts of a car are designed to work well together, whereas the individual parts of Congress are designed to conflict with one another. In other words, the system in place that governs the fiscal decisions is designed to prevent spending, not to enable it. As Calvin Coolidge is reported to have once said, "It is more important to kill bad bills than to pass good ones."

The fiscal decision is designed, from a systems theory approach, to block as many bills as possible through the systems of checks and balances and the splitting of fiscal decisionmaking. The intended result is that the relatively few bills that make it through this gamut can be viewed as good in the sense that many different minority coalitions (including a minority of one at the presidential level) each had at least some ability to stop the bills from having the effect of spending money and thus effecting change.

Splitting this decision among three separate committees, each of which must pass a bill, provides an additional benefit in that, at least in principle, the arrangement should make it difficult for any bill to run the entire gamut of the legislative process. The underlying principle guiding the original writing of the Constitution was one of caution. It was not designed to empower good people or to enable "good" to be done, but rather to provide numerous means through which a small number of politicians could prevent a bill from becoming law.

The Founders—although they did not use these words—were clearly very much aware of the distinction between the productive state, the protective state, and the predatory state—as well as the dangers of the latter.[14] Because of this recognition, a system of checks and balances was designed. Although it is most notably applied to our understanding of the three separate branches of government, the committee system and the splitting of the fiscal decision into three parts constitute yet another system of checks and balances.

We can readily understand this by putting ourselves in the shoes of a well-intentioned member of the U.S. House and understanding the process this imagined person would have to go through to pass a bill that would require some amount of spending. Let's further suppose that whatever this bill would accomplish passes the standard efficiency requirements, that is, that it would provide more dollars in benefits than it costs. We'll also assume that the government is operating with a completely balanced budget and that any increase in spending must also be accompanied by either an equal reduction in spending somewhere else in the budget or an increase in revenues equal to the increased amount of expenditures so as to maintain a balanced budget.

Any member is technically allowed to introduce any piece of legislation on the floor; however, in practice, that person would have to become a member of the relevant committee (and likely subcommittee) that has legislative jurisdiction over bills pertaining to the topic on which the member wishes to increase spending. For example, if the member wished to increase spending on agriculture, he or she would need to be on the Agriculture Committee and, depending on the specifics of the bill, would also need to be on one of the six subcommittees within this committee.

Getting this assignment would give the member at least some ability to influence bills pertaining to agriculture, though still not much, as the committee currently has 46 members. As a result, this member would have to secure the support of at least 23 other committee members before the bill could even be brought to the Speaker and majority leader for them to consider bringing the bill to the floor of the House for a vote.

If the Speaker and the majority leader agree to bring the bill to the floor, they then have the option of bringing the bill to the floor as either closed or open. "Closed" in this context means that no amendments or debate will be allowed, and that the bill goes straight to a yea or nay vote.[15]

"Open," however, means that the bill can be debated on the floor and that amendments can be proposed in line with the rules determined by the Rules Committee. Although the specifics of the rules differ from one session of Congress to the next (and in some cases, the rules differ from bill to bill, as the Rules Committee can meet to amend the rules at any time), some general themes can readily be identified.

First, amendments to the bill must be germane, meaning that any amendment must be relevant to the subject matter of the bill. If a non-germane amendment is offered, any representative can raise a point of order to strike that amendment from consideration. Second, proponents and opponents of the bill are afforded an equal amount of speaking time on the floor, to be divided among as many individual members as the opponents and proponents deem fit, so long as the total amount of time devoted to each side is equal. Once debate has ended, a quorum call is taken to ensure that a majority of the full House is present. Assuming a quorum, a simple yea or nay vote is then taken.

If the bill receives a majority of the votes on the House floor, it is then sent to the Senate for consideration. The rules of the Senate differ markedly from the rules of the House. First, the bill must be placed on the legislative calendar, which is determined jointly between the vice president and the president pro tempore of the Senate. In practice, however, the vice president delegates this power to the president pro tem. Thus, in effect, the president pro tem must agree to put the House bill on the Senate's legislative calendar and then actually bring said bill to the floor for debate.

Once the House bill reaches the floor of the Senate, debate can begin. Unlike the House, debate in the Senate is unlimited, and no rules ensure that proponents and opponents are afforded equal speaking time. The debate does not end unless cloture is invoked. First, 16 senators must sign a cloture motion and present it to the clerk of the Senate, who then reads it. Two voting days must then elapse (e.g., if the cloture motion is submitted on a Monday, the cloture vote would take place on Wednesday in the morning).

To actually invoke cloture requires three-fifths of the "duly chosen and sworn" senators' votes of support. Assuming no vacancies among senators, that means that 60 senators must vote to invoke cloture. Once cloture is invoked, no new amendments may be offered to the bill, and the Senate has 30 hours of debate, after which the bill will be put to a vote, requiring a simple majority to pass. Assuming that the bill passes the Senate, it then goes to the president for final consideration. Should the president agree that the bill is worthwhile and has merit, the president can then sign the bill into law.[16]

Note how many steps must be taken to pass a simple bill. Although the number is impressive in and of itself, we should then multiply it by at least two (and possibly three) since—with the goal being to have a balanced budget—our imagined representative would have to shepherd this authorization bill through the gamut of the legislative process and then shepherd an appropriations bill through that same gamut, which would allow the president to withdraw the money from the Treasury and actually spend it. Our representative would also potentially need to shepherd a revenue bill that would, if necessary, raise the amount of tax revenue necessary to finance the additional spending that has been both authorized and appropriated.

This process is exceedingly difficult to accomplish. The difficulty was intentional. The intent is to provide as many opportunities as possible to prevent a bill from passing and accomplishing its goals. Unfortunately, the process has been corrupted over the years, with corruption leading inexorably to the current fiscal crisis that the United States is experiencing.

A BRIEF HISTORY OF THE FISCAL DECISION

The U.S. legislative system worked remarkably well for many generations. As a result of this and what Buchanan and Wagner refer to as "that old-time fiscal religion," the United States had a long history of running balanced budgets and even ran surpluses in some years.[17] To understand today's fiscal reality, we need to identify the changes in the legislative process that led to the observed pattern of fiscal calamity that we see today. Much began to change around the 1930s and 1940s as a result of two factors: the rise of Keynesianism in the economics profession and the rise of political polarization, especially in the 1980s and 1990s.

THE RISE OF KEYNESIANISM

It is often said that the first law of economics is that scarcity exists, whereas the first law of politics is to ignore the first law of economics. Although pithy, this joke gets at the frustrations that many economists feel when talking with politicians, assuming that they even get an audience at all. Some exceptions do exist, however, perhaps the most notable being that of John Maynard Keynes.[18]

Keynes fundamentally transformed nearly the entire economics profession within just a few short years. That feat alone is noteworthy, but where he lives on perhaps most fully is in the way he fundamentally transformed the economic role of the state. After Keynes, the days where the state's role was primarily that of a referee—tasked with making sure the rules (laws) were both fair and applied equally—were over. Instead, the state's role was expanded to include not only that of referee, but also that of managing the state of the economy writ large through attempts at aggregate demand management.

Keynes's argument can be summarized fairly simply. Governments have both the ability and the duty to use policies (fiscal or monetary) to balance the economy without worrying about balancing their budget. In times of economic hardship, governments have the responsibility to boost aggregate demand by either increasing spending or reducing taxes. In doing so, the government would run a deficit in the current period, which would add to the government's debt.

Conversely, when the economy is booming (or in times of plenty), the government can and perhaps should act as a dampener by reducing spending or raising taxes, which would have them running a surplus in the current period. There is no need to worry, say Keynesians, about the federal budget at any one time because over the length of the entire business cycle (or a sufficient number of business cycles), the federal government's budget will balance itself. Thus, and somewhat paradoxically, Keynes and his followers would likely oppose a constitutional amendment requiring Congress to balance its budget each and every year, as it would effectively take away the ability of the government to engage in the deficit spending that is, in the Keynesian framework, necessary to counter a recession, especially if that recession lasts several years. Two of Keynes's fundamental assertions were (a) spending and production are linked and (b) production and employment are linked, at least in the short run. Taken at face value, these links seem at least somewhat plausible: if consumers are spending more on goods and services, then firms will expand their output. Likewise, if firms are expanding their output, they will need to hire more workers, at least in the short run.

From a policy standpoint that means the state can increase employment in the short run by increasing spending today. What's more, it is argued that this increased pressure to hire will result in increased wages and salaries, which in turn will fuel even more spending on the part of consumers. Consequently, Keynes argued that a *multiplier effect* would occur, whereby each dollar of government spending would increase the total amount of spending by more than a dollar. Using that as an analytic framework for asking the question "Should the government spend money?" the answer is obvious: yes. In the United States, this gave Congress and the president a very powerful justification for the increased spending observed from about 1940 onward.

THE RISE OF POLITICAL POLARIZATION

The second factor that has contributed to the current fiscal shape of the United States lies in the rise of political polarization. Now factions have always been viewed as a danger in American political life, with Madison warning about them extensively in *The Federalist Papers.* Even George Washington warned against the rise of factions in his Farewell Address:

> The alternate domination of one faction over another, sharpened by the spirit of revenge, natural to party dissension, which in different ages and countries has perpetrated the most horrid enormities, is itself a frightful despotism. But this leads at length to a more formal and permanent despotism. The disorders and miseries which result gradually incline the minds of men to seek security and repose in the absolute power of an individual; and sooner or later the chief of some prevailing faction, more able or more fortunate than his competitors, turns this disposition to the purposes of his own elevation, on the ruins of public liberty.[19]

Washington's warning was prescient. In today's political arena, the overwhelming majority of bills passed by Congress are strictly along party lines, a trend that has advanced greatly in recent years. In the early 1970s, votes in Congress were already largely along party lines, with such votes happening approximately 60 percent of the time. Today this figure is closer to 90 percent in both the House and the Senate.[20] As evidence of the decline in even valuing bipartisanship, John McCain was recently referred to as "a traitor to the Conservative cause" for refusing to support a bill to repeal and replace the Affordable Care Act without a bipartisan conversation happening first.

Hebert and Wagner explain partisanship as a result of the increased role that political parties play in society.[21] Where traditional models assume parties to be a sort of simple intermediary that lubricates the political process by disseminating information from politicians to voters,[22] they argue that political parties act as a peculiar sort of interest group in that they present information in such a way as to construct images that resonate particularly well with a certain subset of the population.[23] For example, when discussing subsidizing wind farms, some people might consider the subsidies as filling a gap in research and development in an essential technology, whereas others may consider them as a means of securing additional rents for certain well-connected members of society.[24] Despite what we may hope, there really is no way to definitively prove which vision is the correct one.

The difficulty in exactly characterizing political parties is readily apparent in the context of today's fiscal debate. Tax increases are supported by alleging that some group of citizens is paying less than their fair share of the cost of living in a civilized society, to borrow Oliver Wendell Holmes's phrase. Taxes are opposed by arguing that they would reduce economic growth. Other arguments exist, but these two are probably the most important. These arguments are also completely *orthogonal*, meaning that in no way are they mutually exclusive—both could be true just as easily as both could be false. Each statement is presented not because it is a rejoinder to the other, but because it is well-known that each statement appeals especially well to an identifiable segment of the electorate.

The rise of political polarization has had serious and deleterious effects on the fiscal, political, and social health of the nation, with every four to eight years comprising either mostly increased spending on the war on poverty or mostly increased spending on what could broadly be defined as the war on terrorism. The result is a bloated public sector, which increases spending virtually every year, without a commensurate increase in taxation to finance said expenditures.

One of the most damaging aspects of polarization within any republic comes from the parties' alternating visions of what ought to be done. George Washington again warns us, saying that the alternating dominion of one faction over another makes "public administration the mirror of the ill-concerted and incongruous projects of faction, rather than the organ of consistent and wholesome plans digested by common counsels and modified by mutual interests."[25] In other words, each faction must simply wait until they are the ones in power, at which point they can undo what the previous faction had done and replace it with their own vision, rather than taking a longer-term perspective.

This approach creates difficulties with the administration of virtually every aspect of government, as it becomes a game whereby the ruling faction simply does what it can do when they are able to do so. For example, various provisions in the federal tax code subsidize tobacco cultivation, which encourages consumption through lower prices, whereas other provisions penalize the consumption of tobacco products, thereby discouraging their consumption. Overall the tax code has been used to accomplish myriad incongruent goals, not all related to raising revenues.[26]

BUDGET CHICANERY

Political polarization cannot explain recent transnational deficit phenomena, however. Unfortunately, institutional considerations must account for the persistent deficits we see from governments around the world.[27] Namely, a sort of fiscal commons exists, which can be used jointly by all, in much the same way a public meadow can graze the sheep of all the surrounding farmers. Common-pool resources have many potential management strategies.[28] However, such strategies presume the existence of some sort of entity with some control over the matter, as well as some interest in seeing that the common-pool resource is managed properly.

We see the management of common-pool budget resources most readily in the case of private firms. There, the choice to spend is explicitly linked to the liabilities that choice creates, even if it may not seem so. A firm's budget can be thought of as a common-pool resource, at least at the start of the fiscal year, with that budget being parceled out to various managers in the form of budget numbers such that some amount of petty cash is likely left over. This commons is replenished through commercial activity, that is, by producing a product or service that is then sold to customers. In effect, garnering and maintaining customer support replenish the fiscal commons in the private setting. Managers who consistently go over budget without that additional spending clearly generating sufficient additional revenues will quickly find themselves unemployed, as their actions are tantamount to reducing the amount of resources that can be parceled out. In other words, they are causing the depletion of the firm's common-pool resource. Likewise, even though a manager may wish to overstate the benefits or understate the costs of any proposed project, doing so will not be tolerated for long, as such mistakes are costly and easily attributable to a single source.

In the public setting, the commons refers to the funds available for Congress to spend. Unlike the private setting, where the commons is stocked and replenished through commercial activity, this commons is stocked and replenished by taxation. Here, we can already see a potentially dangerous problem: one way in which would-be elected officials compete for constituent support is through lowering taxes, which is tantamount to reducing the stock of the common-pool resource. Elected officials—through their appointment to various appropriations committees—vie with one another for increased access to this common-pool resource. In doing so, they often prepare cost–benefit analyses. Ideally, only bills whose reported benefits exceed their reported costs should ultimately be supported. However, projecting costs and benefits for bills is fraught with potentials for abuse.

As Block describes: "Advocates of new spending projects will seek projections that will portray them at the lowest possible cost. On the flip side, tax-cut proponents look for projections that minimize revenue loss."[29] This practice isn't in and of itself dishonest—the committees and their members are merely choosing which study to cite in their reports and hearings, as well as carefully choosing witnesses. But selectively presenting evidence advocates a position rather than taking a purely academic approach to the issue. Regardless, numbers are an integral part of the budget process. In particular, two numbers are especially important.

The first number that must be established is a sort of base for comparison purposes. This number, appropriately called the "baseline," is a projection of what will happen if nothing changes in current law. The second number is an estimate of net revenue that would be generated or costs that would be imposed if the proposed legislation were to pass. This number is referred to as the "score." Taken together, these numbers provide the Senate with an estimation of where they are currently heading financially and how the proposed legislation will affect that trajectory. Both numbers are highly important; however, the baseline is perhaps the more important of the two, as a high baseline would reduce the apparent cost of any proposed legislation.

These numbers became particularly important after the 1990 Budget Enforcement Act. That act imposed two restrictions on Congress: First, Congress was not to adopt spending legislation that would cause annual appropriations on discretionary spending to exceed caps established in the budget resolution. Second, all new tax legislation or changes to entitlement programs must be revenue neutral, meaning that decreases in revenue or increases in spending had to be offset by increases in revenue or decreases in spending elsewhere in the budget.

In an ideal world, the economic assumptions and methodologies used to construct these numbers would not matter, but unfortunately, that is not the case: "In the imprecise world of budgetary mathematics, even seemingly small changes in estimation methodologies and economic or behavioral assumptions can lead to significantly different scores."[30] Legitimate differences of opinion will always exist over which assumptions to make or which estimation methodologies to use, but it would be foolish not to acknowledge that assumptions and methodologies can also be chosen merely to suit a particular ideology or to advance a particular agenda.

In addition, the task of classifying an item as taxation or spending is not as straightforward as one would intuitively believe. Both Presidents Ronald Reagan and Bill Clinton, for example, have argued that increases in Social Security benefit taxes should be scored as spending cuts rather than tax increases since the tax increases would effectively reduce the amount of benefit that the recipients actually received.

The timing that is associated with budgetary scoring faces similar but separate problems.[31] It is similar in the sense that it involves the manipulation of numbers, but it differs in that it does not rely on manipulating the numbers' values, nor is it manipulating the categorization of the numbers. Instead, timing can be gamed owing to the fact that budgets are based on fiscal years beginning October 1, whereas many spending programs are based on calendar years. Thus the expense (or revenue) can be reported as occurring in different parts of the calendar year, which correspond to different fiscal years. In the event that a spending program will put an appropriations committee over its cap, the committee can simply report the spending as occurring in a different part of the calendar year and avoid being punished for exceeding its limit during the current fiscal year.

A second source of timing obfuscation can be found in inconsistent uses of the budget window. Budgets are, after all, tied to a specific amount of time. Every household has its own daily budgets, but also weekly, monthly, yearly, and perhaps even lifetime budgets. In setting their budgets, they set aside a certain amount of money that can be spent over the course of a specified amount of time. So too must any committee or office that makes budget projections and recommendations—they must put forth a plan that sets aside a certain amount of money that is available to be spent over a certain amount of time.

In the past, Congress used a short, one-year basis for budgeting purposes. Although it provided Congress with the flexibility to amend the budget resolution each year, it also meant that individual Congresses were not making allowance for the long-run costs of any proposed legislation, instead only making allowance for the current-year costs. This situation created problems in that the long-run costs would get out of hand through the simple fact that few, if any, senators were taking them into account.

A budget resolution that takes into account long-run projections, however, will necessarily be more speculative in nature than a short-term budget, much as how an annual budget at home is much less certain than a daily budget. Long-term planning—while it gains the benefit of taking into account long-run costs—sacrifices the hindsight necessary to easily update figures as new information becomes available.

In 1990, Congress passed the Budget Enforcement Act as a means of settling this debate by moving to a statutory five-year minimum window for purposes of budget resolutions. In 1997, Congress began requesting 10-year budget information from the Congressional Budget Office (CBO); the Office of Management and Budget (OMB) followed suit, similarly supplying 10-year budget information. The important thing here is that the legislative and the executive branches both used the same budget window, the same scoring practices, and so on, in their evaluations. Doing so allows for a more fruitful comparison between the two branches' budget proposals.

The challenge, however, is that no formal rules govern the budget window that must be used other than the five-year minimum. In 2004, for example, the OMB began using a 10-year window in some instances and a 5-year window in others in the same budget proposal. This method made meaningful comparisons and calculations difficult and resulted in charges that the administration was using selective changes in the budget window solely to advance the president's legislative agenda.

A third source of timing difficulty comes from the use of various accounting gimmicks. These can range from the relatively simple to the complex. An example of a simple accounting gimmick comes from the inconsistent use of cash versus accrual accounting. Briefly, cash accounting is a type of accounting practice that records revenues in the period in which they are received and expenses in the period in which they are paid. It does not include revenues that are to be collected in the future, nor does it include expenses that are to be paid in the future in any way.

In contrast, accrual accounting records incomes and expenses when the right to receive or obligation to pay them arises, regardless of whether funds have been received or paid. In the private sector, the accrual method dominates because of its forward-looking nature and is even required in accordance with generally accepted accounting principles established by the Financial Accounting Standards Board.

Congress, however, does not have such a requirement. In general, Congress uses the cash accounting method (though there are exceptions), and OMB/CBO reports are likewise calculated using this method. This method affords legislators several tools of budget chicanery.

Perhaps the easiest one is to simply delay payments or receipts by one day and thus into the subsequent fiscal year. People outside Congress may not notice such a trick, and it can easily be employed to move billions of dollars from one budget year to another. Advance appropriations are similar to this practice: an appropriations bill can be passed in one fiscal year while the authorization bill (and thus the actual spending) can be passed in the subsequent year, again shifting the spending away from one fiscal year and into another. These budget gimmicks are powerful, but they are limited in that they can only move payments and receipts from one year to the next. To move budget items over longer periods, more sophisticated and complex variations need to be employed.

The easiest way to move budget items across longer periods is to phase in programs over time. In doing so, legislators commit to spending over much longer periods than the year in which they are legislating while simultaneously tying the hands of future Congresses (unless the future Congress acts to repeal said program). Alternatively, rather than paying the full cost up front to, say, construct a building, Congress can engage a private contractor to build the building, giving the contractor the title to the building at the end of construction and subsequently paying rent to occupy the space created. This contracting-out method can appear advantageous even if it ultimately costs significantly more than Congress's simply building or buying the building itself. Again, using the cash accounting method, these tricks allow the current Congress to commit to spending programs while reporting only a fraction of that spending in the current year. Under the accrual method, the full cost would be reported immediately regardless of when the money would actually be paid.

Another, slightly more complicated version of this tactic is to pass legislation with a fixed expiration date or sunset, even if the legislation is fully expected to extend beyond the sunset or perhaps even to be made permanent. This trick works because of the methodology that the CBO uses when scoring any proposals. The CBO must, when scoring any proposals, consider them in light of existing law without taking into account future statutory changes to the law. As a result, if a proposal that will reduce revenue includes a sunset provision of three years, the CBO will score it as existing only for those three years, and its score will be improved.

The temporary research and development tax credit may be the most notorious offender of this sunsetting game.[32] Despite widespread bipartisan support, a permanent tax credit for research and development has not been passed; instead, the temporary credit first passed in 1981 has been extended several times such that it is now viewed as virtually a political given.

In summary, the cash accounting method, for all its merits, also provides government agencies with significant scope to engage in budget gimmicks by slightly altering the timing of the spending or revenue collection. Doing so can make it appear as though Congress as a whole is saving significant money on a year-by-year basis while simultaneously increasing long-term spending obligations.

CONCLUSION

This chapter seriously calls into question the ability to properly constrain any legislative assembly from overspending. It is not meant to scare anyone or to imply that the situation is hopeless—as Wagner points out, "What cannot continue, won't continue," and this situation clearly cannot continue indefinitely.[33] This circumstance leads us naturally to questions of prevention and of what will happen if the deficit grows to a point that is untenable.

Much would have to change in the budget process if we are to prevent fiscal disaster. Given the institutional setting of public debt, it is not at all clear how that would be done or if it is even possible. The Founders had a way of doing this through a system of internal checks and balances. That system worked remarkably well for generations. However, in those times, the connection between the general public and their elected officials was much tighter, if only because the population was much smaller and the division of labor much more limited, fostering a greater common knowledge among the public in that everyone had a better understanding of one another. It was also a time when, relatively speaking, the federal government did not do a whole lot. And so reasonable people could evaluate various bills and proposals with much greater ease than they can today.

Finally, that old-time fiscal religion has been broken. Gone are the days when governments were viewed as merely referees within society, making sure that a person's property and contracts were respected. Instead, government has been transformed, rightly or wrongly, into an entity that is expected to provide goods and services to its citizens, or at least some portion of its citizens. What this means for the future of governments and their fiscal health remains to be seen.

CHAPTER NINETEEN

FISCAL FEDERALISM AND DYNAMIC CREDENCE CAPITAL IN THE UNITED STATES

JOHN MERRIFIELD AND BARRY POULSON

For two centuries, the United States maintained arguably the strongest federalist system in the world, grounded in fiscal federalism. The term "fiscal federalism" is used in the broad sense of autonomous and independent branches of government, each responsible for fiscal policies within its own jurisdiction. The basis for this strong federalist system was of course the Constitution, with enumerated powers delegated to the federal government, and remaining powers vested in the states and the people. The strength of this federalist system was decentralized structure, with fiscal autonomy and independence for subnational governments. Elected officials at all levels of government practiced the "old-time fiscal religion" of balanced budgets.[1]

Fiscal federalism was based on a "no-bailout" principle. In the 1840s, a number of states went bankrupt, including Illinois, Michigan, Pennsylvania, and five others. Despite entreaties from insolvent states, the federal government refused to bail them out.[2] The no-bailout principle created the right incentives. After 1840, state and local governments incorporated fiscal rules in their constitutions mandating a balanced budget and limiting debt. Throughout the 19th and early 20th centuries, elected officials learned to live with the constraints imposed by balanced budget rules and debt limits, and citizens gained confidence in the ability of state and local officials to pursue prudent fiscal policies. Banks and other creditors had an incentive to evaluate the creditworthiness of each jurisdiction in extending loans. Credit rating agencies had an incentive to practice due diligence in rating the bonds issued by each jurisdiction. With balanced budget rules and debt limits in place, state bankruptcies were few and far between; the last state to declare bankruptcy was Arkansas during the 1930s.[3]

Before 1934, bankruptcy law applied only to private persons and companies. The relevant federal law, Chapter 9 of the Federal Bankruptcy Code, did not apply to state or local governments. In 1934, Congress extended bankruptcy law to municipal debt, in response to appeals from municipal governments overwhelmed with bonded indebtedness. In 1936, the Supreme Court ruled that law unconstitutional in *Ashton v. Cameron County Water Improvement District*. Also in 1936, Congress passed a new statute that the Supreme Court, in *United States v. Bekins*, ruled constitutional. Since then, local jurisdictions can use bankruptcy law to negotiate with creditors to restructure their debts, and to renegotiate contractual obligations such as pay, retirement, pensions, and health benefits.

Federal bankruptcy law provided for an orderly settlement of municipal debt, and insolvency laws provided for a renegotiation of debt without the government having to enter bankruptcy proceedings. As the creditworthiness of state and local government improved, fiscal federalism strengthened. Over time, with a "no-bailout" principle in place, and governed by bankruptcy laws, citizens gained more confidence that state and local governments would balance their budgets and limit debt, a phenomenon that Blankart refers to as growing "credence capital."[4]

Over the past half century, however, we have witnessed an erosion of fiscal federalism and declining dynamic credence capital. Elected officials at all levels of government abandoned the norm of balanced budgets. A fatal flaw was the rejection of the no-bailout principle; indeed, we have become a bailout society. Municipal governments and school districts are increasingly dependent on state transfers and subsidies; and states such as Connecticut and Illinois have come to rely on bailouts from the federal government. With these bailouts, state and local governments can avoid bankruptcy. This fiscal dependency accelerated with the massive federal bailout of state and local governments during the recent financial crisis.[5]

Credit markets are now signaling to highly indebted state and local governments, and to the federal government, that current fiscal policies are unsustainable. As the debt crisis has intensified, citizens have lost confidence in the ability of elected officials to pursue prudent fiscal policies.

In contrast to the United States, some countries, such as Switzerland, have successfully addressed their debt crisis. Swiss courts have enforced the no-bailout principle, requiring fiscal autonomy and independence for municipal and cantonal governments. With strict bankruptcy laws in place, Swiss subnational and national governments enacted debt brakes, fiscal rules that mandate that governments balance budgets and reduce debt to sustainable levels. As these debt brakes strengthened fiscal federalism, Swiss citizens gained greater confidence in the ability of their elected officials to pursue prudent fiscal policies.[6]

In this chapter, we argue that the United States should follow the Swiss precedent, restoring a strong fiscal federalist system, with fiscal autonomy for state and local governments. A no-bailout principle should be restored, such that state as well as local governments are subject to bankruptcy laws. Like their Swiss counterparts, state and local governments would then have an incentive to enact effective fiscal rules, mandating a balanced budget and reductions in unsustainable levels of debt.

Swiss-style fiscal rules are proposed for the federal government, as well as state and local governments. With these fiscal rules in place, elected officials would have an incentive to address the debt crisis. With effective fiscal rules, and with the enforcement of a no-bailout principle, citizens would gain confidence in the ability of elected officials to pursue prudent fiscal policies. However, after a half century of declining dynamic credence capital, enacting the institutional reforms required for effective fiscal rules in the United States will be a formidable challenge.

EROSION OF FISCAL FEDERALISM

ABANDONING THE OLD-TIME RELIGION OF BALANCED BUDGETS

The U.S. Constitution contains no provisions imposing limits on deficits and debt. However, over the first two centuries of U.S. history, fiscal policies at all levels of government were governed by what economists refer to as the old-time religion of balanced budgets. In periods of military conflict, the federal government often could not increase taxes by a sufficient amount to cover expenses, and it resorted to borrowing. In peacetime, the government was expected to balance the budget, and in some years to generate surplus revenue to pay down the debt. In the long term, federal debt declined both in nominal terms and as a share of gross domestic product (GDP).[7]

Adherence to balanced budgets is evident in the early 20th century. Federal spending and borrowing spiked during World War I, as it had during prior military conflicts. But during the 1920s, federal spending was reduced from $18 billion to $3 billion. As a share of GDP, federal spending fell below 5 percent, comparable with peacetime spending in the 19th century. In the 1920s, the federal government earned surplus revenue used to pay down the federal debt, which was reduced from $25 billion to $17 billion. Federal debt as a share of GDP fell to about 16 percent, comparable with debt levels during peacetime in the 19th century.[8]

The tradition of balanced budgets continued well into the post–World War II years. In some years, Cold War expenditures tipped the federal budget into deficit, but in other years the federal government balanced the budget, including a few years of surplus revenue. Federal debt as a share of GDP declined continuously until the 1970s.[9]

Over the past half century, the federal government abandoned its commitment to balanced budgets. With the exception of a few years in the late 1990s, the federal government has incurred deficits and accumulated debt continuously. The Congressional Budget Office (CBO) projects that under current law, debt will increase to equal the national income over the next decade and will continue to increase to unsustainable levels thereafter.[10]

The past half century has also witnessed an increase in debt incurred by state and local governments. Debt and unfunded liabilities in pension and health benefits for public employees impose heavy burdens on state and local taxpayers. In 2013, state and local governments owed $968 billion in unfunded pension benefits, $587 billion in unfunded health benefits, and $518 billion in outstanding debt.[11] Despite the risk of insolvency, state and local government debt as a share of income is projected to continue to grow in the 21st century.[12] Some states, such as Colorado, have been more successful in enforcing balanced budget rules and tax and spending limits.[13] However, even those states must now address the unsustainable growth of unfunded liabilities in retiree pension and health benefits.

ABANDONING THE NO-BAILOUT PRINCIPLE

Many factors led elected officials to abandon the old-time religion of balanced budgets; however, rejection of the no-bailout principle was a fatal flaw. We can trace that rejection to the Great Depression, when hundreds of municipalities defaulted on the debt they had incurred during the more prosperous years in the 1920s. In some cases, municipalities were able to restructure debt and extend repayment periods, but in many cases the debt went unpaid.[14]

New Jersey and North Carolina responded to the municipal bankruptcies of the 1930s by enacting municipal fiscal emergency laws; these laws allow the state to intervene when municipal governments cannot meet their financial obligations. These interventions include emergency financing, a control board with powers to review and veto local decisions, and adjustment in wages and benefits for employees. Although the laws differ from state to state, they generally allow the state to borrow on behalf of the municipality, essentially bailing it out of its financial difficulties.[15]

The fiscal stress experienced by municipal governments during the financial crisis that began in 2008 led a number of states to pass new fiscal emergency laws. Thirteen states have now passed laws that allow them to deal in general with municipal fiscal emergencies; three states have passed laws addressing specific municipal government emergencies.[16]

Historically, U.S. states and local jurisdictions operated within a strong federalist system, with clear autonomy from the federal government. Over the past half century, however, that fiscal autonomy has eroded significantly. This erosion is reflected in the increased share of state and local expenditures funded from federal government transfers. More importantly, the loss of autonomy is reflected in the increased regulation and control of state and local expenditures by the federal government.[17]

State and local governments are increasingly dependent on federal transfers, especially in funding entitlement programs. That dependence is most evident in the loss of state control over Medicaid. Many state governments accepted the Obama administration policy to expand enrollment in Medicaid, with the provision that the federal government would finance most of the increased cost. Federally mandated spending for welfare and Medicaid programs has thus left state governments with little control over major parts of their budgets.[18]

A discontinuous increase in federal government transfers and bailouts occurred during the recent financial crisis. The George W. Bush administration responded to the 2008 financial crisis by enacting the Emergency Economic Stabilization Act. That act was the basis for the Troubled Asset Relief Program (TARP) that authorized up to $700 billion in subsidies to bail out financial institutions.[19]

The Bush bailout of financial institutions was followed in 2009 by a more ambitious bailout by the Obama administration, including the $830 billion American Recovery and Reinvestment Act (ARRA). The AARA subsidized a wide range of government programs at both the federal and the state level. It also targeted subsidies to two auto firms, Chrysler and General Motors. The government then forced financial institutions that had received TARP funding to purchase the stock of those auto firms, in effect nationalizing the firms. Federal government mandates on the auto industry, and other industries, have continued under the Trump administration.

Fiscal stimulus during the Obama administration was used to subsidize state and local governments.[20] That funding enabled state and local governments to address fiscal stress during the financial crisis, and in some cases to avoid bankruptcy.

Much of that fiscal stimulus was off budget. For example, the federal government subsidized debt issued by state governments as Build America Bonds (BABs). States issuing these bonds received a direct federal subsidy of 35 percent of their interest payment. State governments issued almost $250 billion in BABs in 2009 and 2010. That action allowed the total debt issued by state and local governments to grow during the financial crisis.[21]

But the federal bailout of state and local governments introduced moral hazard, similar to that accompanying bailouts in the financial industry. Anticipating bailouts, municipal governments have less incentive to impose fiscal rules or to pursue prudent fiscal policies. When municipalities receive bailouts, credit rating agencies lump them together, rather than assessing the riskiness of each jurisdiction in issuing debt. The inefficiency and misallocation of lending to municipal governments weaken the public finances of all jurisdictions participating in the bailout.

The bailout of state and local governments by the Obama administration during the Great Recession created even greater dependence on the federal government. Without that federal bailout, many states would have been unable to meet their financial obligations. They are now more dependent on federal government transfers than before the financial crisis.[22]

Recent studies have attempted to estimate the cost of government bailouts during the financial crisis. The Congressional Budget Office estimates that of the $700 billion authorized by the Emergency Economic Stabilization Act, $431 billion was actually spent in bailing out financial institutions.[23] After repayment of those loans, the CBO estimates the cost of TARP at $24 billion. Even this estimate does not fully reflect the cost of these federal loans to private entities (see the discussion of federally subsidized lending by Marvin Phaup in Chapter 15 of this book). The CBO also estimated that the ARRA would increase deficits by $185 billion in 2009, $399 billion in 2010, and $134 billion in 2011, or $787 billion over the 2009–2011 period.[24]

The actual deficits incurred by the Obama administration were unprecedented. In his first year in office, deficits tripled from about $500 billion to almost $1.5 trillion. Deficits remained above $1 trillion a year while those bailout programs were in effect, and then decreased to about $500 billion when they ended. Much of the bailout money was expended off budget, and therefore was not subject to the scrutiny that accompanies the regular budget process.

The inefficiency and misallocation of resources resulting from government bailouts are difficult to measure.[25] But the real cost of federal transfers and bailouts is the impact of these policies on incentives in both the private and the public sector. The perception grows that the federal government cannot constrain debt, exposing the country to increasing risk of default. Credit markets punish this profligacy by charging higher interest rates, reflecting the risk of default in the United States compared with eurozone countries.[26]

State and local governments in the United States are more sensitive to the constraints imposed by credit markets compared with the federal government. Credit ratings on debt issued by state and local governments vary considerably, and the interest rates charged for debt issued by state and local governments vary as well. The financial crisis revealed wide disparities between jurisdictions pursuing prudent and profligate fiscal policies.[27]

AMERICA'S FIRST FAILED STATE: ILLINOIS

Illinois is America's first failed state. The state has accumulated hundreds of billions in debt and unfunded liabilities in public-sector pension and health care plans. The failure of Illinois to address this growing debt crisis is often attributed to a divided legislature and gridlock in the budget process. But a more fundamental flaw is the state's rejection of no-bailout rules, and the growing dependence of both the state government and local governments on federal transfers and bailouts. This flaw can be traced to federal bailouts received during the financial crisis.[28]

Illinois made extensive use of federally subsidized debt in the form of BABs.[29] The direct impact of federal subsidies for bonds was a sharp increase in deficits in 2009 and 2010, boosting total bonds outstanding to $25 billion. This change was followed by a ratcheting up of deficits in subsequent years, reaching a peak of almost $15 billion in 2017. In 2018, it was estimated that Illinois would boost debt by $30 billion.[30]

The state has also assumed liabilities incurred in Chicago and other highly indebted local jurisdictions. The accumulation of debt and unfunded liabilities in pension and health plans in the city of Chicago and in school districts around the state exposed them to the risk of default and bankruptcy. The state of Illinois responded with large bailouts, which in turn further weakened the finances of the state government. The courts have exacerbated this problem, ruling that the Illinois Constitution mandates state bailouts for public-sector pension and health benefits for public employees.

The subsidies received by the state and local governments in Illinois from the fiscal stimulus most likely enabled them to pay bills and avoid bankruptcy. But a credibility problem has emerged from the state of Illinois's bailout of local jurisdictions. Illinois now has the worst credit rating in the municipal bond market. Moody's Investors Service pegs Illinois debt at Baa3, just one grade above junk status. Although Illinois debt trades like junk municipal debt, investors continue to purchase new debt issues. If the state is insolvent and can't meet its financial obligations, the expectation is that the federal government will again bail out the state as it did during the financial crisis.[31]

Fiscal rules in Illinois have been ineffective in constraining deficits and debt. Like 48 other states, Illinois has a balanced budget provision in its state constitution. But in recent years, the state legislature failed to pass a budget—let alone a budget that would balance revenues and expenditures.

In April 2018, a constitutional amendment to cap the rate of growth in spending at the rate of growth in the state economy was introduced in Illinois's legislature.[32] A majority of Illinois state legislators have yet to show support for such a fiscal rule. We question whether any fiscal rules could be effective in constraining deficits and debt in a failed state such as Illinois. The expectation is that the state of Illinois will continue to depend on federal bailouts, and local jurisdictions will continue to rely on state bailouts.[33]

Although Illinois is the worst-rated state in the municipal bond market, other states are also incurring unsustainable debt and unfunded liabilities in pension and health benefit programs for public employees.[34] Most ominous is legislation in California that would by law shift the liabilities of local governments and school districts to the state government. As the bailout of state and local governments becomes more ubiquitous, it will further weaken fiscal federalism.[35]

CONNECTICUT IMPOSES A UNIQUE DEBT BRAKE

Connecticut lawmakers may have come up with a way to prevent the state from foundering on the shores of bankruptcy. Connecticut has unfunded liabilities in pension and health benefits for public employees estimated at $35 billion. With some of the most underfunded benefit programs in the country, municipal governments and school districts are dependent on state bailouts to remain afloat. When the state failed to agree on a budget last year, state aid to municipal governments was frozen. Standard & Poor's downgraded Connecticut's general obligation bonds, citing the fact that the state is guarantor of the city of Hartford's $540 million in debt. In response, the state appointed a commission to study the debt crisis and come up with recommendations for fiscal reform. The commission recommended fiscal discipline measures designed to constrain debt and put fiscal policy on a sustainable path.[36]

This year, with the city of Hartford facing bankruptcy, state legislators came up with a new bond issue that includes covenants imposing a debt brake. The state issued almost $500 million in general obligation bonds that will provide funding for school construction projects as well as grants-in-aid to municipal governments and special districts. The covenants limit state borrowing to no more than $2 billion per year. Bond authorizations may not exceed 1.6 times general tax receipts. State spending is limited to 98 percent to 100 percent of revenues and cannot grow faster than inflation. Excess reserves above the spending limit must be placed in a reserve fund. The state is prevented from changing the formula setting the state debt limit for five years. The state can exceed the debt limit only if the governor declares an emergency, and three-fifths of both chambers of the state assembly vote to increase the cap.[37]

The response to this new bond issue was quite remarkable. The state received orders for three times the number of bonds issued. Oversubscription of the bonds allowed the state to negotiate lower interest rates, significantly reducing the debt service costs. By incorporating a debt brake as a condition for issuing these bonds, credit markets signaled that the state must begin to get its fiscal house in order. Elected officials responded by agreeing on a state budget that eliminated deficits and set aside more than $500 million in the reserve fund.[38]

By imposing a debt brake, Connecticut is following the precedent for new fiscal rules enacted at both the subnational and the national level. What is unique in Connecticut is that the state incorporated the debt brake as a covenant in a bond issue, thus exposing the state to discipline from the bond market. If Connecticut fails to enforce the debt and spending caps, we should expect bond rating agencies to again downgrade general obligation bonds, which will increase the cost of borrowing by the state.

Connecticut may have avoided bankruptcy for now, but the real test will come in the next recession. We should expect municipal governments and school districts in Connecticut to again demand bailouts from the state, and we should expect the state to turn to the federal government for transfers and subsidies, as it did during the financial crisis. Although no state has gone bankrupt since the 1930s, it is difficult to see how heavily indebted states such as Connecticut can stay afloat without fundamental reforms in their fiscal policy.

By enacting their unique debt brake, Connecticut legislators are sending a clear message that the state can no longer afford to bail out municipal governments and school districts. For the debt brake to be successful, the state must begin to impose a no-bailout principle and require local jurisdictions to become financially autonomous and independent in the near term.

Other states and the federal government will be watching the Connecticut debt brake closely. If this experiment with fiscal rules is successful, we should expect a new wave of debt limits and tax and expenditure limits in the states similar to those launched by the tax revolt in the 1970s.

EROSION IN DYNAMIC CREDENCE CAPITAL

A LOSS OF TRUST

The increased dependence of state and local governments on federal transfers and bailouts sends all the wrong signals. State and local governments do not face a hard budget constraint; indeed, they often have an incentive to increase spending in order to qualify for larger federal transfers. Higher levels of debt do not expose them to insolvency and bankruptcy because they now rely on federal transfers and bailouts. State and local governments therefore have an incentive to circumvent balanced budget rules and other rules to constrain spending and debt, and they have little incentive to enact more stringent fiscal rules.

Banks and creditors tend to lump state and local governments together regardless of creditworthiness, because the risk of lending has shifted to taxpayers. For the same reason, credit rating agencies have little incentive to practice due diligence in rating the debt issued by different jurisdictions.

Erosion in fiscal federalism has been accompanied by erosion in dynamic credence capital in the United States. Citizens have likewise lost trust in the ability of elected officials to pursue prudent fiscal policies.[39] The growing debt burden at the state and local level will further undermine efforts to address the debt crisis at the federal level. In a future financial crisis or recession, the expectation is that insolvent state and local governments will again turn to the federal government for transfers and bailouts. In some states, such as Illinois and Connecticut, this will simply ratchet up the level of debt in the long run.

THE GROWING RISK OF DEFAULT

As debt at all levels of government grows, citizens are exposed to increasing risk of insolvency and default, and the outcome is unclear. The loss in dynamic credence capital in the United States is evident in the long-term trend in interest rates. In the late 1970s, the Federal Reserve launched monetary policies designed to stabilize growth in the money supply and rates of inflation. That reform yielded a sharp increase in the interest rate. With some lag, the rate of inflation began a downward trend, accompanied by a decline in long-term interest rates.

FIGURE 19.1
Long-term interest rates forecast, 2018

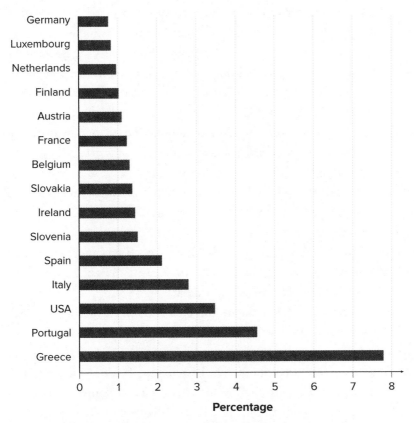

Source: Organisation for Economic Co-operation and Development, *OECD Economic Out-look: Statistics and Projections*, "Long-term interest rates forecast," 2018.

Since the onset of the financial crisis, the Fed has pursued quantitative easing to reduce long-term interest rates even further. However, a divergence in long-term interest rates has emerged between the United States and the eurozone countries. Before the financial crisis, the interest rate on long-term bonds in the United States was below that in the eurozone countries. By 2017, the interest rate on long-term bonds in the United States exceeded that in all the eurozone countries with the exceptions of Portugal and Greece (see Figure 19.1).

For 2018, the Organisation for Economic Co-operation and Development (OECD) projected that the interest rate on long-term U.S. bonds would be 3.44 percent, a rate significantly above that for all the eurozone countries except Greece and Portugal (see Figure 19.1). The average interest rate on long-term debt in the eurozone as a whole was projected at about 2 percent, and the average rate excluding the southern eurozone countries was projected at about 1 percent. Thus the U.S. government pays a premium on long-term bonds between 1.5 percent and 2.5 percent compared with that paid by most eurozone countries.[40]

The conventional wisdom is that the differential in interest rates on long-term bonds between the United States and eurozone countries reflects differences in monetary policy.[41] But as of this writing, the Fed has only begun a policy to boost long-term interest rates, and expectations of the Fed's tightening have had, at most, a modest impact on long-term rates. Most European countries have been more successful in constraining and reducing debt compared with the United States. The higher-risk premium on U.S. long-term bonds compared with eurozone bonds probably reflects investors' loss of confidence in the ability of elected officials in the United States to limit debt.

A number of studies estimate the effects of changes in government debt on interest rates. A study by Turner and Spinelli estimates that each percentage increase in government debt as a share of GDP raises the interest rate differential about five basis points.[42] The impact of debt on interest rates depends on whether it is financed domestically or externally. In the United States, the share of debt financed externally has increased; as a result, the impact of higher debt on interest rates has also increased. This relationship holds even when taking into account the effects of quantitative easing on interest rates. Like the heavily indebted countries in Europe that are dependent on external finance, the United States has become more vulnerable to a financial crisis.[43]

RESTORING FISCAL FEDERALISM AND GROWING DYNAMIC CREDENCE CAPITAL

RESTORING THE NO-BAILOUT PRINCIPLE

It is unclear how to restore fiscal federalism and grow dynamic credence capital in the United States, which is far behind the learning curve compared with the eurozone countries in enacting fiscal rules to effectively constrain debt. The precedent set in some OECD countries is to design and enact new fiscal rules to more effectively limit spending and debt. In the eurozone countries, critics questioned whether these new fiscal rules were credible solutions to their debt crises. They pointed to design flaws in the early debt brakes enacted in Germany and other countries. More importantly, they questioned whether these fiscal rules could be effective without fundamental institutional reforms.[44]

Fundamental to the effectiveness of fiscal rules is a credible no-bailout rule:

> The no-bailout principle in Switzerland has the character of what can be called a "dynamically developing credence capital good." This means that the belief that the policy will be followed grows through its application over time and debases itself when it is disregarded. Each application of the no-bailout rule strengthens the expectation that it will continue to be applied in the future, therefore it is important that the no-bailout principle is continuously applied. Once a bailout takes place it takes time for the markets to believe that it will not happen again and borrowing costs will rise. The key to fiscal responsibility in Switzerland does not rest with balanced budget rules as such, but with a credible no-bailout position. It is not possible to substitute the no-bailout position by a better set of budget constraints and fiscal rules such as the Fiscal Compact. Both are necessary. The problem the Eurozone faces is that once expectations of "no-bailout" have disappeared it is difficult to convince markets that the principle will be followed again.[45]

Growing dynamic credence capital strengthens finances within a federalist system. The more prudent the fiscal policies pursued by a state or local government, the lower its borrowing costs. Profligate state and local governments, on the other hand, face higher borrowing costs, and in some cases insolvency and bankruptcy. Loanable funds tend to flow to the more prudent and creditworthy jurisdictions, promoting capital investment and economic growth. Investments in infrastructure in these jurisdictions attract private investment. This interstate competition for investment and jobs is the basis for a strong federalist system.

Countries such as Switzerland have been successful in using new fiscal rules to address their debt crisis because they have enacted, and carried out, institutional reforms. In fact, when Switzerland began to design and enact more effective fiscal rules, it encountered a dilemma similar to that in the United States. Some Swiss cantons were heavily in debt, and were heavily reliant on the federal government for bailouts. When the Swiss imposed their debt brake, they also imposed constraints on the fiscal policies pursued by cantons. The more profligate cantons were given a fixed number of years to put their fiscal house in order. Over time, those cantons eliminated deficits and reduced their dependence on bailouts from the federal government. As a result of these institutional reforms, Switzerland now has one of the strongest federalist systems in the world, with growing dynamic credence capital.[46]

SWISS-STYLE FISCAL RULES FOR THE UNITED STATES[47]

In our research we explore whether a Swiss–style debt brake tailored to U.S. circumstances is a credible solution to the U.S. debt crisis.[48] Our proposed fiscal rule corrects some of the design flaws in the early debt brakes enacted in eurozone countries. The proposed rule incorporates an expenditure limit with multipliers to allow flexibility in responding to long-term demand for government services. The rules provide for deficit and debt brake multipliers to provide flexibility in meeting fiscal targets.

An emergency fund and capital fund are incorporated in the rules to enable the government to promote economic stability without sacrificing the commitment to reduce the debt burden below a tolerable level in the long term. Once that debt target has been met, the rules provide for a cyclically balanced budget.

However, we agree with critics who argue that the effectiveness of the fiscal rules we propose would require fundamental reform in institutions, and that would be quite challenging in the United States. Historically, U.S. fiscal policies were pursued within a strong federalist system with substantial taxation and expenditure autonomy for state and local governments. However, the erosion of fiscal federalism—with the growing dependence of state and local governments on the federal government—has contributed to the debt crisis. It is unclear how to reverse a half century of declining dynamic credence capital in the United States.

U.S. capital markets are the most efficient in the world at assessing the creditworthiness of borrowers. However, the massive bailouts of borrowers in both the private and the public sector since the financial crisis have introduced moral hazard and undermined this capital market efficiency. When borrowers can count on government bailouts, credit markets have little incentive to practice due diligence in assessing the creditworthiness of potential borrowers. A no-bailout principle may now be needed to restore capital market efficiency before any fiscal rules will be effective. The rules must also restore the role for insolvency and bankruptcy laws.

A no-bailout principle would help restore fiscal autonomy and accountability to state and local governments. Mandatory bankruptcy proceedings for insolvent states as well as local jurisdictions would again create incentives for effective fiscal rules and prudent fiscal policies. Whether or not the judicial system could return to this earlier interpretation of constitutional law is an open question.

Restoring a strong federalist system may also require some heterodox fiscal reforms, and the debt crisis has spurred research into several of such reforms. Restoring fiscal federalism may require shifting taxation and expenditure decisions back to state and local governments. The Reagan administration set a precedent for policies of privatization and devolution of federal programs to the states, with block grants replacing programmatic grants. With waivers from federal regulations, the states experimented with reforms in welfare, Medicaid, and a host of other federal programs. The Reagan administration was also the last to enact reforms that significantly reduced unfunded liabilities in Social Security.[49]

Western states such as Utah have challenged federal government control of mineral and energy resources on public lands, arguing that transfer of ownership and control of public lands to the states would result in more efficient management of these resources. We have called for a New Homestead Act to restore a strong federalist system that was the foundation for rapid economic growth in the 19th century.[50] We have also argued for a Fiscal Responsibility Council and a deficit/debt brake at the national level. Although Congress has considered new fiscal rules, including our proposed deficit/debt brake, it has yet to act on these proposals.[51]

CONCLUSION

The loss in dynamic credence capital in the United States has magnified the difficulties in solving the debt crisis. The expectation is that in a financial crisis the federal government will again suspend any existing fiscal rules as it sees fit. The precedent set during the recent financial crisis favors the massive bailout of corporations and financial institutions, and we should expect the federal government to continue the bailout of state and local governments. Citizens' loss of confidence in the ability of the federal government to constrain debt may now be the biggest hurdle in bringing debt to a sustainable level.

The heavy debt burden now imposed on U.S. citizens exposes the government to risk of default. Higher interest rates on U.S. debt reflect that growing risk and are increasing the debt burden. The ongoing U.S. loss of credence capital makes higher-than-expected interest rates likely. Higher interest rates will make it much more difficult to reduce the U.S. debt burden to a sustainable level.

If the United States experiences a major recession accompanied by significant revenue shortfalls and deficit spending, it will be very difficult for the country to achieve fiscal stabilization. A significant rise in deficits and debt accumulation would be accompanied by increases in interest rates far in excess of those assumed in the CBO's long-term forecasts. Indeed, it is conceivable that in a major recession the United States could experience an increase in interest rates comparable with that experienced by the major debtor countries in the eurozone region.

With an effective debt brake in place, the government would be better able to respond to a recession, military conflict, natural disaster, or other emergencies. Clearly, the fiscal rules now in place have proved to be ineffective and are unlikely to be effective in future years. But the question is whether new fiscal rules, such as those enacted in Switzerland, can be effective in the United States.

We conclude that debt brakes proposed for the United States may not be feasible or credible without fundamental institutional reforms. Restoration of the no-bailout principle could reduce moral hazard and create incentives for elected officials to enact effective fiscal rules. Restoration of a strong fiscal federalist system—with autonomous and independent state and local governments—could reverse the decline in dynamic credence capital. This assessment of the credibility of proposed fiscal rules to solve the debt crisis in the United States absent fundamental institutional reforms may be discouraging to citizens who support these rules. But failure to enact these institutional reforms would expose the country to even greater risks in coming years.

CHAPTER TWENTY

CONTROLLING GOVERNMENT SPENDING: THE DIFFICULTY AND THE HOPE

DWIGHT LEE

If we want things to stay as they are, then things will have to change.

—Giuseppe Tomasi di Lampedusa, *The Leopard*

George Will put it bluntly when he wrote, "America is sleepwalking into the most predictable crisis in its history, the demographically driven crisis of the entitlement state struggling to provide health care for an aging population."[1] And the crisis is not confined to providing health care. It also includes the Social Security payments promised that aging population, which is growing faster than the population responsible for making those payments. Although government Medicare and Social Security obligations are the biggest concerns, other government programs not confined to the aged, such as Medicaid, are also contributing to the problem. Avoiding the crisis Will has warned us about requires looking at many federal spending programs both large and small.

Most people are aware that fiscal responsibility is not the hallmark of the federal government. And a majority would surely agree that our economic future, and that of coming generations, would be more secure if federal spending and the federal debt were reduced. Indeed, for years we have heard from politicians, at least when running for office, that the federal budget needs to be brought into balance and the national debt

FIGURE 20.1

Federal debt held by the public as a percentage of GDP, 1790–2040

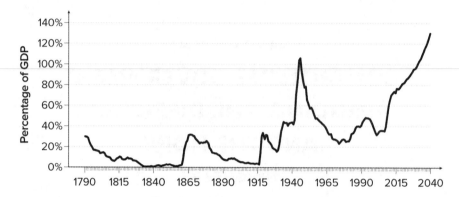

Source: Chris Edwards, "Federal Spending and Debt, 1790 to 2050," *Cato at Liberty* (blog), Cato Institute, September 20, 2013.

Note: GDP = gross domestic product.

reduced.[2] So the public knows what should be done, and most believe that balancing the federal budget is important.[3] Yet it is difficult to convince politicians that deficit spending is not a good idea.

In the over 60 years since 1957 when we had a small budget surplus, the federal budget has been in deficit every year except five. Since the last surplus in 2001, the gross federal debt held by the public has more than doubled as a percentage of gross domestic product (GDP—see Figure 20.1), increasing from 31.4 percent in 2001 to 75.3 percent in 2017.[4] In some ways, this political indifference to voters is surprising. The growth in government spending is reducing the economic productivity needed to sustain itself and also to sustain the growth in our standard of living.

Fiscal changes could be made that would quickly and broadly improve our economic well-being. Those changes would require short-run economic and social adjustments that most would like others to make but would prefer not to make themselves. But the alternative is to continue unsustainable levels of government spending that press down on current prosperity and will eventually necessitate painful economic and social adjustments that can be avoided at far less cost with sensible policy changes today.

Public choice economics provides reasons for believing that politicians are ignoring obvious changes needed to put fiscal policy on a sustainable path; it also explains why the public is letting them get away with it. Broadly speaking, public choice analysis suggests that political decisions tend to concentrate on the short-run benefits of government spending while ignoring its greater long-run costs.[5] But I shall argue that public choice provides reasons to have moderate hope that a fiscal crisis is not as predictable as George Will indicates.

I begin by considering a brief history of federal government spending, which shows an impressive record of fiscal responsibility and economic growth for the first 140 years of U.S. history. The next section considers skeptically the argument that with the right fiscal policies we can depend on economic growth to prevent a fiscal crisis without painful reductions in the growth of, much less cuts in, federal spending. I next examine the bias in favor of expanding government spending well beyond productive limits and consider the importance of constitutional restrictions in moderating that bias. Once a government program has been established, it is well-known that it is difficult to eliminate it, or even reduce it, even if it is obviously wasteful. I then point out that it is often the case that the more wasteful a government program is, the more difficult it is to reduce or eliminate. The penultimate section uses public choice arguments typically viewed as pessimistic regarding controlling government spending to contend that moderate hope for achieving this control is not entirely naive. The final section offers a concluding statement.

A HISTORY OF THE GROWTH IN FEDERAL GOVERNMENT SPENDING

Despite what many believe, the federal government has a long history of impressive fiscal responsibility. From 1790 through the 19th century, peacetime federal spending was consistently less than 3 percent of GDP, with spending little more than that in the 20th century until the 1930s, World War I excluded. Furthermore, during this period, the peacetime budget was almost always in surplus.

A few small peacetime budget deficits did occur during recessions, but that was because of declines in revenue, not because of increased federal spending to stimulate the economy. Of course, large budget deficits from increased spending occurred during wars, but the resulting debt was steadily reduced, sometimes almost entirely, afterward. Following the Civil War, for example, the federal budget was in surplus or was balanced from 1866 until 1893. Starting out as a poor country, the United States had the dominant economy in the world by roughly 1900.

Critical to this fiscal responsibility was the prevailing political ideology that the role of the federal government should be largely limited to enforcing private property rights, protecting citizens against domestic predators and foreign invaders, and providing a few public goods unlikely to be provided through markets. On the other side of this ideological coin was a widespread understanding that some things were simply not the business of the federal government—as reflected in the Ninth and Tenth Amendments to the U.S. Constitution.

That understanding is illustrated by the vetoes of Democratic president Grover Cleveland. For example, in his first presidential term, Cleveland vetoed a bill that called for spending $10,000 to provide seed grain to Texas farmers who were experiencing a serious drought. He sent the bill back to Congress with the same message by which he explained many of his vetoes, that such spending was not permitted by the Constitution.[6] It's difficult to imagine a president routinely vetoing such bills today, as Cleveland did, and being reelected, as Cleveland was.

This record of fiscal restraint shows that the federal government can control peacetime spending at very low levels, run consistent budget surpluses after wars to pay down the debt, and do so while experiencing impressive long-term economic growth. Unfortunately, the prevailing ideology that made this record possible began eroding around the 1890s with the beginning of what is known as the Progressive Era and the growing belief that the wealth being created in the market economy could be increased and allocated more fairly by expanding the economic role of the federal government.[7] And as the limited-government ideology eroded, slowly at first, the ability of the Constitution to sustain that ideology also seemingly eroded. As Henry Simons warned after the erosion had become noticeable:

> Constitutional provisions are no stronger than the consensus that they articulate. At best, they can only check abuses of power until moral pressure is mobilized, and their check must become ineffective if often overtly used.[8]

As late as the early 1930s, however, peacetime federal spending remained less than 5 percent of GDP. Public opinion still exerted strong restraint on government spending early in Franklin Roosevelt's administration in the depths of the Great Depression. Although FDR soon earned his reputation for greatly expanding federal spending, within one month of becoming president he signed the Economy Act of 1933, which dramatically reduced military pensions. This legislation has been described as "the most consequential in pension history."[9] Unfortunately, it was also the last reduction in an entitlement spending program of any consequence. Before the end of Roosevelt's first term, peacetime federal spending had reached 10 percent of GDP, and the Social Security Act was enacted, which was to become the largest government entitlement program in U.S. history. It also coincided with the first U.S. federal spending increase during an economic downturn.

Federal spending as a percentage of GDP during World War II exceeded 40 percent, higher than the 24 percent reached during World War I or the 10 percent reached during the Great Depression. (See Figure 20.2.) If one wanted to be optimistic about the possibility that government spending can be brought down, one could point to the fact that it was decreased dramatically after World War II and since the mid-1950s has oscillated around 20 percent of GDP. This decrease was primarily the result of absolute reductions in federal spending; however, after the late 1950s until the early 1990s, spending increased significantly with only one budget surplus during that time.[10] Yet from the early 1990s until the very early 2000s, federal spending declined noticeably until it started back up in the early 2000s, with a sharp increase once the Great Recession started in 2008. It has dropped since but is still higher than it was before the Great Recession.

FIGURE 20.2

Federal spending as a percentage of GDP, 1790–2040

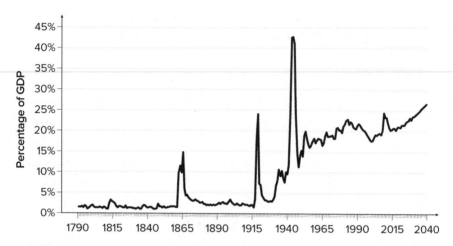

Source: Chris Edwards, "Federal Spending and Debt, 1790 to 2050," *Cato at Liberty* (blog), Cato Institute, September 20, 2013.

Note: GDP=gross domestic product.

One could argue that although federal spending has greatly increased since the mid-1950s, it really hasn't increased much relative to the size of the economy, staying roughly around 20 percent of GDP. One might view this as evidence that we should be able to avoid the crisis George Will has warned us about without slowing government growth. That is, what we need is not fiscal restraint, but government policies that increase economic growth. Let's consider that argument.

CAN WE DEPEND ON ECONOMIC GROWTH TO REDUCE THE THREAT OF CRISIS?

The most obvious problem with depending on economic growth to support growth in federal spending is that federal spending growth is about to escalate. The amount paid to beneficiaries of federal entitlement programs—such as Social Security, Medicare, Medicaid, and others—has increased steadily since 1947, from a little less than 4 percent of GDP to 16 percent in 2015.[11] The number of programs has increased, as has the average value of benefits received by beneficiaries and the percentage of the population receiving those benefits, including more nonpoor than poor. "In 2015, 62 percent of recipient households, encompassing over 100 million U.S. residents, had incomes that were above the poverty line prior to the receipt of entitlements. Thirty-one percent, nearly 60 million persons, were in the upper half of the income distribution."[12]

Two current demographic trends make it even more unlikely that a fiscal crisis can be avoided. First, baby boomers have already started to retire and are demanding their Social Security retirement payments and Medicare benefits, with many millions more right behind them. Meeting their demands will place unprecedented strain on the federal budget. Second, the population of entitlement demanders is growing faster than the population of workers needed to pay for the entitlements. Without the pain from reducing the growth in federal spending, economic growth is highly unlikely to be enough to prevent the far greater pain of George Will's predicted fiscal collapse. Unfortunately, accepting some short-term political pain requires the type of political foresight that hasn't been a notable feature of today's federal fiscal policy. If such foresight had guided political decisions since 1960, we wouldn't be in the sorry fiscal situation we currently find ourselves.

But can't we avoid painful cuts in federal spending with more effective policies to increase economic growth? The government could do many things to increase economic growth, but most require undoing things that impede economic growth, such as excessive regulation and overly complicated taxation, which are beyond the concerns of this chapter. The pro-growth policy that is most likely to generate political enthusiasm is the recommendation to stimulate economic growth by increasing, not decreasing, government spending.

Whether coincidental or not, in the 1960s, politicians became convinced that higher rates of economic growth could be achieved with Keynesian fine-tuning. Buchanan and Wagner argued that Keynesian economics was accepted enthusiastically by politicians because it was an excuse to do what they wanted to do—spend more than they raised in taxes.[13] Yet their enthusiasm was limited to the part about deficit spending when more economic growth was needed.

Since politicians always think more economic growth is needed, they largely ignored Keynes's recommendation for budget surpluses during periods of economic strength. Keynesian economists—anxious to remain politically influential—quickly learned to downplay the fiscal austerity of spending reductions and budget surpluses. For example, Paul Krugman claims that "all of the economic research that allegedly supported the austerity push has been discredited."[14] Krugman acknowledges: "It's true you can't continue to run big budget deficits forever (although you can do it for a long time). . . . At some point you do want to reverse stimulus. *But you don't want to do it too soon.*"[15]

Another problem with increasing growth in federal spending relative to GDP to increase economic growth is that it increases government allocation of resources relative to market allocation. Such a shift in allocating resources is sure to further reduce their marginal productivity, thus slowing economic growth. The loss in the value of economic output will not be fully reflected in the official GDP, however.

As opposed to market output, the value of much government output is measured by the amount spent to provide it instead of how much consumers are willing to pay for it. The rapid economic growth of the American economy during the 1800s—with low federal spending and no attempt to stimulate the economy with increased spending during recessions (some quite serious, though none as long lasting as the Great Depression)—suggests that achieving long-run economic growth doesn't require Keynesian fiscal policy. Indeed, economic growth is more likely to be hampered than helped by Keynesian policies under the influence of political decisions. The only realistic hope for avoiding a fiscal crisis is to start slowing down, or reversing, the growth in government spending. Doing so will both reduce future government obligations and increase the economic growth needed to pay for them.

THE REASONS GOVERNMENT SPENDING INCREASES

Constitutions are important because they help protect the public against excessive taxing and government spending. One might ask why the public needs this protection. If government growth harms the public, voters can vote the big spenders out of office and replace them with those who will tax and spend less. As we saw previously, however, a prevailing ideology in favor of strong constitutional limits on what government can do often erodes over time as the ideology shifts to reflect a public desire for government to tax and spend more. Unfortunately, unless it is strongly restrained by constitutional limits, the democratic political process gives citizens a stronger voice when they want more government than when they want less, even when they would be better off with less. Consider some reasons for this bias in favor of larger government.

Government spending is commonly concentrated on relatively small groups of people organized around narrow interests—such as those in an industry, profession, or government agency—who benefit from the spending. Such groups are strongly motivated to exert political influence to maintain or expand the spending and can do so by virtue of being organized. Since the cost of spending programs in taxes and reduced productivity is spread over the entire population, few are motivated to oppose them. When people incur the cost to influence political decisions, it is usually to support spending and regulations that benefit them, not to oppose those that benefit others. That's why, when political scientist James L. Payne watched 14 congressional hearings during the 1980s (when many were hoping, or fearing, that the Reagan administration would make major cuts in federal spending) and recorded the number of witnesses who favored and opposed government spending programs, he found some striking numbers. Out of 1,060 witnesses, 1,014 supported the program being considered, 7 opposed it, and 39 were neutral.[16]

Of course, politicians are also influenced by large numbers of unorganized voters who can collectively send strong messages to their political representatives without having to travel to Washington or hire K Street lobbyists. Many believe, however, that when voting, people are more concerned with the public interest than when making private, or market, decisions. For example, in response to James Buchanan's being awarded the Nobel Prize in 1986, Steven Kelman wrote an article criticizing the award and public choice in which he argued:

> Government has become, for many, an appropriate forum to dis-
> play their concerns for others. Why? That political decisions involve
> the community as a whole—and often future generations as well—
> encourages people to think about others when taking a stand. This
> is in contrast to personal decisions involving mainly oneself, which
> encourages people to think of themselves.[17]

Kelman's claim cannot be casually dismissed. People are commonly more explicitly responsive to the situation of others when voting than when making market purchases. But that doesn't mean we are more compassionate when voting to help others than when purchasing to help ourselves.

Consider an example. When making a choice for a product in the market, you get what you choose, and you get it only if you choose it—your choice is decisive. When making a choice for a candidate in the voting booth, your favored candidate may or may not be elected, but there is only the tiniest probability that your vote will be decisive. This difference in decisiveness explains why voters are commonly viewed as more morally motivated than are purchasers in the marketplace. How many people who finally find the perfect garment for an upcoming school reunion at a bargain price would refuse to buy it because they think the purchase might increase income inequality? Probably not many. But many people are concerned about income inequality and vote for political candidates who promise to increase their taxes to reduce that inequality with an expensive government program to help the poor.[18]

Many view this difference as evidence that Kelman is right; that people are more willing to sacrifice for others when making political decisions than when making market decisions. But public choice assumes that people are basically the same whether making political or market decisions. It is the incentives that are different in the two settings, not the people. Purchasers have a strong incentive to consider the personal consequences of their purchases because their "vote" is decisive, whereas voters have little if any incentive to consider the personal consequences of their vote since it isn't decisive. Public choice economists view voters as voting expressively, not consequentially. The cost of passing up a bargain on the preferred garment to reduce income inequality may not be very high, but it is a lot higher than the cost of voting to pay more in taxes, even a lot more.

Assume that the cost of not purchasing the preferred garment is $100 in relation to paying more and receiving less pleasure from the garment purchased. But that cost is 100 percent determined by the decision not to make the purchase. Assume the cost to individuals voting for a federal tax increase is $10,000 in present value *if the tax increase is passed.* But their expected cost of voting to pay the additional tax equals $10,000 times the probability that their vote is decisive, that is, determines that the tax will be passed. Assuming their vote is for their representative in the U.S. House, then the probability of their vote's being decisive is approximately 1 in 12.3 million.[19] That means their expected cost of voting to pay $10,000 to reduce income inequality is $10,000 divided by 12.3 million, or a little less than one-tenth of a penny.[20]

Obviously, voting is an important function in a democratic political process. But it is also important to recognize that although voting is essential to a properly functioning democracy, nothing is perfect. And understanding voting's imperfections increases our ability to compensate for them. For example, the work done by public choice economists explains why voting is incapable of protecting the public against government's misuse of the power it needs to perform its essential functions. Among other things, this work emphasizes the importance of political constitutions in disciplining government power. That importance was eloquently stated by James Madison when making the case for ratifying the U.S. Constitution in *The Federalist Papers.* In *Federalist* 51 Madison wrote: "If men were angels, no government would be necessary. If angels were to govern men, neither external nor internal controls on government would be necessary. In framing a government which is to be administered by men over men, the great difficulty lies in this: you must first enable the government to control the governed; and in the next place oblige it to control itself."[21]

Consider an example of how the "generosity" of voters can result in their failure to control government spending. It costs each voter effectively nothing to vote for more spending to achieve noble objectives; however, it is expensive for them to follow up on their vote to see how effective the spending is in realizing those objectives. The fact is, each voter has little incentive to make such an effort since each realizes that it will be ineffective unless a lot of other voters make the same effort, and unneeded if they do.

But there is an unfortunate exception. As opposed to those who vote only with their ballots, organized interest groups and their lobbyists can also "vote" with their political influence, which can have a significant effect on what legislation gets passed and how it is written as it travels though the complicated legislative process. Furthermore, they can use these influential "votes" constantly to affect how the costs and benefits of the legislation are distributed. And because their "votes" are likely to be decisive, it would cost politically influential groups a lot to use them primarily to achieve such noble objectives as helping the poor, providing health care for the sick, protecting American jobs, saving family farms, or reducing global warming. Long after noble-sounding legislation has been largely forgotten by those who voted for it, organized groups will still be giving it close attention to keep it consistent with their private interests, even when that reduces its ability to promote the goals the voters thought they were voting for.[22]

THE DIFFICULTY OF REDUCING GOVERNMENT SPENDING

We have been considering political incentives that motivate increases in government spending even when the social benefits are less than the social costs. This wasteful spending would be less of a problem if the waste was readily recognized and pressures were activated to reduce or eliminate it. Wasteful government spending, however, commonly goes unnoticed by taxpayers, and politicians often have little incentive to reduce waste even when aware of it.

Politicians commonly create wasteful outcomes with spending and regulations intentionally designed to benefit politically influential groups. These groups will fight harder to protect the wasteful programs from which they benefit than they did to get them enacted in the first place, even when the benefits they receive had been largely competed away. Consequently, government has a difficult time providing lasting benefits to special-interest groups, which implies that the more wasteful government spending is, the more difficult it is to eliminate. Gordon Tullock referred to this as a "transitional gains trap."[23]

For example, since the 1930s, the federal government has provided farmers with subsidies and price supports for their crops. The initial effect was to increase the returns to the farmers of targeted crops. But soon competition for the land best suited for growing those crops drove up the price until the return on farming that land declined to the competitive level. Farmers owning the land when the programs started benefited from their land's higher value. But that was not true for farmers who bought their land after the government programs started.

A reasonable measure of the economic waste of the subsidy and price support programs is how much they increase the price of land. That increased price reflects the diversion of investment into producing more of the subsidized crops when it would otherwise have created more value in the production of unsubsidized products. So the more farm programs artificially increase the price of farmland, the more wasteful they are, but the more value farmers will lose in their land if those programs are eliminated. That loss of value would be viewed as horribly unfair, particularly for those who bought their farmland after the subsidy programs started because they had paid for their government benefits in the higher price of the land they bought.

An observation by Adam Smith completes the explanation for why it is easier for politicians to resist creating wasteful programs than to eliminate them after they have been created: "We suffer more . . . when we fall from a better to a worse situation than we ever enjoy when we rise from a worse to a better."[24] In other words, the beneficiaries of an agricultural program may not be any better off because of it, but they will be very much worse off if the program is eliminated and will resist that elimination more strenuously than the efforts they made to get the program passed initially. Furthermore, expressive voters will oppose what they see as the unfairness of eliminating the benefits from those who have paid for them.

A lot of voter sympathy also exists for those who are poor for reasons over which they have little control. Few want to deny them enough government aid to have the basics. Unfortunately, many of the poor receiving public aid would improve their situations with their own productive efforts if the aid would not discourage them from—or punish them for—doing so. In such cases, those who become dependent on welfare programs pay a price for their welfare benefits, and it is a very high price indeed. Thus they would be doubly victimized if those programs were suddenly eliminated or scaled back. Instead of this additional harm being recognized as a measure of the programs' failure, it will be viewed by many as evidence of their success at preventing the harm, even though the harm of the welfare trap would never have occurred without them. But the harm is real and makes it politically difficult to eliminate aid programs once they have been created.

The fact that it is difficult to scale back government spending programs when they do more harm than good is a powerful argument for making it more difficult to pass such programs in the first place. Of course, we have already passed a host of socially harmful programs that cannot be wished away. It would be nice, however, to believe that such spending could be reversed, and reversed widely and sufficiently enough to avoid the fiscal crisis George Will predicted. Let me end with moderate optimism that this is not a completely ludicrous hope.

WITHOUT HOPE THERE IS NO ENTERPRISE

The hope may be naive that politicians will exercise some fiscal responsibility before it is too late to avoid a fiscal crisis, with widespread disappointments and painful adjustments. The most effective thing I can offer is the restoration of an ideological mistrust of centralized government in response to the increasingly irresponsible fiscal policies of the federal government.

Writing in the late 1850s, the French economist Frédéric Bastiat argued that the government (or the state) had become "the great fictitious entity by which everyone seeks to live at the expense of everyone else."[25] Bastiat's statement is an exaggeration because the economy would collapse before we reached such a state. But what is true is that the United States has gone far enough in Bastiat's direction that an increasing number of people are realizing that they are paying more for the benefits of others than the value of the benefits they are receiving. Some of the resentment toward the political process is surely coming from a growing realization that it has maneuvered us into a destructive prisoner's dilemma in which each of us is better off grabbing all the government benefits we can, and all of us are worse off when everyone is doing so.

Government spending may be increasingly recognized as analogous to environmental pollution. Just as public attitudes shifted on environmental pollution—as reflected by a widespread demand for government to restrict everyone's polluting activity—an ideological shift could generate a widespread demand for general reductions in government spending. The biggest problem with this hope takes us back to *The Federalist Papers* and *Federalist* 51. To reduce environmental pollution, government was called on to control others, but reducing fiscal pollution requires the government to control itself.

As with most large-number prisoner's dilemmas, individuals have no incentive to forsake their own government benefits since they have no reason to expect others to follow. But as the fiscal pollution worsens, a crisis point may be reached when political entrepreneurs find it reasonable to put forth a proposal for large numbers of groups to accept reductions in their own federal benefits with the understanding that their reductions will be reciprocated by simultaneous reductions in the federal benefits going to others. Such reductions would be more easily done at a state level despite the serious limits imposed by the fact that much state funding is subsidized, or mandated, by the federal government. But even with no state able to avoid federal fiscal pollution, some states are able to compete successfully for population and tax bases by keeping taxes and the cost of government services relatively low. For example, some states could form consortia to cooperate in reducing their own fiscal pollution.[26] I am unwilling to bet that such a movement will soon be successfully reducing absolute levels of government spending. But I wouldn't rule it out, especially if federal spending continues its upward trend relative to GDP. And if such a movement does appear, it could easily activate a lot of people who are now moderately and quietly sympathetic to reducing the size and intrusiveness of the federal government.

Evidence suggests that people have become less favorable to government growth and spending. Polling data since the 1950s show that a majority of Americans have consistently preferred that the national government do less in general, with this majority trending upward from about 52 percent in 1958 to about 67 percent in 2010. When asked about individual programs, however, the majority favored maintaining or increasing them, but this majority trended downward from about 67 percent in 1958 to about 53 percent in 2010.[27] Public choice analysis would predict this: the general size of government focuses attention on cost, and specific functions of government focus attention on benefits. This trend in favor of a smaller government provides some hope that an ideological shift favoring reductions in federal spending is not absurd.

Even in Europe, where the public is more sympathetic to large central government than in the United States, another study suggests that enough skepticism may exist toward government to encourage ideological resistance to expanding it. Alesina, Carloni, and Lecce looked at 19 OECD countries that quickly reduced large budget deficits by more than 1.5 percent of GDP from 1975 to 2008.[28] Instead of the common view that incumbent governments that reduce budget deficits primarily with spending cuts are more likely to be punished at the polls than those that reduce deficits primarily with tax increases, they found the opposite was true. When the next election came within two years of the deficit reductions, electoral defeat was more likely when deficit reduction was based on tax increases than on spending reduction. Furthermore, the deficit reductions were more durable when achieved by spending reductions.

I am reluctant to sound optimistic about controlling, much less reducing, the size of the federal government relative to GDP. America's experience since the 1930s doesn't suggest a return to a prevailing ideology in favor of reversing our continued dependence on federal spending. Yet this experience hardly supports the hope that expanding, or further centralizing, government spending and power is an effective way of addressing a wide range of social problems.

No one denies that some people have been helped by anti-poverty programs, by mandating Social Security, and by increasing access to medical care. But in each of these cases, and more, the costs have been far higher than necessary to provide help to those who need it most. The dependency that has been created by numerous anti-poverty programs has reduced the incentive for many to take the initiative to improve their lives and those of their families by becoming more productive. Social Security has expanded over time to far more people than would have become poor in their agedness without it. But by reducing the incentive to save for retirement, it has reduced economic productivity and increased the number who would be poor without it. The huge percentage of medical care that is paid for by third-party payments because of Medicare, Medicaid, and the Affordable Care Act has distorted and greatly increased the social cost of health care by largely destroying the market incentives for cost-effective decisions by both consumers and suppliers.

It may now fairly be said, "The harsh reality is that entitlement programs, originally established to 'promote the general welfare,' have become a clear and present danger to the nation's future welfare"; and: "Public dissatisfaction with the entitlement state is mounting. The public is coming to realize that the utopian ideas of the Progressive era . . . have not lived up to their promise. . . . As entitlement costs continue to grow and their harmful consequences become more apparent, public pressure will grow and will ultimately force government to change policies."[29]

Such a result would obviously mean a significant shift in the prevailing ideology in favor of at least significantly slowing down government spending relative to GDP, and possibly reversing that growth. But we must ask: Will this shift be strong enough to overwhelm the reluctance most people have to accept cuts in programs on which they have become dependent? In considering this question, we need to recognize that expressive voting can be a two-edged sword when it comes to government spending.

As discussed earlier, when voting in federal elections, the probability that an individual's vote will determine the election's outcome is effectively zero. But it determines one thing with a probability of 100 percent: how voters feel about how they vote. If voters feel good about taking others into consideration by voting for more government spending to help others, the value of that good feeling will overwhelm their minuscule expected personal financial cost of voting yes for more spending.

But suppose that most voters felt that the most noble thing the federal government can do is to reduce dependence on government by reducing spending and taxing and giving people more freedom and incentive to improve their conditions by engaging in productive cooperation with one another through markets. What if they also understood that when people consider the cost of the products they are voting for with their dollars in the marketplace *they are likewise taking others into consideration*? The market price they are paying for a product gives them the best information available on how much others value another unit of that product. Since we buy another unit of a product only if we value it by more than its price, we refrain from buying another unit when others value it by more than we value it.

Voters with this understanding will get a sense of moral satisfaction from voting against government spending and regulation that exceed their cost of doing so even if they incur a significant loss if enough other people vote the same way. Such an ideological understanding coupled with expressive voting can overcome Tullock's transitional gains trap by allowing the diffused public interest of voters to overpower their more narrowly focused financial interests as beneficiaries of government spending programs.[30]

CONCLUSION

Informed by the fiscal trends at the federal level, it is difficult to be hopeful that a crisis will be avoided. The strength of the American economy is one reason for hope; however, that strength depends on reversing the fiscal trend since the 1930s. The concern is that the strength of the economy depends on a complicated system of institutional arrangements, incentives, and traditions that can continue to generate economic growth for many years after the elements that make that growth possible have started to erode slowly and without notice. As Rosenberg and Birdzell have so portentously pointed out:

> Such a system could run down so slowly, in response to causes separated by so many years from their effect, that by the time its degeneration became apparent, it might be irreversible. Indeed, social systems

can continue to expand long after the events that made their collapse inevitable.[31]

Rosenberg and Birdzell present this statement as "ground for caution," not despair. I have attempted to present an unvarnished view of the difficulty we face in avoiding the seemingly inevitable fiscal crisis, and the social and economic disruption it would cause. But I have tried to do so with the hope that the most predictable crisis in American history is not as predictable as George Will believes it is. No doubt my cautious optimism will remind many of Samuel Johnson's comment when describing his friend's second marriage, "The triumph of hope over experience."[32] I prefer, however, to think of Alfred Marshall's comment, "Without hope there is no enterprise."[33] Few, if any, enterprises are worthier than protecting our liberty and prosperity against the crushing conformity and uninformed control of an ever more centralized and intrusive government.

NOTES

INTRODUCTION

1. John Merrifield and Barry Poulson have published two books addressing this issue: *Can the Debt Growth Be Stopped? Rules-Based Policy: Options for Addressing the Federal Fiscal Crisis* (New York: Lexington Books, 2016) and *Restoring America's Fiscal Constitution* (New York: Lexington Books, 2017).

2. Congressional Budget Office, *2019 Long-Term Budget Outlook*, June 25, 2019.

3. Congressional Research Service, *Statutory Limits on Total Spending as a Method of Budget Control*, March 26, 2016; Congressional Research Service, *Legislative Procedures for Adjusting the Public Debt Limit: A Brief Overview*, by Bill Heniff Jr., (RS21519) May 6, 2016; Congressional Research Service, *A Balanced Budget Constitutional Amendment: Background and Congressional Options*, March 20, 2016.

4. Tom Price, "Proposed Rewrite of the Congressional Budget Process Discussion Draft: Description and Rationale," Committee on the Budget, U.S. House of Representatives, Washington, November 30, 2016; U.S. Government Accountability Office, "Debt Limit: Government Responses to Recent Impasses Underscores the Need to Consider Alternative Approaches," GAO 15-470, 2015 July 9.

5. Pierre Yared, "Rising Government Debt: Causes and Solutions for a Decades-Old Trend," NBER Working Paper No. 24979, National Bureau of Economic Research, August 2018, revised January 2019.

6. Giusseppe Eusepi and Richard Wagner, "Indebted State versus Intermediary State: Who Owes What to Whom?," Constitutional Political Economy 23, no. 3 (2012): 199–212.

CHAPTER ONE

1. Vet Fiscal Rules, www.objectivepolicyassessment.org/vetfiscalrules, describes the model; see also John Merrifield and Barry Poulson, *Restoring America's Fiscal Constitution* (Lanham, MD: Lexington Books, 2017).

2. John Merrifield and Barry Poulson, *Can the Debt Growth Be Stopped?: Rules-Based Policy Options for Addressing the Federal Fiscal Crisis* (Lanham, MD: Lexington Books, 2016); Merrifield and Poulson, *Restoring America's Fiscal Constitution*.

3. John Merrifield and Barry Poulson, "New Constitutional 'Debt Brakes' for Euroland Revisited," *Journal of Applied Business and Economics* 19, no. 8 (2017): 110–132; Merrifield and Poulson, *Restoring America's Fiscal Constitution*.

4. Paul Brandus, "Trump's Intriguing Idea: Cut Debt by Selling Off Federal Assets," *MarketWatch*, March 29, 2017.

5. Most years, the national debt rises by much more than the gap between planned spending and expected revenues.

6. The Swiss debt brake yields approximate budget balance over the business cycle.

7. CBO, *2017 Long-Term Budget Outlook,* March 2017.

8. William F. Shughart II and Carl P. Close. "Liquidating Federal Assets: A Promising Tool for Ending the U.S. Debt Crisis," The Independent Institute, March 6, 2017.

9. Bob Bryan, "Congress Just Reached the Mother of All Budget Deals of the Trump Era—Get Ready for a Wild Thursday," *Business Insider,* Feb 7, 2018.

10. Committee for a Responsible Federal Budget, "Addressing Common Claims about the Budget Deal," *The Bottom Line Blog,* July 25, 2019, https://www.crfb.org/blogs/addressing-common-claims-about-budget-deal; Molly E. Reynolds, "Four Takeaways from This Summer's Budget Deal, *Fixgov* (blog), August 2, 2019.

11. Kimberly Amadeo, "US Economic Outlook for 2019 and Beyond: Experts Forecast Steady Growth." *The Balance,* updated June 25, 2019, https://www.thebalance.com/us-economic-outlook-3305669.

12. Edward C. Prescott and Lee E. Ohanian, "The Good Times Can Roll On: The Economy Isn't on a 'Sugar High.' Pro-Market Policy Improved Incentives to Work and Invest," *Wall Street Journal,* August 23, 2018.

13. Alan Greenspan and Adrian Wooldridge, "How to Fix the Great American Growth Machine: The U.S. Economy Is Losing Its Historic Capacity for 'Creative Destruction.' A Few Key Reforms Are Essential to Keep It on Top," *Wall Street Journal,* October 12, 2018.

14. Phil Gramm and Michael Solon, "Tax Reform Unleashed the U.S. Economy: The Surge in Private Investment Has Brought Big Returns for Households as Well as the Government," *Wall Street Journal,* March 4, 2019.

15. Daniel J. Ikenson, "Ending the 'Chicken War': The Case for Abolishing the 25 Percent Truck Tariff." Cato Institute Trade Briefing Paper no. 17, June 18, 2003.

16. Bob Davis, "U.S. Tariffs on China Aren't a Short-Term Strategy: Trade Officials Don't See the Levies as a Negotiating Tactic in This Case," *Wall Street Journal,* October 6, 2018.

17. Author's calculations are based on CBO, *The 2018 Long-Term Budget Outlook,* June 26, 2018, and CBO, *The 2019 Long-Term Budget Outlook,* June 25, 2019.

18. Benjamin Powell, ed., *The Economics of Immigration: Market-Based Approaches, Social Science, and Public Policy* (Oxford: Oxford University Press, 2015), p. 64.

19. American Immigration Council, "A Guide to S.744: Understanding the 2013 Senate Immigration Bill," Special Report, July 10, 2013.

20. Powell, *The Economics of Immigration,* chapters 3 and 6.

21. Vivek Wadhwa et al., "Skilled Immigration and Economic Growth," *Applied Research in Economic Development* 5, no. 1 (2008): 6–14.

22. Alex Nowrasteh in Powell, *The Economics of Immigration*, p. 56.

23. William A. Galston, "Can America Grow Like It Used To? There Are Reasons to Think Not, Chief among Them the Aging Population," *Wall Street Journal,* May 29, 2018.

24. The Carbon Tax Laffer-curve peak may be below the amount generated by income taxation, and generally the tax rate that delivers the most revenue is above the most efficient (marginal benefit = marginal cost) rate.

25. Estimates are difficult for such a hypothetical situation, but real-world value-added taxes do show significant evasion. See Center for Social and Economic Research, "Study and Reports on the VAT Gap in the EU-28 Member States: 2019 Final Report," Warsaw, Poland, September 4, 2019.

26. See Russell Berman, "All the Trump Budget Cuts Congress Will Ignore," *The Atlantic*, February 12, 2018, to get a solid feel for the difficulty cutting spending, even in a declared fiscal crisis, and to see how the absence of a firm limit on spending, combined with disagreement on priorities, yields increased spending.

27. Berman, "All the Trump Budget Cuts."

28. Lev Borodovsky, "The Daily Shot: The Federal Government Now Pays $1.5 Billion in Interest Every Day," *Wall Street Journal,* October 12, 2018.

29. Akane Otani, "Treasury Yields Rise to Multiyear Highs after Strong Data: Ten-Year Note Yield Settles at 3.159%, the Highest Level in Seven Years," *Wall Street Journal,* October 3, 2018.

30. Based on very old geological surveys that need updating; see Chapter 11, this volume.

31. For example, battery technology is improving significantly. See Christopher Minns, "The Battery Boost We've Been Waiting for Is Only a Few Years Out," *Wall Street Journal*, March 18, 2018. A breakthrough would greatly improve the competitiveness of renewables such as wind and solar.

32. Greg Ip, "A Costly, Deadly Obsession with Coal: The Abundant Fuel Powered the Industrial Revolution, but Has Lost Its Price Advantage and Is Shortening Lives," *Wall Street Journal*, June 6, 2018.

33. For example, The Heritage Foundation, *Blueprint for Balance: A Federal Budget for Fiscal Year 2019* (Washington, The Heritage Foundation, 2018), and The Committee for a Responsible Federal Budget, "Sen. Rand Paul Proposes $500B in Annual Spending Cuts," *The Bottom Line Blog*, January 27, 2011, http://www.crfb.org/blogs/sen-rand-paul-proposes-500b-annual-spending-cuts.

34. Rahm Emanuel, remarks at *Wall Street Journal* CEO Council, November 2008. Clip available at https://www.youtube.com/watch?v=Pb-YuhFWCr4.

35. W. Kurt Hauser, *Taxation and Economic Performance* (Stanford: The Hoover Institution, 1996).

36. Laura Saunders, "Top 20% of Americans Will Pay 87% of Income Tax: Households with $150,000 or More in Income Make Up 52% of Total Income Nationally but Pay Large Portion of Total Taxes," *Wall Street Journal*, April 6, 2018.

37. For example, cuts to the U.S. Department of Education would be politically difficult even though there is no evidence of aggregate academic progress from federal education spending, and states could assume the cost of specific programs deemed effective.

CHAPTER TWO

1. This chapter builds on and updates "Washington's Largest Monument: Government Debt," Cato Institute Tax and Budget Bulletin no. 71, September 2015. The measure of debt used in this essay is "debt held by the public," which includes borrowing from all nonfederal entities such as individuals and other governments. This measure of debt provides the best gauge of the effects of borrowing on credit markets and the economy. Another measure of federal debt is gross debt, which includes debt that the government owes to itself. At the end of fiscal year 2019, gross debt was $23 trillion while debt held by the public was $17 trillion.

2. Numerous books have examined fiscal policies in the early Republic, including John Ferling, *Hamilton and Jefferson: The Rivalry That Forged a Nation* (New York: Bloomsbury Press, 2013); Robert E. Wright, *One Nation under Debt* (New York:

McGraw-Hill, 2008); and Herbert E. Sloan, *Principle and Interest* (Charlottesville: University Press of Virginia, 1995).

3. Thomas Jefferson, Letter to Elbridge Gerry, January 26, 1799, https:// founders.archives.gov/documents/Jefferson/01-30-02-0451.

4. Alexander Balinky, *Albert Gallatin: Fiscal Theories and Policies* (New Brunswick, NJ: Rutgers University Press, 1958).

5. Congressional Budget Office (CBO), *The Budget and Economic Outlook: 2019 to 2029*, January 2019. And see CBO, "Historical Data on Federal Debt Held by the Public," July 2010.

6. Carl Lane, *A Nation Wholly Free: The Elimination of the National Debt in the Age of Jackson* (Yardley, PA: Westholme Publishing, 2014).

7. Lane, *A Nation Wholly Free*.

8. Andrew Jackson, First Inaugural Address, March 4, 1829, https://www.loc .gov/exhibits/treasures/trr075a.html.

9. Lane, *A Nation Wholly Free*.

10. Economists Richard Wagner and Robert Tollison, for example, have said that during America's first 150 years, the prevailing fiscal ethos to balance the budget and cut debt "constituted an unwritten element of our Constitution." Richard E. Wagner and Robert D. Tollison, *Balanced Budgets, Fiscal Responsibility, and the Constitution* (Washington: Cato Institute, 1982), p. 7.

11. Bill White, *America's Fiscal Constitution* (New York: Public Affairs, 2014).

12. Author's calculation using data from the U.S. Treasury and the CBO.

13. CBO, "An Update to the Budget and Economic Outlook: 2019 to 2029," August 2019.

14. James M. Buchanan, *Liberty, Market, and State* (New York: New York University Press, 1986), p. 191.

15. Buchanan, *Liberty, Market, and State,* p. 196.

16. *Budget of the U.S. Government, Fiscal Year 2020, Historical Statistics* (Washington: Government Printing Office, 2019).

17. Joshua Aizenman and Nancy P. Marion, "Using Inflation to Erode the U.S. Public Debt," National Bureau of Economic Research Working Paper no. 15562, December 2009.

18. Aizenman and Marion, "Using Inflation."

19. CBO, "An Update to the Budget and Economic Outlook: 2019 to 2029."

20. CBO, *The 2019 Long-Term Budget Outlook*, June 25, 2019.

21. Author's calculations.

22. Lane, *A Nation Wholly Free*.

23. The "owe it to ourselves" view is identified with economist Abba Lerner writing in the mid-20th century. See Jerry H. Tempelman, "James M. Buchanan on Public-Debt Finance," *Independent Review*, Winter 2007.

24. Paul Krugman, "Nobody Understands Debt," *New York Times*, January 1, 2012. See also Paul Krugman, "Debt Is Money We Owe to Ourselves," *New York Times*, February 6, 2015; and Paul Krugman, "Nobody Understands Debt," *New York Times,* February 9, 2015.

25. Marc Labonte and Gail E. Makinen, "The National Debt: Who Bears Its Burden?," Congressional Research Service, May 1, 2003.

26. Buchanan, *Liberty, Market, and State,* p. 198.

27. Chris Edwards, "Why the Federal Government Fails," Cato Institute Policy Analysis no. 777, July 27, 2015.

28. Estimates are summarized in Christopher J. Conover, "Congress Should Account for the Excess Burden of Taxation," Cato Institute Policy Analysis no. 669, October 13, 2010. See also Edgar K. Browning, *Stealing from Each Other* (Westport, CT: Praeger Publishers, 2008) and Martin Feldstein, "How Big Should Government Be?," *National Tax Journal*, June 1997.

29. Browning, *Stealing from Each Other*, p. 179.

30. Edwards, "Why the Federal Government Fails."

31. The CBO says, "Increased borrowing by the federal government generally draws money away from (that is, crowds out) private investment in productive capital in the long term because the portion of people's savings used to buy government securities is not available to finance private investment. The result is a smaller stock of capital and lower output in the long term than would otherwise be the case (all else held equal)." See CBO, *The 2014 Long-Term Budget Outlook*, July 2014, p. 72.

32. Quoted in Jerry H. Tempelman, "James M. Buchanan on Public-Debt Finance," *Independent Review*, Winter 2007.

33. This is called "Ricardian equivalence." Economist Robert Barro revived interest in the idea that increases in government borrowing would be matched by increases in private saving as individuals looked ahead and sought to offset future taxes. For a discussion, see Robert P. O'Quinn, "Fiscal Policy Choices: Examining the Empirical Evidence," Joint Economic Committee, November 2001.

34. CBO, *The 2014 Long-Term Budget Outlook*, p. 72.

35. Congressional Research Service, "Foreign Holdings of Federal Debt," July 26, 2019.

36. CBO, *The 2014 Long-Term Budget Outlook*, p. 14.

37. Stephen G. Cecchetti, Madhusudan Mohanty, and Fabrizio Zampolli, "The Real Effects of Debt," Bank for International Settlements, September 2011. And see Carmen Reinhart and Kenneth Rogoff, "A Decade of Debt," National Bureau of Economic Research, Working Paper no. 16827, February 2011.

38. Carmen M. Reinhart and Kenneth S. Rogoff, *This Time Is Different: Eight Centuries of Financial Folly* (Princeton, NJ: Princeton University Press, 2009), p. xxxiii.

39. This example loosely follows Buchanan, *Liberty, Market, and State*, p. 202.

40. Buchanan, *Liberty, Market, and State*, p. 215.

41. Government Accountability Office, "Information Technology: Additional Actions and Oversight Urgently Needed to Reduce Waste and Improve Performance in Acquisitions and Operations," GAO-15-675T, June 10, 2015.

42. See the analyses at www.DownsizingGovernment.org.

43. Budget of the U.S. Government, Fiscal Year 2020, Historical Tables (Washington: Government Printing Office, 2019), Table 9.3.

44. Thomas Jefferson, Letter to Spencer Roane, March 9, 1821, https://www.loc.gov/exhibits/jefferson/137.html.

45. See www.DownsizingGovernment.org.

46. Thomas Jefferson, Letter to John Taylor, November 26, 1798, http://memory.loc.gov/service/mss/mtj/mtj1/049/049_0147_0148.pdf. In 1982 the Senate passed a balanced budget amendment, but it failed to gain two-thirds approval in the House. In 1995 a balanced budget amendment passed the House, but it failed in the Senate.

47. Chris Edwards, "Federal Budget Cap at 3%," *Cato at Liberty* (blog), Cato Institute, March 9, 2011.

48. Franklin D. Roosevelt, radio address, July 30, 1932, www.presidency.ucsb.edu/ws/?pid=88406.

CHAPTER THREE

1. International Monetary Fund (IMF), "Assessing Fiscal Space: An Update and Stocktaking," IMF Policy Paper, June 15, 2018.

2. For a recent survey of fiscal rules see Luc Eyraud et al., "Second-Generation Fiscal Rules: Balancing Simplicity, Flexibility, and Enforceability," IMF Staff Discussion Note no. 18/04, April 2018; see also Alberto Alesina and Allan Drazen, "Why Are Stabilizations Delayed?," *American Economic Review* 81, no. 5 (1991): 1170–88; Torsten Persson and Guido Tabelini, *Political Economics: Explaining Economic Policy* (Cambridge, MA: The MIT Press, 2000); Jürgen von Hagen, "A Note on the Empirical Effectiveness of Formal Fiscal Restraints," *Journal of Public Economics* 44 (March 1991): 199–210; Jürgen von Hagen and Ian J. Harden, "Budget Processes and Commitment to Fiscal Discipline," *European Economic Review* 39 (April 1995): 771–779; George Kopits and Steven A. Symansky, "Fiscal Policy Rules," IMF Occasional Paper no. 162, July 22, 1998; George Kopits, "Fiscal Rules: Useful Policy Framework or Unnecessary Ornament?," IMF Working Paper no. 01/145, September 1, 2001; IMF, "Fiscal Rules—Anchoring Expectations for Sustainable Public Finances," IMF Policy Paper, December 16, 2009; Allen Schick, "Stabilizing Public Finance while Responding to Economic

Aftershocks," *OECD Journal on Budgeting*, February 11, 2010; Andrea Schaechter et al., "Fiscal Rules in Response to the Crisis—Toward the 'Next-Generation' Rules. A New Dataset," IMF Working Paper no. 12/187, July 2012; Charles Wyploz, "Fiscal Rules: Theoretical Issues and Historical Experience," in *Fiscal Policy after the Financial Crisis,* eds. A. Alesina and F. Giavazzi (Chicago: University of Chicago Press, 2013).

3. John Merrifield and Barry Poulson, "Swedish and Swiss Fiscal-Rule Outcomes Contain Key Lessons for the United States," *The Independent Review,* 2016; John Merrifield and Barry Poulson, "New Constitutional Debt Brakes for Euroland Revisited," *Journal of Applied Business and Economics* 19, no. 8 (November 1, 2017).

4. Victor Lledó et al., "Second-Generation Fiscal Rules: Balancing Simplicity, Flexibility, and Enforceability," IMF Discussion Note SDN/18/04, April 2018; John Merrifield and Barry Poulson, *Can the Debt Growth Be Stopped? Rules-Based Policy: Options for Addressing the Federal Fiscal Crisis* (New York: Lexington Books, 2016); John Merrifield and Barry Poulson, *Restoring America's Fiscal Constitution* (New York: Lexington Books, 2017).

5. Eyraud et al., "Second-Generation Fiscal Rules."

6. Pierre Yared, "Rising Government Debt and What to Do about It," National Bureau of Economic Research Working Paper no. 24979, August 2018.

7. Giuseppe Eusepi and Richard E. Wagner, *Debt Default and Democracy* (Northampton, MA: Edward Elgar Publishing, 2018).

8. Yared, "Rising Government Debt."

9. Barry Poulson and Jay Kaplan, "A Rent-Seeking Model of TELs," *Public Choice* 79 (April 1994): 117–134; Merrifield and Poulson, *Restoring America's Fiscal Constitution*; Merrifield and Poulson, "New Constitutional Debt Brakes."

10. IMF, "Assessing Fiscal Space."

11. Eyraud et al., "Second-Generation Fiscal Rules"; Yared, "Rising Government Debt"; Merrifield and Poulson, *Restoring America's Fiscal Constitution*; Merrifield and Poulson, "New Constitutional Debt Brakes."

12. Merrifield and Poulson, *Can the Debt Growth Be Stopped?*; Merrifield and Poulson, "Swedish and Swiss Fiscal-Rule Outcomes"; Merrifield and Poulson, "New Constitutional Debt Brakes"; Merrifield and Poulson, *Restoring America's Fiscal Constitution*.

13. Charles B. Blankart, "What the Euro Zone Could Learn from Switzerland," *Institute of Economic Affairs* (blog), May 18, 2015.

14. Merrifield and Poulson, *Can the Debt Growth Be Stopped?*; Merrifield and Poulson, *Restoring America's Fiscal Constitution*.

15. IMF, "Assessing Fiscal Space."

16. Merrifield and Poulson, *Restoring America's Fiscal Constitution*.

CHAPTER FOUR

1. Congressional Budget Office (CBO), *The Budget and Economic Outlook: 2018 to 2028*, April 9, 2018.

2. CBO, *The 2018 Long-Term Budget Outlook*, June 26, 2018.

3. IGM Economic Experts Panel, Taxes and Mandatory Spending, October 25, 2016.

4. Victor Lledó et al., "Fiscal Rules at a Glance," International Monetary Fund (IMF), March 2017.

5. Alberto Alesina, "Fiscal Adjustments—Lessons from Recent History," ECOFIN meeting, April 15, 2010.

6. Jeffrey Frankel, "A Solution to Fiscal Procyclicality: The Structural Budget Institutions Pioneered by Chile," National Bureau of Economic Research Working Paper no. 16945, April 2011.

7. In the remainder of this chapter, I highlight the path of gross and net debt in each individual country example. According to the IMF, "General government gross debt consists of all liabilities that require payment or payments of interest and/or principal by the debtor to the creditor at a date or dates in the future. This includes debt liabilities in the form of SDRs, currency and deposits, debt securities, loans, insurance, pensions and standardized guarantee schemes, and other accounts payable. Thus, all liabilities in the GFSM 2001 system are debt, except for equity and investment fund shares and financial derivatives and employee stock options. On the other hand, general government net debt refers to gross debt of the general government minus its financial assets in the form of debt instruments. Examples of financial assets in the form of debt instruments include currency and deposits, debt securities, loans, insurance, pension, and standardized guarantee schemes, and other accounts receivable. For more information, see the Country/Series-specific notes at the end of your query. To avoid double counting, the data are based on a consolidated account (eliminating liabilities and assets between components of the government, such as budgetary units and social security funds)." IMF *World Economic Outlook*, Frequently Asked Questions; accessed October 15, 2019.

8. Charles Wyplosz, "Fiscal Rules: Theoretical Issues and Historical Experiences," National Bureau of Economic Research Working Paper no. 17884, March 2012.

9. Data from IMF *World Economic Outlook* Database, April 2018.

10. Guillermo Le Fort, "Structural Fiscal Policies to Target in the Chilean Experience," Latin American Debt Management Specialists, April 2006.

11. Frankel, "A Solution to Fiscal Procyclicality."

12. Data from IMF *World Economic Outlook* Database, October 2017.

13. Data from IMF *World Economic Outlook* Database, October 2017.

14. Marina Halac and Pierre Yared, "Fiscal Rules and Discretion under Self-Enforcement," National Bureau of Economic Research Working Paper no. 23919, October 2017.

15. KPMG, "Corporate Tax Rates Table," accessed April 15, 2020, https://home.kpmg/xx/en/home/services/tax/tax-tools-and-resources/tax-rates-online/corporate-tax-rates-table.html.

16. Gram Slattery, "S&P Downgrades Chile Sovereign Debt for First Time in Decades," Reuters, July 13, 2017.

17. Kevin Gray, "Chile Sets New Economic Plans in Motion," *LatinFinance*, May 29, 2018.

18. "Newly-Elected Chilean President Sebastian Piñera Faces a Myriad of Challenges—Economic and Otherwise," Interview with Alejandro Fernández Beros, Chief Economist at Gemines, *FocusEconomics S.L.U.,* March 1, 2018.

19. IMF, *World Economic Outlook*, April 2018.

20. For a full description of the Swiss debt brake, see Alain Geier, "The Debt Brake—the Swiss Fiscal Rule at the Federal Level," Working Paper of the FFA no. 15, February 2011.

21. For a fuller description, see John Merrifield and Barry Poulson, *Can the Debt Growth Be Stopped? Rules-Based Policy Options for Addressing The Federal Fiscal Crisis* (Lanham, MD: Lexington Books, 2016).

22. Merrifield and Poulson, *Can the Debt Growth Be Stopped?*

23. IMF, *World Economic Outlook*, April 2018.

24. Robert Chote et al., "The Fiscal Rules and Policy Framework," *The IFS Green Budget*, January 2009, pp. 81–112.

25. "Cut Spending to Reduce Borrowing," *Financial Times*, January 2, 2007.

26. Chote et al., "The Fiscal Rules."

27. IMF, *World Economic Outlook*, April 2018.

28. HM Treasury, *Budget 2010*, June 2010, 1-2.

29. This is based on the UK Office for Budget Responsibility's calculations. https://obr.uk/download/public-finances-databank/.

30. UK Office for Budget Responsibility, Historical forecast database, September 12, 2017.

31. For more details, read Ryan Bourne, "And They Call It Austerity," in *Taxation, Government Spending and Economic Growth*, ed. Philip Booth (London: Institute of Economic Affairs, 2016).

32. For more details on the UK's longer-term fiscal challenge, read Office for Budget Responsibility, "Fiscal Sustainability Report—July 2018," July 17, 2018.

33. Taxpayers' Alliance, "Highest Tax Burden This Year since 1969–70," July 23, 2018.

34. Office for Budget Responsibility, "Fiscal Sustainability Report."

35. Martin Floden, "Fiscal Consolidation in Sweden: A Role Model?," VoxEU.org, September 25, 2012.

36. IMF, *World Economic Outlook*, April 2018.

37. Lars Calmfors, "The Swedish Macroeconomic Policy Framework," IFN Working Paper no. 1075, 2015.

38. Data come from "General Government Net Debt" and "General Government Gross Debt," IMF *World Economic Outlook*, April 2018.

39. Government Offices of Sweden Ministry of Finance, "The Swedish Fiscal Policy Framework," 2017/18:207, April 12, 2018.

40. This began as a 2 percent surplus target but was reduced to 1 percent following changes to EU regulations about the portion of the old-age pension system counting toward private saving that classified some parts of the pension system as belonging to the private sector.

41. In reality, due to the asymmetric nature of business cycles, ensuring that the surplus target is hit requires the government to target a structural surplus above the target in boom times. For more information, see FÖRDJUPNING, "A New Surplus Target," *The Swedish Economy*, August 2016.

42. Notes from the Swedish National Institute of Economic Research suggest that this should occur "at a rate corresponding to the automatic strengthening of structural net lending that normally occurs in the absence of active fiscal policy decisions." That means that discretionary efforts to reduce structural borrowing should occur at the same rate as cyclical borrowing would usually fall as an economy recovers.

43. The applied budgeting margin is for at least 1 percent of capped expenditure in the current budget year, 1.5 percent for following year, 2 percent the next year, and at least 3 percent for three years ahead.

44. For a discussion of other potential drivers in changes in the gross debt-to-GDP ratio, see FÖRDJUPNING, "A New Surplus Target."

45. Charles Duxbury, "Sweden Seeks to Drop Budget Surplus Target," *Wall Street Journal*, March 3, 2015.

CHAPTER FIVE

1. Congressional Budget Office (CBO), *The Budget and Economic Outlook: 2018 to 2028*, April 9, 2018.

2. CBO, *The 2018 Long-Term Budget Outlook*, June 26, 2018.

3. CBO, *The Budget and Economic Outlook: 2018 to 2028*.

4. CBO, *The 2018 Long-Term Budget*.

5. CBO, *The 2018 Long-Term Budget*.

6. CBO, *The 2018 Long-Term Budget*.

7. Congressional Budget and Impoundment Control Act of 1974, Public Law 93–344, July 12, 1974, 88 Stat. 297.

8. Romina Boccia and Adam Michel, "Pathways for Pro-Growth, Fiscally Responsible Tax Reform," Heritage Foundation Backgrounder no. 3219, May 25, 2017.

9. Debate in the Senate on any reconciliation measure is limited to 20 hours (10 hours on a conference report), and amendments must be germane.

10. Congressional Budget and Impoundment Control Act of 1974.

11. Congressional Research Service, "Congressional Budget Resolutions: Historical Information," RL30297, November 16, 2015.

12. "Debt Ceiling: Timeline of Deal's Development," CNN, August 2, 2011.

13. Bill Heniff Jr., Elizabeth Rybicki, and Shannon M. Mahan, "The Budget Control Act of 2011," *Congressional Research Service*, August 19, 2011.

14. Grant A. Driessen and Megan S. Lynch, "The Budget Control Act: Frequently Asked Questions," Congressional Research Service, https://fas.org/sgp/crs /misc/R44874.pdf, accessed February 23, 2018.

15. Romina Boccia and Justin Bogie, "Reform the Budget Control Act Spending Caps," Heritage Foundation Backgrounder no. 3262, November 1, 2017.

16. Romina Boccia, Justin Bogie, and Paul Winfree, "How Emergency Spending Has Exploded in Recent Years," *Daily Signal*, September 19, 2018.

17. Mike Simpson, "What Are 302(a) Allocations?," https://simpson.house .gov/appropriations/302aallocations.htm.

18. Robert Keith, "The Statutory Pay-As-You-Go Act of 2010: Summary and Legislative History," *Congressional Research Service*, April 2, 2010.

19. Bill Heniff, "Budget Enforcement Procedures: The Senate Pay-As-You-Go (PAYGO) Rule," *Congressional Research Service*, RL31943 (January 9, 2018), https://www.hsdl.org/?abstract&did=807234.

20. Balanced Budget and Emergency Deficit Control Act of 1985, Public Law 99–177.

21. Boccia and Michel, "Pathways for Pro-Growth."

22. Linda K. Kowalcky and Lance T. LeLoup, "Congress and the Politics of Statutory Debt Limitation," *Public Administration Review* 53, no. 1 (January–February 1993); CBO, *Federal Debt and Interest Costs*, May 1993.

23. Romina Boccia, "Blank Check: What It Means to Suspend the Debt Limit," Heritage Foundation Issue Brief no. 4149, February 14, 2014.

24. Jenny Gesley, "Switzerland: Implementation of Article 126 of the Swiss Constitution—The "Debt Brake," June 2016, *The Law Library of Congress*.

25. Adrian Martinez, "The Swiss Debt Brake," PowerPoint presentation, Federal Finance Administration, Bern, March 28, 2018; on file with the author.

26. Expertengruppe Schuldenbremse, "Gutachten zur Ergänzung der Schuldenbremse," Federal Department of Finance, Switzerland.

27. Edward Palmer, "Financial Sustainability of Swedish Welfare Commitments," Policy Research Institute, Ministry of Finance, Japan, *Public Policy Review* 10, no. 2 (July 2014).

28. Romina Boccia and Justin Bogie, "How the Federal Government Can Get Its Spending under Control," *Daily Signal*, July 12, 2016; Romina Boccia, "'Penny Plan' Puts the Spotlight on Out-of-Control Federal Spending," *Daily Signal*, April 26, 2018.

29. H.R. 2471, Maximizing America's Prosperity Act of 2015.

30. Justin Amash, "Business Cycle Balanced Budget Amendment," Power-Point presentation, May 2011.

31. H.R.2560, Cut, Cap, and Balance Act of 2011.

32. A related budget process reform was proposed by the House Committee on the Budget in November 2016. See Committee on the Budget, U.S. House of Representatives, "Proposed Rewrite of the Congressional Budget Process, Summary of Selected Provisions," November 30, 2016, p. 5, https://republicans-budget .house.gov/uploadedfiles/bpr-shortsummary-30nov2016.pdf.

CHAPTER SIX

1. Wikipedia, "Bretton Woods System," https://en.wikipedia.org/wiki/Bretton _Woods_system.

2. Seminal contributions include Finn E. Kydland and Edward C. Prescott, "Rules Rather than Discretion: The Inconsistency of Optimal Plans," *Journal of Political Economy* 85, no. 3 (June 1977): 473–492; Robert J. Barro and David B. Gordon, "A Positive Theory of Monetary Poicy in a Natural-Rate Model," *Journal of Political Economy* 91, no. 4 (August 1983): 589–610; and Alberto Alesina and Guido Tabellini, "Voting on the Budget Deficit," *American Economic Review* 80, no. 1 (1990): 37–49. More recent studies (e.g., Marina Halac and Pierre Yared, "Fiscal Rules and Discretion in a World Economy," *American Economic Reivew* 108, no. 8 [August 2018]: 2305–2334) keep the assumption of distorted government incentives, such as a socially suboptimal predilection for the short term.

3. Mervyn King, "Changes in UK Monetary Policy: Rules and Discretion in Practice," *Journal of Monetary Economics* 39, no. 1 (June 1997): 81–97.

4. Charles Wyplosz, "Fiscal Policy: Institutions versus Rules," *National Institute Economic Review*, no. 191 (2005): 70–84; John B. Taylor, "Swings and the Rules-Discretion Balance," in *Rethinking Expectations: The Way Forward for Macroeconomics*,

eds. Roman Frydman and Edmund Phelps (Princeton, NJ: Princeton University Press, 2013); Jonathan Portes and Simon Wren-Lewis, "Issues in the Design of Fiscal Rules," *The Manchester School* 83, no. S3 (2014): 56–86.

5. Jean-Louis Combes et al., "Inflation Targeting, Fiscal Rules and the Policy Mix: Cross-Effects and Interactions," *Economic Journal* 128, no. 615 (November 2018): 2755–84.

6. For instance, U.S. states have had constitutional balanced-budget amendments since the mid-1800s.

7. Andrea Schaechter et al., "Fiscal Rules in Response to the Crisis—Toward the 'Next-Generation' Rules. A New Dataset," International Monetary Fund (IMF) Working Paper no. 12/187, July 2012.

8. Centre for Economic Policy Research (CEPR), *Independent Fiscal Councils: Watchdogs or Lapdogs?*, eds. Roel Beetsma and Xavier Debrun (London: CEPR Press, 2018).

9. Xavier Debrun et al., "The Functions and Impact of Fiscal Councils," IMF Policy Paper, July 2013; George Kopits, "Independent Fiscal Institutions: Developing Good Practices," *OECD Journal on Budgeting* 3 (2011): 35–52.

10. Wyplosz, "Fiscal Policy."

11. Henrique S. Basso and James S. Costain, "Fiscal Delegation in a Monetary Union: Instrument Assignment and Stabilization Properties," Banco de España Working Paper no. 1710 (2017); Martin Larch and Thomas Braendle, "Independent Fiscal Councils: Neglected Siblings of Independent Central Banks? An EU Perspective," *Journal of Common Market Studies* 56, no. 2 (March 2018): 267–283, in the context of the European Union; and Nicholas Gruen, "Making Fiscal Policy Flexibly Independent of Government," *Agenda: A Journal of Policy Analysis and Reform* 4, no. 3 (1997): 297–307, among others.

12. See, for example, Carlos Eduardo S. Gonçalves and Alexandre Carvalho, "Inflation Targeting Matters: Evidence from OECD Economies' Sacrifice Ratios," *Journal of Money, Credit and Banking* 41, no. 1 (2009): 233–43; Carl E. Walsh, "Inflation Targeting: What Have We Learned?," *International Finance* 12, no. 2 (2009): 195–233; or Combes et al., "Inflation Targeting."

13. Friedrich Heinemann, Marc-Daniel Moessinger, and Mustafa Yeter, "Do Fiscal Rules Constrain Fiscal Policy? A Meta-Regression-Analysis," *European Journal of Political Economy* 51, no. C (2018): 69–92.

14. See Luc Eyraud et al., "Second-Generation Fiscal Rules: Balancing Simplicity, Flexibility, and Enforceability," IMF Staff Discussion Note no. 18/04, April 2018 for fiscal rules; Roel Beetsma et al., "The Rise of Independent Fiscal Councils: Recent Trends and Performance," IMF Working Paper no. 18/68, 2018 for fiscal councils; and Combes et al., "Inflation Targeting," for the combined effects of inflation targeting and fiscal rules.

15. Eyraud et al., "Second-Generation Fiscal Rules."

16. Alberto Alesina and Guido Tabellini, "Bureaucrats or Politicians? Part I: A Single Policy Task," *American Economic Review* 97, no. 1 (2007): 169–79; Simon Wren-Lewis, "Comparing the Delegation of Monetary and Fiscal Policy," in *Restoring Public Debt Sustainability—The Role of Independent Fiscal Institutions,* ed. George Kopits (Oxford: Oxford University Press, 2013).

17. Eyraud et al., "Second-Generation Fiscal Rules."

18. Taylor's (John B. Taylor, "Discretion versus policy rules in practice," *Carnegie-Rochester Series on Public Policy* 39 [1993]: 195–214; John B Taylor, "A Historical Analysis of Monetary Policy Rules," in *Monetary Policy Rules,* ed. John B. Taylor [Chicago: University of Chicago Press, 1999]) observation that episodes of successful monetary policy in the United States were associated with certain patterns in short-term interest rates prompted curiosity about simple rules of thumb for policy rates. The "Taylor rule" quickly gained traction as an informative metric for sound monetary policy, if only for its ability to proxy optimal monetary policy in certain classes of theoretical models (e.g., Michael Woodford, "The Taylor Rule and Optimal Monetary Policy," *American Economic Review* 91, no. 2 [May 2001]: 232–237). Significant and protracted deviations from the rule often raise questions about the appropriateness of monetary policy.

19. See Jean-Maarc Fournier and Philipp Lieberknecht, "A Model-Based Fiscal Taylor Rule and a Toolkit to Assess the Fiscal Stance," February 14, 2020, International Monetary Fund Working Paper, IMF, Wasington, DC, https://www.imf.org/en/Publications/WP/Issues/2020/02/14/A-Model-based-Fiscal-Taylor-Rule-and-a-Toolkit-to-Assess-the-Fiscal-Stance-49025.

20. See among others John B. Taylor, "Reassessing Discretionary Fiscal Policy," *Journal of Economic Perspectives* 14, no. 3 (2000): 21–36; Jasper Lukkezen and Coen Teulings, "A Fiscal Taylor Rule," CPB Netherlands Bureau for Economic Policy Analysis, CPB Background Document, April 23, 2013; Martin Kliem and Alexander Kriwolusky, "Toward a Taylor Rule for Fiscal Policy," *Review of Economic Dynamics* 17, no. 2 (April 2014): 294–302; Nicolas Carnot, "Evaluating Fiscal Policy: A Rule of Thumb," European Economy—Economic Papers no. 526, Brussels: European Commission, August 2014.

21. Eyraud et al., "Second-Generation Fiscal Rules."

22. Angès Bénassy-Quéré et al., "Reconciling Risk Sharing with Market Discipline: A Constructive Approach to Euro Area Reform," CEPR Policy Insight 91, 2018.

23. The classic definition of fiscal rules as a "permanent constraint on fiscal policy" (George Kopits and Steven A. Symansky, "Fiscal Policy Rules," IMF Occasional Paper no. 162, 1998.) echoes this perceived necessity (as does IMF, 2009). William H. Buiter ("Ten Commandments for a Fiscal Rule in

the E(M)U," *Oxford Review of Economic Policy* 19, no. 1 [March 2003]: 84–99) also considers "impartial and consistent" enforcement as one the Ten Commandments for fiscal rules.

24. As defined at Lexico.com, a project of Oxford University.

25. Alberto Alesina and Guido Tabellini, "Voting on the Budget Deficit," *American Economic Review* 80, no. 1 (1990): 37–49.

26. Roel Beetsma and Xavier Debrun, "The New Stability and Growth Pact: A First Assessment," *European Economic Review* 51 (2007): 453–77.

27. In the appendix, we illustrate this situation by assuming that enforcement entails costs in terms of foregone revenues in period 1, possibly because the constraint imposed by the rule affects the quality of fiscal policy. Ben D. Peletier, Rober A. J. Dur, and Otto H. Swank, "Voting on the Budget: Comment," *American Economic Review* 89, no. 5 (December 1999): 1377–1381 develop a full-fledged critique of the Alesina-Tabellini framework in which cutting high-quality expenditure as a result of a balanced-budget requirement is costly.

28. Beetsma and Debrun, "The New Stability."

29. Wolf Heinrich Reuter, "National Numerical Fiscal Rules: Not Complied with, but Still Effective?," *European Journal of Political Economy* 39 (2015): 67–81.

30. Michael Bergman, Michael M. Hutchinson, Svend Hougaard Jensen, "Promoting Sustainable Public Finances in the European Union: The Role of Fiscal Rules and Government Efficiency," *European Journal of Political Economy* 44 (September 2016): 1–19; Heinemann, Moessinger, and Yeter, "Do Fiscal Rules Constrain Fiscal Policy?"; Eyraud et al., "Second-Generation Fiscal Rules."

31. George Kopits and Steven A. Symansky, "Fiscal Policy Rules," IMF Occasional Paper no. 162, 1998.

32. See, for example, Martin Larch, Paul van den Noord, and Lars Jonung, "The Stability and Growth Pact: Lessons for the Great Recession," European Economy, Economic Papers no. 429, December 2010, on the weaknesses of the SGP.

33. See Lars Calmfors ("What Remains of the Stability and Growth Pact," Swedish Institute for European Policy Studies Report no. 9, 2005) for an analysis of the reformed SGP and Roel Beetsma and Xavier Debrun ("The New Stability and Growth Pact: A First Assessment," *European Economic Review* 51, no. 2 (February 2007): 453–477) for a theoretical appraisal.

34. Luc Eyraud and Tao Wu, "Playing by the Rules: Reforming Fiscal Governances in Europe," IMF Working Paper no. 15/67, 2015.

35. Eric M. Leeper, "Monetary Science, Fiscal Alchemy," Proceedings—Economic Policy Symposium, Jackson Hole, WY, Federal Reserve Bank of Kansas City, 361–434, 2010.

36. Luc Eyraud et al. ("How to Calibrate Fiscal Rules: A Primer," IMF Fiscal Affairs Department How-To Notes, March 15, 2018) discuss at length the "hydraulics" behind the calibration of fiscal rules, and in particular the connection between debt and deficit caps.

37. The stability—or mean-reversion—condition is much stronger than solvency (Henning Bohn, "The Behavior of U.S. Public Debt and Deficits, *The Quarterly Journal of Economics* 113, no. 3 (August 1998): 949–963). It is nevertheless at the core of operational debt-sustainability assessments—such as those performed by the IMF—as well as some workhorse models of the fiscal-monetary policy mix (e.g., Eric M. Leeper, "Equilibria under 'Active' and 'Passive' Monetary and Fiscal Policies," *Journal of Monetary Economics* 27, no. 1 (February 1991): 129–147, and related analyses).

38. Under condition (6.3), the long-term debt level will be positive if $\kappa < 0$. Equation (6.4) can be derived by applying (6.1) and (6.2) to steady-state values of the primary balance ($p^\star$) and the public debt ($d^\star$).

39. Jonathan D. Ostry et al., "Fiscal Space," IMF Staff Position Note no. 10/11, 2010; Atish R. Ghosh et al., "Fiscal Fatigue, Fiscal Space and Debt Sustainability in Advanced Economies," *The Economic Journal* 123, no. 566 (February 2013): F4–F30.

40. Huixin Bi, "Sovereign Default Risk Premia, Fiscal Limits, and Fiscal Policy," *European Economic Review* 56, no. 3 (2012): 389–410.

41. Paolo Mauro et al., "A Modern History of Fiscal Prudence and Profligacy," *Journal of Monetary Economics* 76 (2015): 55–70.

42. Xavier Debrun and Tidiane Kinda, "That Squeezing Feeling: The Interest Burden and Public Debt Stabilization," *International Finance* 19, no. 2 (2016): 147–78.

43. See Kathryn Holston, Thomas Laubach, and John C. Williams, "Measuring the Natural Rate of Interest: International Trends and Determinants," *Journal of International Economics* 108, supplement 1 (May 2017): 559–575 for a recent analysis of the determinants of $r^\star$.

44. Debrun and Kinda, "That Squeezing Feeling."

45. In that case, $\dfrac{\partial d^\star}{\partial r^\star} = \dfrac{\kappa \chi}{\left(\gamma^\star\left(1-\lambda\right)-\left(\rho+\chi r^\star\right)\right)^2} < 0.$

46. Debrun and Kinda, "That Squeezing Feeling."

47. Lawrence H. Summers ("Secular Stagnation and Monetary Policy," Federal Reserve Bank of St. Louis *Review* 98, no. 2 (Second Quarter 2016): 93–110) articulates the forces shaping a secular stagnation scenario.

48. Jonathan Portes and Simon Wren-Lewis, "Issues in the Design of Fiscal Rules," *The Manchester School* 8, no. S3 (2015): 56–86.

49. For example, Blanchard, Dell'Ariccia, and Mauro, "Rethinking Macroeconomic Policy," IMF Staff Position Note no. 2010/3, 2010; or IMF, *Now Is the Time: Fiscal Policies for Sustainable Growth*, Fiscal Monitor, April 2015.

50. Frederick van der Ploeg, "Back to Keynes?," *CESifo Economic Studies* 51, no. 4 (2005): 777–822.

51. See for example Axel Leijonhufvud ("The long swings in economic understanding," in *Macroeconomic Theory and Economic Policy: Essays in Honour of Jean-Paul* Fitoussi, ed. K. Vela Velupillai (London: Routledge, 2004), 115–127) on the long swings in macroeconomic thinking between rules and discretion.

52. As shown by Felix Roth ("Political Economy of EMU: Rebuilding Systemic Trust in the Euro Area in Times of Crisis," European Economy Discussion Paper no. 016, European Commission, September 2015), there is a tendency for trust in governments and public institutions such as parliaments to decline significantly in times of crisis.

53. See Richard Rose (*Lesson-Drawing in Public Policy: A Guide to Learning across Time and Space* [Chatham, NJ: Chatham House Publishers, 1993]) for an account of the process of policy learning across time and Lars Jonung ("Looking ahead through the Rear-View Mirror: Swedish Stabilization Policy as a Learnig Process 1975–1995. A Summary," Lund University Department of Economics, 2000) for a case study of Sweden, showing that every major economic crisis has initiated a process, teaching new lessons for the conduct of stabilization policies.

54. Lars Jonung ("Reforming the Fiscal Framework: The Case of Sweden 1973–2013," in *Reform Capacity and Macroeconomic Performance in the Nordic Countries*, ed. Torben M. Andersen, Michael Bergman, and Svend E. Hougaard Jensen [Oxford: Oxford University Press, 2015], chapter 8) describes the rise of the fiscal framework in Sweden as the outcome of budgetary crises in the early 1990s as well as a method to keep the lesson of the crisis alive in the collective memory.

55. Felix Roth, "Political Economy of EMU."

56. We are grateful to Signe Krogstrup and Sebastien Waelti for that suggestion and for sharing their data.

57. See Geert Hofstede, Gert Jan Hofstede, and Michael Minkov, *Cultures and Organizations: Software of the Mind. Revised and expanded,* 3rd ed. (New York: Mc Graw Hill, 2010). A 2015 update of the dataset is freely available on https://geerthofstede.com/research-and-vsm/dimension-data-matrix/ (accessed October 29, 2019).

58. Going even deeper into the roots of attitudes vis-à-vis institutions, some have argued that religion plays a key role in shaping how citizens look upon rules, with Protestants showing a stronger fundamental belief in the importance of legal institutions, in rules, and, specifically, in the rights of creditors (Adrian Chadi

and Matthias Krapf, "The Protestant Fiscal Ethic: Religious Confession and Euro Skepticism in Germany," Universty of Lausanne Department of Economics Working Paper, March 2015).

59. Such lack of ownership can be even more severe if fiscal rules adoption is the result of outside pressure. Rules perceived as forced upon a country could become easy targets in any political blame-game. The same is true if the fiscal rule results from a strategic attempt by one political party to tie the hands of its opponents when they are in office.

60. Eyraud et al., "Second-Generation Fiscal Rules."

61. John B. Taylor, "Discretion Versus Policy Rules in Practice," *Carnegie-Rochester Series on Public Policy* 39 (1993): 195–214.

62. Taylor, "Reassessing Discretionary Fiscal Policy."

63. Kliem and Kriwolusky, "Toward a Taylor Rule"; or Michael Kumhof and Douglas Laxton, "Simple Fiscal Policy Rules for Small Open Economies," *Journal of International Economics* 91 (2013): 113–127.

64. Lukkezen and Teulings, "A Fiscal Taylor Rule"; or Nicolas Carnot, "Evaluating Fiscal Policy."

65. Ben S. Bernanke, "The Taylor Rule: A Benchmark for Monetary Policy?," Brookings Institution blog, April 28, 2015; Jonathan Portes and Simon Wren-Lewis, "Issues in the Design of Fiscal Rules," *The Manchester School* 83, no. S3 (2015): 56–86.

66. IMF, "Fiscal Exit: From Strategy to Implementation," *Fiscal Monitor*, November 2010.

67. IMF, "Now Is the Time: Fiscal Policies for Sustainable Growth," *Fiscal Monitor*, April 15, 2015.

68. IMF, "Analyzing and Managing Fiscal Risks: Best Practices," IMF Policy Paper, May 4, 2016.

69. David Turner et al., "An Investigation into Improving the Real-Time Reliability of OECD Output Gaps Estimates," Organisation for Economic Co-operation and Development Economics Department Working Papers no. 1294, 2016; or Francesco Grigoli et al., "Output Gap Uncertainty and Real-Time Monetary Policy," IMF Working Paper no. 15/14, 2015.

70. For the United States, there is no real-time equivalent to the fiscal series used in Figure 6.6.

71. Turner et al., "An Investigation into Improving the Real-Time Reliability."

72. CEPR, *Independent Fiscal Councils.*

73. See George Kopits, "Independent Fiscal Institutions: Developing Good Practices," *OECD Journal on Budgeting* 3 (2011): 35–52; Roel Beetsma, Xavier Debrun, and Randolph Sloof, "The Political Economy of Fiscal Transparency and Independent Fiscal Councils," ECB Working Paper no. 2091, 2017; Lars Jonung,

"Reforming the Fiscal Framework: The Case of Sweden 1973–2013," in *Reform Capacity and Macroeconomic Performance in the Nordic Countries,* eds. Torben Andersen, Michael Bergman, and Sven Hougard Jensen (Oxford: Oxford University Press, 2015); Roel Beetsma et al., "The Rise of Independent Fiscal Councils: Recent Trends and Performance," IMF Working Paper no. 18/68, 2018.

74. Carnot, "Evaluating Fiscal Policy."

75. We owe this point to Martin Larch.

76. See the directive on national fiscal frameworks, the "Two-Pack" Regulations, or the Fiscal Compact.

77. Debrun et al., "The Functions and Impact of Fiscal Councils"; Kopits, "Independent Fiscal Institutions."

78. Alberto Alesina and Guido Tabellini, "Voting on the Budget Deficit," *American Economic Review* 80, no. 1 (1990): 37–49.

79. This is obtained as $\psi^\star = argmax_\psi W$, taking the policymaker's first order condition on Equation (6.A.5) as a constraint. Under a fiscal rule with enforcement ψ, socially optimal enforcement of the rule (denoted by $\psi^\star$) has to satisfy $\dfrac{\partial W}{\partial \psi} = \left(\pi u'(g_2) + \psi^\star\right)\dfrac{\partial g_1}{\partial \psi} + u'(g_2)\dfrac{\partial g_2}{\partial \psi} = 0$. A period 2 resource constraint implies that $\dfrac{\partial g_2}{\partial \psi} = -\dfrac{\partial g_1}{\partial \psi}$ it immediately follows that $\psi^\star = (1 - \pi)u'(g_2)$.

80. Period 2 resource constraint is not directly affected. If it were (as Peletier et al, "Voting on the Budget: Comment"), it would only magnify the negative "income effect" of enforcement.

CHAPTER SEVEN

1. L. Randall Wray, *Modern Money Theory,* 2nd ed. (Basingstoke, UK: Palgrave Macmillan, 2015), pp. 66–67.

2. U.S. Department of the Treasury. "Debt Limit," https://www.treasury.gov/initiatives/Pages/debtlimit.aspx (accessed August 6, 2018).

3. This estimate slightly overestimates the net interest expense of the consolidated federal government in recent years since it does not account for interest that the Fed pays on deposits by commercial banks or interest that the Fed earns from securities held other than those issued by the Treasury, mainly mortgage-backed securities. In 2017, the latter exceeded the former by about $20 billion. If that amount were netted out from federal interest expenses, the estimate of R for 2017 would have been about a tenth of a percentage point lower than shown. Before 2008, this adjustment would have been insignificant, and it seems likely that it will decrease in coming years as the Fed carries out a planned reduction in its holdings of securities.

4. Herbert Stein, "After the Ball," *The AEI Economist* (December 1984): 2.

5. Joint Resolution Proposing a Balanced Budget Amendment, S.J. Res. 10, 112th Congress, 2011.

6. Ed Dolan, "Freedom, Prosperity, and Big Government," Niskanen Center, April 20, 2017; Ed Dolan, "Quality of Government, Not Size, Is the Key to Freedom and Prosperity," Niskanen Center, April 27, 2017.

7. Rosemarie Fike, "Economic Freedom: Women's Economic Rights—What's Changed and Why Does It Matter?" in *Economic Freedom of the World 2019 Annual Report*, eds. James Gwartney et al. (Vancouver: Fraser Institute, 2019) https://www.fraserinstitute.org/studies/economic-freedom.

8. Ian Vásquez and Tanja Porcnik, *The Human Freedom Index 2019* (Washington, Cato Institute, 2019).

9. Samuel Hammond, "The Free Market Welfare State," Niskanen Center, May 1, 2018.

CHAPTER EIGHT

1. Earl R. Brubaker, "The Tragedy of the Public Budgetary Commons," *The Independent Review* 1, no. 3 (Winter 1997).

2. "Historical Debt Outstanding—Annual," TreasuryDirect, https://www.treasurydirect.gov/govt/reports/pd/histdebt/histdebt.htm.

3. Congressional Budget Office (CBO), "Economic Impacts of Waiting to Resolve the Long-Term Budget Imbalance," Economic and Budget Issue Brief, December 2010.

4. Albert Hirschman, *The Passions and the Interests: Political Arguments for Capitalism Before Its Triumph* (Princeton, NJ: Princeton University Press, 1977).

5. Thomas Jefferson to John Taylor, November 26, 1798, *Founders Online*, National Archives.

6. CNN/ORC Poll, July 2011, https://i2.cdn.turner.com/cnn/2011/images/07/21/rel11b.pdf.

7. Standing Rules of the Senate 113-18 (113 Congress 2013), https://www.rules.senate.gov/rules-of-the-senate.

8. Committee on Rules, U.S. House of Representatives, https://rules.house.gov/resources.

9. H.J. Res. 22, 116th Cong., (2019).

10. "Proposing a Balanced Budget Amendment to the Constitution of the United States: Roll Call Vote No. 138," Office of the Clerk, U.S. House of Representatives, April 12, 2018.

11. "Proposing a Balanced Budget Amendment to the Constitution of the United States: Roll Call Vote No. 858," Office of the Clerk, U.S. House of Representatives, November 18, 2011.

12. Roll Call Vote on S.J. Res. 24, 112th Congress, December 14, 2011.

13. Roll Call Vote on S.J. Res. 10, 112th Congress, December 14, 2011.

14. Chicago Booth, "Balanced Budget Amendment," IGM Forum Survey, November 7, 2017.

15. Budget Contents and Submission to Congress, 31 §USC 1105.

16. CBO, *The Budget and Economic Outlook: 2019 to 2029*, January 2019.

17. Budget Resolution for Fiscal Year 2019, Committee on the Budget, U.S. House of Representatives, June, 2018, https://web.archive.org/web/20181225003716/https://budget.house.gov/budgets/fy-2019-budget/.

18. U.S. Const. art. I, § 8, cl. 2.

19. H.J. Res. 119, 115th Cong., (2017).

20. H.J. Res. 15, 115th Cong., (2017).

21. U.S. Const. art. I, § 9, cl. 7.

22. James M. Buchanan and Gordon Tullock, *The Calculus of Consent: Logical Foundations of Constitutional Democracy* (Ann Arbor: University of Michigan Press, 1962).

23. U.S. Const. art. I, § 7, cl. 2.

24. See "Notes on the Amendments," www.usconstitution.net.

25. H.J. Res. 55, 114th Cong., (2015).

26. Federal Constitution of the Swiss Confederation, Article 126, https://www.admin.ch/opc/en/classified-compilation/19995395/index.html#a126.

27. Global Legal Research Center, "Switzerland: Implementation of Article 126 of the Swiss Constitution—The 'Debt Brake,'" The Law Library of Congress, June 2016.

28. CBO, *The Budget and Economic Outlook: 2019 to 2029*.

29. Unauthorized Spending Accountability Act of 2017, H.R. 2174, 115th Congress (2017).

30. Kurt Couchman, "Congress Can and Should End Government Shutdowns for Good," *Washington Examiner,* February 9, 2018.

31. CBO, "Expired and Expiring Authorizations of Appropriations: Fiscal Year 2018, Revised," July 3, 2018

32. House Committee on Appropriations, State, Foreign Operations, and Related Programs Appropriations Bill, 2019, H.R. Rep. No. 115-829 (2018), 133–34.

33. CBO, *The Budget and Economic Outlook: 2018 to 2028*, Table 2-2.

34. CBO, "Social Security Policy Options, 2015," December 15, 2015.

35. Christopher J. Conover, "Congress Should Account for the Excess Burden of Taxation," Cato Policy Analysis no. 669, October 13, 2010.

36. "Executive Office of the President of the United States, "Tax Expenditures," in *Budget of the United States Government: Fiscal Year 2009* (Washington:

GPO, 2009), pp. 287–328, https://www.gpo.gov/fdsys/pkg/BUDGET-2009 -PER/pdf/BUDGET-2009-PER-8-3.pdf.

37. Kurt Couchman, "A Well-Crafted Budget Amendment Can Succeed," *The Hill*, January 20, 2017.

38. Respectively: Resources, House of Representatives Committee on Rules; Rules of the Senate, https://www.rules.senate.gov/rules-of-the-senate; John Thune, "History, Rules, and Precedents of the Senate Republican Conference," 115th Congress, January 2017; House Republican Conference, "Conference Rules of the 116th Congress, January 2019, https://www.gop.gov/conference-rules -of-the-116th-congress/.

CHAPTER NINE

1. Bureau of the Fiscal Service, Department of the Treasury, "Monthly Statement of the Public Debt of the United States," August 31, 2019.

2. Congressional Budget Office (CBO), *The Budget and Economic Outlook: 2018 to 2028,* April 9, 2018, p. 87. Please note that all references to years in this chapter are for fiscal years, unless noted otherwise.

3. CBO, supplemental data accompanying *The Budget and Economic Outlook: 2018 to 2028* titled "Spending Projections by Budget Account," line 1732, April 9, 2018.

4. Keith Hall, CBO, "The Budget and Economic Outlook: 2018 to 2028," Testimony before the Senate Budget Committee, April 11, 2018, 5–6.

5. A description of the Debt Default Clock is available at the initiative's website.

6. CBO, *The Budget and Economic Outlook: 2018 to 2028*, p. 87. The projected gross debt relative to GDP in 2028 is based on the author's calculation using the CBO data provided in this report.

7. Title III of The Bipartisan Budget Act of 2019 (Public Law 116-37).

8. As noted earlier, gross interest cost projections are provided by the CBO in supplemental data accompanying *The Budget and Economic Outlook: 2018 to 2028*: "Spending Projections by Budget Account," line 1732. CBO also provides the revenue projections in *The Budget and Economic Outlook: 2018 to 2028*, p. 67. The author used these data to calculate the ratio of gross interest costs to total revenues.

9. Again, gross federal interest cost projections are provided in supplemental data accompanying *The Budget and Economic Outlook: 2018 to 2028*: "Spending Projections by Budget Account," line 1732. The CBO also provides the gross debt projections in *The Budget and Economic Outlook: 2018 to 2028*, p. 87. The author used these data to calculate the ratio of gross debt in 2027 to the money raised by

the issuance of new debt by dividing the gross interest cost in that year by gross debt at the end of 2027 minus the gross debt at the end of 2026.

10. CBO, *The Budget and Economic Outlook: 2018 to 2028*, p. 149.

11. CBO, *The Budget and Economic Outlook: 2018 to 2028*, p. 45.

12. CBO provides projections on both gross debt and debt held by the public in *The Budget and Economic Outlook: 2018 to 2028*, p. 87. The author calculated the portion of the gross debt held by the public in 2025 by dividing the dollar level of the debt held by the public by the dollar level of the gross debt in that year.

13. The databases for this factor are (a) Bureau of the Fiscal Service, "Ownership of Federal Securities," Treasury Bulletin, in https://www.fiscal.treasury.gov /fsreports/rpt/treasBulletin/current.htm (accessed September 11, 2018); and (b) Congressional Budget Office, "Budget and Economic Data," https://www.cbo.gov /about/products/budget-economic-data#3 (accessed September 11, 2018).

14. This calculation was made by the Debt Default Clock Review Committee using data found at Department of the Treasury, "Monthly Statement of the Public Debt of the United States," March 31, 2018.

15. CBO, *The Budget and Economic Outlook: 2018 to 2028*, p. 67.

16. CBO, *The Budget and Economic Outlook: 2018 to 2028*, p. 67.

17. CBO, *The Budget and Economic Outlook: 2018 to 2028*, p. 10.

18. For a description of these "extraordinary measures," see Department of the Treasury, "Description of Extraordinary Measures," March 16, 2017, https://www .treasury.gov/initiatives/Documents/Description_of_Extraordinary_Measures _2017_03_16.pdf.

19. CBO, *The Budget and Economic Outlook: 2018 to 2028*, p. 49.

20. CBO, *The Budget and Economic Outlook: 2018 to 2028*, p. 49.

21. The Tax Cut and Jobs Act of 2017, Public Law 115-97.

22. Detailed descriptions of the Compact for America initiative, including the text of the balanced budget amendment it is proposing, are available at the Compact for America Educational Foundation, Balanced Budget Compact Project website https://www.compactforamerica.org/.

23. The House failed to adopt House Joint Resolution 2 by the necessary two-thirds vote on April 12, 2018. See "All Information (Except Text) for H.J. Res. 2—Proposing a Balanced Budget Amendment to the Constitution of the United States," https://www.congress.gov/bill/115th-congress/house-joint -resolution/2/all-info.

24. These five states, in the order they joined, are Georgia, Alaska, Mississippi, North Dakota, and Arizona.

25. Title X of The Congressional Budget and Impoundment Control Act of 1974 (Public Law 93-344; 2 U.S.C. 621 et seq.).

26. For a description of this impasse and the risk of federal default associated with it, see Bob Woodward, *The Price of Politics* (New York: Simon and Schuster, 2012).

27. Section 405 of Title IV of the Congressional Budget and Impoundment Control Act of 1974, Public Law 93–344, U.S.C. 621 et seq.

CHAPTER TEN

1. John B. Taylor, *Getting Off Track: How Government Actions and Interventions Caused, Prolonged, and Worsened the Financial Crisis* (Stanford: Hoover Institution Press, 2009); John B. Taylor, "Swings in the Rules-Discretion Balance," paper prepared for the Conference on the Occasion of the 40th Anniversary of Microeconomic Foundations of Employment and Inflation Theory, New York, November 2010; John B. Taylor, "The Fed Needs to Return to Monetary Rules," *Wall Street Journal*, June 27, 2014.

2. For a discussion of Taylor rules see John B. Taylor, "Discretion Versus Policy Rules in Practice," *Carnegie-Rochester Series on Public Policy* 39 (1993): 195–214; and John B. Taylor, "A Historical Analysis of Monetary Policy Rules," in *Monetary Policy Rule*, ed. John B. Taylor (Chicago: University of Chicago Press, 1999).

3. John Merrifield and Barry Poulson, *Can the Debt Growth Be Stopped? Rules-Based Policy Options for Addressing The Federal Fiscal Crisis* (Lanham, MD: Lexington Books, 2016); John Merrifield and Barry Poulson, *Restoring America's Fiscal Constitution* (New York: Lexington Books, 2017); John Merrifield and Barry Poulson, "Fiscal Federalism and Dynamic Credence Capital in the U.S.," Economics Research Network Economic Policy Paper Series 10, no. 16 (November 2018).

4. See note 2, above.

5. George D. Cohn, director of the National Economic Council, 2017–2018, states that "It's easy to forget but the prevailing wisdom when Mr. Trump took office was that 3% growth wasn't possible and we needed to settle for the 'new normal' of 2%." George D. Cohn, "America Is Competitive Again," *Wall Street Journal*, December 21, 2018.

6. Office of Management and Budget (OMB), *Budget of the United States Government*, Fiscal Year 2019.

7. Congressional Budget Office (CBO), *The 2019 Long-Term Budget Outlook*, June 25, 2019, https://www.cbo.gov/publication/55331.

8. CBO, *The Budget and Economic Outlook 2019 to 2029*, Washington, January 2019.

9. CBO, *The 2019 Long-Term Budget Outlook*.

10. CBO, *The Budget and Economic Outlook 2019 to 2029*.

11. Jean-Marc Fournier and Philipp Lieberknecht, "A Model-based Fiscal Taylor Rule and a Toolkit to Assess the Fiscal Stance," International Monetary Fund (IMF) Working paper no. 20/33, International Monetary Fund, Washington, February 14, 2020, https://www.imf.org/en/Publications/WP/Issues/2020/02/14/A-Model-based-Fiscal-Taylor-Rule-and-a-Toolkit-to-Assess-the-Fiscal-Stance-49025.

12. Taylor, *Getting Off Track*; Taylor, "Swings in the Rules-Discretion Balance"; Taylor, "The Fed Needs to Return to Monetary Rules"; John F. Cogan et al., "Fiscal Consolidation Strategy," *Journal of Economic Dynamics and Control* 37, no. 2 (2013): 404–21; John F. Cogan et al., "Fiscal Consolidation Strategy, an Update for the Budget Reform Proposal of March 2013," https://www.hoover.org/sites/default/files/13104_-_cogan_taylor_wieland_and_wolters_-_fiscal_consolidation_strategy_-_an_update_for_the_budget_reform_proposal_of_march_2013.pdf.

13. Barry Poulson and Hamid Baghestani, "Federal Reserve Forecasts of Nonfarm Payroll Employment across Different Political Regimes," *Journal of Economic Studies* 39, no. 3 (2012): 280–89.

14. Taylor, "Discretion Versus Policy"; John B. Taylor, "Reassessing Discretionary Fiscal Policy," *The Journal of Economic Perspectives* 14, no. 3 (2000): 21–36.

15. For a survey of the literature on rules-based approaches to monetary and fiscal policy, see Xavier Debrun and Lars Jonung, "Under Threat: Rules Based Fiscal Policy and How to Preserve It," *European Journal of Political Economy* 57 (March 2019).

16. Debrun and Jonung, "Under Threat"; Matin Kliem and Alexander Kriwolusky, "Toward a Taylor Rule for Fiscal Policy," *Review of Economic Dynamics* 17 (2013): 294–302; Michael Kumhof and Douglas Laxton, "Simple Fiscal Policy Rules for Small Open Economies," *Journal of International Economics* 91, no. 1 (2013): 113–27; Jasper Lukkezen and Coen Teulings, "A Fiscal Taylor Rule," CPB Netherland Bureau for Economic Policy Analysis, CPB Background Document, April 24, 2013.

17. Debrun and Jonung. (2019; above) generalizes the FTR in the following model:

$$b_t = b_t^\star + \beta y_t$$

where b_t is the nominal budget balance,

$b_t^\star = \frac{-\theta_t^\star}{1+\theta_t^\star} d_{FTR}^\star$ is a long-term objective defined as the nominal balance ensuring the convergence of the public debt-to-GDP ratio to a given number if the output gap is always zero, and $\theta_t^\star$ is the 10-year moving average of nominal GDP growth, β is the deficit allowance for cyclical stabilization, and y_t is the output gap.

18. Debrun and Jonung, "Under Threat."

19. Debrun and Jonung, "Under Threat."

20. Debrun and Jonung, "Under Threat."

21. CBO, *The 2018 Long-Term Budget Outlook*, June 2018; CBO, *The Budget and Economic Outlook: 2019 to 2029*.

22. Nina T. Budina et al., "Fiscal Rules at a Glance: Country Details from a New Dataset," IMF Working Paper 12/187, IMF, Washington, 2012; Victor Lledó et al., "Fiscal Rules at a Glance," IMF Background Paper, International Monetary Fund, Washington, March 2017.

23. For surveys of fiscal rules, see Ayuso Casals, "National Expenditure Rules: Why, How and When," European Economic Commission Economic Papers 473, December 2012; Cordes et al., "Expenditure Rules: Effective Tools for Sound Fiscal Policy," IMF Working Paper 15/29, 2015; Jean-Marc Fournier and Falilou Fall, "Limits to Government Debt Sustainability," OECD Economics Department Working Papers no. 1229, 2015; Falilou Fall et al., "Prudent Debt Targets and Fiscal Frameworks," OECD Policy Paper no. 15, July 2015; Francesca Caselli et al., "Second-Generation Fiscal Rules: Balancing Simplicity, Flexibility, and Enforceability," IMF Staff Discussion Note 18-04, 2018; Luc Eyraud et al., "Second-Generation Fiscal Rules: Balancing Simplicity, Flexibility, and Enforceability," IMF Staff Discussion Note no. 18/04, April 2018; Alberto Alesina and Allan Drazen, "Why Are Stabilizations Delayed?," *American Economic Review* 81 (1991): 1170–1188; Torsten Persson and Guido Tabellini, *Political Economics: Explaining Economic Policy* (Cambridge, MA: The MIT Press, 2000); Jürgen Von Hagen, "A Note on the Empirical Effectiveness of Formal Fiscal Restraints," *Journal of Public Economics* 44, no. 2 (1991): 199–210; Jürgen Von Hagen and Ian J. Harden, "Budget Processes and Commitment to Fiscal Discipline," *European Economic Review* 39 (1995): 771–79; George Kopits and Steven A. Symansky, "Fiscal Policy Rules," IMF Occasional Paper no. 162, 1998; George Kopits, "Fiscal Rules: Useful Policy Framework or Unnecessary Ornament?," IMF Working Paper 01/145, 2001; IMF, "Fiscal Rules: Anchoring Expectations for Sustainable Public Finances," IMF Policy Paper, 2009; IMF Financial Affairs Department, "Now Is the Time: Fiscal Policies for Sustainable Growth," *Fiscal Monitor* IMF, April 15, 2015; "Assessing Fiscal Space—An Update and Stocktaking," IMF Policy Paper, 2018; IMF, "Managing Public Wealth," *Fiscal Monitor*, October 2018; "How to Calibrate Fiscal Rules: A Primer," Fiscal Affairs Department (FAD) How-To Note 8, IMF, March, 2018; Fiscal Rule Dataset, IMF FAD, 2018, http://www.imf.org/external/datamapper/fiscalrules/map/map.htm; Allen Schick, "Post-Crisis Fiscal Rules: Stabilizing Public Finance while Responding to Economic Aftershocks," *OECD Journal on Budgeting*, 2010; Andrea Schaechter et al., "Fiscal Rules in Response to

the Crisis—toward the 'Next-Generation' Rules. A New Dataset." IMF Working Paper 12/187, 2012; Charles Wyplosz, "Fiscal Policy: Institutions versus Rules," *National Institute Economic Review* 191 (2005): 70–84; Charles Wyplosz, "Fiscal Rules: Theoretical Issues and Historical Experience," in *Fiscal Policy after the Financial Crisis,* eds. Alberto Alesina and Francesco Giavazzi (Chicago: University of Chicago Press, 2013).

24. For a discussion of this trade-off, see Marina Azzimonti et al., "The Costs and Benefits of Balanced Budget Rules: Lessons from a Political Economy Model of Fiscal Policy," *Journal of Public Economics* 136 (2016): 45–61; Marina Halac and Pierre Yared, "Fiscal Rules and Discretion under Persistent Shocks," *Econometrica* 82, no. 5 (2014): 1557–614; Marina Halac and Pierre Yared, "Commitment vs. Flexibility with Costly Verification," National Bureau of Economic Research (NBER) Working Paper no. 29936, 2016; Marina Halac and Pierre Yared, "Fiscal Rules and Discretion under Self-Enforcement," NBER Working Paper no. 23919, 2017; Marina Halac and Pierre Yared, "Fiscal Rules and Discretion in a World Economy," *American Economic Review* 108, no. 8 (2018): 2305–2334; Marina Halac and Pierre Yared, "Instrument-Based vs. Target-Based Rules," NBER Working Paper no. 24496, 2018; Manuel Amador et al., "Commitment vs. Flexibility," *Econometrica* 74, no. 2 (2006): 365–396; and Pierre Yared, "Rising Government Debt and What to Do about It," NBER Working Paper no. 24979, August 2018.

25. John Merrifield and Barry Poulson, "State Fiscal Policies for Budget Stabilization and Economic Growth: A Dynamic Scoring Analysis," *Cato Journal* 34, no. 1 (Winter 2014); Merrifield and Poulson, *Can the Debt Growth Be Stopped?*; John Merrifield and Barry Poulson, "A Dynamic Scoring Analysis of How TEL Design Choices Impact Government Expansion," *Journal of Economic and Financial Studies* 4, no. 2 (2016): 60–68; John Merrifield and Barry Poulson, "The Swedish and Swiss Fiscal Rule Outcomes Contain Key Lessons for the U.S.," *Independent Review* 21, no. 2 (Fall 2016): 251–75; John Merrifield and Barry Poulson, "New Constitutional Debt Brakes for Euroland Revisited," *Journal of Applied Business and Economics* 19, no. 8 (2017): 110–32; Merrifield and Poulson, *Restoring America's Fiscal Constitution*; John Merrifield and Barry Poulson, "Fiscal Federalism and Dynamic Credence Capital in the U.S.," Economics Research Network, *Economic Policy Paper Series* 10, no. 16 (November 2018).

26. One of the reasons for the success of fiscal rules in other OECD countries is the provision for emergency funds and escape clauses (Halac and Yared, "Commitment vs. Flexibility"; Stephen Coate and Ross Milton, "Optimal Fiscal Limits with Overrides," December 2018, http://rossmilton.com/optfisclim17.pdf; Victor Lledó et al., "Fiscal Rules at a Glance."

27. "A Greater Role for Fiscal Policy," *Fiscal Monitor*, IMF, April 2017; "Assessing Fiscal Space—an Update and Stocktaking," IMF Policy Paper, 2018.

28. Oliver Blanchard et al., "Rethinking Macroeconomic Policy," *Journal of Money, Credit and Banking* 42, Supplement 1 (2010): 199–215; J. Bradford DeLong and Lawrence H. Summers, "Fiscal Policy in a Depressed Economy," *Brookings Papers on Economic Activity* 1 (2012): 233–297.

29. Marco Bassetto and Thomas Sargent, "Politics and Efficiency of Separating Capital and Ordinary Government Budgets." *Quarterly Journal of Economics* 121, no. 4 (2006): 1167–210.

30. Alain Geier, "The Debt Brake—the Swiss Fiscal Rules at the Federal Level," Federal Department of Finance, Federal Financial Administration Working Paper no. 15, Switzerland, February 2011; Torben M. Andersen, "The Swedish Fiscal Policy Framework and Intermediate Fiscal Policy Targets," *Swiss Journal of Economics and Statistics* 149, no. 2 (2013): 231–48; Frank Bodmer, "The Swiss Debt Brake: How It Works and What Can Go Wrong," *Schweizerische Zeitschrift für Volkswirtschaft und Statistik* 142, no. 3 (2006): 307–30; Tobias Beljean and Alain Geier, "The Swiss Debt Brake—Has It Been a Success?," *Swiss Journal of Economics and Statistics* 149, no. 2 (2013): 115–35.

31. There is an extensive theoretical and empirical literature on debt sustainability. For a survey of this literature in other OECD countries, see Jarmila Botev et al., "A Reassessment of Fiscal Space in OECD Countries," OECD Economics Department Working Papers no. 1352, 2016; Fournier and Fall, "Limits to Government Debt Sustainability; Atish R. Ghosh et al., "Fiscal Space and Sovereign Risk Pricing in a Currency Union," *Journal of International Money and Finance* 34 (2013): 131–163; and Atish R. Ghosh et al., "Fiscal Fatigue, Fiscal Space and Debt Sustainability in Advanced Economies," NBER Working Paper no. 16782, 2011. For a survey of the literature for the United States, see Merrifield and Poulson, *Restoring America's Fiscal Constitution* and vetfiscalrules.net.

32. The dynamic simulation model and the simulation analysis are discussed in detail at the website vetfiscalrules.net, and by Merrifield and Poulson in "New Constitutional Debt Brakes."

33. A similar methodology is used by Alain Geier in "Application of the Swiss Fiscal Rule to Artificial Data: A Monte Carlo Simulation," *Swiss Journal of Economics and Statistics* 148, no. 1 (2012): 37–55.

34. CBO, *The 2019 Long-Term Budget Outlook*.

35. The CBO also projects that under current law rising debt-to-GDP ratios in the long run will result in retardation and stagnation in economic growth accompanied by falling employment.

36. Emmanuel Saez, "Reported Income and Marginal Tax Rates, 1960–2000: Evidence and Policy Implications," NBER Working Paper no. 10273, 2014.

37. Barry Poulson and Jules Gordon Kaplan, "State Income Taxes and Economic Growth," *Cato Journal* 28, no. 1 (Winter 2008): 53–71.

38. For a survey of this literature see Andreas Bergh and Magnus Henrekson, "Government Size and Economic Growth: A Survey and Interpretation of the Evidence," *Journal of Economic Surveys* 25, no. 5 (2011): 872–97.

39. Mike Bird, "Government Bond Jitters Abate," *Wall Street Journal*, January 2, 2019.

40. Matt Welsh, "Trump, on a Future Debt Crisis: 'Yeah, But I Won't Be Here,'" *Reason*, December 5, 2018.

41. Paul Krugman, "On the Debt Non-Spiral, Secular Stagnation Means Even Less Reason to Worry," *New York Times*, September 11, 2018.

42. Krugman, "On the Debt Non-Spiral."

43. Lawrence H. Summers, "Secular Stagnation and Monetary Policy," *Federal Reserve Bank of St. Louis Review* 98 (Second Quarter, 2016): 93–110.

44. Holman W. Jenkins Jr., "High Tax Rates Aren't Optimal," *Wall Street Journal*, January 9, 2019.

45. This simulation analysis makes it clear that the budget rules in the U.S. Congress that preclude analysis of the impact of fiscal policies beyond a 10-year time frame are ill advised. The fiscal rules and fiscal policies advocated in this study could achieve a sustainable debt-to–GDP ratio over three decades. But Congress is precluded from such long-term analysis. The various bills and resolutions promising to balance the budget and reduce debt to a sustainable level within the 10-year time frame are wishful thinking. This helps explain why Congress has virtually abandoned consideration of the fiscal rules and fiscal policies now required to address the debt crisis.

46. The results of this simulation analysis are available at vetfiscalrules.net.

47. Other studies support our assessment that under current law the United States does not have the fiscal space to respond to a major recession. The Federal Reserve Dodd Frank Stress Test for 2018 reveals that in a major recession the United States would experience greater instability than that experienced during the recent financial crisis (Board of Governors of the Federal Reserve System, "*Dodd Franks Act Stress Test 2018 Supervisory Stress Test Methodology and Results*," Washington, 2018). The International Monetary Fund ("Assessing Fiscal Space—An Update and Stocktaking," IMF Policy Paper, IMF, Washington, June 15, 2018) estimates that in such an economic shock the net worth of the federal government would fall about 26 percent by 2020. The negative impact of a major recession on net worth is far greater than the direct impact on deficits alone. See also Yared, "Rising Government Debt."

48. Yared, "Rising Government Debt."

CHAPTER ELEVEN

1. Raúl M. Grijalva and Tom Udall, "Mineral Resources: Mineral Volume, Value, and Revenue," GAO-13-45R, U.S. Government Accountability Office, November 15, 2012.

2. Natalie Kempkey and Matthew Manning, "With Low Oil Prices in 2016, Federal Revenues from Energy on Federal Lands Again Declined," U.S. Energy Information Administration, January 24, 2017.

3. Robert Rapier, "U.S. Increases Dominance in Natural Gas, Produces More Than Entire Middle East," OilPrice.com, July 10, 2019.

4. Candace Dunn and Tim Hess, "The United States Is Now the Largest Global Crude Oil Producer," U.S. Energy Information Administration, September 12, 2018.

5. Linda Doman, "United States Remains Largest Producer of Petroleum and Natural Gas Hydrocarbons," U.S. Energy Information Administration, May 23, 2016.

6. American Chemistry Council, "U.S. Chemical Investment Linked to Shale Gas: $204 Billion and Counting," December 2019.

7. Neil Kornze, director, Bureau of Land Management (BLM), "Recent Management of Oil and Gas Lease Sales by the Bureau of Land Management," Testimony before the Subcommittee on the Interior of the House Committee on Oversight and Government Reform, 114th Cong., 2nd sess., March 23, 2016.

8. U.S. Department of the Interior, "About the Ocean, Great Lakes and Coastal Program," Newswave Newsletter.

9. Bureau of Ocean Energy Management (BOEM), "Map of Undiscovered Technically Recoverable Oil and Gas Resources of the Nation's Outer Continental Shelf, 2016," http://www.boem.gov/2016-National-Assessment-Map/.

10. Institute for Energy Research, "Federal Assets above and below Ground," January 17, 2013.

11. Congressional Budget Office, "Potential Budgetary Effects of Immediately Opening Most Federal Lands to Oil and Gas Leasing," August 2012.

12. Joseph R. Mason, "The Economic Effects of Immediately Opening Federal Lands to Oil, Gas, and Coal Leasing," Institute for Energy Research, December 2015.

13. Jackson Coleman and Stephen Moore, "Untapped Revenue," from the archives of *The Weekly Standard,* March 24, 2017.

14. Kempkey and Manning, "With Low Oil Prices in 2016, Federal Revenues Declined."

15. Brian Park, "U.S. Coal Production, Exports, and Prices Increased in 2017," U.S. Energy Information Administration, February 16, 2018.

16. David Blackmon, "The Drilling Boom on Federal Lands Is Driven More by Price Than Policy," *Forbes*, October 29, 2018.

17. A nautical mile is 6,080.2 feet or approximately 1.15 miles. The exceptions to the three-nautical-mile rule are Florida and Texas, which have boundaries of nine nautical miles. See Submerged Lands Act, 43 U.S.C. §§1301–1315.

18. U.S. Commission on Ocean Policy, "Primer on Ocean Jurisdictions: Drawing Lines in the Water," *An Ocean Blueprint for the 21st Century*, Final Report, July 22, 2004.

19. 43 U.S.C. §§1331 et seq.

20. BOEM, "2017–2022 OCS Oil and Gas Leasing Program."

21. See U.S. Energy Information Administration, "U.S. Crude Oil First Purchase Price," annual view, January 2, 2018.

22. U.S. Department of the Interior, BOEM, "2019–2024 National Outer Continental Shelf Oil and Gas Leasing: Draft Proposed Plan," January 2018, https://www.boem.gov/sites/default/files/oil-and-gas-energy-program/Leasing/Five-Year-Program/2019-2024/DPP/NP-Draft-Proposed-Program-2019-2024.pdf.

23. Nicolas Loris, "Right Reforms for Accessing U.S. Outer Continental Shelf Resources and Unleashing U.S. Energy Production," Heritage Foundation, March 26, 2018.

24. U.S. Department of the Interior, "Secretary Zinke Announces Plan for Unleashing America's Offshore Oil and Gas Potential," press release, January 4, 2018.

25. "Technically recoverable" refers to resources accessible with today's technology. See Sarah J. Hawkins et al., "Assessment of Continuous (Unconventional) Oil and Gas Resources in the Late Cretaceous Mancos Shale of the Piceance Basin, Uinta-Piceance Province, Colorado and Utah, 2016," U.S. Geological Survey Fact Sheet no. 2016-3030, June 2016.

26. Mark A. Kirschbaum et al., "Assessment of Undiscovered Oil and Gas Resources of the Uinta-Piceance Province of Colorado and Utah, 2002," National Assessment of Oil and Gas Fact Sheet, U.S. Geological Survey Fact Sheet no. 157-02, February 2003, p. 2.

27. U.S. Forest Service, "Final Record of Decision: Oil and Gas Leasing on Lands Administered by the White River National Forest," December 3, 2015, pp. 4 and 13, http://www.fs.usda.gov/Internet/FSE_DOCUMENTS/fseprd485176.pdf.

28. Land Management Bureau, "Notice of Availability of the Final Environmental Impact Statement for Previously Issued Oil and Gas Leases in the White River National Forest, Colorado," *Federal Register* 81, no. 151 (August 5, 2016): 51936–37.

29. Forest Service, "Final Record of Decision: Oil and Gas Leasing," p. 7.

30. Rep. Rob Bishop, Letter to Neil Kornze, director, BLM, June 30, 2016. See also David Ludlam, Kathleen Sgamma, and Dan Haley, Letter to Greg Larson, project manager, BLM, June 17, 2016.

31. "Proved reserves" is a very conservative measure referring to resources accessible given current technology, laws, and economic situation. See Marc Humphries, "U.S. Crude Oil and Natural Gas Production in Federal and Non-federal Areas," Congressional Research Service Report no. R42432, October 23, 2018, pp. 2 and 4.

32. Institute for Energy Research, "U.S. Oil Production Up, but on Whose Lands?," September 24, 2012.

33. BLM, "The Federal Land Policy and Management Act (FLPMA) of 1976: How the Stage Was Set for BLM's 'Organic Act,'" http://www.blm.gov/flpma /organic.htm.

34. Forest Service, "Final Record of Decision: Oil and Gas Leasing," p. 12.

35. Forest Service, "Final Record of Decision: Oil and Gas Leasing," p. 12.

36. BLM, "Thompson Divide Drilling History," January 16, 2013.

37. Paul Tolmé, "The Fight over the Thompson Divide," *5280 Magazine*, March 2016.

38. Ryan Summerlin, "'We Weren't Listened to' on Sage-Grouse Policy, Garfield County Says," *Post Independent* (Glenwood Springs and Garfield County, CO), July 11, 2016.

39. Rob Gordon and Nicolas Loris, "Congress' Sneaky Tactic to Grab More Land for the Government," The Daily Signal, December 2, 2014.

40. Nicolas Loris, "The Antiquated Act: Time to Repeal the Antiquities Act," Heritage Foundation Backgrounder no. 2998, March 25, 2015.

41. Jack Spencer, ed., *Environmental Conservation: Eight Principles of the American Conservation Ethic*, The Heritage Foundation, July 27, 2012.

42. 43 U.S.C. § 1332.

43. For more information, see Nicolas Loris, "Removing Restrictions on Liquid Natural Gas Exports: A Gift to the U.S. and Global Economies," Heritage Foundation Backgrounder no. 3232, July 27, 2017.

44. Environmental statutes and regulations internalize the negative externalities associated with the burning of conventional fuels.

45. Jane S. Shaw, "Public Choice Theory," *Concise Encyclopedia of Economics* (Library of Economics and Liberty, 1993).

46. 15 U.S. Code § 717b.

47. Nor does it mean that state regulatory regimes will always make sound policy decisions. New York's ban on hydraulic fracturing and Florida's request for an exemption are examples of that.

48. Marc Humphries, "U.S. Crude Oil and Natural Gas Production in Federal and Nonfederal Areas," Congressional Research Service Report no. 42432, June 22, 2016, https://fas.org/sgp/crs/misc/R42432.pdf.

49. Institute for Energy Research, "Energy Production on Federal Lands Lags Behind Private and State Lands," July 21, 2015.

50. U.S. Energy Information Administration, "Maps: Oil and Gas Exploration, Resources, and Production."

51. Mark Green, "Expanding Offshore Access Is Key to U.S. Energy Security," *API Energy Blog*, May 1, 2017.

52. U.S. Department of the Interior, "Zinke Signs Secretarial Order to Streamline Process for Federal Onshore Oil And Gas Leasing Permits," press release, July 6, 2017.

53. U.S. Department of the Interior, "Final Report: Review of the Department of the Interior Actions that Potentially Burden Domestic Energy," October 24, 2017.

54. Department of the Interior , "Zinke Signs Secretarial Order."

55. Fortune Editors, "What Went Wrong at Solyndra," *Fortune*, August 31, 2011, https://fortune.com/2011/08/31/what-went-wrong-at-solyndra/.

56. Richard Valdmanis, "Drillers Give Tepid Response to Record U.S. Offshore Lease Sale," *Reuters*, March 21, 2018.

57. Myron Ebell, director, Center for Energy and Environment, Competitive Enterprise Institute, Testimony on draft bill, Enhancing State Management of Federal Lands and Waters Act, before the Subcommittee on Energy and Mineral Resources, House Committee on Natural Resources, 115th Cong., 2nd sess., June 14, 2018, https://cei.org/sites/default/files/20180614_-_Myron_Ebell_Energy _and_Mining_Subcommittee_testimony.pdf.

58. David Blackmon, "Gilmer: We Should View the Permian Basin as a Permanent Resource," *Forbes*, August 17, 2017.

59. U.S. Department of the Interior, "They Said It Couldn't Be Done: Trump Admin Dominates with Billion-dollar Oil and Gas Sale," press release, September 6, 2018.

60. Holly Fretwell and Shawn Regan, "Divided Lands: State vs. Federal Management in the West," Property and Environment Research Center, PERC Public Lands Report, March 2015, Figure 1.

61. For more information, see Nicolas D. Loris, "Chapter 5: Economic Freedom, Energy, and Development," in *2015 Index of Economic Freedom*, ed. Terry Miller and Anthony B. Kim (Washington: The Heritage Foundation and Dow Jones & Company, Inc., 2015), https://www.heritage.org/index/pdf/2015/book/chapter5.pdf.

62. Fretwell and Regan, "Divided Lands," Figure 1.

63. Eric C. Edwards, Trevor O'Grady, and David Jenkins, "The Effect of Land Ownership on Oil and Gas Production: A Natural Experiment," Utah State University Working Paper, December 2016.

64. Elizabeth Malm, "Federal Mineral Royalty Disbursements to States and the Effects of Sequestration," The Tax Foundation Fiscal Fact no. 371, May 30, 2013.

65. Michael Giberson and Shawn Regan, "Public Interest Comment in Response to U.S. Department of Interior's Advanced Notice of Proposed Rulemaking," submitted in response to *Federal Register* 80 (June 5, 2015): 22148, https://www.regulations.gov/document?D=BLM-2015-0002-0019.

66. Giberson and Regan, "Public Interest Comment."

67. U.S. Department of Energy, "Strategic Petroleum Reserve Profile," Office of Fossil Energy, accessed March 29, 2020, http://fossil.energy.gov/programs/reserves/spr/.

68. Philip Verleger, "Measuring the Economic Impact of an Oil Release from the Strategic Petroleum Reserve to Compensate for the Loss of Venezuelan Oil Production," Appendix 4 in "U.S. Strategic Petroleum Reserve: Recent Policy Has Increased Costs but Not Overall U.S. Energy Security," Report prepared by the Minority Staff, Permanent Subcommittee on Investigations of the Senate Committee on Governmental Affairs, 108th Cong., 1st sess., March 5, 2003.

69. Timothy J. Considine and Kevin M. Dowd, "A Superfluous Petroleum Reserve?," *Regulation* 28, no. 2 (Summer 2005): 18–25.

70. Timothy J. Considine, "Is the Strategic Petroleum Reserve Our Ace in the Hole?," *The Energy Journal* 27, no. 3 (2006): 91–112.

71. Reid Stevens, "The Strategic Petroleum Reserve and Crude Oil Prices," University of California, Berkeley, November 15, 2014.

72. Considine and Dowd, "A Superfluous Petroleum Reserve?"

73. Anthony Andrews and Robert Pirog, "The Strategic Petroleum Reserve: Authorization, Operation, and Drawdown Policy," Congressional Research Service Report no. R42460, June 18, 2012.

74. Katharine Seelye and David Sanger, "The 2000 Campaign: The Vice President; Gore Asks Release of U.S.-Stored Oil to Stabilize Price," *New York Times*, September 22, 2000, https://www.nytimes.com/2000/09/22/us/2000-campaign-vice-president-gore-asks-release-us-stored-oil-stabilize-price.html.

75. David E. Sanger, "Politics or Policy?," *New York Times,* September 23, 2000.

76. U.S. Department of Energy, "Strategic Petroleum Reserve Test Sale 2014," Report to Congress, November 2014.

77. U.S. Department of Energy, "Price Competitive Sale of Strategic Petroleum Reserve Petroleum; Standard Sales Provision," Final Rule, *Federal Register* 70, no. 129, July 7, 2005.

78. Department of Energy, "Strategic Petroleum Reserve Test Sale 2014."

79. Department of Energy, "Strategic Petroleum Reserve Test Sale 2014."

80. Department of Energy, "Strategic Petroleum Reserve Test Sale 2014."

81. U.S. Energy Information Administration, "Petroleum and Other Liquids: U.S. Field Production of Crude Oil," https://www.eia.gov/dnav/pet/hist/LeafHandler.ashx?n=PET&s=MCRFPUS2&f=M.

82. In the event of noncompliance with the treaty, the IEA's Governing Board could administer corrective measures if it felt the integrity of the collective global inventories and ability to coordinate might be at risk as a result of the noncompliance. However, the board is not likely to dismiss a noncomplying member.

CHAPTER TWELVE

1. Congressional Budget Office, *The 2019 Long-Term Budget Outlook*, June 25, 2019, https://www.cbo.gov/publication/55331.

2. Much of the rest of the projected increase is from higher interest payments on the debt.

3. This figure is taken from the summary of the Social Security and Medicare 2018 annual reports. See Social Security and Medicare Boards of Trustees, "Status of the Social Security and Medicare Programs: A Summary of the 2018 Annual Reports," Social Security Administration, 2018, p. 4, https://www.ssa.gov/oact/TRSUM/tr18summary.pdf.

4. See Social Security Administration, "2018 OASDI Trustees Report," Table VI.G10, 2018; and Boards of Trustees, Federal Hospital Insurance and Federal Supplemental Medical Insurance Trust Funds, "2018 Annual Report," 2018.

5. From Office of Management and Budget, "Historical Tables," 2018, Table 1.2.

6. This is not exact for several reasons. The normal eligibility age for Social Security is now 66 and not everyone eligible retires. Some recipients are under age 65 (e.g., surviving spouses and children and disability insurance recipients). There are administrative costs as well. However, spending on these other individuals is small relative to regular benefits. Thus, Social Security spending per senior is a reasonably accurate indicator of benefits per recipient.

7. From Social Security Administration, "2018 OASDI Trustees Report," Social Security Area Population, Table V.A3, 2018. Figure 12.2 is drawn from the intermediate forecast.

8. For Medicare spending, data are from Board of Trustees, Federal Hospital Insurance and Federal Supplemental Medical Insurance Trust Funds, "2018 Annual Report." Premiums paid by recipients are not deducted from the Medicare spending data.

9. Medical price inflation historically has been substantially higher than overall inflation. However, in the past eight years, the two rates have been quite comparable. Thus increases in real Medicare benefits per senior prior to recent years will be understated. For future years, I rely on the Board of Trustees (2018) forecast. It may also be the case that unrestrained Medicare spending is a cause of the higher medical price inflation.

10. The stability of relative generosity makes sense, absent major changes in Social Security benefit rules. Benefits are a fraction of real lifetime earnings, which corresponds closely to GDP per capita.

11. Relative generosity does not fall in the simulations because forecasted GDP never falls. Thus, I abstract away from a possible decline in GDP due to a recession.

CHAPTER THIRTEEN

1. Bruce Lindsay, "FEMA's Disaster Relief Fund: Overview and Selected Issues," Congressional Research Service Report no. 43537, May 7, 2014.

2. Lindsay, "FEMA's Disaster Relief Fund."

3. Lindsay, "FEMA's Disaster Relief Fund."

4. U.S. Department of Homeland Security, "Disaster Relief Fund: Monthly Report as of September 30, 2018," Federal Emergency Management Agency (FEMA), October 5, 2018.

5. Bruce Lindsay, William Painter, and Francis McCarthy, "An Examination of Federal Disaster Relief under the Budget Control Act," Congressional Research Service Report no. 42352, November 8, 2013, updated February 24, 2016, https://www.fas.org/sgp/crs/misc/R42352.pdf.

6. Congressional Budget Office (CBO), "Discretionary Appropriations, Fiscal Year 2018, with Cap Adjustments," October 5, 2018, https://www.cbo.gov/system/files?file=2018-10/FY%202018%20House%202018.9.30.pdf.

7. Bruce Lindsay and Justin Murray, "Disaster Relief Funding and Emergency Supplemental Appropriations," Congressional Research Service Report no. 40708, April 12, 2011.

8. Justin Bogie, "A Primer on Disaster and Emergency Appropriations," Heritage Foundation Issue Brief no. 4524, March 2, 2016.

9. Office of Management and Budget, "The Statutory Pay-As-You-Go Act of 2010: A Description."

10. Veronique de Rugy and Allison Kasic, "The Never-Ending Emergency: Trends in Supplemental Spending," Mercatus Working Paper no. 11-30, August 2011.

11. FEMA, "Disaster Declarations by Year: 1988."

12. The Stafford Act of 1988 amended the Disaster Relief Act of 1974 by linking the presidential declaration of an emergency or disaster to a response of the Federal Emergency Management Agency.

13. David Inserra, "FEMA Reform Needed: Congress Must Act," Heritage Foundation Issue Brief no. 4342, February 4, 2015.

14. FEMA, "Disaster Declarations by Year: 2017."

15. FEMA, "Disaster Declarations by Year: 2018."

16. CBO, "Supplemental Appropriations in the 1980s," February 1990, https://www.cbo.gov/system/files?file=2018-05/1980s.pdf.

17. CBO, "Supplemental Appropriations in the 1990s," March 2001, https://www.cbo.gov/system/files?file=2018-07/1990s.pdf.

18. CBO, "Supplemental Appropriations 2000–Present," October 5, 2018, https://www.cbo.gov/system/files?file=2018-10/FY%202018%20House%202018.9.30.pdf.

19. Lindsay, "FEMA's Disaster Relief Fund."

20. CBO, "Status of Appropriations FY 2015–2019," https://www.cbo.gov/topics/budget/status-appropriations.

21. CBO, "Supplemental Appropriations in the 1990s."

22. CBO, "Supplemental Appropriations 2000–Present."

23. Nicole Ogrysko, "Trump Asks Civilian Agencies for Help to Offset New $44 Billion Disaster Relief Package," *Federal News Network*, November 20, 2017.

24. Government Accountability Office (GAO), "Disaster Recovery: Better Monitoring of Block Grant Funds Is Needed," GAO-19-232, March 2019.

25. GAO, "Disaster Assistance–Flood Insurance."

26. CBO, "Table 1. Authorizing Divisions: CBO Estimate for Senate Amendment 1930, The Bipartisan Budget Act of 2018," February 8, 2018.

27. CBO, "Table 1. Authorizing Divisions."

28. Congressional Research Service, "Army Corps of Engineers: FY2018 Appropriations," In Focus no. IF10671, April 2, 2018.

29. Justin Bogie, "Earmarks Won't Fix the Broken Budget and Appropriations Process," Heritage Foundation Backgrounder no. 3353, September 20, 2018.

30. William Painter and Jared Brown, "FY2013 Supplemental Funding for Disaster Relief," Congressional Research Service Report no. R42869, February 19, 2013.

31. CBO, "The Federal Government's Spending and Tax Actions in Response to the 2005 Gulf Coast Hurricanes," August 1, 2007.

32. GAO, "Hurricane Katrina and Rita Disaster Relief," Testimony Before the Subcommittee on Investigations, House Committee on Homeland Security, House of Representatives, GAO-06-844T, June 14, 2006.

33. Jeff Zeleny, "$700 Million in Katrina Relief Missing, Report Shows," *ABC News*, April 3, 2013.

34. CBO, "Funding for Overseas Contingency Operations and Its Impact on Defense Spending," October 23, 2018.

35. Committee for a Responsible Federal Budget, "What's an Emergency?," June 22, 2010.

36. GAO, "Principles of Federal Appropriations Law," 3rd ed., vol. I, January 2004.

37. Painter and Brown, "FY2013 Supplemental Funding for Disaster Relief."

38. Painter and Brown, "FY2013 Supplemental Funding for Disaster Relief."

39. Bogie, "Earmarks Won't Fix the Broken Budget and Appropriations Process."

40. FEMA, "Per Capita Impact Indicator and Project Thresholds," October 1, 2019.

41. Lynn M. Williams and Susan B. Epstein, "Overseas Contingency Operations Funding: Background and Status," Congressional Research Service Report no. R44519, February 7, 2017.

42. Williams and Epstein, "Overseas Contingency Operations Funding."

43. National Flood Insurance Act of 1968, as amended, 42 U.S. Code 4001 et seq.

44. National Flood Insurance Act of 1968, as amended.

45. Congressional Research Service, "Introduction to the National Flood Insurance Program," Congressional Research Service Report no. 44593, August 16, 2016.

46. U.S. Department of Homeland Security, "Answers to Questions about the NFIP," FEMA F-084, Federal Emergency Management Agency, March 2011.

47. CBO, "Table 1. Authorizing Divisions."

CHAPTER FOURTEEN

1. U.S. Const. art. I, § 9, cl. 7 https://www.archives.gov/founding-docs/constitution-transcript.

2. See Budget and Accounting Act of 1921, Public Law 67-13, 67th Cong., 1st sess., June 10, 1921; and Congressional Budget and Impoundment Control Act of 1974, Public Law 93-344, 93rd Cong., 2nd sess., July 12, 1974.

3. The budget resolution data for fiscal years 1999 through 2019 are compiled from Congressional Research Service published historical data for 1999 through 2016 combined with widely available budget resolution data for fiscal years 2017–2019. See Bill Heniff Jr., "Congressional Budget Resolutions: Historical Information," Congressional Research Service Report no. RL30297, November 16, 2015.

4. Joseph Scherer, "The Report of the President's Commission on Budget Concepts: A Review," Federal Reserve Bank of New York Monthly Review, December 1967.

5. Fair Credit Reform Act, 15 U.S.C.§1681, https://fiscal.treasury.gov/files/ussgl/fcra.pdf.

6. James C. Capretta, "How Congress Can Fix Its Trillion Dollar Accounting Error," American Enterprise Institute, July 11, 2018.

7. Capretta, "How Congress Can Fix Its Trillion Dollar Accounting Error."

8. Congressional Budget Office (CBO), "How CBO Produces Fair-Value Estimates of the Cost of Federal Credit Programs: A Primer," July 12, 2018, p. 2.

9. CBO, "Fair-Value Estimates of the Cost of Federal Credit Programs in 2019," June 29, 2018, p. 2.

10. CBO, *The Budget and Economic Outlook: 2018 to 2028,* April 9, 2018, Table A-1, p. 94.

11. The CBO constructs its baseline in accordance with provisions set forth in the Balanced Budget and Emergency Deficit Control Act of 1985, as amended, and the Congressional Budget and Impoundment Control Act of 1974, as amended.

12. CBO, *The Budget and Economic Outlook: 2018 to 2028.*

13. Paul Winfree, Justin Bogie, and Romina Boccia, "How Emergency Spending Has Exploded in Recent Years," Heritage Foundation Commentary, September 19, 2018.

14. Justin Bogie, "Congress Must Stop the Abuse of Disaster and Emergency Spending," Heritage Foundation Backgrounder no. 3380, February 4, 2019.

15. Keith Bea, "Federal Emergency Management Agency Funding for Homeland Security and Other Activities," Congressional Research Service Report no. RL31359, April 9, 2002, p. 24; and Committee for a Responsible Federal Budget, "What's an Emergency?," June 22, 2010.

16. Jason Pye, "Only in Washington Can Limiting the Growth of a Government Program Be Called a 'Spending Cut,'" *FreedomWorks Blog*, June 29, 2017.

17. CBO, "Expired and Expiring Authorizations of Appropriations: Fiscal Year 2018, Revised," July 3, 2018, p. 2, https://www.cbo.gov/publication/54126.

18. Government Accountability Office, "Principles of Federal Appropriations Law," 3rd ed., vol. I, January 2004.

19. Congressional Budget and Impoundment Control Act of 1974.

20. A Bill to Assure that Congress Acts on the Budget Resolution, S. 1681, 112th Congress (2011–2012).

21. Romina Boccia, "Sen. Braun to Congress: No Budget? No Pay for You," Heritage Foundation Commentary, February 14, 2019.

CHAPTER FIFTEEN

1. Abba Lerner, "Functional Finance and the Federal Debt," *Social Research* 10, no. 1 (February 1943): 38–52.

2. J. W. Mason and Arjun Jayadev, "Lost in Fiscal Space: Some Simple Analytics of Macroeconomic Policy in the Spirit of Tinbergen, Wicksell and Lerner," Washington Center for Equitable Growth Working Paper, November 2016.

3. David Colander, "Functional Finance," in *An Encyclopedia of Keynesian Economics*, ed. Thomas Cate, G. C. Harcourt, and David Colander (Cheltenham:

Edward Elgar Publishing, 1997), http://community.middlebury.edu/~colander/articles/functional%20finance%20article.pdf.

4. Daniel Shaviro, "The Long-Term Fiscal Gap: Is the Main Problem Generational Inequity?," *George Washington Law Review* 77, no. 5/6 (September 2009): 1298–357.

5. Jude Wanniski, "Taxes and a Two-Santa Theory," *National Observer*, March 6, 1976.

6. Eugene Steuerle, "Did the Congress and the President 'Give' Us a Tax Cut?," *Tax Vox Blog*, February 5, 2008.

7. John L. Mikesell, *Fiscal Administration*, 9th ed., chap. 3 (Boston: Wadsworth Cengage Learning, 2014).

8. Gross outlays are netted against collections from commercial-type transactions such as sales of assets or services.

9. For specific instances of the strategic budget use of asset sales, specifically discrete sales from the Strategic Petroleum Reserve, conditional on high prices, see the Bipartisan Budget Act of 2015 (PL 114-74), Sections 403 and 404, and the Bipartisan Budget Act of 2018.

10. For an accessible, detailed description, see Community Living Assistance Services and Supports Act, www.wikipedia.org.

11. Congressional Budget Office, "Memorandum to Sen. Harry Reid, Majority Leader," March 11, 2010.

12. Marvin Phaup, "Budgeting for Mandatory Spending: Prologue to Reform," *Public Budgeting & Finance* 39, no. 1 (Spring 2019): 24–44.

13. This recommendation was made by the Committee for a Responsible Federal Budget in a *Memorandum* 'Including Debt Targets in the JSC's Budget Process Reform Package," October 30, 2018.

14. Office of Management and Budget, *A Budget for a Better America: Analytical Perspectives, Fiscal Year 2020 Budget of the U.S. Government* (Washington: Government Printing Office, 2019), p. 77.

CHAPTER SIXTEEN

1. The GRPF is distinct from the oft-related principle that public budgets should be balanced *over the course of a business cycle*, with deficits incurred during recessions (as revenues decline) and surpluses incurred during expansions (with proceeds used to repay debt). The GRPF pertains to the *use* made of funds (whether for investment or consumption) borrowed publicly at long maturities. Cyclical issues are relevant to the Golden Rule of Public Finance (GRPF) analysis because in recent decades debt-financed consumption, more than infrastructure spending, has become the preferred fiscal prescription for curing recessions; and surpluses are rare, so debts incurred are rarely reduced. The norm of "balance the budget

over the cycle" also has faded. Strict adherence to a GRPF, which forbids deficit spending for ordinary outlays, implies that deficits caused by recessions necessitate spending cuts, tax hikes, or both, typically a pro-cyclical (thus inadvisable) policy mix. The GRPF also is unrelated to the "golden rule of capital accumulation," embedded in models of "steady state" economic growth beginning in the 1950s.

2. For defenders in recent decades, see Harley L. Lutz, *Public Finance*, 4th ed. (New York: Appleton-Century Company, Inc., 1947); James M. Buchanan, *Public Principles of Public Debt*, vol. 2 of *The Collected Works of James M. Buchanan* (Indianapolis, IN: Liberty Fund, 1958); James M. Buchanan, *Public Finance in Democratic Process*, vol. 4 of *The Collected Works of James M. Buchanan* (Indianapolis, IN: Liberty Fund, 1967); James M. Buchanan and Richard E. Wagner, *Democracy in Deficit: The Political Legacy of Lord Keynes*, vol. 8 of *The Collected Works of James M. Buchanan* (Indianapolis, IN: Liberty Fund, 1977); Richard E. Wagner, *Deficits, Debt and Democracy: Wrestling with Tragedy on the Commons* (Northampton, MA: Edward Elgar Publishing, 2012); John Merrifield and Barry Poulson, *Restoring America's Fiscal Constitution* (New York: Lexington Books, 2017); and Richard M. Salsman, *The Political Economy of Public Debt: Three Centuries of Theory and Evidence* (Northampton, MA: Edward Elgar Publishing, 2017).

3. See Joseph A. Schumpeter, "Gladstonian Finance," in pt. 3, chap. 2 of *History of Economic Analysis* (Oxford: Oxford University Press, 1954), p. 402–05; and Salsman, *The Political Economy of Public Debt*, pp. 86, 166–67. William Gladstone (1809–1898) was Britain's prime minster or chancellor of the exchequer in two-thirds of all years from 1852 to 1894; he extolled (and practiced) limited government, sound money (the gold standard), sound finance (balanced budgets), and free trade.

4. For a comprehensive survey of fiscal rules in 96 nations, see Victor Lledó et al., "Fiscal Rules at a Glance," International Monetary Fund, March 2017. The survey reveals that in recent decades only six nations adopted anything like a GRPF: Costa Rica (p. 22: since 2001), Germany (p. 32: 1969–2010), Japan (p. 43: 1947–1974), Luxembourg (p. 48: 1990–2003), Malaysia (p. 49: 1959–present), and UK (p. 75: 1997–2008). In none of the six cases was an enforcement mechanism found that might rectify rule breaches.

5. Jonathan Gruber, *Public Finance and Public Policy*, 5th ed. (New York: Worth Publishers, 2016).

6. That citizens should only pay for what they get and get what they pay for, regarding public goods—termed the benefits principle—is another bygone fiscal rule. It has been displaced by "ability to pay," the principle that richer citizens should pay disproportionately more for public goods, in excess of value received, while poorer citizens should receive value from public spending in excess of what they might pay for them (if anything).

7. Significantly, in private-sector transfers to heirs governed by wills, probate courts permit the deceased to transfer positive- but *not* negative-net-worth estates; if private debts are bequeathed, they must be accompanied by assets of equal or greater value. No such protection is afforded future generations that are compelled to service public debts incurred by ancestors; they may receive public assets that are worth less than the debts.

8. See Richard A. Musgrave, *The Theory of Public Finance* (New York and London: McGraw-Hill, 1959). The influential public finance text succinctly captured the theoretical shift in the 20th century, with "The Benefit Approach" (chap. 4) followed by "The Ability-to-Pay Approach" (chap. 5). As a Keynesian social democrat, Musgrave favored the latter principle. The most influential previous public finance text—Lutz, *Public Finance*—defended the benefit principle. Whereas Lutz favored a limited state, Musgrave did not.

9. The U.S. Constitution refers to the public debt, but only to say that Congress has the power to incur it and raise taxes to repay it (Art. I, Sec. 8) and that it is valid regardless of how or when it is incurred (Art. VI).

10. Policymakers are understandably reluctant, amid recessions, to narrow budget deficits by spending restraint and/or tax hikes, so they resist austerity budgets. Yet studies of fiscal consolidation show that while tax hikes make recessions worse, spending restraint does not. See Alberto Alesina and Silvia Ardagna, "Large Changes in Fiscal Policy: Taxes versus Spending," in *Tax Policy and the Economy*, vol. 24, ed. Jeffrey R. Brown (Chicago: University of Chicago Press, 2010); and Jamie Guajardo, Daniel Leigh, and Andrea Pescatori, "Expansionary Austerity: New International Evidence," International Monetary Fund Working Paper no. WP/11/158, July 2011.

11. The Stability and Growth Pact caps the budget deficits and public debts of each of each member state (28 of them) at 3 percent and 60 percent of GDP, respectively. A member state that breaches the caps must take corrective action by an Excessive Deficit Procedure and, failing that, faces fines and economic sanctions. But there is no strict enforcement of the pact. Since 2008 at least a quarter of the members has been perpetually noncompliant. Sweden and Luxembourg are the only member states that have never breached the caps since the pact was formed in 1998.

12. On the many ways John Maynard Keynes and the Keynesians undermined fiscal rectitude, see Buchanan and Wagner, *Democracy in Deficit: The Political Legacy of Lord Keynes*. Yet Keynes also worried if public debt wasn't used for public investment; see Elba K. Brown-Collier and Bruce E. Collier, "What Keynes Really Said about Deficit Spending," *Journal of Post Keynesian Economics* 17, no. 3 (1995): 341–55.

13. James M. Buchanan, "Fiscal Nihilism and Beyond," chap. 19 in *Public Finance in Democratic Process*, vol. 4 of *The Collected Works of James M. Buchanan* (Indianapolis, IN: Liberty Fund, 1967).

14. See Giuseppe Eusepi and Richard E. Wagner, *Public Debt: An Illusion of Democratic Political Economy* (Northampton, MA: Edward Elgar Publishing, 2018).

15. See Robert J. Barro, "The Ricardian Approach to Budget Deficits," *Journal of Economic Perspectives* 3, no. 2 (1989): 37–54.

16. See James M. Buchanan, "The Ethics of Debt Default," in *Deficits*, ed. James M. Buchanan, Charles K. Rowley, and Robert D. Tollison (Oxford, UK: Basil Blackwell, 1987). See also a tardy but able rebuttal by Giuseppe Eusepi and Geoffrey Brennan, "The Public-Debt Trap," in *The Reason of Rules: Constitutional Political Economy*, vol. 10 of *The Collected Works of James M. Buchanan* (Indianapolis, IN: Liberty Fund, 2002), pp. 104–6.

17. See Jerome Roos, *Why Not Default? The Political Economy of Sovereign Debt* (Princeton, NJ: Princeton University Press, 2019). Roos contends that "the profound transformation of the capitalist world economy over the past four decades has endowed private and official creditors with unprecedented structural power over heavily indebted borrowers, enabling them to impose painful austerity measures and enforce uninterrupted debt service during times of crisis—with devastating social consequences," in the publisher's summary. https://press.princeton.edu/books/hardcover/9780691180106/why-not-default.

18. Office of Management and Budget, "Historical Tables," Table 3.1—Outlays by Superfunction and Function: 1940–2024. Spending on Human Resources includes spending on education, training, employment, social services, health care, income security, Medicare, and Social Security.

19. What I call "the paradox of profligacy"—successively lower sovereign bond yields despite successively higher public leverage in recent decades—is attributable partly to lower inflation and partly to central bank policies that impose near-zero interest rates and "financial repression." See Salsman, *The Political Economy of Public Debt*, pp. 25, 247–53.

20. Office of Management and Budget, "Historical Tables," Table 9.1—Total Investment Outlays for Physical Capital, Research and Development, and Education and Training: 1962–2020.

21. See Federal Reserve Bank of St. Louis, "Shares of Gross Domestic Product: Gross Private Domestic Investment;" See U.S. Bureau of Economic Analysis, "Shares of Gross Domestic Product: Gross Private Domestic Investment," https://fred.stlouisfed.org/series/A007RE1A156NBEA.

22. Federal Reserve Bank of St. Louis, "State and Local Government Gross Investment." See U.S. Bureau of Economic Analysis, "State and Local Government Gross Investment," https://fred.stlouisfed.org/series/SLINV.

23. Federal Reserve Bank of St. Louis, "Business Sector: Real Output Per Hour of All Persons," https://fred.stlouisfed.org/series/OPHPBS; from U.S. Bureau of Labor Statistics, "Business Sector: Real Output Per Hour of All Persons."

24. See Awaworyi Churchill and Siew Ling Yew, "Are Government Transfers Harmful to Economic Growth? A Meta-Analysis," *Economic Modelling* 64, no. C (2017): 270–87. The authors examine the "common perception . . . that government transfers are harmful to economic growth" and find that they are "more detrimental to economic growth in developed countries compared to less-developed countries because such transfers can have a non-monotonic effect on growth. When government transfers are substantial, as they are in developed countries, they tend to reduce growth."

25. Luc Eyraud et al., "How to Select Fiscal Rules: A Primer," International Monetary Fund How-To Notes, March 2018, p. 5.

26. Achim Truger, "Implementing the Golden Rule for Public Investment in Europe: Safeguarding Public Investment and Supporting the Recovery," WWWforEurope, Policy Paper no. 22, March 2015.

27. Truger, "Implementing the Golden Rule for Public Investment in Europe."

28. In truth, little public infrastructure is built without heavy reliance on the private sector for materials, equipment, factories, transportation, architectural-engineering services, and labor; the biggest public roles are in permitting, planning, and funding.

29. Barro (2003) finds that "for given per capita GDP and human capital, [economic] growth depends . . . negatively on the ratio of government consumption to GDP." Robert. J. Barro, "Determinants of Economic Growth in a Panel of Countries," *Annals of Economics and Finance* 4, no. 2 (2003): 231.

30. See Leland B. Yeager, ed., *In Search of a Monetary Constitution* (Cambridge, MA: Harvard University Press, 1962); and Lawrence H. White, Viktor J. Vanberg, and Ekkehard A. Köhler, eds., *Renewing the Search for a Monetary Constitution: Reforming Government's Role in the Monetary System* (Washington: Cato Institute, 2015).

31. James M. Buchanan and Roger D. Congleton, *Politics by Principle, Not Interest: Towards Nondiscriminatory Democracy* (New York: Cambridge University Press, 1998).

32. On the generality standard, see also James M. Buchanan, "Three Amendments: Responsibility, Generality, and Natural Liberty," Cato Unbound, December 4, 2005, https://www.cato-unbound.org/2005/12/04/james-m-buchanan/three-amendments-responsibility-generality-natural-liberty.

33. The normalization of envy and exploitation of "the most advantaged," embodied in John Rawls's theory of justice, is discussed (and heartily endorsed) by Jeffrey Edward Green. See John Rawls, *A Theory of Justice* (Cambridge, MA: Harvard University Press, 1971); Jeffrey Edward Green, "Rawls and the Forgotten Figure of the Most Advantaged: In Defense of Reasonable Envy Toward the Superrich," *American Political Science Review* 107, no. 1 (2013): 123–138.

34. See recent polls of academic "experts" conducted by the University of Chicago's Booth School of Business on the gold standard (IGM Forum Survey, "Gold Standard," January 12, 2012) and a balanced budget amendment (IGM Forum Survey, "Balanced Budget Amendment," November 7, 2017).

CHAPTER SEVENTEEN

1. David Primo, *Rules and Restraint: Government Spending and the Design of Institutions* (Chicago: University of Chicago Press, 2007), p. 109.

2. Vincent Ostrom, *Intellectual Crisis in American Public Administration* (Tuscaloosa: University of Alabama Press, 1974).

3. Carl Schmitt, *The Concept of the Political* (1932; repr., Chicago: University of Chicago Press, 1996).

4. Schmitt, *Concept of the Political*; Richard E. Wagner, *Deficits, Debt, and Democracy: Wrestling with Tragedy on the Fiscal Commons* (Cheltenham, UK: Edward Elgar, 2012).

5. Adam Smith, *An Inquiry into the Nature and Causes of the Wealth of Nations* (1776; repr., New York: Modern Library, 1937), p. 424.

6. Mark Blaug, *Economic Theory in Retrospect* (Cambridge: Cambridge University Press, 1997), p. 642.

7. James M. Buchanan and Richard E. Wagner, *Democracy in Deficit: The Political Legacy of Lord Keynes* (New York: Academic Press, 1977).

8. Michael C. Munger and Kevin M. Munger, *Choosing in Groups: Analytical Politics Revisited* (Cambridge: Cambridge University Press, 2015).

9. Vilfredo Pareto, *The Mind and Society* (1915; repr., New York: Harcourt Brace, 1935).

10. Friedrich Wieser, *Das Gesetz der Macht* (Vienna: Julius Springer, 1926); Bertrand de Jouvenel, *On Power: Its Nature and the History of Its Growth* (London: Hutchinson, 1948).

11. George Stigler and Gary Becker, "De Gustibus Non Est Disputandum," *American Economic Review* 67 (1977): 76–90.

12. Stigler and Becker, "De Gustibus Non Est Disputandum."

13. Gaetano Mosca, *Elementi di scienza politica*, 4th ed. (Bari: G. Laterza, 1947); Pareto, *Mind and Society*.

14. Duncan Black, *Theory of Committees and Elections* (Cambridge: Cambridge University Press, 1958); Anthony Downs, *An Economic Theory of Democracy* (New York: Harper & Row, 1957).

15. Kenneth E. Boulding, *The Image: Knowledge in Life and Society* (Ann Arbor: University of Michigan Press, 1956).

16. Richard E. Wagner, *Fiscal Sociology and the Theory of Public Finance* (Cheltenham, UK: Edward Elgar, 2007), pp. 125–54.

17. Carolyn Webber and Aaron Wildavsky, *A History of Taxation and Public Expenditure in the Western World* (New York: Simon and Schuster, 1986).

18. Roger Koppl, *Big Players and the Economic Theory of Expectations* (New York: Palgrave Macmillan, 2002).

19. Henry Maine, *Ancient Law* (London: John Murray, 1861).

20. Bruce Bueno de Mesquita et al., *The Logic of Political Survival* (Cambridge, MA: MIT Press, 2003).

21. Robert Michels, *Political Parties: A Sociological Study of the Oligarchical Tendencies of Modern Democracy* (New York: Collier Books, 1962).

22. Bertrand de Jouvenel, "Seminar Exercise: The Chairman's Problem," *American Political Science Review* 55, no. 2 (1961): 368–72.

23. Giuseppe Eusepi and Richard E. Wagner, "Tax Prices in a Democratic Polity: The Continuing Relevance of Antonio de Viti de Marco," *History of Political Economy* 45, no. 1 (2013): 99–121; Manuela Mosca, *Antonio de Viti de Marco: A Story Worth Remembering* (Basingstoke, UK: Palgrave Macmillan, 2016).

24. Antonio de Viti de Marco, *Il carattere teorico dell'economia finanziaria* (Rome: Pasqualucci, 1888); Antonio de Viti de Marco, *First Principles of Public Finance*, trans. Edith Pavlo Marget (New York: Harcourt, Brace, 1936).

25. Antonio de Viti de Marco, *Un trentennio di lotte politiche* (Roma: Collezione Meridionale Editrice, 1930).

26. Roy Harrod, *The Life of John Maynard Keynes* (London: Macmillan, 1951).

27. Frank H. Knight, *Intelligence and Democratic Action* (Cambridge, MA: Harvard University Press, 1960).

28. Richard E. Wagner, "A Macro Economy as an Ecology of Plans," *Journal of Economic Behavior and Organization* 82, nos. 2–3 (2012): 433–44.

29. Mitchel Resnick, *Turtles, Termites, and Traffic Jams* (Cambridge, MA: MIT Press, 1994).

30. Resnick, *Turtles, Termites, and Traffic Jams*.

31. Wagner, "Macro Economy as an Ecology of Plans."

32. Robert J. Barro, "Are Government Bonds Net Wealth?," *Journal of Political Economy* 82, no. 6 (1974): 1095–118.

33. John J. Seater, "Ricardian Equivalence," *Journal of Economic Literature* 31, no. 1 (1993): 142–90.

34. Wagner, "Macro Economy as an Ecology of Plans."

35. James M. Buchanan, *Cost and Choice* (Chicago: Markham, 1969).

36. James M. Buchanan, *Public Finance in Democratic Process: Fiscal Institutions and Individual Choice* (Chapel Hill: University of North Carolina Press, 1967).

37. See Richard E. Wagner, "Liability Rules, Fiscal Institutions, and the Debt," in *Deficits*, ed. James M. Buchanan, Charles K. Rowley, and Robert D. Tollison (Oxford: Oxford University Press, 1986), pp. 374–90.

38. Albert Hirschman, *Exit, Voice, and Loyalty* (Cambridge, MA: Harvard University Press, 1970).

39. Spencer H. MacCallum, *The Art of Community* (Menlo Park, CA: Institute for Humane Studies, 1970).

40. Marta Podemska-Mikluch and Richard E. Wagner, "Dyads, Triads, and the Theory of Exchange: Between Liberty and Coercion," *Review of Austrian Economics* 26, no. 2 (2013): 171–82.

41. Richard E. Wagner, *Public Debt and the Corruption of Contract*, published simultaneously as *Il debito pubblico e la corruzione delle promesee* (Milan: Bruno Leoni Institute, 2017).

42. Charles Fried, *Contract as Promise: A Theory of Contractual Obligation* (Cambridge, MA: Harvard University Press, 1981).

CHAPTER EIGHTEEN

1. Richard E. Wagner, *Deficits, Debt, and Democracy: Wrestling with the Tragedy of the Fiscal Commons* (Cheltenham, UK: Edward Elgar, 2012), p. 7.

2. Antonio de Viti de Marco, *First Principles of Public Finance*, trans. Edith Pavlo Marget (New York: Harcourt, Brace, 1936).

3. James M. Buchanan, "The Pure Theory of Government Finance: A Suggested Approach," *Journal of Political Economy* 57, no. 6 (1949): 495–505; James M. Buchanan, *Public Finance in Democratic Process: Fiscal Institutions and Individual Choice*, vol. 4, *The Collected Works of James M. Buchanan* (Indianapolis: Liberty Fund, 1967).

4. Geoffrey Brennan and James M. Buchanan, *The Reason of Rules: Constitutional Political Economy*, vol. 10, *The Collected Works of James M. Buchanan* (Indianapolis: Liberty Fund, 2000).

5. Wagner, *Deficits, Debt, and Democracy*.

6. Giuseppe Eusepi and Richard E. Wagner, *Public Debt: An Illusion of Democratic Political Economy* (Cheltenham, UK: Edward Elgar, 2017).

7. David J. Hebert, "The Spontaneous Order of Politics," in *Austrian Economics: The Next Generation*, ed. Steven Horwitz (Bingley, UK: Emerald Publishing, 2019), pp. 131–44.

8. Buchanan, *Public Finance in Democratic Process*.

9. David J. Hebert, "The Chairman's Solution," *Journal of Public Finance and Public Choice* 34, no. 1 (2019): 71–82.

10. James M. Buchanan and Richard E. Wagner, *Public Debt in a Democratic Society* (Washington: American Enterprise Institute for Public Policy Research, 1967).

11. Hebert, "Chairman's Solution," pp. 72–73.

12. Bertrand de Jouvenel, "Seminar Exercise: The Chairman's Problem," *American Political Science Review* 55, no. 2 (1961): 367–72.

13. David Ricardo, "Essay on the Funding System," in *The Works of David Ricardo, with a Notice of the Life and Writings of the Author,* ed. J. McCulloch (Indianapolis: Liberty Fund, 1888).

14. James M. Buchanan, *The Limits of Liberty: Between Anarchy and Leviathan,* vol. 7, *The Collected Works of James M. Buchanan* (Indianapolis: Liberty Fund, 1975).

15. During his tenure as Speaker of the House, Paul Ryan brought significantly more bills to the floor as "closed" than any previous Speaker. Whether this is a symptom of increased partisanship in Washington or a contributing factor to that partisanship remains to be determined.

16. Christopher M. Davis, *Invoking Cloture in the Senate* (Washington: Congressional Research Service, 2017).

17. James M. Buchanan and Richard E. Wagner, *Democracy in Deficit: The Political Legacy of Lord Keynes,* vol. 8, *The Collected Works of James M. Buchanan* (Indianapolis: Liberty Fund, 1977).

18. In *Democracy in Deficit*, Buchanan and Wagner provide the most cogent exploration of the legacy of John Maynard Keynes (hence the oft-neglected subtitle of the book, *The Political Legacy of Lord Keynes*).

19. George Washington, "Farewell Address, 19 September 1796," Founders Online, National Archives, https://founders.archives.gov/documents/Washington/99-01-02-00963.

20. Logan Dancey and Geofffrey Sheagley provide a telling analysis of party-line voting in the United States. Dancey and Sheagley, "Partisanship and Perceptions of Party-Line Voting in Congress," *Political Research Quarterly* 71, no. 1 (2018): 32–45.

21. David J. Hebert and Richard E. Wagner, "Political Parties: Insights from a Tri-Planar Model of Political Economy," *Constitutional Political Economy,* 29, no. 3 (2018): 253–67.

22. Gordon Tullock, *The Politics of Bureaucracy* (Washington: Public Affairs Press, 1965); John H. Aldrich, *Why Parties? The Origin and Transformation of Political Parties in America* (Chicago: University of Chicago Press, 1995); E. E. Schattschneider, *Party Government: American Government in Action* (New York: Farrar and Rinehart, 2004).

23. Hebert and Wagner, "Political Parties."

24. Randall G. Holcombe describes a similar process in *Political Capitalism: How Economic and Political Power Is Made and Maintained* (Cambridge: Cambridge University Press, 2018).

25. Washington, "Farewell Address, 19 September 1796."

26. Deborah Paul and David Hebert extend this type of logic to all bills. Deborah L. Paul, "The Sources of Tax Complexity: How Much Simplicity Can Fundamental Tax Reform Achieve?," *North Carolina Law Review* 76, no. 1 (1997): 151–220; Hebert, "Spontaneous Order of Politics."

27. Richard E. Wagner, "Grazing the Budgetary Commons: The Rational Politics of Budgetary Irresponsibility," *Journal of Law and Economics* 9 (1992): 105–19; Richard E. Wagner, *Deficits, Debt, and Democracy*; Jody W. Lipford and Bruce Yandle, "Grazing the State and Local Fiscal Commons: Do Different Tax Prices Lead to More or Less Grazing?," *Public Finance Review* 42, no. 4 (2013): 466–86.

28. Elinor Ostrom, *Governing the Commons: The Evolution of Institutions for Collective Action* (Cambridge: Cambridge University Press, 1990).

29. Cheryl D. Block, "Budget Gimmicks," in *Fiscal Challenges: An Interdisciplinary Approach to Budget Policy* (Cambridge: Cambridge University Press, 2008), pp. 39–67.

30. Block, "Budget Gimmicks."

31. Block, "Budget Gimmicks."

32. Block, "Budget Gimmicks."

33. Richard Wagner, "Fiscal Crisis as Failure of Progressivist Democracy," George Mason University Working Paper in Economics no. 15-26, March 2015.

CHAPTER NINETEEN

1. For a discussion of fiscal federalism and budget constraints, see Jonathan Rodden, "Reviving Leviathan: Fiscal Federalism and the Growth of Government," *International Organization* 57, no. 4 (2003): 695–729; Jonathan Rodden, Gunnar S. Eskeland, and Jennie Litvack, eds., *Fiscal Decentralization and the Challenge of Hard Budget Constraints* (Cambridge, MA: MIT Press, 2003); David Wildasin, "The Institutions of Federalism: Toward an Analytical Framework," *National Tax Journal* 57, no. 2 (2004): 247–72; Barry R. Weingast, "Second Generation Fiscal Federalism: The Implications of Fiscal Incentives," *Journal of Urban Economics* 65, no. 3 (2009): 279–93; and Barry R. Weingast, "Second Generation Fiscal Federalism: Political Aspects of Decentralization and Economic Development," *World Development* 53 (2014): 14–25.

2. Paul Studenski and Herman Krooss, *Financial History of the United States* (New York: McGaw-Hill, 1963).

3. Studenski and Krooss, *Financial History.*

4. The concept of dynamic credence capital was first introduced by Charles Blankart. He argues that a "[no] bailout rule is a necessary condition for fiscal autonomy of state and local governments. With a no bailout rule, state and local governments have an incentive to enact fiscal rules to constrain spending and debt." See Charles B. Blankart, "The Process of Government Centralization: A Constitutional View," *Constitutional Political Economy* 11, no. 1 (2000): 27–39; Charles B. Blankart, Erik R. Fasten, and Achim Klaiber, "Föderalismus ohne Insolvenz?," *Wirtschaftsdienst* 86, no. 9 (2006): 567–71; Charles B. Blankart, "An Economic Theory of Switzerland," CESifo Working Paper no. 3646, March 2011; and Charles B. Blankart, "Swiss Role: What the Eurozone Could Learn from Switzerland," *CESifo Forum* 16, no. 2 (2015): 39–42. For a discussion of fiscal federalism in the eurozone countries, see John Merrifield and Barry Poulson, "New Constitutional Debt Brakes for Euroland Revisited," *Journal of Applied Business and Economics* 19, no. 8 (2017): 110–32.

5. The relationship between fiscal federalism and the size of government is explored in Philip Grossman, "Fiscal Decentralization and Government Size: An Extension," *Public Choice* 62, no. 1 (July 1989): 63–66; Philip J. Grossman and Edwin G. West, "Federalism and the Growth of Government Revisited," *Public Choice* 79, nos. 1–2 (1994): 19–32; Wallace E. Oates, "Toward a Second Generation Theory of Federalism," *International Tax and Public Finance* 12, no. 4 (2005): 349–73; and Dwight R. Lee, "Reverse Revenue Sharing: A Modest Proposal," *Public Choice* 45, no. 3 (1985): 279–89.

6. John Merrifield and Barry Poulson, "The Swedish and Swiss Fiscal Rule Outcomes Contain Key Lessons for the U.S.," *Independent Review* 21, no. 2 (2016): 251–74; John Merrifield and Barry Poulson, *Can the Debt Growth Be Stopped? Rules-Based Policy Options for Addressing the Federal Fiscal Crisis* (New York: Lexington Books, 2016); John Merrifield and Barry Poulson, *Restoring America's Fiscal Constitution* (New York: Lexington Books, 2017); Merrifield and Poulson, "New Constitutional Debt Brakes."

7. Barry Poulson, *Economic History of the United States* (New York: Macmillan, 1981).

8. Poulson, *Economic History of the United States*.

9. Merrifield and Poulson, *Can the Debt Growth Be Stopped?*; Merrifield and Poulson, *Restoring America's Fiscal Constitution*.

10. Gross debt—which includes intergovernmental debt as well as debt held by the public—now exceeds national income. Since interest cost arises from gross debt, this is even stronger evidence of an unsustainable debt burden. Congressional Budget Office, 2018 Long-Term Budget Outlook, June 26, 2018, https://www.cbo .gov/publication/53919.

11. Pew Charitable Trusts, "Long Term Obligations Vary as a Share of Resources," March 1, 2018.

12. Long-term obligations have increased as a share of state resources, and vary considerably among the states. Federal Reserve, *Financial Accounts of the United States: Flow of Funds, Balance Sheets, and Integrated Macroeconomic Accounts, Fourth Quarter 2017*, March 8, 2018, https://www.federalreserve.gov/releases/z1/; Pew Charitable Trusts, "Long Term Obligations"; Robert W. Wassman and Ronald C. Fisher, "State and Local Government Debt 1992–2008," Tax Notes, August 15, 2011.

13. John Merrifield and Barry Poulson, "State Fiscal Policies for Budget Stabilization and Economic Growth: A Dynamic Scoring Analysis," *Cato Journal* 34, no. 1 (Winter 2014): 47–81.

14. Eric A. Scorsone, "Municipal Fiscal Emergency Laws: Background and Guide to State-Based Approaches," Mercatus Center (George Mason University) Working Paper no. 14-21, July 2014.

15. Scorsone, "Municipal Fiscal Emergency Laws."

16. Scorsone, "Municipal Fiscal Emergency Laws."

17. Ben Canada, "Federal Grants to State and Local Governments: A Brief History," *Congressional Research Services RL 30705*, February 2019.

18. Kaiser Family Foundation, *Medicaid Financing: An Overview of the Federal Medicaid Matching Rate*, September 2012.

19. Congressional Budget Office (CBO), *Report on the Troubled Asset Relief Program*, October 12, 2012, https://www.cbo.gov/publication/43662.

20. CBO, "CBO's Estimates of ARRA's Economic Impact," CBO Blog, February 22, 2012, https://www.CBO.GOV/publication/43014.

21. U.S. Treasury Department, *Treasury Analysis of Build America Bonds Issuance and Savings*, May 16, 2011.

22. CBO, *Report on the Trouble Asset Relief Program*; Congressional Budget Office, *The Budget and Economic Outlook: 2016 to 2026*, January 2016, https://www.cbo.gov/publication/51129.

23. CBO, *Report on the Troubled Asset Relief Program*.

24. CBO, *Budgetary Impact of ARRA*.

25. Merrifield and Poulson, *Can the Debt Growth Be Stopped?*; Merrifield and Poulson, *Restoring America's Fiscal Constitution*.

26. Jarmila Botev, Jean-Marc Fournier, and Annabelle Mourougane, "A Re-assessment of Fiscal Space in OECD Countries," Organisation for Economic Co-operation and Development (OECD) Economics Department Working Papers no. 1352, November 23, 2016; Atish R. Ghosh et al, "Fiscal Fatigue, Fiscal Space and Debt Sustainability in Advanced Economies," National Bureau of Economic Research Working Paper no. 16782, February 2011; Falilou Fall et al, "Prudent Debt Targets and Fiscal Frameworks," OECD Economic Policy Papers no. 15, July 1, 2015; Falilou Fall and Jean-Marc Fournier, "Macroeconomic Uncertanties, Prudent Debt

Targets and Fiscal Rules," OECD Economics Department Working Papers no. 1230, June 29, 2015; Stephanie Lo and Kenneth Rogoff, "Secular Stagnation, Debt Overhand and Other Rationales for Sluggish Growth, Six Years On," Bank for International Settlements Working Paper no. 482, January 16, 2015; Christiane Nickel and Andreas Tudyka, "Fiscal Stimulus in Times of High Debt: Reconsidering Multipliers and Twin Deficits," *Journal of Money, Credit and Banking* 46, no. 7 (October 2014): 1313–1344; OECD, *Global Economic Outlook*, June 2016; OECD, *Interim Economic Outlook*, September 21, 2016; David Turner and Francesca Spinelli, "The Effect of Government Debt, External Debt and Their Interaction on OECD Interest Rates," OECD Economics Department Working Papers no. 1103, December 11, 2013.

27. Ronald C. Fisher and Robert W. Wassmer, "The Issuance of State and Local Debt During the United States Great Recession," *National Tax Journal* 61, no. 1 (March 2014): 113–150; Daniel J. Nadler and Sounman Hong, "Political and Institutional Determinants of Tax-Exempt Bond Yields," Program on Education Policy and Governance, Harvard Kennedy School Report No. 11-04, 2011; Robert W. Wassmer and Rondald C. Fisher, "State and Local Government Debt, 1992–2008," *State Tax Notes* 427 (August 2011): 427–436.

28. Gunjan Banerji, "Deficit-Ridden Illinois to Test Its Appeal," *Wall Street Journal*, April 25, 2018.

29. U.S. Treasury Department, *Treasury Analysis of Build America Bonds Issuance and Savings*.

30. Gunjan Banerji, "Deficit-Ridden Illinois to Test Its Appeal."

31. Gunjan Banerji, "Deficit-Ridden Illinois to Test Its Appeal."

32. Joe Tabor, "A constitutional amendment to impose fiscal discipline on state lawmakers is gaining bipartisan support," IlliniosPolicy.org, April 27, 2018.

33. Thirty-two states have enacted some form of state tax and expenditure limit as a constitutional or statutory measure. See John Merrifield and Barry Poulson, "State Fiscal Policies for Budget Stabilization and Economic Growth: A Dynamic Scoring Analysis," *Cato Journal* 34, no.1 (2014): 47–81. Even if Illinois were to enact an expenditure limit, it is difficult to see how this fiscal rule could be effective without fundamental institutional reform. After half a century of declining dynamic credence capital, Illinois is the poster child for a failed state.

34. Andrew G. Biggs, "Understanding the True Cost of State and Local Pensions," American Enterprise Institute, *State Tax Notes*, February 13, 2012.

35. *Wall Street Journal*, "Obama's Debt Interest Bomb," Opinion/Review & Outlook, April 10, 2017.

36. Heather Gillers, "State Promises Thrift in Selling Bonds," *Wall Street Journal*, June 6, 2018, pp. B1–B2; Office of the State Treasurer Denise L. Nappier, "Connecticut General Obligation Bond Sale Oversubscribed: Investor Demand Strong,"

news release, June 8, 2018, https://www.ott.ct.gov/pressreleases/press2018/PR060 82018TreasuryCompletesSuccessfulBondSale.pdf.

37. Gillers, "State Promises Thrift in Selling Bonds"; Office of the State Treasurer, "Connecticut General Obligation Bond Sale Oversubscribed."

38. Office of the State Treasurer, "Connecticut General Obligation Bond Sale Oversubscribed."; Paul Burton, "Connecticut's proposed bond covenants could set precedent, S&P says," The Bond Buyer, March 29, 2018; Paul Burton, "Budget Covenant Grabs Spotlight in Connecticut's GO Sale," The Bond Buyer, June 4, 2018.

39. Surveys reveal a loss of trust in U.S. institutions. A Gallup poll revealed that after a 50-year decline, just 14 percent of respondents said that the federal government could be trusted a great deal. A survey by the University of Chicago Booth/Kellogg School shows that only 22 percent of Americans trust the nation's financial system. "George Washington: Lack of Trust—Caused by Institutional Corruption—Is Killing the Economy," *Naked Capitalism* (blog), May 5, 2012, https://www.nakedcapitalism.com/2012/05/george-washington-lack-of-trust -caused-by-institutional-corruption-is-killing-the-economy.html.

40. OECD, *Global Economic Outlook*; OECD, *Interim Economic Outlook*.

41. *Wall Street Journal*, "Obama's Debt Interest Bomb," Opinion/Review & Outlook.

42. Turner and Spinelli, "The Effect of Government Debt."

43. Turner and Spinelli measure the interest rate growth differential as the difference between the interest rate on 10-year bonds and a smoothed OECD estimate of nominal potential growth. For non–euro area countries, an increase in the government debt-to-GDP ratio (above the 75 percent threshold) raises interest rates by 2½ basis points if financed domestically, and 3½ to 5 basis points if financed externally. This helps explain why in countries such as Japan, with debt financed domestically, the impact of debt on interest rates is moderated. Turner and Spinelli, "The Effect of Government Debt."

44. Merrifield and Poulson, "Swedish and Swiss Rule Outcomes"; Merrifield and Poulson, "New Constitutional Debt Brakes."

45. Blankart, "Swiss Role," pp. 40–41.

46. Merrifield and Poulson, "Swedish and Swiss Rule Outcomes"; Merrifield and Poulson, "New Constitutional Debt Brakes."

47. Numerous resolutions proposing new fiscal rules as amendments to the Constitution have been introduced in Congress over the years, but none has received the two-thirds vote in both houses required to submit the amendment to the states for ratification. The most recent resolution—proposing a balanced budget amendment—failed in the House in April 2018.

48. Merrifield and Poulson, *Restoring America's Fiscal Constitution*; Merrifield and Poulson, "New Constitutional Debt Brakes."

49. The theme of competitive federalism is explored by Albert Breton in "Towards a Theory of Competitive Federalism," *European Journal of Political Economy* 3, no. 1–2 (1987): 263–329; and *Competitive Governments: An Economic Theory of Politics and Public Finance* (New York: Cambridge University Press, 1996). See also Giampaolo Garzarelli, "Cognition, Incentives, and Public Governance: Laboratory Federalism from the Organizational Viewpoint," *Public Finance Review* 34, no. 3 (2006): 235–57; and Giampaolo Garzarelli and Lyndal Keeton, "Laboratory Federalism and Intergovernmental Grants," *Journal of Institutional Economics* 14, no. 5 (2017): 949–74.

50. Merrifield and Poulson, "Swedish and Swiss Rule Outcomes"; Merrifield and Poulson, "New Constitutional Debt Brakes."

51. Transplanting the Swiss debt brake to the United States must take into account the unique political and economic institutions in these countries. For a discussion of the difficulties in institutional transplants, see Daniel Berkowitz and Katharina Pistor, "Legal Transplants, Legal Irritants and Economic Development," in *Corporate Governance and Capital Flows in a Global Economy*, ed. Peter K. Cornelius and Bruce Kogut (New York: Oxford University Press, 2002); and Daniel Berkowitz, Katharina Pistor, and Jean-François Richard, "The Transplant Effect," *American Journal of Comparative Law* 51, no. 1 (2003): 163–204.

CHAPTER TWENTY

1. George F. Will, "The Slovenly Institution That Is Congress." *Washington Post*, July 25, 2017.

2. The discussion will focus on controlling federal spending. State and local governments are not notable for their fiscal responsibility, but one should recognize that some of their fiscal inefficiencies are the direct result of federal spending and tax policies. See J. R. Clark and Dwight R. Lee, "Tax Reform as a Discovery Process," in *For Your Own Good: Taxes, Paternalism and Fiscal Discrimination in the Twenty-First Century*, ed. Adam Hofer and Todd Nesbit (Fairfax, VA: Mercatus Center, George Mason University), pp. 289–302.

3. Roper Center for Public Opinion Research, "Taxes and Spending," *In the Balance: The Public, the Budget and the Deficit Blog*, January 29, 2015, https://ropercenter.cornell.edu/in-the-balance-the-public-the-budget-and-the-deficit/.

4. Federal Reserve Bank of S. Louis, "Gross Federal Debt Held by the Public as Percent of Gross Domestic Product," July 26, 2019, https://fred.stlouisfed.org/series/FYPUGDA188S.

5. Wilkinson, who is well versed in public choice, has argued, "The only really reliable method to shrink government (and not just the *rate* of government growth) is to shrink the economy." Will Wilkinson, "What If We Cannot Make

Government Smaller?," Niskanen Center, Washington, October 19, 2016, https://www.niskanencenter.org/cant-make-government-smaller/.

6. Robert Higgs, *Crisis and Leviathan: Critical Episodes in the Growth of American Government* (Oxford: Oxford University Press, 1987), pp. 83–84.

7. Higgs, *Crisis and Leviathan*, chap. 6.

8. Henry Simons, *Economic Policy for a Free Society* (Chicago: University of Chicago Press, 1951), p. 20.

9. John F. Cogan, *The High Cost of Good Intentions: A History of U.S. Federal Entitlement Programs* (Stanford, CA: Stanford University Press, 2017), p. 71.

10. Kimberly Amadeo, "U.S. Budget Deficit by Year Compared to GDP, Debt Increase, and Events: Is the U.S. Deficit Really That Bad?, *The Balance*, July 11, 2019.

11. See Cogan, *High Cost of Good Intentions*, p. 379. Entitlements do not include all transfers. Cogan's definition of a federal entitlement is given on page 10 and can exclude a number of expensive programs commonly thought of as entitlements.

12. Cogan, *High Cost of Good Intentions*, p. 381.

13. James M. Buchanan and Richard E. Wagner, *Democracy in Deficit: The Political Legacy of Lord Keynes* (New York: Academic Press, 1977).

14. Paul Krugman, "The Case for Cuts Was a Lie. Why Does Britain Still Believe It? The Austerity Delusion," *The Guardian*, April 29, 2015, https://www.theguardian.com/business/ng-interactive/2015/apr/29/the-austerity-delusion.

15. See Krugman, "The Austerity Delusion" (emphasis added).

16. James L. Payne, *The Culture of Spending* (San Francisco: Institute for Contemporary Press, 1991), p. 13, Table 1.1.

17. Steven Kelman, "'Public Choice' and Public Spirit," *Public Interest* 87 (1987): 80.

18. Amanda Holpuch, "Forty Millionaires Ask New York to Raise Taxes on Wealthy in '1% Plan for Fairness,'" *The Guardian* (U.S. edition), March 16, 2016.

19. This is a close approximation of the probability that one vote will break a tie in the votes of the other 200,000 voters when one candidate is favored over the other by 51 percent to 49 percent. See Geoffrey Brennan and Loren Lomasky, *Democracy and Decision: The Pure Theory of Electoral Preference* (Cambridge: Cambridge University Press, 1993), p. 57, Table 4.1. The assumption of 200,001 voters is somewhat less than the number expected to vote in a congressional election in a presidential election year.

20. Since the legislation is not sure to pass even if their candidate is elected, the probability is actually less than 1 in 12.2 million that their vote will be decisive in getting the legislation passed. This means that their costs of voting for the candidate are even less than stated above.

21. Alexander Hamilton, John Jay, and James Madison, *The Federalist*, Gideon ed., edited with an introduction, reader's guide, constitutional cross-reference, index, and glossary by George W. Carey and James McClellan (Indianapolis: Liberty Fund, 2001), https://oll.libertyfund.org/titles/788#Hamilton_0084_925.

22. The fact that a vote is so unlikely to have any effect on the outcome of an election not only reduces the voters' cost of voting for an expensive program, it also reduces their motivation to become informed on the likely effect of the program they feel so sanctimonious about voting for. Many noble-sounding government programs would fail to achieve the virtuous results expected even if they were not sabotaged by organized interest groups. For an informative discussion of voter ignorance, see Ilya Somin, *Democracy and Political Ignorance: Why Smaller Government Is Smarter* (Stanford, CA: Stanford University Press, 2016).

23. Gordon Tullock, "The Transitional Gains Trap," *Bell Journal of Economics* 6, no. 2 (1975): 671–78.

24. Adam Smith, *The Theory of Moral Sentiments* (1759; Indianapolis: Liberty Fund, 1982), p. 213; this is now referred to as *loss aversion* and is commonly though mistakenly attributed to behavior economists.

25. Frédéric Bastiat, *Selected Essays on Political Economy*, ed. George B. de Huszar (Irvington-on-Hudson, NY: Foundation for Economic Education, 1995), p. 144.

26. Connecticut, Delaware, Maine, Maryland, Massachusetts, New Hampshire, New York, Rhode Island, and Vermont have formed a consortium to reduce greenhouse gases. It shouldn't be difficult to form state consortia to reduce fiscal pollution that would benefit their citizens more than one to reduce carbon dioxide pollution. See Colin A. Young, "9 States, Including Mass., Agree to Accelerate Emission Reductions in Next Decade" WBUR, August 23, 2017, http://www.wbur.org/news/2017/08/23/9-states-including-mass-agree-to-extend-carbon-reduction-goals-to-2030.

27. See Matt Grossman and David A. Hopkins, *Asymmetric Politics: Ideological Republics and Group-Interest Democrats* (Oxford: Oxford University Press, 2016), p. 56, Figure 2-13.

28. Alberto Alesina, Dorian Carloni, and Giampaolo Lecce, "The Electoral Consequences of Large Fiscal Adjustments," National Bureau of Economic Research Working Paper no. 17655, December 2011.

29. Cogan, *High Cost of Good Intentions*, p. 385.

30. Keynes gave us cautious hope in this regard when he wrote: "I am sure that the power of vested interests is vastly exaggerated compared with the gradual encroachment of ideas. Not, indeed, immediately, but . . . soon or late, it is ideas, not vested interests, which are dangerous for good or evil." Let's hope it is the good ideas that prevail in the long run. John Maynard Keynes, *The General Theory*

INDEX

Note: Page numbers followed by "f" or "t" indicate figures and tables, respectively. Page numbers with "n" or "nn" indicate notes.

ABOUT THE EDITORS

JOHN MERRIFIELD is professor emeritus of economics at the University of Texas at San Antonio. He co-edits the *Non-Partsian Education Review* and is the president of the nascent Institute for Objective Policy Assessment (www.objectivepolicyassessment.org). He earned a PhD in economics from the University of Wyoming in 1984. Professor Merrifield has authored 5 books, co-edited 3 more, and published 56 peer-reviewed journal articles and has written multiple chapters in edited volumes concerning topics as wide-ranging as education economics, urban and regional economics, environmental and natural resource economics, and public finance.

BARRY POULSON is professor emeritus at the University of Colorado Boulder and a visiting professor at several universities, including the University of North Carolina; Cambridge University; and Universidad Carlos Tercera, Madrid, Spain. His main area of expertise is economic development and economic history. His current focus is on fiscal policies and fiscal constitutions. He was the vice chair of the State Treasurer's Advisory Group on Constitutional Amendments in Colorado. Professor Poulson is an adjunct scholar of the Heritage Foundation and senior fellow of the Independence Institute.

ABOUT THE CONTRIBUTORS

ROMINA BOCCIA is a leading fiscal and economic expert focusing on limiting federal spending and the national debt. She is a member of the Alumni Board at the Foundation for Economic Freedom and previously worked at the Heritage Foundation. Boccia has been published in the *Washington Post*, the *Atlantic*, the *Washington Times*, and the *Washington Examiner*.

JUSTIN BOGIE is a policy analyst focusing on fiscal affairs at the Heritage Foundation. He researches the federal budget, appropriations, the national debt, and budget reform issues. He has appeared on Fox Business Network and C-SPAN. Bogie regularly contributes to *The Hill*, the *National Interest*, and the *Washington Examiner*. He has also been featured on CNN and Fox News and in the *Washington Post*.

RYAN BOURNE is the R. Evan Scharf Chair for the Public Understanding of Economics at the Cato Institute. He has a BA and an MPhil in economics from Cambridge University. Bourne writes about economics with a focus on fiscal policy, inequality, and minimum wage. He writes for the *Daily Telegraph* and the blog *ConservativeHome* and has appeared on BBC News, CNN, Sky News, CNBC, and Fox Business Network. Before joining the Cato Institute, Bourne worked at the Institute of Economic Affairs and the Centre for Policy Studies.

KURT COUCHMAN is a director of government relations for a non-profit organization that advocates for fiscal responsibility. Before that, he was vice president of public policy at Defense Priorities, a Washington, DC–based organization seeking a more prudent foreign policy. Couchman has also served three members of Congress, including as a legislative assistant to Justin Amash and as legislative director to Rep. Dave Brat. He has spearheaded campaigns for balanced budget amendments and other budget reform initiatives. Couchman has a master's degree in economics from George Mason University.

XAVIER DEBRUN is the deputy chief of fiscal policy and surveillance in the Fiscal Affairs Department of the International Monetary Fund (IMF). He joined the IMF in 2000 and has worked in the Research Department and the Fiscal Affairs Department. Debrun was an associate professor of economics at the Graduate Institute in Geneva, which is also where he completed his PhD. His research interests include international policy coordination, the economics of monetary unions, and macro-fiscal issues.

ED DOLAN holds a PhD in economics from Yale University. He taught at Dartmouth College, the University of Chicago, George Mason University, and Gettysburg College. Dolan has also taught in Moscow, Budapest, Prague, and Stockholm. He is currently a senior fellow at the Niskanen Center and lives in northwest lower Michigan.

CHRIS EDWARDS is the director of tax policy studies at the Cato Institute and editor of www.DownsizingGovernment.org. He is a top expert on federal and state tax and budget issues. Before joining Cato, Edwards was a senior economist on the congressional Joint Economic Committee, a manager with PricewaterhouseCoopers, and an economist with the Tax Foundation. Edwards has testified to Congress on fiscal issues many times, and his articles on tax and budget policies have appeared in the *Washington Post*, the *Wall Street Journal*, and other major newspapers. He is the author of *Downsizing the Federal Government* and coauthor of *Global Tax Revolution*.

JOHN GAREN is the BB&T Professor of Economics in the Gatton College of Business and Economics at the University of Kentucky and is the founding director of the Institute for the Study of Free Enterprise. Garen received his PhD from Ohio State University in 1982. He taught at the University of Chicago, the Mercatus Center at George Mason University, National Sun Yat-Sen University, and National Taiwan Normal University. Garen's research interests include the economics of organizations, labor and human resource economics, and the role of government in society.

DAVID J. HEBERT is an associate professor of economics and director of the Center for Markets, Ethics, and Entrepreneurship at Aquinas College. Previously, he was an assistant professor at Ferris State University and at Troy University.

LARS JONUNG is an emeritus professor at the Knut Wicksell Centre for Financial Studies at Lund University in Sweden. He was chair of the Swedish Fiscal Policy Council for 2012–2013. Jonung was a research adviser focusing on economic and financial affairs in Brussels from 2000 to 2010. He served as chief economic adviser to Prime Minister Carl Bildt. His research covers monetary and fiscal policy, inflationary expectations, the euro, the economics of European integration, and the history of Swedish economic thought.

DWIGHT LEE is a research fellow at the Independent Institute and the William J. O'Neil Endowed Chair Global Markets and Freedom and Scholar in Residence at Southern Methodist University. He received his PhD in economics from the University of California, San Diego, and has taught at the University of Georgia, Washington University, George Mason University, Virginia Polytechnic Institute and State University, University of Colorado, San Diego State College, and the American Institute of Banking.

NICK LORIS is an economist who focuses on energy, environmental, and regulatory issues. He is the deputy director of the Thomas A.

Roe Institute for Economic Policy Studies and Herbert and Joyce Morgan Fellow at the Heritage Foundation. Loris has testified before both House and Senate committees. He has been published in the *Wall Street Journal* and the *New York Times* and has appeared on CNN, Fox News, MSNBC, and National Public Radio.

MARVIN PHAUP is a professor at the Trachtenberg School of Public Policy and Public Administration at the George Washington University. His research aims to improve the performance of federal budgeting measured by efficiency, equity, and stabilization. Before joining the Trachtenberg School in 2007, he headed the financial studies/budget process group at the Congressional Budget Office. He was part of the team that developed the Federal Credit Reform Act of 1990. Phaup was a consultant to the Peterson-Pew Commission on Budget Reform, the Organisation for Economic Co-operation and Development, and the International Monetary Fund.

RICHARD M. SALSMAN is an assistant professor of political economy at Duke University, teaching in the Philosophy, Politics, and Economics program. He is an American Institute for Economic Research senior fellow and a member of the John Locke Foundation. He is also the president of InterMarket Forecasting Inc. Previously, Salsman was an economist at Wainwright Economics and a banker at the Bank of New York and Citibank.

BAKER SPRING is a policy analyst specializing in national security, foreign policy, treaty ratification, arms control, nonproliferation policy, missile defense, and defense budget issues. He has extensive experience in working with members of Congress at the staff level as a policy analyst on Capitol Hill and as a fellow with the U.S. Senate Committee on the Budget.

RICHARD E. WAGNER is a professor of economics at George Mason University. He works primarily in the fields of public finance and public choice. Wagner received his doctorate in economics from the University of Virginia, studying under James M. Buchanan. He has been published in the *American Economic Review*, the *Journal of Law and Economics*, *Public Choice*, the *Journal of Monetary Economics*, *Policy Studies Journal*, the *Cato Journal*, the *European Journal of Law and Economics*, and the *Review of Political Economy*, among others. He serves in an advisory capacity for several think tanks and is on the editorial board of *Constitutional Political Economy*, the *Journal of Public Finance and Public Choice*, the *Cato Journal*, *Public Finance and Management*, and the *Review of Austrian Economics*.

About the Cato Institute

Founded in 1977, the Cato Institute is a public policy research foundation dedicated to broadening the parameters of policy debate to allow consideration of more options that are consistent with the principles of limited government, individual liberty, and peace. To that end, the Institute strives to achieve greater involvement of the intelligent, concerned lay public in questions of policy and the proper role of government.

The Institute is named for *Cato's Letters*, libertarian pamphlets that were widely read in the American Colonies in the early 18th century and played a major role in laying the philosophical foundation for the American Revolution.

Despite the achievement of the nation's Founders, today virtually no aspect of life is free from government encroachment. A pervasive intolerance for individual rights is shown by government's arbitrary intrusions into private economic transactions and its disregard for civil liberties. And while freedom around the globe has notably increased in the past several decades, many countries have moved in the opposite direction, and most governments still do not respect or safeguard the wide range of civil and economic liberties.

To address those issues, the Cato Institute undertakes an extensive publications program on the complete spectrum of policy issues. Books, monographs, and shorter studies are commissioned to examine the federal budget, Social Security, regulation, military spending, international trade, and myriad other issues. Major policy conferences are held throughout the year, from which papers are published thrice yearly in the *Cato Journal*. The Institute also publishes the quarterly magazine *Regulation*.

In order to maintain its independence, the Cato Institute accepts no government funding. Contributions are received from foundations, corporations, and individuals, and other revenue is generated from the sale of publications. The Institute is a nonprofit, tax-exempt, educational foundation under Section 501(c)3 of the Internal Revenue Code.

Cato Institute
1000 Massachusetts Avenue NW
Washington, DC 20001
www.cato.org